MONUMENTS AND MEMORY, MADE AND UNMADE

Monuments and Memory, Made and Unmade

EDITED BY

Robert S. Nelson and Margaret Olin

The University of Chicago Press
Chicago and London

The University of Chicago Press, Chicago 60637
The University of Chicago Press, Ltd., London
© 2003 by The University of Chicago
All rights reserved. Published 2003
Printed in the United States of America
12 11 10 09 08 07 06 05 04 03   1 2 3 4 5

ISBN: 0-226-57157-2 (cloth)
ISBN: 0-226-57158-0 (paper)

Library of Congress Cataloging-in-Publication Data

Monuments and memory, made and unmade / edited by Robert S. Nelson and
    Margaret Olin.
        p. cm.
    Includes bibliographical references and index.
    ISBN 0-226-57157-2 (cloth : alk. paper)—ISBN 0-226-57158-0 (pbk. : alk. paper)
    1. Monuments. 2. Monuments—Conservation and restoration. 3. Historic sites.
    4. Historic sites—Conservation and restoration. 5. Memory—Social aspects.
    I. Nelson, Robert S., 1947– II. Olin, Margaret Rose, 1948–

    CC135 .M647 2003
    306.4'7—dc21

                                                                        2003010129

Part of chapter 6 was published in a different version as Margaret Olin, "Touching
Photographs: Roland Barthes's 'Mistaken' Identification," *Representations* 80 (2002):
99–118.

"The World Trade Center," by David Lehman, is taken from *Valentine Place* (New
York: Scribner, 1996). © 1996 by David Lehman. First published in *The Paris Review*
no. 136 (fall 1995): 74. Reprinted by permission of the author. All rights reserved.

♾ The paper used in this publication meets the minimum requirements of the American
National Standard for Information Sciences—Permanence of Paper for Printed Library
Materials, ANSI Z39.48-1992.

Remembering the victims of 9/11 and its aftermath

||||||| Contents

A monument is only venerable in so much as a long history of the past has imprinted the black of centuries on its vaults.

Chateaubriand (1802)

Monuments in the sense of this law are . . . works of the human hand since whose
inception at least sixty years have passed.

Alois Riegl (1903)

At the beginning of the twentieth century, Alois Riegl, the first Con-
servator General of monuments in the Austro-Hungarian Empire,
drafted a law that attempted to define what Europeans had begun to
appreciate a century earlier.[1] Then romantics, like Chateaubriand,
had argued that old buildings and the signs of their age should be
cherished as tangible evidence of a past whose remoteness made it all
the more desirable.[2] Riegl and other professionals, engaged in the
study and preservation of monuments, sought to translate the romantic into the practical. Because European cities were then being
rapidly modernized, officials had the responsibility to decide what to
tear down and what to rebuild and in what style. Riegl wrote sug-
gestively about how to select works of the human hand for protection

and added a theoretically innovative essay about balancing the values of one monument against those of another.

This essay, "The Modern Cult of Monuments: Its Character and Its Origin," had a greater impact than Riegl's attempt at legislation, which never became law. The article traced a historical development from the "intentional monument," whose significance is determined by its makers, to the "unintentional monument," a product of later events.[3] He regarded his own subject, history, as but one player in this field of values, destined, he thought, to fade away over time. Its legacy would be a love for the signs of the passage of time as well as an enthusiasm for the new. A century later, the disciplines of history and art history are flourishing, and so is a mixture of historic preservation and technologically innovative architecture that characterizes contemporary attempts to reformulate "the city of collective memory," to evoke a recent study.[4] Riegl's involvement in the legal and practical issues of monument preservation typifies art history's investment in the making and unmaking of monuments, its own and those of others. Then as now, the discipline's definition of a monument is potentially no less inclusive than Riegl's: a monument is what art history chooses to celebrate and proclaim a monument. Both Riegl and art history, however, lessen the threat of their definitions by limiting monuments, in practice, to aesthetically significant objects of enduring value. Economic, legal, and political forces further constrain the actual designation of a monument.

The century that separates our project from Riegl's reflections was not sympathetic to "intentional" monuments, if one excepts the flurry of projects after World War I. Thanks to modernism, art history lost interest in studying such monuments,[5] favoring instead the unintentional, "enduring evidence or example."[6] After the nineteenth century, most art historians thought monuments were no longer a proper object of study.[7] For its part, history remained a resolutely textual discipline, even if the later scholars submerge themselves in a considerably wider range of archives than those that the nineteenth-century historian Leopold von Ranke chose to study. Until the Viet Nam Memorial was erected in Washington, D.C., after much controversy, recent monuments in the United States failed to achieve widespread public acceptance. Modernist architects disdained older traditions, especially the classical so beloved by monument designers through the 1930s. Yet what never abated was that which the monument satisfied: the desire to commemorate, to mark a place, to represent the past to the present and future, to emphasize one narrative of the past at the expense of others, or simply to make the past past. Now that modernism has waned, postmodernism and its concern for visual reference have stimulated a new interest in the topic. Contributions as diverse as James E. Young's studies of Holocaust memorials or Michele H. Bogart's work on public sculpture have lent new academic legitimacy to monuments.[8] At an increasing pace, diverse regions and periods and different notions of the monumental are being recorded and analyzed.[9]

"By common consent, the postmodern age is obsessed with memory," according to one author.[10] Particularly important in this regard has been collective memory, a mingling of the public and the private. Anthropologists have stressed the relation of memory to ritual and habit[11] and have explored the relations between personal and communal memory.[12] Decades ago, Maurice Halbwachs underscored the social character of memory and enabled it to be studied as a historical process.[13] Halbwachs's work had a lasting impact, especially in France. Recently, Pierre Nora, the editor of a fascinating study of the construction of French memory, introduced the notion of *"lieux de mémoire,"* or sites "where memory is crystallized, in which it finds refuge." These *lieux* range from gastronomy to the Tour de France and include physical monuments such as medieval cathedrals and the Eiffel Tower. They are to be distinguished from what he calls *"milieux de mémoire,* settings in which memory is a real part of everyday experience," such as a family, church congregation, or village.[14] Combining some of these concerns with the insights of Frances Yates's *The Art of Memory,*[15] Patrick Hutton has interpreted the writing of history as an art of memory.[16] The general subject of history and memory has become a scholarly growth industry and the title of a journal.[17]

A desire to explore these discourses further and within the context of art history has inspired this book. The twelve chapters that follow serve as case studies toward a larger history of the monument and its function in society. While mainly written by art historians, ours is not an exclusively art historical book and does not remain centered on the artwork itself. Essays instead explore the rhetoric of the monument and examine the processes that allow it to function. How does the monument come into being? How does it serve to coalesce memory, both personal and corporate? Once created, how does the monument affect society?

More than most works of art or architecture, not to mention ordinary objects, monuments enjoy multiple social roles. As things, they share their status with other objects: the term monumentality suggests qualities of inertness, opacity, permanence, remoteness, distance, preciosity, and grandeur. Yet monuments are prized precisely because they are not merely cold, hard, and permanent. They are also living, vital, immediate, and accessible, at least to some parts of society. Because a monument can achieve a powerful symbolic agency, to damage it, much less to obliterate it, constitutes a personal and communal violation with serious consequences. While the destruction of mere things is commonplace in our takeout and throwaway world, attacking a monument threatens a society's sense of itself and its past.

This potential to redirect cultural memory tempts some people to destroy or appropriate what has been built, protected, or restored with great care. The phenomenon is universal, and includes Aztec temples in Mexico after Cortez, Christian churches in Constantinople after the Ottoman conquest, or, in recent memory, mosques in Bosnia and statues of Lenin in the Soviet Union. Yet while physical destruction and social disruption have undeniable personal and economic costs, they also can inspire the creation of monuments, as well as their study and preservation. The period after the French Revolution, for example, saw the formulation of concepts crucial to the notion of the historical monument and its preservation.[18] Because social turmoil breaks continuity with tradition and the immediate past, new monuments can represent an uncontested version of the past.

Memory and monument are to each other as process and product, although not necessarily as cause and effect, for circularity often obtains. The two terms are etymologically related and descend from notions of remembering. "Memory" derives from an Indo-Germanic root to which terms in Sanskrit are related. Hence the words are similar in European languages: e.g., in ancient Greek μνημεῖον, any memorial, remembrance, a monument of the dead, and μνῆμη, memory; or in Russian памятник, monument, memorial, and память, memory. The English "monument" is from the Latin *monumentum* and has cognates in French, Italian, and the other Romance languages. The German *Denkmal,* with the root "to think," is an exception to the pattern, although it has the same range of meanings as monument in other European languages. The anomalous character of the German word has a simple explanation: Martin Luther invented it for his Old Testament of 1523.[19]

While the term monument is Indo-European, all complex societies, it may be argued, invest cultural and actual capital in structures akin to monuments; hence the global scope of the volume. Our focus on social process and agency extends the range of possible artifacts well beyond the prototypical classical monument and its numerous progeny, especially the public sculpture of modern cities. While existing for millennia, the historic monument in Western Europe and America has come down to us trailing the clouds of the Enlightenment and the nation-state. Monuments are sanctioned by regional and national organizations, canonized by UNESCO and its system of World Heritage sites,[20] and sustained by global tourism. Monuments in turn support all of the above. They also link worlds that do not share common values. Europeans and Americans protested the destruction of the monumental Buddhas at Bamiyan, Afghanistan, in March 2001, for example, and six months later, terrorists based in Afghanistan attacked American monuments.

Our book considers three broad processes relevant to the creation and sustenance of monuments—Travel, Time, and Destruction/Reconstruction—and ponders these issues across different periods and cultures. To continue with the example of Bamiyan, it once was a place of pilgrimage for Buddhists and remembered by and defined through its colossal statues. Shortly after their destruction, a replica was being planned in Sichuan, China.[21] Yet it is doubtful if the modern copy will function in the same way as the ancient originals. Past pilgrimages to Bamiyan were communal; modern tourism aspires to be personal and individual, even if the reality is otherwise. Mass tourism or the packaged tour enjoys less prestige. Yet it can govern the experience of the monument and its physical structure.[22] Monuments are important, because people want to see them, and when that quest is realized actually or virtually, monuments become social agents. If the Bamiyan statues were rebuilt in China or Afghanistan, the modern subjectivities that inform global tourism, especially the romantic appreciation of the marks of time, would find the copy wanting. Therefore the new statue's relation to temporal structures, whether personal, religious, or national, would inevitably differ from that of the old.

Like most monuments, Bamiyan might be discussed under any of our three rubrics. But categorization is heuristically useful. The book's three-part narrative parallels the ritual stages that Arnold van Gennep proposed long ago: the rite of separation (Travel), the rite of transition or the crucial liminal period of transformation (Time), and the rite of incorporation (Destruction/Reconstruction).[23] But the analogy is only approximate, because van Gennep and later scholars of ritual focused on human interaction and performance. These aspects are important to us only in so far as they inform a particular type of object, the monument.

Throughout our work, we have labored against what might be called the "black hole" phenomenon, that is, the power of monuments to control everything within their orbit, like a star so massive that its gravitational force sucks everything back to itself, even light. What begins as independent study of monuments can turn into commemoration and hagiography, as aura overwhelms analysis. Pierre Nora also struggled with this issue,[24] which pertains as well to our most recent experience with monuments—the gradual rise of the World Trade Center in New York to the status of an international monument, its tragic destruction, and present proposals for its reconstruction and commemoration. Shortly after the collapse of these massive structures, the architectural critic

Paul Goldberger predicted that "now that the World Trade Center has become a martyr to terrorism, . . . architectural criticism of it will cease altogether."[25]

Because the WTC seemed to us a particularly informative example of the change from building to monument, we have added an epilogue about this metamorphosis. Strictly speaking only a person becomes a martyr, but the Pulitzer Prize–winning critic did not err, and the WTC is on its way to sainthood. Like all socially vital monuments, the WTC has become a social hybrid, part object, part subject, able to act upon and for people, as if animate. A monument, a *Denkmal,* is something to think with and to stimulate our memory. As an inanimate object, closely allied with the human, it constitutes a special type of tool. The socially vital monument coalesces communal memories and aspirations and becomes a mechanism for the projection of personal values and desires, a theme shared by all essays in our volume.

Like those things that Bruno Latour calls "quasi-objects, quasi-subjects," monuments are examples of a premodern cultural hybrid that modernity in its most powerful phases attempted to purify and neuter. Denying their composite character strips monuments of their animism, so redolent of "primitive" societies, and makes them civilized but dead. Latour found that hybrids trace and enact social networks,[26] and similarly in our volume essay after essay reveals the intricate relations that operate around and through the monument. To be vital, the monument must exist within an actual, present-oriented network of relationships. Unlike a lifeless art object suspended on the white walls of a museum, the monument does not privilege the past at the expense of the present. Rather it engages both to make claims for and against the future. The second section of our book explores this control and negotiation of time.

Social processes surrounding the monument begin even before it is seen. Travel to the monument, like all forms of pilgrimage, transforms object and beholder. The round trip, the full rite de passage, as van Gennep analyzed it,[27] remakes the memories of individuals and connects both object and beholder to larger social structures, thereby inculcating senses of personhood and history that society deems important. Journeys to see monuments began centuries ago but accelerated with the Grand Tour, when generations of young male English aristocrats were introduced, for example, to the art and pleasures of Venice.[28] Today college students of either gender and their obligatory backpacks continue the tradition on Eurail passes, as do retired people, who prefer standard luggage and Mercedes buses. At whatever stage of life, people travel to find something desired, in this case, a cultural, social, or aesthetic ideal that the monument is thought to provide. If that fantasy is unfilled and the enchantment of the monument dispelled, tourism plummets. Consequently, tourism and terrorism are to each other as matter to antimatter. Because destruction is part of the history of monuments, our volume concludes with that which can alter and even obliterate the old and contribute to the new.

The twelve chapters and epilogue illustrate that a monument's power pertains to its beauty, design, size, expense, location, or age value—the black of centuries that Chateaubriand appreciated and that some preservationists today would like to clean.[29] However, each author ultimately defines a monument less by what it looks like than by what it does. This is the final contribution of our volume. It may be argued that the monument is a particularly motivated form of an art object, as understood by the anthropologist Alfred Gell. Rather than a means of symbolic communication, the art object, he contends, is a means of acting, a way of transforming the world. If one grants that aesthetic success and cultural significance are socially determined, rather than intrinsic, for example, to the nature of material or talent, then Gell is correct to insist that the art object "is a function of the social-relational matrix in which it is embedded . . . [and] has no 'intrinsic' nature, independent of the relational context."[30]

The monument expresses the power and sense of the society that gives it meaning, and at the same time obscures competing claims for authority and meaning. Designed to be permanent, the actual monument, as our volume illustrates, changes constantly as it renegotiates ideals, status, and entitlement, defining the past to affect the present and future. Deprived of its enabling and enabled social networks and left untended, monument and memory disappear. When the grand monument vanishes, as an English poet from the time of the monument's apotheosis put it,

> Nothing beside remains. Round the decay
> Of that colossal wreck, boundless and bare
> The lone and level sands stretch far away.[31]

Nothing remains, unless, of course, the vast desert or the colossal wreck becomes a monument itself by virtue of the evocative rhetoric of a celebrated "monument" of English literature. But this last sense of monument we do not pursue, concerned, as we are, with the rhetoric of the monument, not rhetoric as monument.

A project with several beginnings, this book has followed sundry paths over the past few years in response to different places, people, and events. Many have contributed to its rites and facilitated its passage. In 1999, our previous work on the theory of monuments and art history and our experiences in writing about individual monuments led us to propose a session for the annual meeting of the College Art Association. The topic, "Places of Memory," derived from the volumes of Pierre Nora, produced a flood of submissions. We are grateful to the Art History Session chairs, Sarah Blake McHam and Betsy Rosasco, for allowing our single session to grow into two. Thanks to fellowships, we were then working in a new monument, the J. Paul Getty Museum and the Getty Research Institute, an aesthetic Valhalla on a mountain in Los Angeles. Michael Roth, then director of the scholar program, facilitated our work, along with Sabine Schlosser and Charles Salas, and the GRI graciously funded a follow-up seminar in the spring of 2000.

From these events and thanks to discussion with colleagues elsewhere, scholars from diverse specialties began to see the potential for a volume about the social lives of monuments. In June 2001, the now well-defined group assembled at the Sterling and Francine Clark Art Institute in Williamstown, Massachusetts, to discuss drafts of their essays. Our gracious hosts were the Research and Academic Programs and its director Michael Ann Holly, aided by Darby English. At Williamstown, we agreed that the final versions of our chapters would be due in September 2001, a fateful month for one building that we had given no thought to when we launched our project in New York two years earlier. What has become known as 9/11 caused some of us to mention that difficult time in our essays and the editors to prepare an epilogue.

At all stages in our project, we received advice and help. We are pleased to acknowledge especially Michele Bogart, Zeynep Çelik, Thomas Cummins, Georges Didi-Huberman, Chloé S. Georas, Tom Gunning, Charles Merewether, Keith Moxey, Ernst Osterkamp, Todd Porterfield, Polly Nooter Roberts, Catherine Soussloff, Leslie Topp, Heghnar Watenpaugh, Irene Winter, James E. Young, and Robert Nelson's research assistant, Simone Tai. Two anonymous readers read the manuscript for the University of Chicago Press and offered insightful criticisms. At the Press, Susan Bielstein offered her support and critical eye, and Anthony Burton expertly chaperoned the book through the arduous process of publication. Jill Shaw prepared the index. Special thanks are due to Jonathan and Gary Worchester.

It is traditional to end acknowledgments even closer to home. In recent months, our children, subjected to incessant dinner-table discussions, began referring to our "obsession," and indeed there is something about monuments that is obsessive and also fascinating and appealing. Yet although a monument may be part object and part subject, as we have explained, it is hardly huggable. We thank our children for patiently going about their business of providing us warmth, joy, and another point of view.

NOTES

1. [Alois Riegl], *Entwurf einer gesetzlichen Organization der Denkmalpflege in Österreich* (Vienna: k.k. Zentral-Kommission, 1903). Although anonymous, the draft is generally attributed to Riegl. The epigraph is from p. 93, para. 1.

2. Chateaubriand, *Génie du christianisme* (Paris: Garnier Flammarion, 1966), 1:400 (see epigraph).

3. "Der moderne Denkmalkultus, Sein Wesen und seine Entstehung" was first published to accompany the draft for a law. It was republished in Riegl's collected essays, *Gesammelte Aufsätze,* ed. Karl M. Swoboda (Vienna: Benno Filser, 1929), 144–93; translated as "The Modern Cult of Monuments: Its Character and Its Origin," by Kurt W. Forster and Diane Ghirardo in *Oppositions* 25 (1982): 21–51.

4. M. Christine Boyer, *The City of Collective Memory: Its Historical Imagery and Architectural Entertainments* (Cambridge: MIT Press, 1994).

5. Marita Sturken and James E. Young, "Monuments," *Encyclopedia of Aesthetics,* vol. 3 (Oxford: Oxford University Press, 1998), 272–78; James E. Young, "Monuments and Memory," in *Critical Terms for Art History,* ed. Robert S. Nelson and Richard Shiff, 2d ed. (Chicago: University of Chicago Press, 2003), 234–47.

6. "Monument" in the *Oxford English Dictionary,* on-line version.

7. H. W. Janson, *The Rise and Fall of the Public Monument* (New Orleans: Graduate School Tulane University, 1976).

8. James E. Young, *At Memory's Edge: After-Images of the Holocaust in Contemporary Art and Architecture* (New Haven: Yale University Press, 2000); idem, *The Texture of Memory: Holocaust Memorials and Meaning* (New Haven: Yale University Press, 1993). Michele H. Bogart, *Public Sculpture and the Civic Ideal in New York City, 1890–1930* (Chicago: University of Chicago Press, 1989).

9. Erik Iversen, *Obelisks in Exile,* 2 vols. (Copenhagen: Gad, 1968); Samir al-Khalil, *The Monument: Art, Vulgarity, and Responsibility in Iraq* (Berkeley: University of California Press, 1991); Michael Herzfeld, *A Place in History: Social and Monumental Time in a Cretan Town* (Princeton: Princeton University Press, 1991); Wu Hung, "Tiananmen Square: A Political History of Monuments," *Representations* 35 (Summer 1991): 84–117; Kirk Savage, *Standing Soldiers Kneeling Slaves: Race, War and Monument in Nineteenth-Century America* (Princeton: Princeton University Press, 1997); Sergiusz Michalski, *Public Monuments: Art in Political Bondage, 1870–1997* (London: Reaktion Books, 1998); Kevin D. Murphy, *Memory and Modernity: Viollet-le-Duc at Vézelay* (University Park: Pennsylvania State University Press, 2000); Françoise Choay, *The Invention of the Historic Monument* (New York: Cambridge University Press, 2001); Françoise Bercé, *Des monuments historiques au patrimoine du XVIIIe siècle à nos jours* (Paris: Flammarion, 2000); Hans-Rudolf Meier and Marion Wohlleben, eds., *Bauten und Orte als Träger von Erinnerung: Die Erinnerungsdebatte und die Denkmalpflege* (Zürich: Hochschulverlag AG an der ETH, 2000). We are grateful to Geza Hájós for the latter reference.

10. Daniel J. Sherman, *The Construction of Memory in Interwar France* (Chicago: University of Chicago Press, 1999), 1.

11. Paul Connerton, *How Societies Remember* (New York: Cambridge University Press, 1989).

12. Most recently Jennifer Cole, *Forget Colonialism? Sacrifice and the Art of Memory in Madagascar* (Berkeley: University of California Press, 2001).

13. Maurice Halbwachs, *On Collective Memory* (Chicago: University of Chicago Press, 1992).

14. Pierre Nora, *Realms of Memory: Rethinking the French Past,* trans. Arthur Gold-hammer, 3 vols. (New York: Columbia University Press, 1996–98), 1:1. The series is now being published by the University of Chicago Press, beginning with *Rethinking France,* vol. 1 (Chicago: University of Chicago Press, 2001). For a general overview of these volumes and Nora's central concepts, see Nancy Wood, "Memory's Remains: *Les lieux de mémoire,*" *History and Memory* 6 (1994): 123–51.

15. Frances A. Yates, *The Art of Memory* (Chicago: University of Chicago Press, 1966).

16. Patrick H. Hutton, *History as an Art of Memory* (Hanover: University Press of New England, 1993).

17. *History and Memory* 1 (1989); David Thelen, *Memory and American History* (Bloomington: Indiana University Press, 1990); John Bodnar, *Remaking America: Public Memory, Commemoration, and Patriotism in the Twentieth Century* (Princeton: Princeton University Press, 1992); Jacques Le Goff, *History and Memory* (New York: Columbia University Press, 1992); Patrick J. Geary, *Phantoms of Remembrance: Memory and Oblivion at the End of the First Millennium* (Princeton: Princeton University Press, 1994); Matt K. Matsuda, *The Memory of the Modern* (New York: Oxford University Press, 1996); Susan A. Crane, *Museums and Memory* (Stanford: Stanford University Press, 2000), and idem, *Collecting and Historical Consciousness in Early Nineteenth-Century Germany* (Ithaca: Cornell University Press, 2000). The journal *Representations* devoted an issue to memory and monuments, translating Nora's introduction to *Les lieux de mémoire:* "Between Memory and History: *Les Lieux de Mémoire,*" *Representations* 26 (1989): 7–25. The journal returned to the topic of memory in two other issues: "Monumental Histories," 35 (summer 1991) and "Grounds for Remembering," 69 (winter 2000).

18. Boyer, *City of Collective Memory,* 377–79; Jukka Jokilehto, *A History of Architectural Conservation* (Boston: Butterworth Heinemann, 1999), 69–75.

19. *Trübners Deutsches Wörterbuch,* vol. 2 (Berlin: Walter de Grunter, 1940), 42; Helmut Scharf, *Kleine Kunstgeschichte des Deutschen Denkmals* (Darmstadt: Wissenschaftliche Buchgesellschaft, 1984), 8.

20. E.g., the International Council on Monuments and Sites, founded in 1965. See the discussion in the useful general book by Jokilehto, *History of Architectural Conservation,* 287–89.

21. *New York Times,* October 6, 2001.

22. An excellent account of these processes is found in Tim Edensor, *Tourists at the Taj: Performance and Meaning at a Symbolic Site* (New York: Routledge, 1998).

23. Arnold van Gennep, *The Rites of Passage* (Chicago: University of Chicago Press, 1960), 11.

24. Pierre Nora, "The Era of Commemoration," *Realms of Memory,* 3:609–37.

25. Paul Goldberger, "Building Plans: What the World Trade Center Meant," *New Yorker,* September 24, 2001, 78.

26. Bruno Latour, *We Have Never Been Modern* (Cambridge: Harvard University Press, 1993).

27. Van Gennep, *Rites of Passage.*

28. Bruce Redford, *Venice and the Grand Tour* (New Haven: Yale University Press, 1996).

29. David Lowenthal, *The Past Is a Foreign Country* (New York: Cambridge University Press, 1985), 125–82.

30. Alfred Gell, *Art and Agency: An Anthropological Theory* (New York: Oxford University Press, 1998), 7.

31. Percy Bysshe Shelley, "Ozymandias," in *The Complete Poetical Works of Percy Bysshe Shelley,* ed. Neville Rogers (Oxford: Clarendon Press, 1975), 2:320.

PART I

Travel

Most monuments are the still center of a whirlwind of movement. Travelers visit them; they and others move through and around them. Rituals are performed within them, religious or secular. Not planning to return to their distant goal, many of the travelers make records of their comings and goings. These postcards and snapshots taken back from the trip become the record of the trip itself. And indeed, these treasured tokens, which determine what the monument is and how the trip is remembered, are records of the movement and the interaction with the monument as much as or more than they are records of the object of veneration itself.

The pictorial record of the trip is perhaps the defining characteristic of the monument. After all, people come from far and wide to visit ordinary buildings, often to do business in them, to obtain a passport, for example, or make payments. But seldom do they take home tokens or photographs from such trips. Urban federal buildings, for example, rarely become monuments unless they are destroyed by terrorists, after which postcards of them start to appear in the personal collections of tourists.

The relation of the monument to movement, however, predates postcards and snapshots. The first two chapters in this section, which is arranged chronologically, concern travelers armed with diaries and drawing tools, with which they made written and visual records of journeys to a monument. These accounts demonstrate the need to bear witness by traveling to the site of a monument.

Stephen Bann examines the use of travel to recover that which one has lost at home. John Bargrave, later an antiquarian and collector, traveled to Bourges, France, in 1645, in forced exile and in mourning for a lost society in Canterbury. His was not a touristic journey but a journey of exile that made the Cathedral of Bourges into a template of the cathedral at Canterbury, the foreign monument providing an opportunity to reflect on the one at home. His abrupt juxtapositions of travel views with descriptions of historical events that, in emblematic mode, recall current or recent events turned the cathedral into a monument of recent destruction in its own home and the lost home of the exile. This personal quest caused the exile to view the destination as a site of personal memory, quite distinct from the prescribed "itinerary" of modern tourism. Such travel activates reflection. Having arrived at Bourges Cathedral, the monumental goal of his journey, he not only took away tokens, he left one. He climbed to its top, a great cathedral skyscraper like the tall buildings of modern cities, and left an inscription, stating his presence.

The Chinese scholar-painter Huang Yi, subject of Lillian Tseng's essay, visited ancient sites more than a century after Bargrave's visit to Bourges. Huang, like Bargrave an antiquarian, made inferences about the dates of the stele he visited from their inscriptions. The object of the trip was to return with accurate rubbings. He made drawings that documented himself as a traveler among the stele, and, in a different pictorial act of remembering, he relived his reunion with his friend Wu Yi in Wu Yi's studio, which he treated like a monument. Not only did the completed album attest to the monumentality of the stele (and studio) represented; it functioned as a connecting link between friends. As Huang sent it to them, one at a time, they inscribed it with commentary and returned it, so that it could travel to others.

Not drawings but photographic postcards are the currency of exchange in Robert Nelson's essay about religious and secular tourism to the church of Hagia Sophia in Istanbul. The albums of the previous essays were perhaps at least as important as the trip itself. Here, however, a complex interplay between guidebooks and those responsible for making the monument live up to the guidebooks leads to changes in the cityscape, in an era when the simulacrum begins to replace the existing monument.[1] The monuments themselves are created for their photogenic, commodifiable presence, and this creation extends to the city itself, as tourist zones fill the areas around monuments. The private meaning that the cathedral had for Bargrave and that the stele had for Huang became public in accordance with changes in the nature of travel, as modern mass tourism began to envelop the entire world.

Touristic ambling, however prescribed by guidebooks and travel companies, does not resemble the precisely structured ritual processions that took place at the monument during the Middle Ages, when the monument was inextricably embedded in a living milieu rather than a tourist bubble. Twentieth-century tourists travel to enjoy spectacle. But the icons staring back at the beholder eleven centuries earlier were in the same space as, as well as dressed like, the beholder. They were people then, not exhibits.

Finally, the Internet and television, the subject of Mitchell Schwarzer's essay, become tourist media and suggest a very different experience for the traveler. Tactile experience was the hallmark of the travels of Bargrave, who left his mark on the cathedral, and Huang, who took rubbings from stele. Tactile experience accompanied optical experience as well, as the tourist ambled through landscapes, savoring the atmosphere. But as landscape becomes mediascape, the monuments are those structures repeatedly shown on television. Pilgrimage becomes instantaneous. The past becomes a media spectacle. The travels that Bargrave made and that the tourist flaneur enjoyed are now most frequently done on-line. One's fellow travelers are not a few English aristocrats or fellow antiquarians, or even a group of American tourists, but millions. And yet one generally surfs alone.

With the introduction of first the train, then the airplane, and finally travel by mouse click and remote, monuments have become increasingly easier to access. Travels have become easier to represent as well. Personal diaries have grown scarcer; first the novel, then photographic and electronic media have taken over. Along with these changes in travel and its representation, the private experience has given way increasingly to the public, bringing about a change in audience that modifies the way a monument can interact with society.

Consequently, the nature of travel to monuments has implications for the other categories in the volume. As we have seen, the personal travels of Bargrave and Huang touch on themes of destruction and mourning: coping with grief and loss were part of the purpose of their trips. In the case of Bargrave, iconoclasm continued to play an important role in his later travels. In mourning for the Cathedral of Canterbury, stripped of precious relics of Saint Thomas's Shrine, he brought back from his travels first pictures but later relics and curiosities. The tourist monument, on the other hand, is threatened with what Jaś Elsner (in part 3) calls "ritual desecration," when monuments are secularized. Even in the moving landscape of today, the monument is endangered: it becomes little more than an obstacle, as travel becomes an end in itself (even when the traveler does not move).

Travel has implications for time as well. The past from which Bargrave drew moral lessons, and which Huang sought to recover and understand, becomes the indistinguishable spectacle of pastness for the modern tourist. Internet and television travel also have implications for time. They inculcate a fragmented notion of time that no longer fits into a past (whether recoverable with difficulty or remembered), a present, or a future. All is present. The technological present becomes our collective memory.

NOTE

1. Jean Baudrillard, "The Precession of Simulacra," trans. Paul Foss et al. (New York: Semiotext(e), 1983), 1–80.

Scaling the Cathedral:
Bourges in John Bargrave's Travel Journal for 1645

STEPHEN BANN

Much has already been written about the importance of the cathedral for French authors in the postrevolutionary period. From Hugo and Balzac to Proust, it acquired the character not just of a polyvalent symbol condensing themes of historical rupture and change, but indeed of a central metaphor for the all-embracing and, so to speak, architectural ambitions of the modern writer. For Hugo, who wrote eloquently in the Restoration period about the need to rehabilitate monuments destroyed by the Revolution, the image of the cathedral symbolized the transition from a premodern culture in which public messages were transmitted by the emblematic facades of great buildings to a situation in which the individual creator strives to achieve mass communication through the written text. As he memorably commented: "Le livre tuera l'édifice." A century after Hugo, Proust—having spent several years of his youth pondering the literary resurrection of a great French cathedral in Ruskin's *The Bible of Amiens*—further radicalized Hugo's message by claiming, in *A la recherche du temps perdu,* that the only ground for such a new symbolic architecture is the fertile soil of individual reminiscence. Julia Kristeva paraphrases Proust's message in the form of an imperative addressed to the modern reader: "If you will only be so good as to open up your memories of felt time, *there* will rise the new cathedral."[1]

This study, though written in the light of such modern developments, seeks to elaborate a rather different equation between history and memory, writing and the cathedral, in the context of a historically specific economy of the verbal and the visual sign. I am indebted to studies of the early modern period which anchor speculations of this kind in concrete objects and particular life experiences, from Jonathan Spence's already classic account of the career of a Jesuit father, Matteo Ricci, at the Chinese court to Juliet Fleming's recent speculation on graffiti and other forms of writing in Tudor and Stuart England.[2] Both the subjective processing of the otherness of the foreign land and the specific conditions of material inscription in the early modern period will be recurrent issues in the argument that follows.

The most direct point of reference, however, is my own work on the cleric, collector, and traveler John Bargrave (1610–80). In my earlier study of Bargrave, I tried to tease out the connections between his extensive travels throughout Europe during the period of the English Civil War, his formation of a "cabinet of curiosities" which has survived almost intact up to the present day, and his need to bear witness through these activities to the historical predicament in which he found himself. For Bargrave, as I argued, the gradual formation of a collection was, in a sense, a secular act of mourning for the antebellum society that he, and his family, had irretrievably lost. The recent reappearance of the original manuscript of Bargrave's French travel journal of 1645 provides a remarkable opportunity to extend this earlier investigation. A happy survival from what Fleming calls the "paper-short" situation of early modern England, this journal commemorates the very first expedition which Bargrave made to the continent, in the early stages of the English Civil War. It combines moral reflection and travel narrative with a significant number of visual illustrations penned by Bargrave that possess, in my view, an emblematic as well as a descriptive character. For the history of tourism as a mode of condensing memory in pregnant images and commentary, it is (as I hope to show) an early and exemplary text.[3]

Here we must recognize both a direct link with and a difference from the postrevolutionary French examples with which I began this essay. It is indeed crucial to note that this journal was written in the early stages of the English Revolution—a conflict in which John Bargrave and his whole family were directly or indirectly involved, and which precipitated this particular journey, as it did all of his continental travels between 1645 and 1660. I take it for granted that his account of France in 1645 reflects the conflictual situation in which he found himself at the outset of the struggle. It was colored inevitably by his strongly held ideological views on religious, political, and broadly cultural matters.

I go further, however, in proposing a dominant theme in Bargrave's *imaginaire* that recalls the role of the cathedral for French writers living in the aftermath of the Revolution. Balzac is said to have compared his life's achievement as a writer to the Cathedral of Bourges, thus indicating a kind of counterflow of artistic genius with which he hoped to recuperate the symbolic achievement of the now demythologized architectural structure. Bargrave had no such ambition, for his collection or for his journal. But the expedition of 1645 that gave rise to the latter can surely be viewed as a tale of two cathedrals. The symbolic center of his early life had undoubtedly been the great metropolitan cathedral of Canterbury, in whose shadow he had received his first schooling, and at which his redoubtable Royalist uncle, Isaac Bargrave, presided as dean between 1625 and 1643. His decision to make Bourges the focal point of his French journey—at a point when Dean Bargrave had paid with his life for his stalwart opposition to the Parliament—must have been inspired by the desire to recover the center which he had recently lost. What I term "scaling the cathedral" amounts to a kind of calibration of the new site by analogy with the earlier one. In other words, I suggest that it is by minutely describing his discoveries, and relating them implicitly to his earlier experience, that Bargrave strives to recover his psychological equilibrium. Bourges is a new site to him, certainly, but it is also qualified to serve as a site of memory.

Why then, precisely, did John Bargrave set out for France in 1645, and how should we interpret his decision to choose Bourges? The first question can soon be answered in terms of the genuine emergency in which he found himself after the death of his uncle, the dean, in January 1643 and his expulsion in the following year from the fellowship which he occupied at the Cambridge college of Peterhouse. Dean Bargrave's death appears to have been a direct consequence of the period of three months' imprisonment without trial that he suffered at the hands of the Long Parliament. He had taken a leading role in organizing the Royalist opposition in east Kent, and several members of his family were participants in the first Kent rebellion of 1643, itself a prelude to the much bloodier Rebellion of 1648, which has been termed "the last great local insurrection in English history."[4] As a younger son, who had been schooled for an academic and ultimately an ecclesiastical career, John Bargrave had no direct part to play in the increasingly bellicose machinations of his elder brother and his close male relatives. The path to Paris had already been taken by a number of prominent Royalists, who feared for their safety in Britain and were able to plot with impunity in the capital city of the neighboring great power. Bargrave records in his journal for May 31, shortly after his own arrival in Paris: "I had an opportunity to talke above an houre with the Marquess of Newcastle and after that with the Earle of Yarmouth and the Lord German whoe for the memorie of my uncle the Deane of Canterburie used me exceeding courteously."[5] It is typical of Bargrave that he should take pride in the credit accruing to his name from his uncle's courageous reputation, and he would certainly have exchanged political views with these prominent exiles. But the purpose of his own journey was not to serve as a Royalist agent.

In fact, the very first dated entry of the journal, recording his departure from Dover on May 23, conveys the practical objective. It mentions that he is traveling in the company of "2 young gentle-men, viz Mr Alexander Chapman, and Mr John Richards," to whom he is acting as "Governor." His equally young nephew, John Raymond, is also of the party. One may imagine that the disruption of courses at the University of Cambridge, following the mass ejection of recalcitrant fellows, had left many young undergraduates in the lurch. Indeed Raymond himself, who had taken up his foundation scholarship at Peterhouse only in January 1643, must have had his studies rudely curtailed. The journey to Bourges, via Paris, was thus a supervised excursion, involving a move to an alternative scene of instruction. The address which Bargrave provides for direction of his correspondence on the opening page of the journal indicates his arrangement to take lodgings in the academic quarter of the city. It reads: "Monsieur Bargrave gentilhomme Anglais demeurant au logis de Monsr Taupin rue des Juifs proche les grandes escoles." The latter term is glossed by the further reference to the schools that Bargrave provides in his "prospect" of Bourges: "The grand escole for the civil and canon law and physic." Elsewhere in the journal he refers to it simply as "the university."

The analogy with Cambridge is thus plain from the start. When Bargrave records his attendance at academic ceremonies at the university, he remarks: "All wch forms differeth but little from that of Cambridge, that of the girdle being excepted." Yet it would not have made much sense for him to choose Bourges for this visit if what was required was an academic community in close contact with Cambridge. There was probably no reciprocal agreement between the institutions, such as the one that allowed Bargrave and his two academic traveling companions to be matriculated at the University of Padua on a later visit to Italy in 1647.[6] Bourges must surely have caught his attention, at least in part, because of its strong parallels with Canterbury. It was an ancient Gallo-Roman town, the former capital of one of the provinces of Aquitaine, with many vestiges of the Roman occupation still visible in its extensive fortifications. Bargrave, who took the trouble to sign himself "Gentleman of England and Kent" on the title page of his *College of Cardinals,* would have been very sensitive to such signs of provincial pride.[7] Since medieval times, moreover, Bourges had been capital of the Berry and the site of an archbishopric, with an imposing Gothic cathedral. If only ecclesiastical connections were important to him, Bargrave might well have selected Sens, whose cathedral had strong architectural links with Canterbury, and whose archdiocese traditionally encompassed the diocese of Paris. But Sens, awkwardly placed on the border between Ile-de-France and northern Burgundy, had few of the characteristics of a provincial capital which Bourges, the center of the former royal *apanage* of the ducs de Berry, unquestionably possessed.

A further factor of interest is that Bourges and its surrounding region had suffered sorely in France's own recent civil war, the Wars of Religion, which extended well into the seventeenth century. The only major excursion that Bargrave and his party made during their visit was to see the town of Sancerre, on the Loire about thirty miles from Bourges, where the ruinous state of the buildings provoked Bargrave's reflections:

> There is likewise a poore peece of a Monestery of the Augustinians, wch wee going to see, The father that showed us the Garden told us that it was at that time 22 yeares since the Prince of Condé (now living) caused that City to be so ruined—a Cause d'Heretiques—by reason that the Huguenots in the Civil Warre hell owt the seige so slowly that the histories admire it, saying that they eate man's flesh a long time before they were betrayed.[8]

It is straight after this chilling revelation that Bargrave chooses to adorn the journal with one of his most elaborate sketches: a view of the town of Sancerre, with fortifications clinging precariously around the hill, and a motif of vines and bunches of grapes filling the mound in a highly formalized way. The village of Saint Thibault and the winding course of the Loire can be seen in the background. What, if any, is the connection between the fragment of recent history that Bargrave has just retailed, and the view that he sketches in? In order to begin to answer this question, which poses in a brutal way the status of visual reference in Bargrave's text, we need to look first of all at the ideology that he explicitly represents. This has an important role both in determining the way in which the traveler ought to behave and in conferring the obligation to convey points of note to an eventual audience.[9]

John Bargrave's philosophy of travel, as defined in the opening pages of his journal, has a strong ethical dimension, which is inseparable from its political dimension. It is consonant with the middle-of-the-road Anglicanism of his uncle Dean Isaac, and of such close allies of the dean as Matthew Wren, bishop of Ely, who was left high and dry with the increasing polarization of the English political class into Puritan and High Church, or Laudian, factions.[10] But it can also be equated with the highly influential definition of the "gentleman" provided by Henry Peacham in his early-seventeenth-century treatise *The Compleat Gentleman*. The connection lies in a common abhorrence of extremes, whether in actions or opinions, and in the maintenance of courteous and discreet behavior at all times. Bargrave's own formulation is as follows:

> The traveller must not make comparisons, especially (such as most are subject unto) concerning, and preferring theire owne countrie in every thing. . . .
>
> Courtesie is the chiefest cognisance of a gentleman with joyned such that discretion may travaile without a passport: and he is the cheapest friend who is gayned only be courtesie.
>
> If his apparell be fashionable it matters not how plaine it be; it being a ridiculous vanity to go gaudy amongst strangers, it is as if one should light a candle to the Sunn.[11]

Maybe Bargrave himself could be accused of breaking his own rule when he comments, on his visit to Notre-Dame on June 14 during the Paris stay, that it is "but smalle (two or 3 such might almost stand in Pauls at London)"! But his measurements in this case are not entirely fanciful. Bargrave's mother was the daughter of a wealthy London haberdasher, and he was very well acquainted with Old Saint Paul's, up to its destruction by fire in 1666 the longest church in northern Europe. Moreover, he goes on to commend Notre-Dame's adornments of "hangings and pictures, and sculptures whereof the most stately and magnificent is the story of St Christopher at the entrance of the Church."

Being courteous and discreet should not however inhibit communication. Bargrave proves himself to be dedicated to social intercourse, even with (and perhaps particularly with) those who do not share his point of view, and he is no less eager to see and record for his future readers all exotic features of note. Here again, there is a pithy sentence from the first page of the French journal that sums up his philosophy: "The Life of a Traveller should be spent either in Reading/Meditation/Discourse by such he doth converse with ye Deade/Himself/Living." It is a characteristic initiative when, on August 28, 1645, Bargrave sallies out to debate the fine points of the doctrine of transubstantiation with the Jesuits of Bourges, at that date quite newly installed in their splendid new college next to the Renaissance Hôtel des Echevins. This was not in fact an encounter with complete strangers: the two Jesuits were Father Carew, an Englishman, and Father Sproud, a Scot, and the debate, though animated, appears to have been friendly. More daring and more risky in its undertaking must have been Bargrave's eventually fulfilled ambition to converse with Bourges's most eminent inhabitant, a prince of the blood and the governor of the city—the very prince de Condé who had so cruelly punished the town of Sancerre. Bargrave seems to court impudence when blithely asking the prince "why hee was in so little a house," but the Machiavellian reply which he receives seems to indicate that his powerful interlocutor did not take the question amiss.[12]

Bargrave takes pains to record his conversations with the great, especially when they touch upon political issues close to his heart.[13] But this discursive exchange does not elucidate the role of the visual interpolations, exceptional though they may be, which he inserts in his text. It does not explain the juxtaposition of his view of Sancerre, precariously perched on its hill, with the previously quoted passage describing the extremities of the siege (fig. 1.1). Yet I would assert that these sketches are not simply random images of record, however much their placing within the travel narrative necessarily has to follow the protocols of chronological sequence. They are put there to demonstrate exemplary truths. In accordance with the seventeenth-century usage, they are more precisely emblematic, since they invite us to meditate on a truth that is not susceptible to being placed directly before our eyes. They conjoin history and memory, and this is precisely through the abrupt collocation of dis-

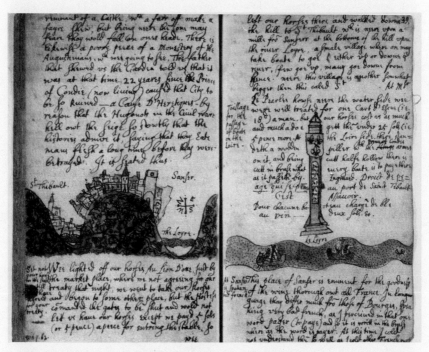

Fig. 1.1. View of Sancerre (left-hand page) and pillar with the arms of the prince de Condé (right-hand page). From Bargrave's 1645 Journal. Courtesy Dean and Chapter of Canterbury Cathedral.

parate elements that force a certain effort of reflection and reminiscence upon the reader. What I am describing here is, of course, the classic mode of operation of the emblem, with its image, motto, and moral in dynamic conjunction. My suggestion is that Bargrave makes the disparate registers of inscription in his journal operate in a similar way.

In the case of the view of Sancerre, the chilling reference to the Wars of Religion is placed in such a way that we cannot treat the image as simply topographic. We have to think more about the inhumanity that took place twenty-five years before. What makes the conjunction of images and text all the more pointed, and indeed personalized, is the "wodden piller" with the arms of the prince de Condé which balances the image of the hill of Sancerre on the adjoining page. This is, on the topographic level, no more than an illustration of the post marking the toll fees owed by boats traveling up the Loire. But Bargrave has purposefully emended his text to show that this bears not "the Kings armes" but those of the prince de Condé. Thrown into juxtaposition with the reference to Condé's role in the "ruin" of Sancerre, the post becomes an emblem of his implacable authority.

That John Bargrave himself had a strong sympathy with the Huguenots can be easily demonstrated. He knew several of the prominent French émigré Protestants who had joined the Christian community in Canterbury, and his uncle had personally (though unsuccessfully) attempted to safeguard their forms of worship when Archbishop Laud insisted on imposing uniformity.[14] But my concern here is not to validate Bargrave's politics. It is to make a point about his use of the interaction of verbal and visual signs. The two visual interpolations—which Bargrave presumably added shortly after his visit to Sancerre, and maybe sketched out at the time—create a place for attention and at the same time a disclosure of ideological depth. What needs to be said is conveyed obliquely, not only because of the risk of surveillance and possible confiscation of the precious little book, but because this is the way to activate memory and provoke fruitful reflection.[15]

The implication of my argument is that Bargrave practices a kind of "wild" emblematics. This is not a particularly hazardous suggestion, given the specificity and sparsity of visual references over the period and the intrinsic unlikelihood that such images would have served an unproblematic aim of description. What we must accept, at the very least, is the fact that Bargrave as traveler and journal writer took careful steps to improve his ability to produce images. In 1645, he had not progressed beyond the use of what appear to be color washes. Yet even this implies a decision to load painting materials into the baggage of the impecunious scholar. On later trips to the continent, Bargrave became more ambitious. A helpful note by another English traveler,

Richard Symonds, confirms that Bargrave and his nephew John Raymond acquired the skill of employing black lead "to take off Intaglios" (i.e., etchings) in Germany, most probably on their return journey from Italy in 1647.[16]

Yet Bargrave did not claim, in 1645 or indeed at any later date, to be an artist. What is clear from the outset—and demonstrated in the survival of the unique French journal of 1645—is that he acquired and developed technical skills in order to give his text the function of visibility and hence of memorability. These images arrest us in our reading—just as we may imagine that the original objects, sites, and ceremonies stopped Bargrave the traveler in his tracks. Each can serve as a trigger to set off a concatenation of ideas, which both question and reinforce the Anglican ideology of the subject.[17]

This, at any rate, is my hypothesis, and it needs to be discussed further in some detail before I examine the major construct of the journal, which is Bargrave's description of Bourges Cathedral. In the chronology of the journey through France, Bargrave's images are initially not very ambitious. First in order comes the simply traced picture of a monk in his habit, completed at Orléans on the journey from Paris to Bourges. Bargrave describes its raison d'être in this way: "In the Cloister [of the Capucins] on the left hand there is the picture of a monk walking in a groave, which for the habit's sake I heere set down." In this case, then, the purpose is not to reproduce the image as such but simply to provide documentation on the dress of a monastic order. But it seems to be the case that Bargrave was already reflecting on his own drawing skills, or the lack of them, at this stage of the journey. He goes on to call attention to a "peece" which is "excellent drawne by one of ye monks, and all the sentences which are very well written."

Bargrave clearly has gained confidence as a draftsman by July, when he has become established at Bourges, and he uses a two-page spread to memorialize two specific and contrasting characteristics of his new habitation. On the left-hand page, there is a brief description of the local use of "sabots or wooden shoes" which he chooses both to illustrate with a vigorous sketch and to relate to the commonly heard French proverb: "Je vous entends—Vous avez des sabots. That is I understand you or I heare you—You have wodden shoes: that is, now you speak owt, or, now you speake to the purpose." Sharing this page is a famous curiosity of Bourges, "the thigh boane of a Gyant," which hangs in the "midst of the cloister before the St Chapell" and is shown to us hanging from its chain, next to two empty chains which once carried other gigantic limbs. On the facing page, then, there comes a full set of sketches of the "Rarities" in the Sainte Chapelle itself, which Bargrave describes as being by repute "the rarest and richest in all France except St Dennis [i.e., the royal abbey of St. Denis]" (fig. 1.2).[18]

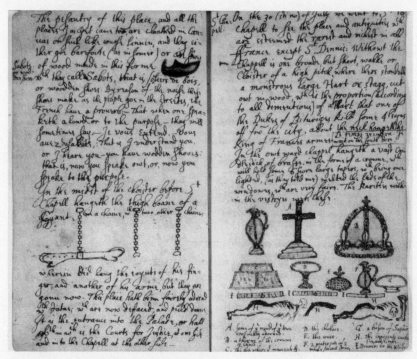

Fig. 1.2. "Sabot" (left-hand page) and "Rarities" of the Sainte Chapelle, Bourges (right-hand page). From Bargrave's 1645 Journal. Courtesy Dean and Chapter of Canterbury Cathedral.

Given the future role of Bargrave as a collector of "rara," or curiosities, it is difficult to ignore the interesting range of objects chosen for this two-page spread, several of which might later have found a suitable home in one of his cabinets. It is also tempting to read an ideological point into the very juxtaposition of these three categories of objects: the functional shoes are juxtaposed with the monstrous relic of the giant, and both of these placed opposite still venerated objects of religious cult—some of which share the physical properties of the "curiosity." Canterbury Cathedral had been stripped, as a result of Henry VIII's brusque decision, of the precious relics and other appurtenances of Saint Thomas's shrine that had so powerfully contributed to the cathedral's medieval splendor. This loss was still reverberating in the mid-seventeenth century when iconoclasm was once again revived as a destructive force in English culture. Bargrave's journal puts on record (in advance of his routine as a collector) both his attraction to the ambiguous category of the "curiosity" and his repulsion from what he would later call the "folly" of superstition. The visual collocation starkly intensifies, and in the same process suspends, the potential contradictions.

I can anticipate the objection that it would be over ingenious to apply throughout Bargrave's journal the kind of hermeneutic interpretations that I have been suggesting here. Certainly not all the images included lend themselves to this type of analysis. Indeed, the most prevalent class of image featured—and perhaps the kind which Bargrave considered himself socially as well as technically most qualified to record when he left England supplied with his range of colors—is the heraldic coat of arms. But even here there is an underlying special reason why Bargrave breaks off the text and engages in a work of visual representation. Bargrave's father had acquired armigerous status only in 1611, the year after John's birth, and his sense of being a "gentleman" was closely bound up with the need to display the evidence of this status. Dean Isaac Bargrave had placed the recently granted arms in a prominent position on the vaulting of the cloisters of Canterbury Cathedral. When John Bargrave went on to visit Italy in 1646, he commissioned a triple portrait of himself and his companions in which the Bargrave arms were prominently displayed, and this chivalric accessory was repeated when, in 1650, he had another portrait done on his return to Rome.[19] In the 1645 French journal, the care taken over the sketching of the arms of the city and "university" of Bourges—not to mention the whole-page display of the Bourbon lilies and resplendent escutcheon of the prince de Condé—must surely be seen in part as confirming, by association, his own proud claim to bear arms. A "gentleman" of reduced means, he sets all the more store by the distinction that elevates him above the common run of humanity.

Yet the more ambitious sketches in the journal suggest much more than the message of nobility by association. For example, perhaps the most technically ambitious and elaborate of all of them, almost a full page, is the record of a civic ceremony on August 3, the feast day of the patron of Bourges Cathedral, Saint Stephen, which provided the occasion for a gathering of "4 or 5 thousand people in the market place called Les Arens" (fig. 1.3). Bargrave shows himself to be interested in the persistence of this place-name which dates back to the original Roman Arena: "In this place the auncient Romans had an Amphitheatre. Of such there is now no token, but the name and the common peoples talke of it." He is also concerned to convey his perceptions of the governance of the city, choosing to depict the very moment when the "Maior" lights an elaborate bonfire with his torch, and glossing it with a description of civic ceremonial which would have awakened his recollections of Canterbury.

Yet the prime point of the image is surely that Bargrave is witnessing the commemoration of a recent historical event, which is vividly evoked in the firing of cannon and the flames about to take hold of a towering structure on the

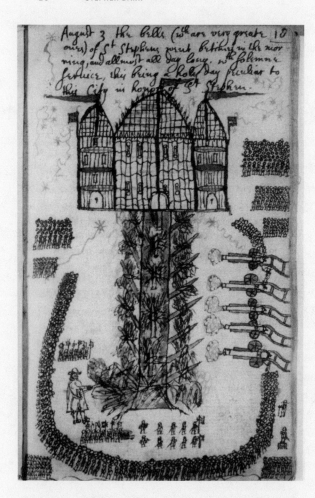

Fig. 1.3. Ceremony in the marketplace, August 3, 1645. From Bargrave's 1645 Journal. Courtesy Dean and Chapter of Canterbury Cathedral.

top of which is the "neate form of a castle, made of small osiers."[20] Although it took place at Bourges, this was a ceremony which celebrated the capture of "Mardick" (i.e., Fort-Mardyck) in the vicinity of Dunkerque, in the course of the current war between the French and the incursive Spanish troops in the Low Countries. The interest of the good citizens of Bourges in this far-off battle can be explained by the fact that the victor was none other than the brilliant general Louis II de Bourbon, future fourth prince de Condé and heir of the resident governor. For Bargrave, whose sense of the pitiful state of his own war-wracked country was inextricably bound up with his view of the shifting panorama of European politics, this victory over the Spaniards could at least substitute provisionally for the absence of news from home.

Most mysterious among the larger images in the journal, and apparently unexplained by any relevant textual reference, is the competently sketched "wine presse of St Stevens the Cathedral at Bourges," in which the tonal treatment of the wooden members gives a reasonable impression of three-dimensionality (fig. 1.4). The little captions by Bargrave suggest that this vast apparatus housed in the cathedral incorporated collection boxes "pour St Clare" (the female order of Franciscans) and the Carmelites. But Bargrave has chosen to decorate the central chamber with a wine-red motif of clustered grapes. The fact that this repeats almost identically the motif that he uses to cover the hill of Sancerre suggests that Bargrave is not merely acknowledging the excellence of the wines of the region but also making a reference to the biblical significance of the vine. As it appears in Psalm 80, the vine is an emblem of the continuing strength of God's people under tribulation: "Return, we beseech thee, O God of hosts: look down from heaven, and behold, and visit this vine." In John 15. 5, Christ picks up this quotation when he proclaims: "I am the vine, ye are the branches."

This suggestion that Bargrave foregrounds aspects of an image in order to provoke a biblical reminiscence is quite coherent with the way he himself

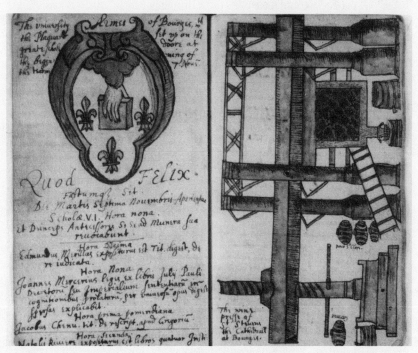

Fig. 1.4. Arms of the University of Bourges (left-hand page) and "wine presse of St Stevens the Cathedral," Bourges (right-hand page). From Bargrave's 1645 Journal. Courtesy Dean and Chapter of Canterbury Cathedral.

chooses to interpret a major work of sculpture installed in the crypt of the cathedral. Before we examine this, however, it is important to make some preliminary points about the way in which Bourges Cathedral is introduced into the text. My interpretation of this section of the travel journal, which in a real sense marks the climax of Bargrave's journey, is inseparable from broader considerations relating to the visual and verbal components of the text. Bargrave himself assures us elsewhere that, in all his journeys to Italy, he would treat the ascent of Mount Vesuvius as the limit and turning point of his entire itinerary.[21] Bourges Cathedral plays an analogous role in the French journal. Although it does not signify his turning back to his homeland, it does serve as a kind of internal metaphor for the whole enterprise, bringing together its manifold ethical, historical, and religious undertones.

It is in fact right at the start of his stay in Bourges, on July 23, that Bargrave determines that he will go "up to the topp of ye steeple," that is to say the northwest tower of the cathedral, known then as now as the "Tour de Beurre." From that high point, he proceeds to sketch a view of his surroundings, or as he puts it, "the prospect of the City as I have figured it in the next page." "Prospect" would have been the customary way in which artists skilled in perspective described their city views in the seventeenth century. Bargrave was probably quite familiar with engravings such as Matthew Merian's *Prospect of London* (1638), though he would not yet have had the chance to see Wenceslaus Hollar's famous view from the tower of St. Saviour's, Southwark, published in Antwerp only in 1647. Bargrave's "prospect," also taken from a church tower, makes no attempt to achieve correct perspectival recession, except perhaps in the case of a few scraggy trees and a crudely drawn extramural church, shown in the top right-hand corner. It is more in the nature of a map, showing as it does the main thoroughfares and buildings of the city, and supplying them with a key, so that they can be identified in the subsequent text (fig. 1.5).[22]

This is not to say that Bargrave was ignorant of the different points of view from which the city of Bourges could be more advantageously viewed. Indeed he goes on to comment specifically that Bourges's northward-looking situation ensures that "the view of it is very faire and pleasant as one cometh to it from Orléans or Issodunum [Issoudun]," but that from the south side "there is no prospect." Evidently he was in agreement with the anonymous local artist of the period whose prospect from the northern approach, across the River Yèvre, is still to be seen at Bourges in the foyer of the Hôtel Lallemand (Musée des arts décoratifs). (The eighteenth-century engraving illustrated here chooses a similar viewpoint, though from a greater distance [fig. 1.6].) Bargrave could easily have imitated this type of conventional view, in much the same way as

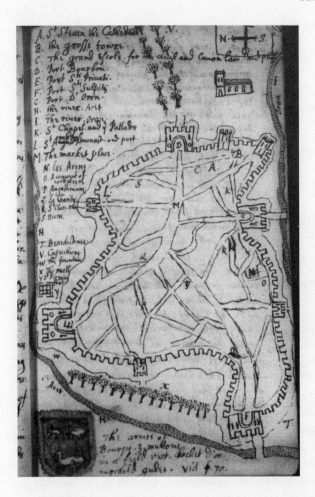

Fig. 1.5. "Prospect" of Bourges from the Cathedral tower. From Bargrave's 1645 Journal. Courtesy Dean and Chapter of Canterbury Cathedral.

he sketched the distant prospect of Sancerre. But it is consistent with the symbolic importance invested in his visit to the cathedral that the Tour de Beurre should be the marker from which he takes his bearings within the city. This comes across very clearly when we learn that he does not just descend from the heights with his prospect but insists on leaving signs of his passage behind:

> When I was on the steeple . . . at one of the corners there is a pinnacle which hath a bell for a clock, and on the out side on the topp standeth a large Pelican double gilded which is the wether-cock, I climb'd up to it . . . and turned it rounde many times with my hand, and then on the inside of the pinnacle and steeple I writt with a black led penn Noli altum sapere, adding my name, though I took not the literall counsel.

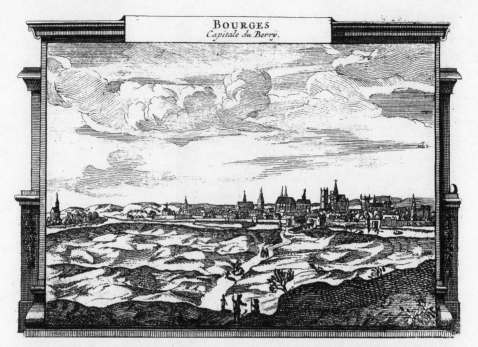

Fig. 1.6. "Bourges. Capitale du Berry," an eighteenth-century view. The "Tour de Beurre" of the Cathedral is clearly visible beyond the bridge and town gate to the right of the picture. Author's collection.

Bargrave's graffito takes the form of a proverb, loosely related perhaps to the opening verses of Psalm 131 according to the Book of Common Prayer: "Lord, I am not high-minded: I have no proud looks. I do not exercise myself in great matters: which are too high for me." But he appreciates the ironic twist in the fact that he has already defied the injunction to avoid heights. Coupled with his remarkable agility in activating the weathercock (symbolic of Christ's sacrifice) at some risk to himself, this passage could be said both to represent and to perform an act of subjective inscription. The black-leaded text is probably no longer to be found on the "inside" of the still existent "pinnacle." But the ink of the journal brings it back to us again.

In this respect, one might suggest that Bargrave's performance hardly corresponds with what Juliet Fleming, with much justification, sees as the prevalent tone of graffiti writing in this period: "predicated on a socially constituted subject and on notions of authorship that were collective, aphoristic and inscriptive, rather than individualist, lyric and voice-centred."[23] If we put the matter another way, it is surely legitimate to see this sequence of purposeful actions by Bargrave, and their written form as they survive in his journal, precisely as a strategy of grafting the individual onto the collective, the lyric onto the aphoristic, and the voice-centered onto the inscriptive. As a traveler and (in a real sense) a temporary exile from his country, Bargrave responded to the inducement to explore this additional register of self-reflexivity. One might even conclude that he has actualized this reflexivity specifically through the possibilities of inscription afforded by the journal.

Scarcely has Bargrave recorded these exploits on the dizzy heights of the building when he decides to descend, literally and conceptually, to the depths. "I was not then so high, but anon was as lowe. For when we were come downe, wee went to the Sepulcher, a church underneath the quire of the Cathedrall, going through a darke vault to it." In this new atmosphere, the paradox of representation is acutely developed, as Bargrave successively considers the textual source of the sculptural group of the Burial of Christ to be seen there, and the material constituents of the work in so far as it is accessible to the touch. First, he cites verses from all four Gospels to provide the material referring to Joseph of Arimathea's role in Christ's burial (though he gets the chapter reference slightly wrong in Luke and the verse reference slightly wrong in Mark, which may suggest that he was recalling these texts from memory). Then he goes on to ask questions about its material:

> [W]ee were shewed the Sepulture, which indeed Death drawne to the Life by the arte of a most dexterous hand. There is St. Mat. 27,57 St Mar 15,23 Lu 24,50 John 19 38 very exquisitely expressed in statue worke (Religione intuentibus incubit) he that shewed it, was all the while on his knees before it but answered to the question propounded, he saide it was all of marble, but the proportions being gilded, rich and color'd I could not discerne well, but to the touch it seemed to be stoane. I was much taken with the aptness of the place, and the fullness of the representation.

At the center of this complex little passage, there is the Latin tag which proclaims the unmediated effect of a lifelike spectacle: "It instills those who look upon it with religion." But this commonplace remark is relativized by the hint that the guide is merely superstitious in kneeling before the work. The "Sepulture" should be understood not as a presence but as a material representation, accessible to "touch," and perfectly well adjusted to its infernal context.[24]

Bargrave's account of his visit to the cathedral at Bourges is therefore expressed in terms of a scaling of heights and a descent to depths; it relies on the description of acts of subjective inscription and symbolic interpretation that foreground his own liminal position as a foreigner—one who can stand both inside and outside the closed circuit of dogma. Of a more systematic enumeration of the features of the main body of the church—the choir, the nave, and the distinctive double aisles on each side of it—there is little to be read here, and nothing to be seen. Admittedly the main adornment of the choir, the *jubé* or choir screen, was vandalized by the Protestants during the Wars of Religion and would be put back in place by the canons only in 1653. Bargrave does not seem to be aware of its existence. However, before making another hair-raising climb across the exterior of the building, he does examine the fifteenth-century tympanum illustrating the Last Judgment over the main West Door. With his usual insistence on an individualistic reading, he interprets even the fragmentary state of some of the figures as lending an additional, expressive dimension of pathos to their apocalyptic attitudes:

> The owt side of the west-end is very stately and magnificent, having one large doore in the midst over which Semicirque is wonderfully sett forth the Day of Judgement in statue worke, but much defaced by the civill wars. Yet I fancied one part of it to be more glorious by its intended ruine. For the story representing the rysing from the graves, the figures being mutilated, and deprived of severall limbs, this man seemeth to looke for his arme that he hath lost; that for his legg, a third for his hand, and a forth for his heade: some for one part some for another.

It is, as Bargrave significantly notes, the civil wars in France that have caused this mutilation. He would have been right to anticipate similar destructive frenzies in the war that was breaking out in his native land and would not spare the cathedral church of Canterbury. But even the "intended ruine" can be redeemed if we read the whole scene not as evidence of malevolent destruction but as a passionate search of the "figures" for their missing fragments—"some for one part some for another." Bargrave's own future activity in building up his collection, piece by piece, in his enforced separation from his native land also seems "glorious" (that is to say, redemptive) in this light.

The Restoration of the Stuart monarchy in 1660 caused John Bargrave to return home precipitately from his fourth visit to Rome, and his appointment to a canonry at Canterbury Cathedral in 1662 ensured that he had space to store and display his collection. At this period, the cult of the beheaded Charles I, King and Martyr, was widely promoted by the Anglican Church, and paintings reflecting the well-known iconography of the monarch laying down his earthly crown and taking up a heavenly one were put up in a number of English cathedrals. The example commissioned for Canterbury, which still hangs in the north choir aisle, contains, however, one significant local variant. In the distant landscape to one side of the kneeling monarch there is a striking image of the cathedral itself, like a city set on a hill, lit with shafts of heavenly light.

This discussion has been concerned with a very different scenario: not the triumphant image of the cathedral transcending its earthly situation, but on the contrary Bargrave's dogged attempt to vindicate his ethical and political concerns through a journey of exile, and the record which he made of it. Bourges would not replicate Canterbury, but it would provide a kind of sounding board against which to measure his intimate concerns. His intention was thus to make his experience resonant, through the inquiring narrative of his travels, and through the symbolic weight that he attached to incidents and images met with along the way. Although such a travel journal would customarily be annexed to the prehistory of the "Grand Tour," it is difficult to transpose such an achievement into the very different society of the eighteenth century, let alone into the more recent context of mass tourism where rigid guidelines have replaced the plasticity of the individual quest. Nevertheless, the image of the cathedral as monument and memorial survives, and not only in the all-encompassing literary worlds of Hugo, Balzac, or Proust. The shattered steel ribbing of the twin towers of the World Trade Center (fig. E.4) evokes the Gothic tracery of the destroyed cathedral of Coventry, as both the recent and the remote disaster are assimilated into the common texture of memory.

NOTES

1. The general topic is well covered by the recent collection of essays edited by Ségolène Le Men, *La cathédrale illustrée de Victor Hugo à Claude Monet* (Paris: CNRS, 1998). For Hugo, see "Sur la destruction des monuments en France," in *Oeuvres complètes,* ed. Jean Massin (Paris: Club français du livre, 1969), 2:572; also the excellent analysis in Jeffrey Mehlman, *Revolution and Repetition: Marx/Hugo/Balzac* (Berkeley: University of California Press, 1977), 72–73. For Proust, see John Ruskin, *La Bible d'Amiens,* translation, notes, and preface by Marcel Proust (Paris: 10/18, 1986); also Julia Kristeva, *Proust and the Sense of Time,* trans. and with an introduction by Stephen Bann (London: Faber, 1993), 7.

2. See Jonathan Spence, *The Memory Palace of Matteo Ricci* (London: Faber, 1985); Juliet Fleming, *Graffiti and the Writing Arts of Early Modern England* (London: Reaktion, 2001).

3. The Bargrave journal is a small, parchment-bound notebook titled on its cover "A part of my Journal of France 1645 John Bargrave The First Part." It came to light in the Canterbury Cathedral Archive (U11/8 IRBY Deposit) after the publication of my own study, *Under the Sign: John Bargrave as Collector, Traveler and Witness* (Ann Arbor: University of Michigan Press, 1994). Although it may be assumed that the written records of later continental journeys by Bargrave were employed in the composition of the *Itinerary . . . through Italy* published under the name of his nephew, John Raymond, in 1648, as well as in his compilation *Pope Alexander the Seventh and the College of Cardinals* (Camden Society, 1867), none

of the corresponding manuscripts have been found. The recently published travel diary of his cousin Robert Bargrave, which covers the period 1646–57 and intersects at two points with the travels of John, survives in a fair copy, which was either compiled from a collection of notes or written up from an earlier, lost draft. See the editorial comments of Michael G. Brenan, in *The Travel Diary of Robert Bargrave Levant Merchant 1647–1656* (London: Hakluyt Society, 1999), 38–51.

4. See Brenan, *Travel Diary*, 10–14, for a succinct account of "The Bargraves and the Civil War."

5. The journal is not regularly paginated, and references will therefore be made in the text to the dating of the individual entries, where a page number is not provided.

6. See Bann, *Under the Sign*, 15.

7. Ibid., 6: "Generosum Anglum Cantianum."

8. John Bargrave, Journal, opp. p. 39.

9. Although the travel journal does not, of course, address a specific audience, it may be claimed that Bargrave's work in writing and collecting was always implicitly didactic and, moreover, related to his conception of himself as a witness of history. See Bann, *Under the Sign*, 99–130.

10. See ibid., 51–57.

11. John Bargrave, Journal, first inside page.

12. The visit takes place toward the end of Bargrave's stay, on September 17. The prince's reply is, basically, that he is acutely conscious of the perils of his position as second in line to the throne, after the duc d'Orléans, and in the absence of any other heirs in the next generation. He is therefore unwilling to run the risk of "seditions from the people, or emulations from the greater ones," and chooses his lodging by virtue of its proximity to the "Gross Towre," in case of emergency.

Henri II, third prince de Condé, was born on September 1, 1588, and died on December 26, 1646, not much more than a year after his conversation with John Bargrave. He had become governor of Berry in 1616, and despite acting as a mediator between the Court and the Huguenots in 1616, he captured and sacked the latter's stronghold of Sancerre in 1621.

13. A specially relevant instance is his altercation with the "Grand Duke" of Tuscany, on a later Italian journey, when he takes the ruler to task for including a portrait of Oliver Cromwell in his celebrated gallery. See Bann, *Under the Sign*, 11–12, for the relevant passage from Bargrave's *College of Cardinals*.

14. Ibid., 55–56.

15. Two instances can be cited of Bargrave's later productions which reinforce this point. First, there is the frontispiece to the *Itinerary*, in which Bargrave and his nephew seem to have infiltrated a visual allegory on the rivalry of Venice and Counter-Reformation Rome, which is not discussed in the text. Secondly, there is the case of Bargrave's only recorded engraving, which represents the entry of Queen Christina of Sweden into the Catholic church at Innsbruck in 1655. He has pasted the only known copy of his portrait of the renegade queen into a page of the *College of Cardinals*, which juxtaposes it with violent and abusive references to her train. See Bann, *Under the Sign*, plates 23, 25, and pp. 109, 115–16. It is worth pointing out that the prince de Condé may have also excited Bargrave's special attention because he betrayed the faith of his ancestors: though the son and grandson of Calvinists, he gained the reputation of being the most intolerant of Catholics.

16. See Bann, *Under the Sign*, 146 n. 1. Richard Symonds notes that Raymond learned to print from such "intaglios" with the addition of black lead. It is likely that this method was studied on their return journey in order to find a way of printing from the drawings of Italian

monuments that Bargrave and Raymond had completed over the previous year. Presumably these are the numerous images that appear as print illustrations to the *Itinerary*.

17. There is no space here for me to develop further the distinctive nature of Bargrave's Anglicanism. For a comparable figure of the period, whose ideology is also expressed in the interstices of his signifying practice, see my essay "Izaak Walton et John Donne," in *John Donne*, ed. Jean-Marie Benoist (Paris: Cahiers de l'H, 1983), 31–38. Among Walton's well-known collection of *Lives* is one devoted to Bargrave's connection, Sir Henry Wotton.

18. John Bargrave, Journal, 15–16. I am told by Mme. Béatrice de Chancel-Bardelot, conservateur-en-chef of the Musées de Bourges, that the visual record of the relics is exceptional, if not unique, for the period.

19. For the two portraits, see Bann, *Under the Sign*, plates 2 and 14.

20. John Bargrave, Journal, 10.

21. See Bann, *Under the Sign*, 71.

22. A seventeenth-century map of the Siege of Autun, in the collection of the Musée Rolin, Autun, is similar in its mixture of graphic and diagrammatic features.

23. Fleming, *Graffiti*, 41.

24. The work can still be seen in the crypt of Bourges Cathedral.

2

Retrieving the Past, Inventing the Memorable:
Huang Yi's Visit to the Song-Luo Monuments

LILLIAN LAN-YING TSENG

This is an essay about an album made by a Chinese literati painter, Huang Yi (1744–1801), to commemorate his visit to ancient monuments in between Mount Song and the River Luo in north China. More than a simple pictorial recollection of a recent visit to remote monuments, the album is unusually engaged in various acts of remembrance. This composite of image and text—pictures and their corresponding postscripts are mounted in pairs—contains both visual and textual evidence of remembering. Before making the album, the painter carefully kept a diary during his journey. Both that immediate record and the later recollection of the journey in album form uncover the fear of forgetting and the need to produce mementos. Having finished the album, the painter further circulated it among his friends, which proclaims the desire to be remembered. After the painter's death, the album then became the remembered as it gave rise to replicas that marked the copiers' attempt at remembering.

From the album and the web of remembrance it spins, this essay explores the convergence of memory studies and visual culture, two fields of inquiry which emerged less than two decades ago. I consider how a visual mode of representation—as opposed to textual or oral—helps to shape memory. Focusing on the album that comprises both pictures and postscripts, I examine the potential competition between image and text in articulating the references of remembrance. Comparing the album with the diary, I show that the later pictorial recollection, free to re-organize the experiences of the past, conveys more psychological than factual aspects of remembrance. Furthermore, the format of a Chinese album allows the unlimited expansion of colophons, where the viewer often makes his comments while absorbing the opinions inscribed by others. Taking advantage of this format, I discuss how spectatorship may consolidate our understanding of the collective memory shared by a definable or even intimate social group.

Through the case study, this essay also reflects on the possible dialogues between monuments and memories. I am particularly concerned with the fluid relationships between the two. Based on the painter's postscripts, I investigate what the represented monuments in the album were intended to commemo-rate—the historical past revealed by monuments, or the historiographical commentary on that past derived from the studies of monuments. With the aid of the viewers' inscriptions, I analyze how, by bringing the inaccessible monu-ments to the forefront, the painter and his album could be monumental. My essay further ponders the replaceability of a monument by means of represen-tation and reproduction as two modes of remembrance—the monuments, pri-marily erected by the ancients to commemorate specific persons or events, could be in turn the objects of commemoration once they were represented in the album. Likewise, the pictorially represented monument, originally made by the painter to commemorate his personal journey, could itself become the object of commemoration once it was reproduced by later copiers.

Image and Text

After his ascent of the sacred Mount Song and his journey to the ancient cap-ital Luoyang in 1796, Huang Yi produced an album with twenty-four leaves illustrating the twenty-four places he had visited.[1] The locations he repre-sented are all legendary, including mountain scenery (e.g., "Stone Gurgle"), religious sites (e.g., the White Horse Temple, Longmen Grottoes, and Shaolin Monastery) and ancient ruins (e.g., the three Han gate-towers). The way he chose to represent these monuments—using ink on paper with looser brush-work known as the Dong-Ju style—is also familiar in the traditional genre of Chinese literati landscape painting. What distinguishes his album from others is the depiction of the travelers' peculiar attention to monuments.

Huang Yi appears on one leaf as a traveler halfway up a mountain, climb-ing with a companion to a monastery (fig. 2.1). The travelers, placed between a village at the foot and a monastery at the summit, are making a pilgrimage

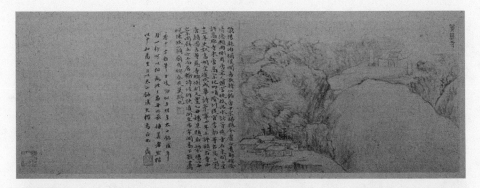

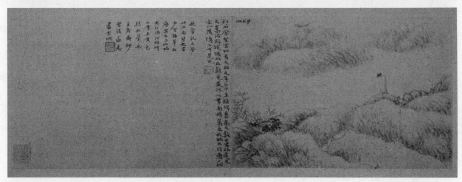

Fig. 2.1. (top) Huang Yi, "Visiting Steles in the Song-Luo Area," *The Dengci Monastery,* 1796. Palace Museum, Beijing.

Fig. 2.2. (bottom) Huang Yi, "Visiting Steles in the Song-Luo Area," *Mount Mang,* 1796. Palace Museum, Beijing.

from the secular to the sacred, while enduring great hardship as suggested by the steep cliffs with no visible path. Normally, the faraway religious complex would be a desirable reward for such a harsh journey, but not for Huang Yi. On another leaf, Huang showed himself and his companions approaching a peak floating above clouds, where only an imposing stone stele towers into the sky (fig. 2.2). Evidently, what captivated Huang was not the well-known mountain scenery but the stele standing alone for centuries. Likewise, what motivated him in the previous pilgrimage was not the monastery but the two steles outside. He labeled this album "Visiting Steles in the Song-Luo Area," and thus paid particular homage to stone steles.

The moss-covered surface or torn body of a stone stele bears witness to time, and its engraved texts commemorate either persons or events from the past. Such nostalgia inspired by a stele can be both sentimental and intellectual. The tomb with carved words in Poussin's *The Arcadian Shepherds* may provide clues to the painter's intentions and abundant material for scholarly reflection,[2] but the steles in Huang Yi's album are all blank, devoid of writing. The intentional blankness—contrary to the commemorative nature of steles—only provokes the viewer to search for some text, to read the titles at the upper corners of the paintings and to go through the postscripts immediately following the images. For example, the depiction of approaching an imposing stele is entitled "Mount Mang." A short postscript states that "at the site of the Huisheng Temple at Mount Mang, there is a stele inscribed by Shi Zhongli in the first year of the Yuanyou reign (1086). It is quite lofty and could be seen from a distance" (fig. 2.2). Both title and postscript supplement the image, specifying the location and identification of the represented monument. For the ascent scene, the title "Dengci Monastery" is given, and the long postscript states in part that Huang "visited the Dengci Monastery. . . . To the east of the monastery stands the stele [written] by Emperor Gao of the Tang (r. 650–83) to commemorate [his father's] achievements.[3] At the back of the stele are engraved the names of his accompanying subjects such as Li Ji (594–669), below which are Emperor Ming's poem on his stay at Chenggao inscribed by Shi Shu in the thirteen year of the Kaiyuan reign (725)[4] and Wang Ping's inscription in the fourth year of the Chongning reign (1105). To the west of the monastery stands a stele inscribed by Yan Shigu (581–645) to commemorate [the establishment of] the Dengci Monastery.[5] It contains a side inscription by a man named Yang in the Yichou year of the Yuanfeng reign (1085)" (fig. 2.1). Rather than simply indicating location and identification, the postscript paraphrases the inscriptions on the two steles outside the monastery. The concern over precise names and dates on the steles gives Huang's nostalgia a scholarly quality and makes the viewer wonder what are more important—images of visiting steles or postscripts about inscriptions on the visited steles.

In any case, Huang Yi's passion was to record the engraved texts that recounted the past. His interests also extended to other comparable monuments with ancient texts. On one leaf of the album, Huang portrayed himself in a group pointing to a pair of architectural remains identified by the title as "Kaimu Stone Gate-Towers" (fig. 2.3). The postscript reports that "the Kaimu Gate-Towers are several steps east of the Chongfu Temple. The inscription with the seal characters in the second year of the Yanguang reign (123) is [mainly] on the northern wall of the western gate-tower.[6] There are two remaining lines on the eastern side of the same gate-tower. I used to send craftsmen to make rubbings of this [inscription], in which preceding [the characters] '*kai mu miao xing*' is a line [containing] '*chuan jun yang.*' Now [I] see [even] before it appears a line [containing] '*er yue.*' [I] suspect this could be the year and month that the gate-towers were constructed. With rubbings carefully

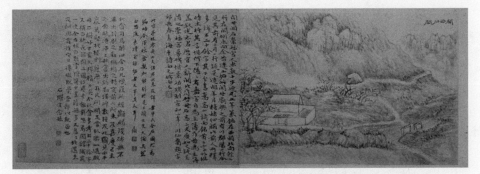

Fig. 2.3. Huang Yi, "Visiting Steles in the Song-Luo Area," *The Kaimu Stone Gate-Towers,* 1796. Palace Museum, Beijing.

made on fine paper, I could identify twenty more words than my predecessors had done." The statement reveals that Huang's visit to the stone steles in the Song-Luo area was no less than a field trip. He did research beforehand, and once there carefully examined objects and made records. The almost archaeological approach to monuments explains the reason why Huang Yi always appears with a team in the album. On the leaf entitled "Yi Que," Huang is shown seated in one of the Longmen Grottoes, supervising the production of rubbings from what he has inspected.[7]

The postscript to the Kaimu Stone Gate-Towers further discloses Huang's true interests in the engraved texts that recount the past. The gate-towers were built for the Kaimu Temple dedicated to Qi's mother, who was the wife of Yu, the founder of the Xia dynasty.[8] Yu was a legendary figure believed to regulate rivers and prevent floods in remote antiquity. By honoring his achievements with inscriptions on the western gate-tower, those living during the Han reign prayed for timely winds and rains.[9] When Huang read these inscriptions, what he recalled was not the historical past—neither Xia nor Han—to which the texts refer, but the historiographical past to which the texts lead: he recollected the rubbings he had examined and relived the scholarship he had learned. His greatest pleasure came from the discovery of what had been ignored, or rather forgotten, such as the twenty more newly recognized words on the gate-tower.

Both image and text in the album thus work together to substantiate Huang's nostalgic journey to the Song-Luo area. On the one hand, the blankness of the painted steles (and other comparable monuments) indicates the status of forgetting—people (Huang Yi and other scholars) no longer remembered, or remembered correctly, what had been engraved on them. The lengthy postscripts, on the other hand, display the efforts of remembering—how Huang reclaimed the forgotten past, and reclaimed more of it than anyone else, through his travels in the wilds, his survey of stone monuments, and his devotion to textual studies.

Painting and Diary

The album not only shows how Huang Yi recalled the remote past but also presents how he recollected the recent journey. According to his postscript in the album's colophon, Huang spent about forty days in October and November of 1796, traveling to and around the Song-Luo area. Highly satisfied with the results, especially the gains of more than four hundred rubbings, Huang expressed his elated mood through the twenty-four pictures based on his travel notes, pictorial or textual. Whether he sketched along the way is unknown, but he did keep a diary during the journey, which later circulated and was published in 1854, half a century after his death.[10]

The diary begins with an entry dated October 6, the day that Huang Yi arrived at Xiangfu. No account is given of his journey from Ji'ning, where he held office (fig. 2.4).[11] The diary proceeds with Huang's movement westward along the Yellow River, through Zhengzhou and Xingyang to Yanshi. It describes how Huang spent one week at Mount Song, ascending from Yanshi on October 10 and returning to the same town on October 19. Next comes a description of Huang's journey from Yanshi to Longmen, leaving on October 21, stopping at Luoyang, and returning to Yanshi on October 27. The diary ends with entries on Huang's homeward trip via Mengxian, Huaiqing, Weihui, Dongming, Caojun, and Juye. Huang appears to have traveled overland back to Ji'ning, which took him twelve days, from October 29 to November 9. Very likely Huang made the round trip between Ji'ning and Yanshi (approximately five hundred miles) with the simple donkey carts depicted in the album.[12]

The diary details where Huang Yi visited, what he examined, purchased, and was given, and with whom he worked, consulted, and traveled. It became the source for his postscripts to the twenty-four pictures. For example, from the entry dated October 8, the day he visited the Dengci Monastery, we learn that he indeed "climbed a high mound" to reach the monastery, that the inscription with the names of accompanying subjects on the back of the stele was "too high to make a rubbing," and that in addition to the two steles outside flanking the monastery, another stele "erected in the fifth year of the Wuping reign (574) in the [Northern] Qi dynasty was on the wall of the rear hall."[13] The three pieces of information are mentioned in the diary but omitted in the postscript to the picture entitled "Dengci Monastery" (fig. 2.1).

The twenty-four pictures depict highlights of the diary. Unlike the diary, the pictures are scene-oriented and either condense explorations of different

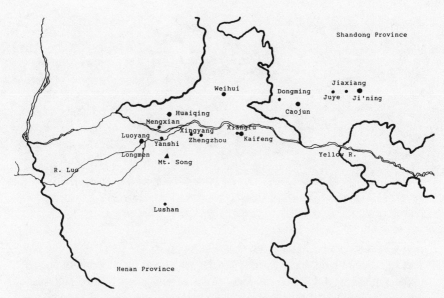

Fig. 2.4. Places Huang Yi visited in his journey to the Song-Luo monuments. Drawn by Lillian Lan-ying Tseng.

days into one scene or divide a single day's adventure into two or three scenes.[14] For instance, Huang recalled his journey to Mount Song on October 13 in three leaves depicting the Songyang Academy, the Kaimu Gate-Towers (fig. 2.3), and the Taishi Gate-Towers.[15] In contrast, the leaf entitled "Little Rock Mountain Studio" combines Huang's experiences on October 19 and 28 into one scene (fig. 2.5).

The diary and the paintings differ regarding Huang's relationship with his friends, which may reveal Huang's specific state of mind when he recalled his journey.[16] From the diary, it appears that Huang formed equally strong friendships with Wang Fu and with Wu Yi (1745–99), two old cronies who received him at Yanshi.[17] Wang Fu supplied Huang with a sedan chair, servants, and local guides for the ascent of Mount Song, invited him to visit Longmen, hosted parties for him, and accommodated him at Yanshi. In return, Huang made and presented Wang with a long handscroll entitled "Looking at Ancient Relics at Longmen."[18] Wu Yi received Huang in his studio, accompanied him to the Longmen Grottoes, and gave him a considerable number of rubbings as gifts.[19] From the album, however, we gain a very different picture because Wu Yi is mentioned in seven postscripts while Wang Fu's name appears only in two. Huang Yi lingered so much with his memory of Wu Yi when he made the album that he overlooked others who had also participated in activities as recorded in his diary.

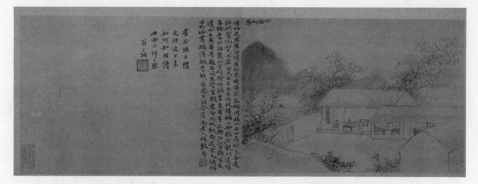

Fig. 2.5. Huang Yi, "Visiting Steles in the Song-Luo Area," *The Little Rock Mountain Studio,* 1796.
Palace Museum, Beijing.

Why was Huang Yi so immersed in his memory of Wu Yi? Wu, one year
younger than Huang, was a learned scholar with great enthusiasm for ancient
texts, publishing books on classics, ritual canons, and bronze and stone
relics.[20] He was one of the sponsors who financially supported the restoration
of the Wu family shrines in 1787, a project initiated by Huang Yi after he had
excavated them in the previous year.[21] We are not sure if Wu Yi was ever introduced to the spectacular Han relics in situ, but he left some comments on
the carvings of the Front Chamber.[22] Because of shared common interests,
Huang Yi was very fond of this friend.[23] Huang once presented Wu Yi with his
copy of a carved figure from the Zhu Wei shrine, claiming that he had discovered a likeness between the figure and his friend.[24] More often, they exchanged
their opinions about textual research by circulating rare books and rubbings.[25]
Since Wu came from Yanshi at the foot of Mount Song, Huang often asked for
Wu's help in gathering rubbings of the ancient steles in that area.[26] Dissatisfied
with the rubbings made by others, Huang decided to visit the Song-Luo monuments in person.[27] According to Huang's diary, when he arrived at Yanshi on
October 9, Wu Yi was compiling local gazetteers in Lushan.[28] However, Wu
was soon fetched home and received Huang in his studio after Huang's descent
of Mount Song on October 19. They traveled together to Luoyang to visit the
Longmen Grottoes. Wu then went back to Yanshi on October 23, leaving
Huang behind to make rubbings.[29] On October 27 and 28, Wu again received
Huang at Yanshi on Huang's way back to Ji'ning.[30]

The leaf entitled "Little Rock Mountain Studio" was meant to depict Wu
Yi's reception of Huang Yi in his scholarly studio at Yanshi (fig. 2.5). This is
the only leaf that has nothing to do with any well-known mountain scenery or
historical sites in the Song-Luo area. The absence of the major theme, stone
steles, makes the viewer turn to the postscript. There, Huang reports that Wu

built his studio to store his precious acquisition, a third-century stone stele commemorating the Jin general Liu Tao. The studio name, "Little Rock," referred exactly to this stele. In the studio, Wu introduced two cherished antiques to Huang, the Jin stele and also an ancient jade tablet.[31] Next, Huang mentions the rubbings that Wu generously gave him, including one hundred pieces made from the Longmen Grottoes. Huang also recounts that they went to a local school, making some rubbings from Wu's collection displayed there. This is the only leaf with a postscript that provides more information than the diary.[32] With the aid of the postscript, the leaf on the Little Rock Mountain Studio became the epitome of Huang and Wu's friendship, which was rooted in their pursuit of ancient texts.

This was not the first time Huang Yi depicted Wu Yi's Little Rock Mountain Studio. Between 1792 and 1793, Huang Yi had made a painting for Wu Yi, portraying Wu studying in his mountain dwelling.[33] It was an unusual painting made for a special friend at a crucial moment. Wu Yi, then the Boshan magistrate, had been impeached for punishing the notorious prime minister He Shen's ruffians in the summer of 1792, when they were sent to capture bandits but instead molested people of Boshan county.[34] Removed from office, Wu announced his intention to retire to his hometown at the beginning of 1793 and asked his friends to inscribe their poems on the painting made by Huang Yi.[35] According to the poems, Huang painted Wu studying alone in his Little Rock Mountain Studio as an icon of Confucian dignity. His painting not only indicated that scholarly reclusion was no less than an official career, but also suggested that the strength of a true scholar could not be easily sapped by the peremptory working of political power.

Nevertheless, Wu Yi did not retreat to his hometown as he wished in 1793. He went back to Boshan to comfort local people who esteemed him and strongly petitioned for his case, but he was soon compelled to take a teaching position at a local academy in Dongchang.[36] He then led a vagrant life, working as a private tutor in Bozhou and as an academy lecturer in Linqing.[37] Wu Yi was unable to return to Yanshi until 1796, when he received an invitation to compile local gazetteers in Lushan.[38] His official grievance was finally redressed in December of 1799 after He Shen was proved guilty of many crimes. But the justice came too late—Wu had died in November.[39] The mishap in the last decade of Wu's life added a tragic ending to the profile of a learned scholar and upright officer, and earned him respect and regret from his friends and followers.[40]

Huang Yi's reunion with Wu Yi at the foot of Mount Song was memorable. It took place in 1796, when Wu had just returned to his hometown after an exile of four years. They met in the Little Rock Mountain Studio, which

Huang had heard of and even pictured but had never personally visited. Representing the Little Rock Mountain Studio in the 1796 album, Huang did not merely depict their recent scholarly exchange. He must have recalled another painting of this studio he made for Wu at a very trying moment about four years earlier. Huang's memory of Wu is thus tangled with great admiration for his knowledge on the one hand and with deep sorrow for his misfortune on the other.[41]

With the diary and the painting both available, we can study the different ways Huang Yi remembered his journey to the Song-Luo area. The diary was a day-to-day account of his travel, while the painting revealed more of a mental recapture of this trip. Huang's passion for ancient texts not only led him on a pilgrimage to ancient monuments, but also aroused his deep sympathy for Wu Yi in his resettlement at the foot of Mount Song. The impact of their reunion was so strong that Huang could not help revisiting their meetings by including in the album Wu's Little Rock Mountain Studio, a private space but treated with no less care than the noted sights of the Song-Luo area and the famed sites from the Han to the Tang dynasties. Huang's fusion of interests in monuments and concern for an old friend is, however, unclear in his daily textual record. Only in the pictorial representation do we detect the psychological aspect of remembering.

Painter and Viewer

Huang Yi might have kept his diary to himself, but he showed his painting to friends. After finishing the album at Ji'ning in December 1796, Huang immediately sent it to Weng Fanggang (1733–1818) in Beijing. Weng, eleven years older than Huang, was also a learned scholar with great enthusiasm for ancient texts, particularly those from the Han dynasty. The two first met in 1777 when Huang obtained rare rubbings of the Han Xiping Stone Classics erected in the late second century, which Weng then borrowed for making copies and reengraving onto stones.[42] From then on, Huang shared all of the Han texts he collected with Weng, including rubbings of the steles of Master Wei and Fan Shi he procured in 1783, and rubbings of the steles of Master Zhu, Lingtai, and the gate-towers of Wang Zhizi he acquired in 1785.[43] For these two Han devotees, the most exciting event was Huang's unearthing of the Wu family carved stones in 1786, for which Weng erected a commemorative stele.[44] In 1789, Weng published *Records of the Han Bronze and Stones*, which incorporated all of the Han carvings that Huang had shared with him and presented them in a broader context.[45] In the 1802 epitaph he composed for Huang Yi,

Weng retrospectively described himself as "the person who knew Huang most profoundly if friendship can be evaluated by stones and inks."[46]

Having received Huang's album at the beginning of 1797, Weng not only displayed it at a gathering celebrating the birthday of the great Song writer Su Shi (1036–1101),[47] but also wrote down his comments next to Huang's post-scripts leaf by leaf. One was made during the festival on the night of January 16, while another was inscribed in the format of a long poem after waking up the following morning.[48] His inscription for "Little Rock Mountain Studio" is especially touching: "[I] was wondering what Xugu's [Wu Yi] recent progress in studying the Three Ritual Canons might be. My heart leapt because of reading this painting" (fig. 2.5). Apparently, Weng Fanggang knew Wu Yi well. That his heart "leapt" while looking at the depiction of Wu's studio may have been caused by his eagerness to learn of Wu's academic achievement. More likely, it implies his eagerness to know of Wu's return to Yanshi. Weng was one of the few friends willing to inscribe their poems on the painting Huang made for Wu in 1793, the year in which Wu was removed from office.[49] Weng's response not only confirms his understanding of Huang Yi's motivations in recalling his journey, but also indicates that his own memory—contributing a poem similarly representing Wu's studio years ago—was evoked by such an understanding. Both men shared a close friend, and the album was a bridge between them.

In the spring of 1797, Huang Yi showed the album to Sun Xingyan (1753–1818) when Sun visited him at Ji'ning. Sun was also a scholar intensively interested in visiting steles. He compiled his *Records of Bronze and Stones at Liquan* as early as 1784,[50] but his most ambitious work was *Records of Visiting Steles around the World* published in 1802.[51] Although he applauded Huang's project of restoring the Wu family shrines and donated three thousand *qian* in 1787,[52] he did not examine the stone carvings in person until he took an official position in Shandong province in 1795. When he arrived, Huang led him to the site at Mount Ziyun and made a commemorative painting. Sun composed a poem for this special tour,[53] to which Huang also responded with a poem.[54] With Huang serving as his guide, Sun visited two other famous Han relics, the stone shrines attributed to Zhu Wei and to Guo Ju. Both were represented in a series of paintings Sun hired a painter to make in his late years.[55] The two men thus cemented their friendship when they both held posts in Shandong, and Sun even placed the woodblocks for printing his collected poems under Huang's trusteeship.[56] Twice in 1797, Sun looked at the album of the Song-Luo monuments while visiting Huang: in April, he inscribed the title of the album with huge seal characters and left a short poem after the title in May. Sun was also a good friend of Wu Yi, but unlike Weng, he did not openly express his feelings in his written comments.[57]

Huang Yi next sent his album far south to Liang Tongshu (1723–1815) and Xi Gang (1746–1804), who lived in Hangzhou, Huang's hometown on the shore of the West Lake. The son of Liang Shizheng, who compiled the most monumental catalogues of Emperor Qianlong's (r. 1736–95) collections,[58] Liang Tongshu was a local celebrity. Renowned as a calligrapher and a connoisseur of antiques, he was very likely Huang's mentor in Hangzhou.[59] Xi Gang and Huang Yi were the same age. Both enjoyed equal fame as two of the Four Masters of the Xiling School, distinguished by their seal carvings.[60] Liang received Huang's album at the beginning of 1799 and quickly passed it on to Xi Gang, and both left their inscriptions on the colophons.

After the album returned from the south, Huang showed it to Song Bao-chun (1748–1818) during Song's visit in March of 1799. How Song became friends with Huang is unclear, but it was probably because Song was one of Weng Fanggang's followers.[61] We do know that Huang once carved a seal for Song in 1777[62] and that Song financially supported Huang's project of restoring the Wu family shrines in 1787.[63] Close to both Weng and Huang, Song was also the person who inscribed the epitaph Weng made for Huang onto a gravestone in 1802.[64] In 1799, Song twice appreciated Huang's album, composing a long poem in March and writing it down on a colophon later in October.

In the winter of 1799, Huang presented the album to Wang Niansun (1744–1832), who was traveling through Ji'ning. In the Qing dynasty, Wang was one of the authorities on ancient vocabulary and texts. His annotations of the two principal ancient dictionaries, *Erya* and *Guangya,* were highly regarded, as were his commentaries on Han and pre-Han texts.[65] In charge of the waterways in Shandong, Wang visited Huang in 1799 and wrote his comments on the leaf depicting the Kaimu Gate-Towers. Wang was the first officer to call for the impeachment of the prime minister He Shen after the death of Emperor Qianlong. He must have been aware of Wu Yi's tragedy.[66]

Finally, Huang showed his album to Li Rui (1769–1817) and asked him to leave a poem on a colophon in the fall of 1800. Li, whose specialties were mathematics and astronomy, was a disciple of the erudite historian Qian Daxin (1728–1804) and was therefore familiar with the practice of visiting steles.[67] Four months prior to Li's arrival at Ji'ning, Qian wrote a preface to Huang Yi's forthcoming catalogue entitled *Characters Inscribed on Bronzes and Stones Collected in the Little Penglai Pavilion.*[68]

By sending the album to Beijing and Hangzhou and showing it to visitors, Huang Yi actively circulated his pictorial recollection of his journey to the Song-Luo monuments. Its reception varied. As a simple travel record, the album easily led the viewers' attentions to the represented sights. For Sun Xingyan, who had visited the Song-Luo area, the album, with its faithful depiction of famous scenes, "suddenly revived his memory of a comparable trip in the past." For those who had never been to these places, the album stimulated their imaginations, making them "do their roaming from their bed." "Roaming from the bed [woyou]" is a quote taken from an anecdote of the Taoist/Buddhist painter Zong Bing (375–443), meaning that even if one is not allowed to wander among sacred mountains, he can still contemplate the Way by roaming from his bed in a chamber with painted landscape.[69] Weng Fanggang used this metaphor to express his great pleasure in viewing Huang's album: "Taking the composition of inscriptions as 'roaming from the bed,' [I] am not even bothered by the baggage."[70] Wang Niansun and Liang Tongshu also adopted the same figure of speech. Confined to the south, Liang Tongshu and Xi Gang were especially grateful that the album brought the remote scenery to the forefront. It is apparent from the shared cultural legacy of "roaming from the bed" that Huang's album was influential in shaping the viewers' memory of the Song-Luo sights.

Huang's principal motive for the journey, however, was not to see the sights but to examine the sites. His friends, all keen on ancient texts, showed their penetrating evaluations. Song Baochun described his experience of viewing the album as "appreciating steles while reading paintings." Sun Xingyan, in his eulogy for Huang, wrote that his friend's "talent is not limited to calligraphy, poetry, and painting; [his] touching stone steles with yellow silks even excels the ancient people." Because of its cultural impact, Xi Gang ranked Huang Yi's album higher than Wang Lü's (c. 1332–c. 1391) renowned album depicting his journey to Mount Hua, noting that "the rubbings [Huang] obtained can correct the errors of historical writings."[71] For example, as Wang Niansun stated, Huang was able to obtain more than twenty previously unrecognized characters from the Han Gate-Towers and to rectify placements that had been mistaken since Chu Jun's illustrations (fig. 2.3).[72] As Weng Fanggang nicely put it, Huang achieved "what Gu Yanwu [1613–82], Wang Shu [1668–1743] and Wu Yujin [1698–1773] could not complete, and his work was satisfying where Niu Zhenyun's [1706–58] Illustrations of Bronze and Stones was comparatively insufficient" (fig. 2.3).[73] In the Qing dynasty, Gu, Wang, and Wu were the pioneers in establishing the practice of visiting steles,[74] while Chu and Niu were the first who employed image to explain text in recording steles.[75] This is probably the highest compliment Huang could have received. Weng was so excited about Huang's breakthrough with the Han Gate-Towers, which occurred seven years after his publication of Records of the Han Bronze and Stones, that he claimed on a colophon that he had not felt such delight at a Su Shi birthday celebration for many years.

When Huang Yi searched for ancient texts on stone steles, what he recalled was not the historical past to which the texts refer but the historiographical past to which the texts lead. His attitude toward monuments, as con-
solidated in his postscripts, inevitably influenced his viewers. When his friends
looked at the image of visiting steles and then looked into the text annotating
steles, what came to mind was not the historical past the steles intended to
commemorate, but the historiographical past in which the steles were unin-
tentionally situated. Therefore, by representing the Song-Luo sites, the album
itself became a site for historiographical commemoration. By retrieving the engraved past on steles, Huang Yi himself became a monument in the history of
studying ancient texts.

From sight-seeing to site-examining, from retrieving the past to inventing
the memorable, the viewers' receptions of the 1796 album fully corresponded
to the painter's intention. Huang's active circulation of the album and the ad-
vantages associated with this particular format, which allowed the exchanges
of opinions through the accumulation of visible colophons, undoubtedly contributed to the shaping of the collective memory of the Song-Luo monuments.
As Maurice Halbwachs clarified in his discussions of collective memory, "It is
not because memories resemble each other that several can be called to mind at
the same time. It is rather because the same group is interested in them and is
able to call them to mind at the same time that they resemble each other."[76] For
Huang and his friends, an intimate group of cultivated literati in eighteenth-
century China, their great interests in learning ancient texts, in competing
with the ancients, and in rewriting history should be the key foundations of
this collective memory.[77] As Li Rui observed in his inscription for the album,
"Few in the world could harp on the same tune [as Huang], [probably only]
Qian Daxin in the south and Weng Fanggang in the north."

Original and Copy

Huang Yi's memory of the Song-Luo monuments is sustained not only in his
diary and album but also in the four hundred rubbings he brought back. As
stated in his diary, Huang's motive for the journey was to examine the monuments in person and to obtain more accurate rubbings of the monuments.[78]
One-fourth of the rubbings were provided by Wu Yi, but the rest were made
on site by local assistants and the two craftsmen who accompanied Huang
from Ji'ning.[79] These rubbings—direct impressions of stone steles—were the
most reliable reproductions of monuments in an age when photography was
not yet known (fig. 2.6).[80] They therefore provided Huang Yi with a sense of
possessing the monuments after the journey, and of possessing the authority

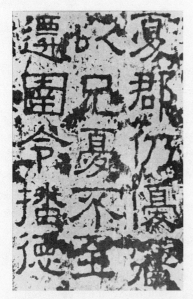 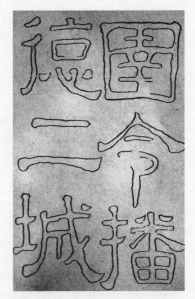

Fig. 2.6. (left) Detail of the Stele of Master Zhao. Rubbing. From *Sudao quanji* (Taipei: Dalu, 1989).

Fig. 2.7. (right) Detail of the Stele of Master Zhao. Double-lined traced copy. From Huang Yi, *Xiaopenglai ge jinshi wenzi,* 1800 edition. Harvard-Yenching Library, Cambridge.

to construct the memory of the monuments, especially for those who had never been to the sites. Huang's diary ends with the gratification he felt in distributing duplicate rubbings to his good friends at Ji'ning.[81]

However, the duplicate rubbings were, after all, limited in numbers. Huang further circulated his acquisitions through his own copies of rubbings. By tracing the contours of impressed characters, Huang made the copies in a special manner called "delineation with double lines" (*shuanggou*). The double-lined traced copies could not compete with rubbings in terms of reliability, but they were capable of mass production. Huang Yi published his collection of Han rare rubbings by having his double-lined traced copies transferred onto woodblocks for printing (fig. 2.7).[82] Although Huang's acquisitions from the Song-Luo area came too late to be included in this project, we learn from Xi Gang's inscription that Huang did make some double-lined traced copies after his Song-Luo rubbings. We also learn that Huang Yi shared his journey with Xi Gang by sending him his album and his double-lined traced copies, but not the rubbings, as if to declare that the reproduced monuments (the rubbings) were more valuable than the represented monuments (the album).

Judging from the three products resulting from Huang's visit to the Song-Luo monuments—painting, diary, and rubbings—we may conclude that while the painting and diary allowed him to relive his memory of the visit, the rubbings retained his memory of the visited monuments. Intellectually, the reproductions of monuments (rubbings) were regarded more highly than the representations of monuments (painting and diary). The first-hand reproductions (rubbings) were also considered superior to the second-hand reproductions (double-lined traced copies). When the monuments became inaccessible (away from sites), the rubbings substituted for them. Likewise, when the rubbings became unavailable (too precious to be given away), the double-lined traced copies easily replaced them. Memory, either recollected by the painter or reshaped among the viewers, thus alternatively circulated in the variants of the original and of the copy.

Just as Huang tried to retain the memory of stone steles through rubbings and double-lined traced copies, his album, like ancient steles, also led to attempts at reproduction and became a monument for later generations. We learn from Chen Gong's inscription in 1839 that he obtained Huang Yi's depiction of Mount Song in a smaller album. He speculated that the smaller album must have been a later copy, because it contained several scenes unseen in the 1796 album, and because Weng Fanggang's inscriptions appeared inauthentic.[83] Without further information, we cannot be sure of what motivated the production of this mixed copy. The only traceable case is the album of Wu Dacheng (1835–1902), a copy made in 1891.

Wu Dacheng was a leading officer at the late Qing court. In public, he was an entrusted envoy negotiating the national boundaries with the imperialistic forces.[84] He won universal praise for his 1886 mission to the northeastern border, because he prevented the invasion from Russia and triumphantly erected as a landmark a bronze pillar, on which he inscribed with seal characters the statement that "this pillar can only be erected; it cannot be moved."[85] In private, Wu Dacheng was an amateur literati artist and avid collector of ancient bronzes, jades, and rubbings.[86] He first saw Huang Yi's album in Beijing in the spring of 1891, but could not afford the high price quoted by the dealer and thus yielded to another collector, Fei Nianci. In the fall, Fei happened to stop by Wuxian where Wu was then living. Fei lent Wu the album for ten days to make a copy.[87]

One may be amazed at how closely Wu Dacheng's copy resembles Huang Yi's work (fig. 2.8). To an untrained eye, the compositions, brushwork, and calligraphic styles—including all the inscriptions left by various writers—are so skillfully imitated as to be indistinguishable from those of the original, were it not for the seal "Dacheng" stamped on the bottom corner of each leaf. Part of the reason why Wu Dacheng could make an excellent copy in such a short span of time is that he was experienced in imitating Huang Yi's painting and callig-

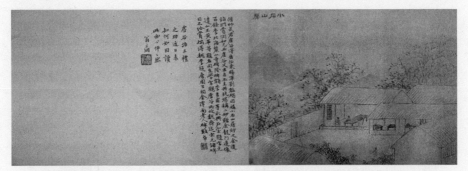

Fig. 2.8. Wu Dacheng, Copy of Huang Yi's "Visiting Steles in the Song-Luo Area," *The Little Rock Mountain Studio,* 1891. From Wu Dacheng, *Kezhai lin huang xiaosong sima songluo fangbei tu ershisi zhong* (Shanghai: Youzheng, 1917).

raphy. Three years before, in 1888, Wu had had a chance to reproduce Huang's 1788 album, based on a contemporary painter Gu Yun's (1835–96) copy.[88]

What prompted Wu Dacheng to copy Huang Yi's work, even from an indirect source? The renowned artist Wu Changshi (1844–1927), who successfully established a personal style through the studies of stone steles, remarked, "If one puts his hand to ancient steles, to whom could he possibly talk? [Wu Dacheng] was thinking of Qiu'an [Huang Yi] while displaying his interest in Yunhu [Gu Yun]."[89] For anyone in the late Qing who was fascinated with ancient steles, Huang Yi from the previous century was a model to follow. When Huang Yi's work was unavailable, Gu Yun's copy could well be a vehicle for such historical contemplation. However, in view of the fact that the album Gu copied was nothing but ordinary landscape, one can imagine Wu Dacheng's excitement over viewing Huang Yi's original album of the Song-Luo steles, even if only for ten days.

If the primary motivation behind Huang Yi's visit to the Song-Luo steles was to retrieve the remote past engraved on stones, Wu Dacheng's copy revisited the recent past created by Huang and his peers. According to Zhang Yu, who added an inscription to the copy at the request of the painter, the leaf on the Little Rock Mountain Studio strongly reminded Wu Dacheng of the days when he held an official position in Henan province. Wu Dacheng longed for Wu Yi's famed collection at Yanshi, only to find that both his steles and his rubbings had gotten scattered and lost. With much effort, Wu Dacheng found and purchased the third-century stele after which Wu Yi had named his studio at Huixian, a city situated one hundred miles away from Yanshi. As Huang Yi stated in his postscript, Wu Yi had shown him two of his most cherished objects—the third-century stele and an ancient jade tablet. Even though he was never able to locate the exact jade tablet mentioned by Huang, Wu Dacheng, an experienced collector who owned many excellent jade tablets, still considered himself as Wu Yi's equal in this regard.[90] Evidently, what Wu Dacheng intended to reconstruct were not the ancient texts on the monuments, but the antiques collected by Huang Yi and his peers. By copying Huang Yi's album, Wu Dacheng turned Huang's textual studies into utter antiquarianism.

Unlike rubbings or double-lined traced copies, Huang Yi's original album on the Song-Luo monuments was a unique object, owned by one person and viewed by his close friends. Wu Dacheng's faithful copy undoubtedly enhanced its circulation,[91] although it was always regarded as inferior to the original.[92] Nevertheless, it is Wu Dacheng's copy that was first published after the introduction of collotype to China in the early twentieth century. With the photomechanical reproduction, Wu Dacheng's copy has monopolized our memory of Huang Yi's album since its first publication in 1917.[93] As Walter Benjamin argued, "By making many reproductions it [the technique of reproduction] substitutes a plurality of copies for a unique existence. And in permitting the reproduction to meet the beholder or listener in his own situation, it reactivates the object reproduced."[94] Once we move beyond the cultural conventions of the traditional Chinese literati, we become uncertain about how multiple memories of multiple monuments are perceived, as the "aura" of Huang Yi's album through Wu Dacheng's copy spreads through mass media and to the reader of this essay.

NOTES

1. The album is currently part of the Palace Museum collection in Beijing. Twenty-three leaves of the album have been reproduced in reduced scale in *Zhongguo gudai shuhua tumu* (Beijing: Wenwu, 2000), 23:234–36.

2. Louis Marin, "Towards a Theory of Reading in the Visual Arts: Poussin's *The Arcadian Shepherds,*" in *Calligram: Essays in New Art History from France,* ed. N. Bryson (Cambridge: Cambridge University Press, 1988), 63–90.

3. The stele was erected in the fourth year of the Xianqing reign (659). Henan sheng wenwu ju, ed., *Henan beizhi xulu* (Zhengzhou: Zhongzhou, 1992), 161.

4. Emperor Ming was an alternative title for Emperor Gao.

5. The stele was destroyed during the Cultural Revolution. Henan sheng wenwu ju, *Henan beizhi xulu,* 149.

6. Huang's postscript says "the fifth year of the Yanguang reign." However, according to rubbings, it should be the second year. See Lü Pin, ed., *Zhongyue han san que* (Beijing: Wenwu, 1990), plates 127, 128.

7. See *Zhongguo gudai shuhua tumu,* 23:235, fig. 9.

8. Since the temple was erected to worship Qi's mother, it should be called "Qimu." To avoid referring to Emperor Jing of the Han, Liu Qi, "Qimu" was then changed to "Kaimu."

9. For the transcriptions and rubbings, see Lü Pin, *Zhongyue han san que*, 39–43, plates 127, 128.

10. The diary was first published in 1854 by Wu Chongyao. For the course of circulation, see Wu's postscript to Huang Yi, *Songluo fangbei riji*, reprinted in *Shike shiliao xinbian*, ser. 3, vol. 28 (Taipei: Xinwenfeng, 1986), 605.

11. Ibid., 597–604. The dates used in this essay are all transferred from the Chinese lunar calendar to the Western solar calendar. Noticeably, Huang's diary records only thirty-five days from October 6 to November 9, while his postscript in the colophon states that it took about forty days to make the journey. The difference should be caused by the days spent on the trip from Ji'ning to Xiangfu, which Huang excluded in his diary but included in his postscript.

12. For example, the leaf entitled "The Autumn Scenery at Mount Taihang." See *Zhongguo gudai shuhua tumu*, 23:236, fig. 20.

13. Huang Yi, *Songluo fangbei riji*, 597.

14. We are not sure if Huang produced the twenty-four leaves in chronological order, because the current sequence agrees with neither its previous documentation nor its later copy. For the current sequence, see *Zhongguo gudai shuhua tumu*, 23:234–36. For the sequence published with Weng Fanggang's inscriptions, see Weng Fanggang, *Ti songluo fangbei tu*, reprinted in *Shike shiliao xinbian*, ser. 3, vol. 28, 589–93. For the sequence in Wu Dacheng's copy, see Wu Dacheng, *Kezhai lin huang xiaosong sima songluo fangbei tu ershisi zhong* (Shanghai: Youzheng, 1917).

15. *Zhongguo gudai shuhua tumu*, 23:235, figs. 16, 17, 18.

16. He Shaoji, who had the good fortune to view both the diary and the painting, noticed the differences between the two in his 1857 inscription for the album. However, he mentioned only that the diary was more accurate as to the dates of Huang's visits to steles, while the album presented more thoroughly the stories of Huang's efforts to obtain rubbings.

17. Wang Fu was called by friends Wang Qiucheng, while Wu Yi was called by friends Wu Xugu.

18. Huang Yi, *Songluo fangbei riji*, 597, 600–602. Huang Yi pictured himself on a sedan chair on the leaf entitled "Huanyuan Pass."

19. Ibid., 600–602.

20. Wu Yi, *Yanshi jinshi ji* and *Yanshi jinshi yiwen ji*, both first published around 1788, both reprinted in *Shike shiliao xinbian*, ser. 2, vol. 14; Wu Yi, *Anyang xian jinshi lu*, first published in 1819, reprinted in *Shike shiliao xinbian*, ser. 1, vol. 18. Yanshi and Anyang are both in Henan province.

21. Weng Fanggang, "Chongli han wushici shi ji" (1787), rubbings, collection of the Fu Ssu-nien Library in Taipei. This text was later included in Weng Fanggang, *Fuchuzhai wenji*, 1878 ed., collection of the Fu Ssu-nien Library in Taipei, 5:15b–16a, but all the sponsors' names were omitted by this publication. For Huang Yi's excavation of the Wu family shrines, see Wu Hung, *The Wu Liang Shrine: The Ideology of Early Chinese Pictorial Art* (Stanford: Stanford University Press, 1989), 4–7.

22. Wu Yi, "Han wushi qianshishi huaxiang," in his *Jinshi san ba*, first published in 1843, reprinted in *Shike shiliao xinbian*, ser. 1, vol. 15, 575–76.

23. Wei Chengxian, "Yong shifan jijiu yun ti xugu shanju dushu tu," in *Shoutang yishu*, ed. Wu Muchun, 1843 ed., collection of the Harvard-Yenching Library in Cambridge, pt. 1, 9b.

24. The painting was reproduced in *Shoutang yishu*. After Wu Yi's death in 1799, the painting became the major source for Wu's friends to express their grief. See Wu Muchun, *Shoutang yishu*, pt. 1, 1a–5a.

25. Wu Yi, "Da huang xiaosong shu," in *Shoutang wenchao,* first published in 1843, reprinted in *Congshu jicheng chubian* (Shanghai: Shangwu, 1935), 3:48–49.

26. Wu Yi, "Yu huang xiaosong shu," in *Shoutang wenchao xuji,* 1843 ed., collection of the Fu Ssu-nien Library in Taipei, 9:8a–b. Wu instructed his brother to make rubbings for Huang.

27. Huang Yi, *Songluo fangbei riji,* 597.

28. Ibid. Since Wu Yi was compiling local gazetteers in Lushan, Wang Fu was the person who assisted Huang to ascend to Mount Song from Yanshi.

29. Ibid., 600–601. Wang Fu was then in Luoyang. It is because of Wang Fu's invitation that Wu Yi accompanied Huang Yi to Luoyang. Then Wu Yi and Wang Fu returned to Yanshi together, leaving Huang at Longmen to make rubbings.

30. Ibid., 602. It was at the parties hosted by Wang Fu that Wu Yi and Huang Yi met on October 27 and 28.

31. For the jade tablet, see Wu Yi, "Gu yugui tushuo," in *Shoutang wenchao,* 1:10–11.

32. The postscript basically combines the activities on October 19 and 28 and is more specific on the rubbings Wu gave Huang.

33. Weng Fanggang, "Xugu shanju dushu tu bing xu," in Wu Muchun, *Shoutang yishu,* pt. 1, 6a.

34. Wu Yi had been the magistrate of Boshan county since the winter of 1791. Sun Xingyan, "Wu xugu zhuan;" in *Soutang yishu,* pt. 2, 8a–11a; Fa Shishan, "Wu xugu zhuan," ibid., 12a–14b; Zhao Xihuang, "Wu zhengjun zhuan," ibid., 15a–17b; Jiang Fan, "Hanxue shicheng ji," ibid., 18a–20b; Yu Pengnian, "Wu xugu aici," ibid., 21a–23a.

35. The poems were included in Wu Muchun, *Shoutang yishu,* pt. 1, 6a–10a.

36. Wu Muchun, "Xugu fujun xingshu," in ibid., pt. 2, 29a–37b.

37. Ibid., 34b.

38. Ibid., 35a.

39. Ibid., 35b–36b.

40. Zhu Gui, "Zhizuzhai wenji muzhi," in Wu Muchun, *Shoutang yishu,* pt. 2, 2a–4a; Yao Nai, "Xibaoxuan wenji mubiao," in ibid., 5a–b.

41. In 1797, not long after the album was produced, Huang Yi was said to have made Wu Yi's portrait in the format of a hanging scroll. See *Zhongguo gudai shuhua tumu,* 23:372.

42. Weng Fanggang, "Huang qiu'an debei shier tu xu," in his *Fuchuzhai wenji,* 2:7b; Weng Fanggang, "Huang qiu'an zhuan," ibid., 13:6b. The fragments were reproduced in Huang Yi, *Xiaopenglai ge jinshi wenzi,* 1800 ed., collection of the Harvard-Yenching Library in Cambridge, "Shijing canbei." It also included three of Weng Fanggang's comments.

43. Huang Yi, "Weijun bei," "Fanshi bei," "Zhujun bei," "Lingtai bei," "Wang Zhizi que," in his *Xiaopenglai ge jinshi wenzi.*

44. Weng Fanggang, "Chongli han wushici shi ji," *Fuchuzhai wenji,* 5: 15b–16a.

45. Weng Fanggang, *Lianghan jinshi ji,* first published in 1789, reprinted in *Xusiu siku quanshu,* vol. 892 (Shanghai: Shanghai guji, 1997). In 1790, Weng left an inscription to commemorate his visit to the carved stones at Ji'ning. See Weng Fanggang, "Guan ji'ning xuegong zhubei tiji," rubbings, collection of the Fu Ssu-nien Library in Taipei.

46. Weng Fanggang, "Huang qiu'an zhuan," *Fuchuzhai wenji,* 13:7b.

47. Friends invited to the gathering included the calligrapher Yi Bingshou (1753–1815) and the famous Yangzhou painter Luo Pin (1733–99). Yi Bingshou left an inscription, listing the names of the invited viewers. In Weng's inscription to the leaf entitled "Fengxian Temple," Luo Pin was said to admire Huang's depiction of the gigantic statues.

48. The inscription for the leaf entitled "Fengxian Temple" was made on January 16; the inscription for the leaf entitled "Shaoshi Gate-Towers" was composed on January 16 but inscribed on January 17. The dates of the remaining inscriptions were not specified.

49. Wu Yi, *Soutang yishu,* pt. 1, 6a–b.

50. Sun Xingyan, *Liquan jinshi zhi,* first published in 1784, reprinted in, *Shike shiliao xinbian,* ser. 3, vol. 31 (Taipei: Xinwenfeng, 1986).

51. Sun Xingyan, *Huanyu fangbei lu,* first published in 1802, reprinted in *Congshu jicheng chubian,* vols. 1583–87 (Shanghai: Shangwu, 1937).

52. Weng Fanggang, "Chongli han wushici shi ji" (rubbings).

53. Sun Xingyan, *Sun yuanru xiansheng quanji* (Shanghai: Shangwu, 1935), 436.

54. Huang Yi, *Qiu'an yigao* (Shanghai: Juzhen fangsong yinshuju, 1918), Qiushi, 4b.

55. Sun Xingyan, *Sun yuanru xiansheng quanji,* 493.

56. Gong Qing's postscript to *Jishang tingyun ji,* in Sun Xingyan, *Sun yuanru xiansheng quanji,* 448.

57. Sun Xingyan left his poem on the 1793 painting Huang Yi made for Wu Yi; Sun also composed a long biographical essay for Wu after his death. For both, see Wu Muchun, *Shoutang yishu,* pt. 1, 6b–7a; pt. 2, 8a–11b. In addition, fifteen letters Wu wrote to Sun were preserved in Wu Yi, *Shoutang wenchao xuji,* 10:1a–10b.

58. Such as *Shiqu baoji, Midian zhulin,* and *Xiqing gujian. Shiqu baoji* and *Midian zhulin* were reprinted in *Yingyin wenyuange sikuquanshu,* vols. 823–25 (Taipei: Shangwu, 1983); *Xiqing gujian* was reprinted in *Yingyin chizaotang sikuquanshu huiyao,* vols. 243–44 (Taipei: Shijie, 1986).

59. For calligraphy, see Liang Tongshu, *Pinluo'an lunshu,* published in 1889, reprinted in *Congshu jicheng xinbian,* pt. Yishu, vol. 52 (Taipei: Xinwenfeng, 1985); for connoisseurship, see Liang Tongshu, *Gu yaoqi kao* and *Gu tongqi kao,* both in *Yushi guqi pulu* (Taipei: Shijie, 1962).

60. See Xiling yinshe, ed., *Xiling sijia yinpu* (Hangzhou: Xiling yinshe, 1964).

61. Li Yusun, *Jinshixue lu* (Shanghai: Shangwu, 1937), 52.

62. Xiling yinshe, *Xiling sijia yinpu,* 74.

63. Weng Fanggang, "Chongli han wushici shi ji" (rubbings).

64. Weng Fanggang, "Huang qiu'an zhuan," *Fuchuzhai wenji,* 13:7b.

65. Lu Xinyuan, *Jinshixue lu bu,* 1879 ed., collection of the Harvard-Yenching Library in Cambridge, 6a. For Wang's scholarship, see Fang Junji, *Gaoyou wangshi fuzi xue zhi yanjiu* (Taipei: Wenshizhe, 1974).

66. Zhao Erxun et al., *Qingshi gao* (Beijing: Zhonghua, 1998), 481:13211.

67. Ibid., 507:13982.

68. Qian Daxin's preface was written on June 27, 1800. See Huang Yi, *Xiaopenglai ge jinshi wenzi,* v–vi.

69. Kiyohiko Munakata, "Concepts of *Lei* and *Kan-lei* in Early Chinese Art Theory," and Susan Bush, "Tsung Ping's Essay on Painting Landscape and the 'Landscape Buddhism' of Mount Lu," in *Theories of the Arts in China,* ed. S. Bush and C. Murck (Princeton: Princeton University Press, 1983), 105–31, 132–64.

70. Weng Fanggang's inscription for the leaf entitled "Autumn Color of Mount Taihang."

71. For more discussions of Wang Lü's work, see Kathlyn Maurean Liscomb, *Learning from Mount Hua: A Chinese Physician's Illustrated Travel Record and Painting Theory* (Cambridge: Cambridge University Press, 1993).

72. *Illustrations of Bronze and Stones,* first published in 1745, reprinted in *Siku quan-shu cunmu congshu,* vol. 278 (Tai'nan: Zhuanyan, 1996). It was illustrated by Chu Jun and explained by Niu Zhenyun.

73. Weng Fanggang's inscription for the leaf entitled "Kaimu Gate-Towers."

74. For the practice of visiting steles in the early Qing, see Qianshen Bai, "Fu Shen and the Transformation of Chinese Calligraphy in the Seventeenth Century," Ph.D. diss., Yale University, 1996, 187–205.

75. See n. 72.

76. Maurice Halbwachs, *On Collective Memory* (Chicago: University of Chicago Press, 1992), 52.

77. For the development of historical studies in this period, see Tu Wei-yun, *Qianjia shidai de shixue yu shijia* (Taipei: Xuesheng, 1989); for its cultural atmosphere, see Chen Jin-ling, *Qingdai qianjia wenren yu wenhua* (Beijing: Renmin jiaoyu, 2001).

78. Huang Yi, *Songluo fangbei riji,* 597.

79. Ibid., 597, 602. In his postscript to the leaf "Little Rock Mountain Studio," Huang related that Wu Yi gave him more than one hundred rubbings.

80. When engravings are thin and light, rubbings still provide clearer views than photos do.

81. Huang Yi, *Songluo fangbei riji,* 603.

82. Huang Yi, *Xiaopenglai ge jinshi wenzi,* first published in 1800.

83. Chen Gong left his inscription on a colophon of the 1796 album.

84. Yu Yue, "Kezhaigong muzhiming," in Wu Dacheng, *Danren ziyicao* and *Kezhai shi-cun* (Wuxian: Meijing shuwu, 1938).

85. Zhao Erxun, *Qingshi gao,* 153:4502–4; Wu Dacheng, *Huanghua jicheng* (Changchun: Jilin wenshi, 1986).

86. Tian Shiyi, *Jinshi zhushu mingjia kaolue* (Ji'nan: Shandong shengli tushuguan, 1935), 53a–b; Wu Dacheng, *Wu kezhai chidu* (Shanghai: Shangwu, 1930).

87. Zhang Yu's inscription for Wu Dacheng's copy in 1893, in Wu Dacheng, *Kezhai lin huang xiaosong sima songluo fangbei tu ershisi zhong* (Shanghai: Youzheng, 1917).

88. Wu Dacheng, *Wu kezhai lingu shanshui ce* (Tokyo: Bansuiken, 1939).

89. Ibid. Wu Changshi left a poem on one of the colophons in 1888.

90. Zhang Yu's inscription for Wu Dacheng's copy, in Wu Dacheng, *Kezhai lin huang xiaosong sima songluo fangbei tu ershisi zhong.* For Wu's connoisseurship in ancient jades, see Wu Dacheng, *Guyu tukao* (Ji'ning: Ji'ning jieshu, 1889).

91. Wu Dacheng, *Kezhai lin huang xiaosong sima songluo fangbei tu ershisi zhong.*

92. Walter Benjamin, "The Work of Art in the Age of Mechanical Reproduction," in *Illuminations: Essays and Reflections,* ed. Hannah Arendt (New York: Schocken Books, 1969), 217–51.

93. Huang Yi's album became part of the collections of the Palace Museum in Beijing after 1949. It was never well published until 2000. Even in the recent publication, the leaf entitled "Little Rock Mountain Studio" and all the inscriptions on the colophons are omitted. See *Zhongguo gudai shuhua tumu,* 23:234–36.

94. Benjamin, "Work of Art in the Age of Mechanical Reproduction," 221.

Tourists, Terrorists, and Metaphysical Theater at Hagia Sophia

ROBERT S. NELSON

To introduce modern and medieval experiences of Hagia Sophia/Aya Sofya in Constantinople/Istanbul as a monument, I will begin with a work of fiction that itself is a sign and symptom of the modern practices of leisure and memory, the spy novel. The master of the genre was and is John Le Carré, even if the popularity of such fiction and the nature of his creations have changed with the end of the Soviet Union and the rise of diverse political strife not so easily explained in terms of the Manichaean dualism of the cold war. At each stage of his career, Le Carré has written against and with the current political scene, and his illusions are enabled by veristic details of character and place. These, in turn, may serve to illustrate a recent stage in the social life of Hagia Sophia, the cathedral of Byzantine Constantinople from 537 to 1453, thereafter Aya Sofya, the principal imperial mosque of Ottoman Istanbul, and since 1934 a national museum. When the mosque was secularized, it was officially recognized as an art monument of universal significance. Thus Hagia Sophia exemplifies some of the social processes by which a building becomes symbolically important.

After September 11, 2001, the world has been reminded yet again that such monuments can also be sites of social conflict. Throughout

its long history, Hagia Sophia was repeatedly contested. Built after and in response to the Nika riot of the *populus* of Constantinople in 532, the Greek
church became Latin following the fall of the city to the Crusaders in 1204,
then Greek again after the Byzantine reconquest in 1261, and finally Ottoman
after the sack of the city in 1453. Shortly after his victory, Mehmed the Con-
queror wandered about "paradise-like" Hagia Sophia and decided to make it
his mosque.[1] Today new conflicts have emerged in and around the modern national monument that appears to be a tourist idyll. A monument is serene,
beautiful, secure, coherent, powerful, and permanent, characteristics that do
not apply to the quotidian world, whether modern or medieval; hence the
great appeal of monuments like Hagia Sophia.

Near the beginning of *The Little Drummer Girl* (1983), Le Carré presents
a brief vignette that incorporates Hagia Sophia. The larger story in which it is
embedded involves a contest between intelligence agents for Israel and Germany and a close-knit group of Palestinians, understood by one side to be terrorists and the other side to be freedom fighters. In the passage that follows,
Le Carré sets the stage for the later kidnapping of the Palestinian Yanuka in
Greece. PreviouslyYanuka had flown to Istanbul, "checked into the Hilton on
a Cypriot diplomatic passport and for two days gave himself to the religious
and secular pleasures of the town." Designed in 1951 and opened in 1955, the
Istanbul Hilton had long been the most prestigious hotel in the city, "a little
America" and a bulwark against communism, according to Conrad Hilton.
Its prime location insured that the Istanbul Hilton remained important, even
as newer hotels were built.[2] As for Yanuka's urban pleasures, he prays at the
mosque of Suleiman and visits the tourist areas at the end of the old city of
Istanbul/Constantinople. There he lingered in the park (fig. 3.1) between the
mosque of Sultan Ahmet, known to tourists as the Blue Mosque, and the former Byzantine church, then Ottoman mosque, now the modern museum of
Hagia or Saint Sophia:

> In the gardens of Sultan Ahmed Square he sat on a bench among the or-
> ange and mauve flower beds, gazing benignly at the surrounding domes and
> minarets that made the perimeter, and also at the clusters of giggling Ameri-
> can tourists, particularly a group of teenage girls in shorts. . . . He bought
> slides and postcards from the child hawkers without caring about their outra-
> geous prices; he wandered round the Saint Sophia, contemplating with equal
> pleasure the glories of Justinian's Byzantium and of the Ottoman conquest. . . .
> But his most devout concentration was reserved for the mosaic of Augus-
> tine and Constantine presenting their church and city to the Virgin Mary, for
> that was where he made his clandestine connection: with a tall, unhurried

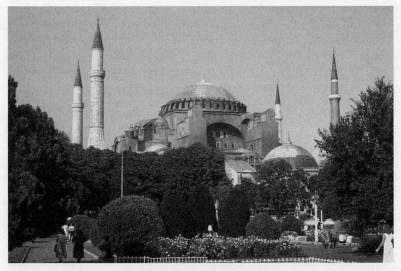

Fig. 3.1. Hagia Sophia from the south. Photograph by Robert S. Nelson.

man in a windjacket who at once became his guide. Until then Yanuka had resolutely refused such offers, but something this man now said to him— added no doubt to the place and time of his approach—persuaded him immediately. Side by side, they made a second, cursory tour of the interior, dutifully admired the early unsupported dome, then drove together along the Bosphorus in an old American Plymouth, till they came to a car park close to the Ankara highway. The Plymouth drove off; Yanuka was once more alone in this world—but this time as owner of a fine red Mercedes car, which he calmly took back to the Hilton and registered with the concierge as his own.[3]

We later learn that the Mercedes was packed with two hundred pounds of Russian plastic explosives, and thereafter the plot begins to run its course. That story is left to readers of the novel. Of present concern are this vignette and its potential for introducing modern appreciations of Hagia Sophia circa 1980. To the present author, someone who has visited Istanbul over many years, Le Carré's scene setting seems correct down to the smallest detail with one large and glaring exception: the description of the Byzantine mosaic in the southwest vestibule of Hagia Sophia. The emperor at the left of the lunette (fig. 3.2) is not Augustine but Justinian, the sixth-century builder of Hagia Sophia, who for that reason holds a model of his donation to the Virgin and child. Otherwise, Le Carré's sketch of Yanuka's actions in and around Hagia Sophia is accurate and constitutes useful evidence for its status as a monument and the

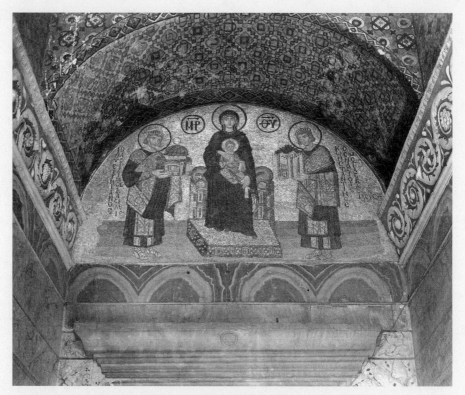

Fig. 3.2. Hagia Sophia, mosaic in the southwest vestibule. Courtesy of Dumbarton Oaks, Byzantine Photographs and Fieldwork Archives, Washington, D.C.

uses made of such a building within the modern city. In this incident, Yanuka, though a terrorist or a fighter against Zionism, assumes the pose of a tourist, the perfect disguise for someone in an area that has tourists en masse when it has flowers in bloom.

The protagonist's use of the city for "religious and secular pleasures" corresponds to modern norms of travel by Western Europeans and Americans since the Grand Tour, although both functions were not always combined in one location. In the eighteenth and nineteenth centuries, Venice, for example, had educational, cultural, and erotic connotations for the English, as Bruce Redford has explored, whereas for Westerners in general, Jerusalem became a place for religious tourism by mass audiences from the later nineteenth century.[4] In the same period, Istanbul was a crossroads for steamship lines and above all a place for business, as befitted the capital of the Ottoman Empire. Yet with the coming of a direct rail connection to Western Europe in the late nineteenth century, Istanbul was successfully marketed and redefined as a place of exoticism and eroticism in sources as diverse as travel posters, travel writing, and mystery novels (e.g., Agatha Christie's *Murder on the Orient Express* [1933]).⁵ A commonplace in such representations is the Westerner looking at and admiring the monuments and people of Istanbul, especially the women. In his novel, Le Carré makes a clever twist on that old theme. Here it is the Muslim, not the Westerner, who looks at women—those American teenagers inappropriately dressed for this culture, another accurate detail.

Like a dutiful Western tourist, Yanuka pauses beneath the mosaic in the southwest vestibule (fig. 3.3), for some years the entrance to the building, as it was in the Middle Ages. In this relatively narrow space and beneath the mosaic, Yanuka meets his associate. As the two discuss their future exchange of the car and its explosives, they look at a symbolic scene of exchange, Justinian presenting his church of Hagia Sophia and Constantine his city of Constantinople to the enthroned Virgin and child (fig. 3.2). The encounter in this place is a clever foretelling of what is to come in the novel, as well as the typical response of actual tourists.

Yanuka stops and contemplates the mosaics of Hagia Sophia as if in an art gallery, and a guide accosts him just as guides accost all unaccompanied visitors as soon as they enter the building. Also like the good tourist, Yanuka has previously enjoyed the sights and smells in the nearby park (fig. 3.1) and has bought slides and postcards. If he were a true tourist, he would later show the slides to his friends, and either mail or keep the postcards. Such photographic souvenirs are ways of remembering the site and introducing it to others with the result that the site becomes understood through and by the photographic image. Photographic postcards have been a major aspect of tourism since the late nineteenth century, and Istanbul came to be included in this particular aspect of the economy of travel images in the early twentieth century.⁶ Such representations stimulate interest in seeing Hagia Sophia and the mosque of Sultan Ahmet and define them as the principal sights of Istanbul. The city in turn comes to be known through its monuments, and once these monuments are widely enough known, they can serve as a realistic locale for a spy novel.

Essential to the formation of a tourist site, according to the seminal book of Dean MacCannell, is this relationship between the place, its markers or denotators, and the tourist,⁷ a peculiarly visual and objectifying process that John Urry has explored further in his *Tourist Gaze*.⁸ For the tourist to admire a tourist attraction a number of factors must come into play. The purity of the monument must not be compromised by untidy surroundings, a constant concern of the tourist industry.⁹ The floral gardens that Le Carré describes are, therefore, appropriate for a tourist attraction. In Le Carré's novel, the hawkers of photographs and the images they sell further promote the site, but what

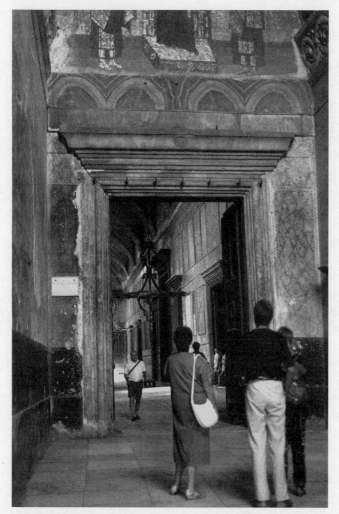

Fig. 3.3. Hagia Sophia, southwest vestibule and inner narthex. Photograph by Robert S. Nelson.

actually leads tourists to this specific place are guidebooks. Accompanied first by engravings, later by photographs, and now by photographic reproductions of engravings,[10] guidebooks structure the tourist experience and stimulate interest in the monuments of the city. Whereas governments can decree that a structure should be a monument, guidebooks and other such markers make it a social reality.

The fictionalized Yanuka acts as if directed by a guidebook, for he retraces the usual paths of tourism in Istanbul. He is described as visiting two of the principal sights of the city, the mosque of Suleiman and the group of buildings at the eastern end of the peninsula. Since the nineteenth century, guidebooks have directed tourists to these areas, using variations on the "star system," that device used by Baedeker and others to rank the most important sights.[11] In Yanuka's case, he starts with the mosque of Suleiman, perhaps because he is presented as a Muslim tourist. Guidebooks for Westerners since the nineteenth century have favored the eastern section of the city with the nearby Ottoman palace, Hagia Sophia, and the Sultan Ahmet. If interested, tourists continue to the mosque of Suleiman.[12] Guidebooks also direct visitors to hotels, which until recently were located, like the Hilton in which Yanuka stays, in the more westernized Pera and Galata. The commercial center of the city since the nineteenth century, this area is separated from the old city and its monuments by a small body of water, the Golden Horn, and its heights offer picturesque views of the distant domes and minarets of the old city.

In the two paragraphs of *The Little Drummer Girl*, Le Carré presents Yanuka in the guise of one final type of Westerner relevant to the modern use of the city and its monuments, namely the *flâneur,* that peripatetic wanderer about the streets of nineteenth-century Paris. Described and celebrated by Charles Baudelaire as the quintessential expression of modernity, the *flâneur* and his role in defining and expressing the significances of the modern city, its spaces, wares, and peoples have also interested Walter Benjamin and others. For Baudelaire, the perfect *flâneur* was the

> passionate spectator [for whom] it is an immense joy to set up house in the heart of the multitude, amid the ebb and flow of movement, in the midst of the fugitive and the infinite. To be away from home and yet to feel oneself everywhere at home; to see the world, to be at the centre of the world, and yet to remain hidden from the world. . . . The spectator is a *prince* who everywhere rejoices in his incognito. . . . He is an 'I' with an insatiable appetite for the 'non-I,' at every instant rendering and explaining it in pictures more living than life itself, which is always instable and fugitive.[13]

This figure of the *flâneur* was at the center of Benjamin's grand project to analyze the Parisian arcades as the characteristic manifestation of modern urban society and economy. Working from Baudelaire, whom he quotes, Benjamin understood that Paris for the *flâneur* divides into "its dialectical poles. It opens up to him as landscape, even as it closes around him as a room."[14]

While John Le Carré may or may not have known Baudelaire's essay or Benjamin's ill-fated project, the *flâneur* is a well-established motif of modern literature and, more important, a feature of modern life.[15] With his accurate eye for the uses of the city, Le Carré has disguised Yanuka well as a tourist *flâneur*. The Palestinian gazes passively at domes, minarets, and teenage girls from the safe space of his bench in a room-like park and then wanders about Hagia Sophia. Seen but unseen, Yanuka occupies the center of an idyllic scene and by his gaze converts buildings into pictures. He stands beneath an actual picture, the Byzantine mosaic, and enacts its language of exchange. This sight-seer is also a sight maker, for the *flâneur*/tourist commodifies what is seen, reenacting the processes by which certain places are marked for tourism and reproduced in travel advertisements in order to generate tourist dollars.

Travelers to present-day Istanbul know that only parts of the city encourage the wanderings of the *flâneur*. Today, one pleasant place to stroll is the ancient Hippodrome, located to the south and west of Hagia Sophia and Sultan Ahmet and connected to the park between the two buildings and to the Divanyolu, the ancient and medieval Mese, or the main street of the old city. The latter route also is recommended, for it has sidewalks and streetlights. But elsewhere in the old city, walking is more difficult and seldom undertaken by Western tourists, now or in the past. Yanuka, for example, is not described as wandering between the mosques of Suleiman and Sultan Ahmet. He instead sits in the park of Sultan Ahmet and walks around Hagia Sophia. The reason that the Parisian *flâneur* of Baudelaire and Benjamin is at home here and not elsewhere in the old city is that the park and the adjacent Hippodrome were designed for just such promenades by the French architect and town planner Joseph Antoine Bouvard at the beginning of the twentieth century.

But the process of urban transformation began earlier. Long before academics became interested in what has been called "tourist bubbles,"[16] or self-contained, well-marked, and well-maintained precincts for tourists, the area around Hagia Sophia was made into what Europeans had come to see. The basic history of this section of Istanbul has been studied in admirable detail by Zeynep Çelik. Following a disastrous fire in 1865, the Divanyolu was widened and provided with sidewalks "just like in European cities," the mayor of Istanbul proudly remarked. At its eastern terminus, a small square was opened up to the southwest of Hagia Sophia (fig. 3.4). On the southern flank of the then mosque, a tree-lined street was created, and subsidiary structures began to be removed around Hagia Sophia in accordance with the most advanced French notions that monuments should be freestanding to be seen properly.[17]

In the first half of the nineteenth century and earlier, the eastern end of Hagia Sophia was the more ceremonially significant space, because it formed one side of an open space before the main gate to the Ottoman palace, but gradually European artists and photographers came to see the picturesque potential of viewing the building from the Hippodrome. Only from that vantage

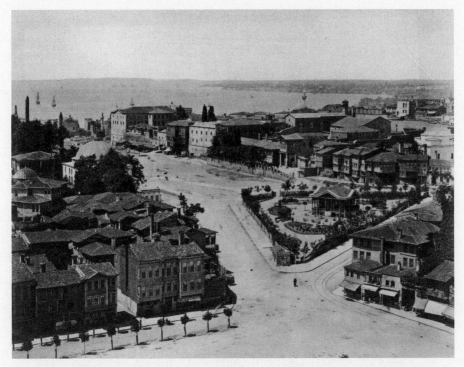

Fig. 3.4. Hippodrome, late nineteenth–early twentieth century. Courtesy of the Research Library, Getty Research Institute, Los Angeles, Pierre de Gigord Collection (96.R.14).

point could the whole building be properly seen and visualized,[18] according to the evolving European aesthetics of the city. But the view from the southwest ultimately was also not adequate, and this and other monuments in Istanbul did not meet the expectations of European travelers. One criticized the government "for not planning and improving the places that catch a traveler's eye . . . and for not cleaning and repairing the streets of the city."[19] And indeed in the later nineteenth century, the Hippodrome was a dusty, ill-kept open space, punctuated by the obelisk.

Responsive to Western criticism, the sultan asked his ambassador to France to find someone to make the necessary improvements, and in 1901 Bouvard was engaged. Working only from photographs of the city, Bouvard proposed to raze a neighborhood of tall, wooden apartment buildings between Hagia Sophia and Sultan Ahmet (fig. 3.4) in order to join this space to the Hippodrome and thereby turn the whole turned into a classic French garden. In their totality, Bouvard's ideas were impractical, but aspects were soon implemented. In 1910 the wooden housing was removed, and by the 1920s the

Hippodrome and adjacent area had been turned into a Parisian park (fig. 3.1). Its Egyptian obelisk, which had been set on a sculpted base in late antiquity, now formed an elegant decoration for urban promenades. An ancient hippodrome began to resemble the Place de la Concorde, and the classical became neoclassical.[20]

A decade later, on November 24, 1934, the Turkish Republic decreed that the mosque of Aya Sofya was to be turned into a museum, because of its "historical significance." With the conversion of "this unique architectural monument of art," humanity will "gain a new institution of knowledge," according to the proclamation.[21] The official confirmation of the building's status as a monument was the culmination of social and cultural processes that began decades before and one aspect of the secularization and modernization of Turkey that followed the end of the Ottoman Empire and the creation of the republic in 1923 and the abolition of the caliphate in the next year. In the decade that followed, the state took over the education that had formerly been religious, outlawed the fez and turban, adopted the international calendar, turned the Topkapi Sarai into a museum, had the Qur'an translated into Turkish, and decreed that Turkish should be written in Latin letters. In 1932, the call to prayer was chanted in Turkish for the first time from the minarets of the mosque of Aya Sofya.[22]

Only three years later, Aya Sofya opened as a museum on the first of February 1935, and immediately *Cumhuriyet,* the principal newspaper of Istanbul, reported that passengers from a German ship toured the building.[23] Atatürk himself visited later that month.[24] The same newspaper reported that to prepare for the conversion, the museum directorate had removed the mosque's rugs and straw mats, thus exposing the marble floor beneath, and had taken away the racks where visitors deposited their shoes before entering the mosque, as well as "some extras that were added after Aya Sofya became a mosque."[25] During the fall of the preceding year, the newspaper recorded that the authorities had closed the coffee shops in Aya Sofya's courtyard because they were "dirty" and gave some permission to reopen only when they agreed to sell "candy and postcards." Also for the benefit of tourists, the municipality built a public restroom in the corner of Sultan Ahmet Park "to emulate European examples," and its cleanliness was praised in the newspaper.[26]

By such measures, large and small, a monument and a tourist attraction were created, and an active, living building of the present—the mosque of Aya Sofya—was turned into an artifact of the past, as secular modernism became the official aesthetic of the Turkish Republic during the 1930s.[27] The transformation of the areas around Hagia Sophia began with the creation of the square at the southwest corner in the later nineteenth century and the park of

Sultan Ahmet about 1910, and it has continued in recent years. To the north of Hagia Sophia, an entire tourist street has been constructed. Old wooden Ottoman houses have been gentrified beyond recognition, and a deluxe hotel and restaurant installed inside a false front of domesticity.[28] To the east of Hagia Sophia, in the square where once pashas and ambassadors entered and exited the sultan's palace, tour buses now congregate, children sell postcards, and taxi drivers stand ready to charge the unsuspecting at least double the normal fare. To the west are rug shops and a youth hostel; east of Sultan Ahmet, a large rug bazaar has opened. The space of tourists and all those that cater to them—the tourist bubble—thus continues to grow, and the present-day museum of Aya Sofya, neither the fully reconstructed Hagia Sophia nor the former mosque of Aya Sofya, resides entirely within that bubble, with many implications for history, tradition, collective memory, and social control. But before considering these issues, a different perspective is useful.

Eleven hundred years before Yanuka or his creator visited Istanbul, another Palestinian came to Constantinople. His name was Harun-ibn-Yahya, and he was not a disguised tourist but a Byzantine prisoner from Ashkelon. Ibn-Yahya recounts the wonders of the city and describes an imperial procession to Hagia Sophia that began at the imperial palace, a now vanished compound of gardens, pavilions, churches, and receptions rooms, located south and east of Hagia Sophia and in part under Sultan Ahmet.[29] From the palace, the procession crossed a forum, the Augusteum, which more or less corresponded to the present-day park of Sultan Ahmet (fig. 3.1), and entered the church through the southwest vestibule (fig. 3.2). In the space where Yanuka or John Le Carré would stroll, ibn-Yahya saw something rather different:

> [The emperor] commands that on his way from the Gate of the Palace to the Church for the common people [Hagia Sophia], which is in the middle of the city, be spread mats and upon them there be strewn aromatic plants and green foliage, and that on the right and left of his passage the walls be adorned with brocade. Then he is preceded by 10,000 elders wearing clothes of red brocade . . . , 10,000 young men wearing clothes of white brocade . . . , 10,000 boys wearing clothes of green brocade . . . , 10,000 servants wearing clothes of brocade of the color of the blue sky [and carrying] axes covered with gold . . . , 5,000 chosen eunuchs wearing white Khorasanian clothes of half silk . . . [and carrying] golden crosses . . . , 10,000 Turkish and Khorasanian pages wearing striped breast-plates [and carrying] spears and shields wholly covered with gold . . . , a hundred most dignified patricians wearing clothes of colored brocade . . . [and carrying] gold censers perfumed with

aloes . . . , twelve chief patricians wearing clothes woven with gold . . . [and
carrying] golden rod[s] . . . , a hundred pages . . . wearing clothes trimmed
with borders and adorned with pearls; they carry a golden case in which is the
Imperial robe for the Emperor's prayer. . . . Then comes the Emperor wearing
his festival clothes, that is, silk clothes woven with jewels; on his head there is
a crown.[30]

As he suggests, ibn-Yahya was both an observer and a participant in the
imperial procession to Hagia Sophia, and his account is accurate, if one disregards the enormous number of participants cited, merely a way of saying that
the numbers were large. According to another source, the tenth-century *Book
of Ceremonies,* preparations for the procession started the day before the event
with orders to the city officials to clean the streets and to decorate them with
fragrant flowers, standard procedures for important processions.[31] The emperor began the following day at the throne room of the palace, the octagonal
Chrysotriklinos, where he prayed in the apse that contains an image of Christ
seated on a throne. From an epigram inscribed "around the ceiling" of the
Chrysotriklinos, we know that during the years 856–66 this image of Christ
was placed above the actual imperial throne and that the Virgin, as a "divine
gate," was represented above the entrance.[32] Leaving the Chrysotriklinos with
an escort, the emperor visited different sites in the palace, where various members of the palace community greeted him, making the deep obeisance of the
proskynesis and pronouncing acclamations to him.

After he crossed the Augusteum, the emperor entered the southwest
vestibule of the Great Church and passed beneath the mosaic that Le Carré
misidentified (fig. 3.2). At the inner narthex of Hagia Sophia, he met the
patriarch, and they processed together to the Imperial Door, the tallest and
symbolically most important of those leading into the narthex and the one
reserved for the emperor (visible at a distance in fig. 3.3). Pausing at this
threshold (fig. 3.5), the patriarch pronounced a prayer and the emperor prayed
and three times made the deep bow of proskynesis. Prayers completed, both
men and their entourages paraded across the nave to the sanctuary.[33]

The rites at the Imperial Door took place beneath another mosaic (fig.
3.6). At the center, Jesus Christ sits on a jeweled throne, gestures with his right
hand, and holds a book inscribed with words from the Gospel of John (20.19,
26; and 8.12): "Peace to you, I am the light of the world." Flanking medallions
depict, at the right, a winged figure with a staff or an angel and, at the left, a
woman with a veil, probably the Virgin Mary. Below her kneels an unidenti-
fied emperor with a plain nimbus. Above the door itself is a broad, projecting
lintel, clad in bronze and decorated with an image of a throne on which an-

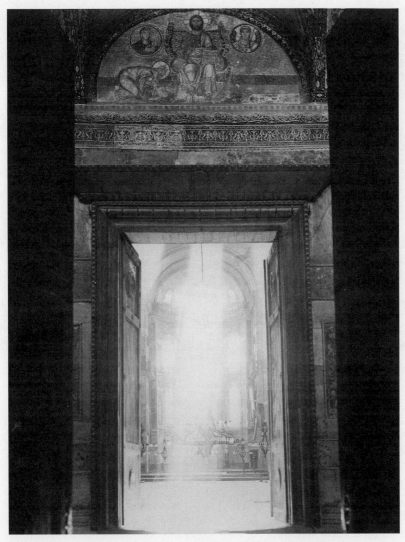

Fig. 3.5. Hagia Sophia, Imperial Door. Courtesy Dumbarton Oaks, Byzantine Photographs and Fieldwork Archives, Washington, D.C.

other book is open to a version of John 10.9, "The Lord said, I am the door of the sheep, if anyone enters by me he will go in and out and find pasture." The relief and the mosaic are more or less contemporary and date to the late ninth or early tenth century.[34]

The events at this portal, as described in the *Book of Ceremonies,* provide an experiential frame for the imagery above and vice versa. That context, it

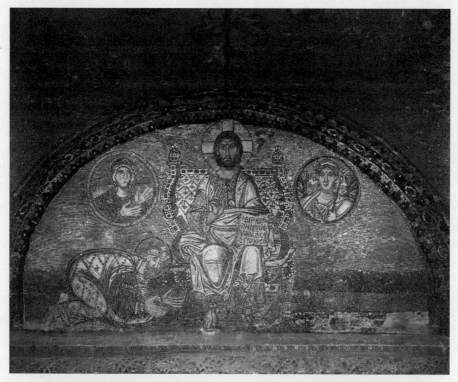

Fig. 3.6. Hagia Sophia, mosaic over the Imperial Door. Courtesy Dumbarton Oaks, Byzantine Photographs and Fieldwork Archives, Washington, D.C.

must be emphasized, is that of a very particular audience, the emperor and the normally male members of the imperial court, who took part in these processions. The social dynamic involved is what anthropologists understand as ritual, in which place and time are restructured by and for participants as they affirm and interiorize an external system of value.[35] In the words of the medieval *Book of Ceremonies,* the imperial rituals make the empire "appear to our subjects more majestic and, at the same time, more pleasing and admirable," and, performed correctly, that is, "with proportion and order," they represent "the harmony and movement that the Creator gives to this entire universe."[36] Thus the political rituals depend upon and reenact the prevailing cosmology of the day, becoming what Clifford Geertz terms "metaphysical theatre . . . designed to express a view of the ultimate nature of reality."[37] Processing in this context from the Chrysotriklinos to Hagia Sophia was an acknowledgment and acceptance of one's place within a social hierarchy, as the outsider ibn-Yahya implicitly recognized.

The mosaic above the Imperial Door contributed to this production of so-cial meaning. For its principal audience, the emperor and court, the figure of Christ, seated on a jeweled throne with a lyre-shaped back, may have had other associations. A rather similarly posed Christ on a lyre-backed throne occupied one side of the gold coins of contemporary emperors, coins that because of their high value would have been seen only by the elite. Both representations also probably resembled a mosaic in the Chrysotriklinos of the Imperial Palace.[38] In the latter, the enthroned Christ was placed above the actual throne of the emperor, and the Chrysotriklinos was the place where imperial proces-sions to Hagia Sophia began but also where they ended. The *Book of Cere-monies* specifies that before the emperor retired to his apartment, he would pray once more in its apse, "in which is represented as divine and human the holy image of our Lord and God seated on a throne."[39] Associating palace and cathedral, the similar image at Hagia Sophia joined visually what the cere-mony linked ritually.

Somewhat different associations and memories accompanied the mosaic that Le Carré misidentified (fig. 3.2), the vestibule lunette most likely made later in the tenth century. As others have observed, the central group of the Vir-gin and child, especially details of the pose of the two figures, closely resembles the apse mosaic, the church's most prominent public image that was inaugu-rated in the presence of the emperors by the Patriarch Photios in 867.[40] Be-holders entering the church were prepared for and reminded of their goal, the apse and altar, by this first appearance of the Mother of God, the protective guardian of the city of Constantinople. The emperor would walk through this door below this representation of imperial donations, process to the Imperial Door, turn right, walk east, and deposit his offering to the same church be-neath the mosaic of the apse. To associate the generosity and piety of the de-picted rulers with the living emperor below, Justinian and Constantine are dressed in the manner of medieval, not late antique, emperors. Both wear a version of the *loros*, a long gilded sash that became a major feature of impe-rial regalia only in the period of the mosaic.[41] Moreover, the model of Hagia Sophia in Justinian's hands is represented from the point of view of an impe-rial procession from the palace, for the church is shown from the south, so that the depicted and actual apses share the same orientation.

By these means at this threshold and again at the Imperial Door, ritual action and mosaic representation proclaim and instantiate imperial legitimacy and construct subject positions for elite audiences. Le Carré uses the vestibule mo-saic in a similar manner, when he makes Yanuka's rendezvous there foretell the later exchange of the Mercedes, but the medieval and modern uses and implications of the mosaic and these spaces could hardly be more different. When medieval emperors looked at the anonymous emperor in the Imperial Door mosaic or at Justinian and Constantine in the preceding vestibule, they saw persons dressed more or less as they were, so that identification was encouraged, the city's history was evoked, and its performative spaces were charged with meaning.[42] Yanuka's relation to the past is different: "He wandered round the Saint Sophia, contemplating with equal pleasure the glories of Justinian's Byzantium and of the Ottoman conquest." The pleasure would hardly be the same for someone identifying with either the Byzantine or the Ottoman period, but to the tourist/*flâneur,* all is equally distant and potentially edifying and pleasurable.

For such an audience, Hagia Sophia can be understood as what Pierre Nora has termed a place or site of memory (*lieu de mémoire*), as opposed to an environment of memory (*milieu de mémoire*), the way the church functioned, I would argue, in the Middle Ages.[43] *Lieux de mémoire* belong to our world of tourism, monument commissions, history, and art history; *milieux de mémoire* to past, distant, or at least different societies in which communal memory has not lost its powers to bind and inspire. A *lieu de mémoire* is isolated and separated from contexts and perceived individually and privately, even if it is regarded as national patrimony, and for this reason it can be conserved, studied, described, reproduced, visited, viewed from afar and understood to be in the past. Thus it belongs to history and is regarded as fixed in time, usually at the moment of its creation.

A *milieu de mémoire* is communal, belongs to public life, functions through a network of associations with diverse places, spaces, and groups, relies upon metonymic constructions, and, like human memory, condenses, abridges, alters, displaces, and projects fragments of the past, making them alive in the present for particular groups. Experienced dynamically and not viewed passively, reproduced mechanically, or studied abstractly, *milieux de mémoire* change and evolve. Existing in the present, their representations favor the present tense, as in the book that Christ displays above the Imperial Door. In contrast, *lieux de mémoire,* like the discourses that conserve and analyze them, employ the past tense to describe the depersonalized object and assume that a gulf separates past and present. In the case of Hagia Sophia, simple age, not to mention the Ottoman Conquest, played a role in this process, but the reconstitution of the building as a museum and a monument constituted a further break from either its Byzantine or its Ottoman past and marked its demise as a living, social organism.

Facilitating the distancing process, photography preserves what Benjamin terms the trace of the object but denies its aura, allowing us to look at the object, to see it clearly, but to feel no connection with it. What is seen in the photograph, whether a building or a person, cannot, figuratively or literally, look back or cause us to use our other senses to reconsider what we have seen. The trace may be associated with the *lieu de mémoire* and is an aspect of voluntary memory, as Benjamin explains. Aura, its antithesis, promotes a Proustian involuntary memory and offers the sensation of connection, as if the object could return the gaze.[44] Benjamin puts it simply and in a way that applies to the modern and medieval perceptions of Hagia Sophia: "In the trace, we gain possession of the thing; in the aura, it takes possession of us."[45] If Benjamin had looked at Byzantine mosaics, he would have found what he imagined and desired, for these staring frontal figures do indeed confront the viewer/believer. In the lunette over the Imperial Door, Christ gestures to the beholder and speaks to him or her directly ("I am the light of the world . . ."). Believers acknowledge that address, the implicit aura, the presence of the holy, by gesturing to the image or, if it is within reach, by kissing and touching it. In contrast, *flâneurs* gaze from a safe distance, and tourists take or buy pictures to preserve and possess the sight.

Distance from the building and its past is achieved through other means as well. Yanuka, like tourists, but also most art historians, is a visitor to Istanbul. While tourists stay for only a short time and art historians linger as long as they can, each resides there within some aspect of the tourist bubble, even if it is the academic version, the research institute. In accounts written of the monument, travel to and from the object of study is normally suppressed and the fiction is maintained that author and reader enjoy instant, magical access.[46] Such work occludes the modern processions and processes that render a monument like Hagia Sophia personally meaningful for modern scholars (grant application, research permit, journey, interview with curator, and so on).

Finally rupture and distance are achieved by the reorganization of the spaces around Hagia Sophia. Like other medieval cathedrals, it was once surrounded by structures of various sorts, so that distant views and the picturesque aesthetic they promote were not possible. To perceive the building, one had to enter it, submit to its liminal processes, and thereby enact tradition and memory. With its many icons, gold and silver liturgical furnishings, countless lamps and candles, clouds of incense, and scores of resplendent clergy and court members attending on days of high ceremony, the medieval Hagia Sophia was grand, imposing, moving, beautiful, vital, and politically significant. But it was not a modern monument, as Christine Boyer describes, one of those "didactic artifacts . . . treated with curatorial reverence . . . isolated ornaments; jewels of the city to be placed in scenographic arrangements and iconographically composed to civilise and elevate the aesthetic tastes and morals of an aspiring urban elite."[47] By stripping Hagia Sophia of attendant structures and landscaping nearby areas, modern town planners constructed what the Turkish Republic decreed. This is the space into which Le Carré's protagonist wanders one fine day, a place of private not communal memory, modern not medieval, seen not experienced, and thereby appropriate for tourism, for art history, and for the ritual processes that create and affirm modern memory.

The first version of this essay, written before September 11, 2001, ended here. But even without that tragedy questions linger and prompt a coda. What exactly is the nature of the object that I have described? Can a strongly ideological text, such as the *Book of Ceremonies,* provide evidence for Hagia Sophia *"wie es eigentlich gewesen,"* or "as it actually was," Ranke's famous principle of historicism from an age of realism? Surely many in Byzantium did not share the same enthusiasm for protocol as court officials, and few inside and fewer outside Constantinople witnessed such processions. They could only marvel at the mosaics of Hagia Sophia and imagine their possible meanings, much as they concocted stories about ancient sculpture in the streets of Constantinople.[48]

Moreover, what is the relevance of a short passage in a spy novel to the modern life of the building in Istanbul? Ranke and his modern successors would not approve of the use of a novel as a historical source, and there are indeed dangers here.[49] But is the monument not itself a type of realist fiction, real because tangible and visible, but fictive because it was more symbolic than utilitarian in both the medieval and modern eras? In the course of its long life, Hagia Sophia changed from a *milieu* to a *lieu* of memory. If in both regimes it was a socially bonding and consensus-producing cultural agent, what has it been protecting societies against? What does it hide? Why must the objects of tourism or ritual be pure and flower bedecked and thus different from the rest of the world? To answer for Hagia Sophia would require another essay, but fragments of that story may be presented here.

Born out of political conflict in the sixth century, Hagia Sophia as a monument contained, framed, and denied social violence from that moment to the present. Before and during World War I, the Ottoman government proposed to dynamite the building if Turkey were attacked.[50] Afterward when Istanbul was occupied by the Entente, the English government, or at least its foreign minister, Lord Curzon, wanted to take the building from the Muslims and turn it back into a church, and the Turkish authorities stationed soldiers in the narthex in fear that the Greek population of Istanbul would try to retake the mosque by force.[51] Such was also the goal of the ill-fated military conquest of Turkey by the Greek government a few years later. Rallying the Turkish population, Atatürk expelled the Greek invasion, but then abolished the sultanate and the caliphate and secularized the mosque of Aya Sofya. Only two years before, seventy thousand people had celebrated Ramadan inside and outside that mosque.[52]

Cumhuriyet was mainly silent about these events, but that in itself seems suspicious, and social conflict can be detected here and there on its pages. For example, one article attempted to dispel rumors that the mosque would be damaged or altered by the restoration work of the Byzantine Institute of America from 1931. It also refuted another concern that the latter's motives were religious, i.e., Christian, and reassured readers that the work was being undertaken solely "for the sake of knowledge and art."[53] In more recent years, Islamic parties and factions in Turkey have sought to make Aya Sofya a mosque again and a small area has been reserved for Muslim prayers.[54] It was presumably because the building was a symbol of the power of the secular state that Kurdish dissidents set off a bomb inside the museum in 1994.[55] In the summer of 1999, Turkish tour guides were still recalling that event as they regaled bewildered cruise ship passengers with their joy at the recent capture of the Kurdish leader. For their part, the Turkish authorities bedecked the processional path to Hagia Sophia with photographic displays of the alleged mistreatment of Turks fleeing ethnic violence in Bulgaria. One wonders how many tourists bothered to ask what all this had to do with what they had come to see, Justinian's Great Church.

But all is surely relevant for the recent history of Hagia Sophia as a modern monument and evidence of the building's civic significance. To counter this modern history, artists, art historians, historians, novelists, and poets have long labored to produce visual and verbal evocations of the building's past magnificence, from the widely read Byzantine poems of William Butler Yeats, to the stunningly beautiful book by Cyril Mango,[56] and to the latest cybernetic fiction of Richard Powers.[57] In "Sailing to Byzantium," the aging Irish poet yearned for the "holy city of Byzantium," filled with "monuments of unaging intellect." He prayed to be gathered there into "the artifice of eternity," and to sing, like the mechanical bird Yeats imagined in the palace of the Byzantine emperor,

> To lords and ladies of Byzantium
> Of what is past, or passing, or to come.

Hearing a different bird or drummer at great monuments, terrorists strive to replace the dreams of poets, tourists, *flâneurs,* and historians with visions of other worlds. To do so, they too effect rupture, unfortunately actual rather than symbolic, as they flail away at society's aspirations and symbols. But from such violence, dreams and memories can emerge undamaged, even strengthened. Sadly, buildings and the people inside are more vulnerable.

NOTES

1. On the Ottoman history of the building, see the fundamental study of Gülru Necipoğlou, "The Life of an Imperial Monument: Hagia Sophia after Byzantium," in Robert Mark and Ahmet Ş. Çakmak, eds., *Hagia Sophia from the Age of Justinian to the Present* (New York: Cambridge University Press, 1992), 195–225. Surely the most handsome book ever to be published on Hagia Sophia is Cyril Mango, *Hagia Sophia: A Vision for Empires* (Istanbul: Ertuğ and Kocabiyik, 1997). A useful general study is Rowland J. Mainstone, *Hagia Sophia* (New York: Thames and Hudson, 1988). In *Hagia Sophia, 1850–1950: Holy Wisdom Modern Monument* (Chicago: University of Chicago Press, forthcoming), I discuss modern reactions to the building.

2. On the Hiltons of the 1950s, see the excellent new book of Annabel Jane Wharton, *Building the Cold War: Hilton International Hotels and Modern Architecture* (Chicago: University of Chicago Press, 2001). Significantly, as her frontipiece indicates, an early advertisement for the Istanbul hotel associates it with the Blue Mosque.

3. John Le Carré, *The Little Drummer Girl* (London: Hodder & Stoughton, 1983), 58–59.

4. Bruce Redford, *Venice and the Grand Tour* (New Haven: Yale University Press, 1996); Arie Shachar and Noam Shoval, "Tourism in Jerusalem: A Place to Pray," in Denis R. Judd and Susan S. Fainstein, eds., *The Tourist City* (New Haven: Yale University Press, 1999), 198–211.

5. Sophie Basch et al., *Le Voyage à Constantinople: l'Orient-Express* (Brussels: Snoeck-Ducaju & Zoon, 1997).

6. Robert Ousterhout and Nezih Başgelen, *Monuments of Unaging Intellect: Historic Postcards of Byzantine Istanbul* (Istanbul: Tür Tanitim Advertising Services, 1995).

7. Dean MacCannell, *The Tourist: A New Theory of the Leisure Class* (Berkeley: University of California Press, 1999), 41–56,109–33.

8. John Urry, *The Tourist Gaze: Leisure and Travel in Contemporary Societies* (London: Sage Publications, 1990). See also the essays in *Unpacking Culture: Art and Commodity in Colonial and Postcolonial Worlds*, ed. Ruth B. Phillips and Christopher B. Steiner (Berkeley: University of California Press, 1999). Particularly relevant to a tourist destination such as Hagia Sophia is Tim Edensor, *Tourists at the Taj: Performance and Meaning at a Symbolic Site* (New York: Routledge, 1998).

9. John Urry, *Consuming Places* (New York: Routledge, 1995), 209.

10. E.g., John Freely, *Blue Guide: Istanbul* (New York: W.W. Norton, 1988).

11. Discussed in M. Christine Boyer, *The City of Collective Memory: Its Historical Imagery and Architectural Entertainments* (Cambridge: MIT Press, 1994), 237–38; Francis Haskell, *Rediscoveries in Art: Some Aspects of Taste, Fashion and Collecting in England and France* (Ithaca: Cornell University Press, 1976), 169–71.

12. Today's standard, the *Blue Guide,* first takes the reader to the precincts of the Hagia Sophia and then devotes a chapter to the latter and three others to the general area here: Freely, *Blue Guide: Istanbul,* 65–143. In 1849, when the English author and popular enter-

tainer Albert Smith visited Istanbul, he also went first to this area, landing at the palace, touring Hagia Sophia and afterward the Mosque of Sultan Ahmet. His group was going on to the Mosque of Suleiman, but learning that the other mosques were similar to what he had seen, Smith begged off and went riding instead: Albert Smith, *A Month at Constantinople* (London: David Bogue, 1850), 96–101.

13. Charles Baudelaire, "The Painter of Modern Life," in *The Painter of Modern Life and Other Essays,* trans. and ed. Jonathan Mayne (New York: Da Capo, 1964), 9–10.

14. Walter Benjamin, *The Arcades Project,* trans. Howard Eiland and Kevin McLaughlin (Cambridge: Harvard University Press, 1999), 417.

15. Keith Tester, ed., *The Flâneur* (New York: Routledge, 1994).

16. Dennis R. Judd, "Constructing the Tourist Bubble," in *Tourist City,* ed. Dennis R. Judd and Susan S. Fainstein (New Haven: Yale University Press, 1999), 35–53.

17. Zeynep Çelik, *The Remaking of Istanbul: Portrait of an Ottoman City in the Nineteenth Century* (Seattle: University of Washington Press, 1986), 55–62.

18. This point will be developed in my forthcoming book about the modern Hagia Sophia.

19. Çelik, *Remaking of Istanbul,* 110.

20. On this general matter, see ibid., 110–15.

21. Nurettin Can Gulekli, *Eski Eserler ve Müzelerle ilgili Kanun Nizamname ve Emirler.* (Ankara: Milli Eğitim Basımevi, 1948), 64–65. The passages translated here are the work of Dr. Jessica Tiregol, my research assistant, while a fellow at the Getty Research Institute. I am most grateful for Dr. Tiregol's aid with this decree and for her research on Turkish newspapers, as reported below.

22. Bernard Lewis, *The Emergence of Modern Turkey,* 2d ed. (Oxford: Oxford University Press, 1968), 256–79, 415–16; Niyazi Berkes, *The Development of Secularism in Turkey* (Montreal: McGill University Press, 1964), 486–90.

23. *Cumhuriyet,* February 2, 1935.

24. Thomas Whittemore, *The Mosaics of St. Sophia at Istanbul: Second Preliminary Report Work Done in 1933 and 1934* (Oxford: Oxford University Press, 1936), 7.

25. *Cumhuriyet,* January 28, 1935.

26. Ibid., November 9 and 21, 1934.

27. On this process more generally, see Sibel Bozdoğan, *Modernism and Nation Building: Turkish Architectural Culture in the Early Republic* (Seattle: University of Washington Press, 2001).

28. Zeynep Çelik, "Urban Preservation as Theme Park: The Case of Soğukçeşme Street," in Zeynep Çelik et al., eds., *Streets: Critical Perspectives on Public Space* (Berkeley: University of California Press, 1994), 83–94.

29. Wolfgang Müller-Wiener, *Bildlexikon zur Topographie Istanbuls* (Tübingen: Ernst Wasmuth, 1977), 229–237 with bibliography.

30. A. Vasiliev, "Harun-Ibn-Yahya and His Description of Constantinople," *Seminarium Kondakovianum 5* (1932): 158–59; Ahmad M. H. Shboul, in *Oxford Dictionary of Byzantium* (Oxford: Oxford University Press, 1991), 903.

31. Albert Vogt, *Constantin VII Porphyrogénète, Le livre des cérémonies,* vol. 1, pt. 1 (Paris: Société d'édition "Les Belles Lettres," 1967), 3–4; Michael McCormick, *Eternal Victory: Triumphal Rulership in Late Antiquity, Byzantium, and the Early Medieval West* (Cambridge: Cambridge University Press, 1986), 207.

32. Vogt, *Livre des cérémonies,* vol. 1, *Commentaire,* 8–9; Cyril Mango, *The Art of the Byzantine Empire, 312–1453: Sources and Documents* (Englewood Cliffs, N.J.: Prentice-Hall, 1972), 184.

33. On the imperial procession recently, see George P. Majeska, "The Emperor in His Church: Imperial Ritual in the Church of St. Sophia," in *Byzantine Court Culture from 829–1204,* ed. Henry Maguire (Washington, D.C.: Dumbarton Oaks, 1997), 5–6; and Gilbert Dagron, *Empereur et prêtre: étude sur le "césaropapisme" byzantin* (Paris: Gallimard, 1996), 106–12.

34. On the relief: Paul A. Underwood, "Notes on the Work of the Byzantine Institute in Istanbul: 1957–59," *Dumbarton Oaks Papers* 14 (1960): 212–13; Maria Andaloro, "Polarità bizantine, polarità romane nelle pitture di Grottaferrata," in *Italian Church Decoration of the Middle Ages and Early Renaissance,* ed. William Tronzo (Baltimore: John Hopkins University Press, 1989), 15. On the mosaic: Robin Cormack, "Interpreting the Mosaics of S. Sophia at Istanbul," *Art History* 4 (1981): 138–41; and "The Mother of God in the Mosaics of Hagia Sophia at Constantinople," in *Mother of God: Representations of the Virgin in Byzantine Art,* ed. Maria Vassilaki (Milan: Skira, 2000), 114.

35. Catherine Bell, *Ritual Theory, Ritual Practice* (New York: Oxford University Press, 1992), 109–10.

36. Vogt, *Livre des cérémonies,* 1.1:2.

37. Clifford Geertz, *Negara: The Theatre State in Nineteenth-Century Bali* (Princeton: Princeton University Press, 1980), 104.

38. James D. Breckenridge, "Christ on the Lyre-Backed Throne," *Dumbarton Oaks Papers* 34–35 (1980–81): 247–60; Philip Grierson, *Catalogue of the Byzantine Coins in the Dumbarton Oaks Collection and in the Whittemore Collection,* vol. 3, pt. 1 (Washington: Dumbarton Oaks, 1973), 154–55.

39. Vogt, *Livre des cérémonies,* 1.1:17.

40. Cormack, "Mother of God," 112–13.

41. See Grierson, *Catalogue,* vol. 2, pt. 1, 78–80.

42. There are useful essays on these problems in general in Barbara A. Hanawalt and Michal Kobialka, eds., *Medieval Practices of Space* (Minneapolis: University of Minnesota Press, 2000), especially that of Michael Camille, who also contrasts the medieval and the modern (pp. 1–36).

43. Pierre Nora's grand project has been condensed and focused in the English edition: *Realms of Memory: Rethinking the French Past,* trans. Arthur Goldhammer, 3 vols. (New York: Columbia University Press, 1996–98) . In his original introduction and the new preface to the translation, Nora discusses the two types of memory (pp. xv–xxiv, 1–20). The general project owes much to the pioneering investigation of communal memory by Maurice Halbwachs during the 1920s and 1930s, some of which is available in his *On Collective Memory* (Chicago: University of Chicago Press, 1992).

44. Walter Benjamin, "On Some Motifs in Baudelaire," in *Illuminations: Essays and Reflections,* ed. Hannah Arendt (New York: Schocken Books, 1969), 186–89.

45. Benjamin, *Arcades Project,* 447.

46. These and other issues are explored in James Clifford, *Routes: Travel and Translation in the Late Twentieth Century* (Cambridge: Harvard University Press, 1997), 17–39.

47. Boyer, *City of Collective Memory,* 34.

48. Cyril Mango, "Antique Statuary and the Byzantine Beholder," *Dumbarton Oaks Papers* 17 (1963): 53–75

49. See the discussion of history and fiction in David Lowenthal, *The Past Is a Foreign Country* (New York: Cambridge University Press, 1985), 224–31.

50. See the memoir of Henry Morgenthau, *Ambassador Morgenthau's Story* (Garden City, N.Y.: Doubleday, 1918), 198. The American archaeologist Thomas Whittemore wrote to

Isabella Stewart Gardner on March 8, 1913, that the Turks were threatening to destroy Hagia Sophia. Archives of the Isabella Stewart Gardner Museum, Boston.

51.   Philip Mansel, *Constantinople: City of the World's Desire, 1453–1924* (New York: St. Martin's Griffin, 1995), 383–84; Henri Mylès, *La fin de Stamboul* (Paris: E. Sansot, 1921), 165–66.

52. *Cumhuriyet,* February 4, 1932

53. Ibid., November 14, 1932.

54. Mansel, *Constantinople,* 431.

55. *Chicago Tribune,* August 29, 1999.

56. See n. 1.

57. Richard Powers, *Plowing the Dark* (New York: Farrar, Straus & Giroux, 2000).

The Moving Landscape

MITCHELL SCHWARZER

For millennia, people throughout the world have made sense of them-selves in gardens, fields, roads, and monuments built into raw land. Landscape humanizes land. It extends mind, body, and technology into nature. It constructs social and temporal awareness out of wood, water, and wilderness. For a shorter amount of time, no more than a couple of thousand years, people in selected parts of the world have additionally made sense of themselves in two-dimensional landscapes made up of paint on a surface. This flexible theater of landscape brushes in clouds and ruins, distant epochs and faraway regions. Such painterly landscapes eventually influenced the design of land, con-fusing the here-and-now with the representational. But in all cases—in the flesh, represented on canvas, influenced by canvas—landscapes deepen a person's line of perception in a present moment.

For the shortest amount of time, consisting of less than the past 150 years, people in the industrial world have made sense of them-selves in landscapes that move. Through technologies of mechanized transportation and image reproduction, moving landscapes continue to expand humanity's external consciousness, but they also now split apart the internal one. Contemporary moving landscapes on the roadside and on screens sever the place of viewing from the objects or events viewed. Such was also the case with paintings. But because of the reality effect of moving imagery, the moving landscape rockets eyes and minds away, keeps them going, and yet, paradoxically, often leaves the body and its other senses where they are. From cars or on television, it is almost possible to say that people become the fixed monument around which landscape swirls.

This phenomenon is very apparent in digital culture. What happens, for instance, when I type the word *landscape* into the newest and largest memory bank in history, the Internet? When we click from one site to the next, there is always a moment when the screen is blank or in flux. I await the chosen site, and if I become conscious of the wait, I resign myself to the frustrating possibility of a screen headed by the words "this page cannot be displayed." That's what happened on the afternoon of August 18, 2001 when I typed the domain names "landscape.org" and "landscape.net" onto the address bar. The server could not be found. For more than a moment, another website was unavailable. "Landscape.com" quickly brought a white page with the title "landscape.com is undergoing further development." Below, a line suggested clicking on a link to find what I was looking for. In a drab grid were listed nine categories: hobbies, health, gifts, travel, home, entertainment, finance, shopping, and computing, plus an adult site, "over 18 only." At the bottom of the page, a search box, "goto.com," brought another hindrance to the effort. The original sponsor of "landscape.com" had probably gone out of business. Checking with "register.com" revealed that the current site was now owned by "anything.com." "Landscape.com" had become a holding or redirection page offering not specific products or ideas but predetermined search categories.

Each of the nine categories of "landscape.com" contained six subcategories. Under the home section, gardening was listed after home loan, home buying, and home improvement, and before pets and interior design. When I clicked on gardening I was faced with a list with fifteen websites, the first of which was called "pre-screened home gardeners." And when I clicked on this site I landed in "servicemagic.com," offering prescreened contractors matched to me. Below the title "landscape, decks & fences" was a list of fifteen more subcategories, starting with "fences" and ending with "yard preparation and soils." The subcategory "yard preparation and soils" presented yet five more options: landscape grading, mulch delivery, sand delivery, topsoil delivery, and fill dirt delivery. Finally, clicking on any of these headings revealed a set of questions that could, presumably, had I the inclination, lead to some action in the land.

Using the word *landscape* as a domain name curiously reminds us of landscape's original Germanic roots, as listed in the *Oxford English Dictionary*: *landtschap, lantschape, landscap*. Landscape is not something in and of itself but the creation or organization of land, a process. With respect to the Internet, then, landscape consists as much of the spaces between screens as the contents of the screen. What defines the digital landscape most is movement. On this brief journey, from the initial domain name "landscape.com" streamed hundreds of potential landscapes, strings of words and pictures that grew out of each other only to implicate the word *landscape* in mobile perception.

Landscape has long been one of those words, like *nature* or *culture,* that possess such an abundance of definitions that what unravels off the tongue, if not the eyes and screen, is all over the place. Landscape can be a picture or view of scenery or nature; the artistic or architectural design of land; the layout and measurement of cities or regions; patrimony over lands indicative of heritage; the study of the environment or an ecological system. Among these varied definitions, I believe, there is a central philosophical divide. Is landscape an issue of sensation or of taste? Or, to put it another way, is landscape a totality or a qualification of totality? Can all the aspects of landscape be dotted with significance, the smallest shed or alley something to be accounted for? Or is landscape that which is artistically elevated, where selected works and monuments assume center stage?

In the first part of this essay I will examine how the word *landscape* conjures notions of both bucolic vistas and raw terrain. Until the twentieth century, landscape referred primarily to painting and garden design. It was the greenhouse of collective memory, the exemplary place where the trees of Eden and the stones of antiquity might be cultivated and witnessed in the present moment. During the twentieth century, the interpretation of landscape expanded from the scenographic utopias of the fine arts. Scholars and writers within the fields of geography (and later architecture) shifted the arc of understanding and appreciation away from excellence and escape and toward everyday happenings. Landscape, in this other rendition, takes in the vulgarity and commonness that make up the ambient environment.

If landscape's definition now takes in the everyday world, it will be my contention in the second part of this essay that this encounter has been reconfigured by technology. As theorists from Walter Benjamin to Jean Baudrillard note, the landscapes of modernity and postmodernity are perceived less and less on their own terms, in concentrated on-site viewing, and more and more through vehicular and camera movement. At one time, most people experienced landscapes by moving through them. In today's world of computers, film, and television, automobiles, high-speed rail, and airplanes, people sit down and the landscape moves.

Car commercials epitomize the moving landscape. They compose a disproportionately large share of the production resources and airtime of television advertising. But, more importantly, after the MTV videography revolution of the 1980s, car commercials make up the principal stage for television's rapid-fire visuality. Crossing the screen faster than a speeding locomotive, able to leap over states or countries in a single bound, television's cars, trucks, and SUVs fragment the spatial continuum of landscape into a mountainous swell of imagery, sights without measure, an oceanic voyage with little hope of landfall.

From Pictures to Geographies

In an essay, "Urbanism and Semiology," Françoise Choay distinguishes two types of landscape on the basis of legibility: closed and open systems. She calls closed systems those premodern places that signify through the interplay of their proper elements without help from supplementary verbal or graphic systems.[1] In a precise place, for a distinct cultural group, the elements of landscape constitute an integral system of communication. People are born into this system, learn to communicate, think, and experience within it, and derive their fundamental sense of identity and temporality from it. Here are found the tangible accompaniments to belief and religion: a sacred grove of trees or columns, stepped heights, large stones atop a grave. These landscapes once composed most of nature and culture, albeit within the confines of a small territory and homogeneous community. Often a society's ancestors were affixed to the land, and aspects of landscape down to the smallest detail were points of entry into experiences of multiple temporalities.[2] Often landscape was the collective memory bank.[3] In ancient Japan, for instance, all aspects of nature were the grounds of spirits, or *Kami,* who deepened the thickness and hence memory of every conscious act.

When certain societies became larger and more complex (e.g., the civilizations of the Nile, Euphrates, Indus, and Hwang Ho valleys), hierarchies emerged within nature and hence landscape. In these centralized states, the greatly extended landscape was far too large for lucid communication. Whole stretches had to be profaned or ignored, assumed into the ordinary; in turn, selected places and things, especially the expensive and painstaking creations of art and architecture, became the exceptional and typically restricted sites of large-scale collective communication.

First in China during the Tang dynasty, and then in the West during the Renaissance, landscape went off-site. Most frequently, it was identified with the painterly reproduction of mountains, river valleys, and the seaside. In Europe, the word *landscape* took the meaning of a picture of pastoral scenery or an actual view onto land turned into scenery. Like the other fine arts—painting, sculpture, or architecture—of which it was a part, landscape design bettered nature. It turned wild or worked places into pleasure grounds. To have a sense of landscape was to engage only a small portion of the land or water: the ability to discriminate, to love the cultural transformation and reassemblage of natural phenomena as wondrous phenomena. In terms of memory, landscape painting most frequently attempted to resurrect aspects of classical antiquity or biblical times and construct a contemporary experience less from a place's actual history than from literary and pictorial conventions.[4] On canvases by Salvator Rosa or Claude Lorrain, prized aspects of nature and culture—classical temples, giant trees, distant cities, harbors opening onto great bays, polychromatic skies—were arranged to produce an impression of antique wildness, the spatial underside of time's passage. Indoors, hanging on walls, such paintings extended illusory perspectival views where nature was carefully cultivated and aged.

Later, out of doors, especially in such eighteenth-century English gardens as Stourhead or Stowe, landscape became a walking tour into the classical past. The counterpart to the Grand Tour of Italy or Greece was the sightsee on a baronial estate, where an arrangement of statues, temples, and other edifices produced close at hand a sequence of faraway temporal allusions. Actual nature was reworked into shapes and spaces that matched the dreams of painting and literature; a woodland in dreary cloud-covered northern Europe could become an expansive meadow opening onto allusions from sunlit lands—a second coming of Arcadia or the Virgilian Roman countryside of villas and vineyards.[5] In the garden, landscape design irrigated any contemporary place and time with waters from an epic past.[6]

In spirit if not form, these elevating practices continued into the twentieth century. The everyday landscapes of modernity, now made more threatening by the disorder of rampant industrialization, repulsed scores of writers, architects, and painters. No wonder that most of the modern avant-gardes carried over an idealizing, if not classicizing, outlook on landscape. While their palette featured irregular geometries or industrial materials, the binary character of the term landscape as a concept of betterment remained. In the mechanized tracks of the twentieth century as much as the floriferous paths of the seventeenth and eighteenth centuries, landscape fled the world at hand for utopian imagining.

Still, no matter how tightly these landscape paintings, gardens, and sites were linked to the stories of a people, establishing and maintaining their uniqueness invariably required greater levels of interpretation and connoisseurship. Landscape is both a place seen and a way of seeing. The landscapes of cosmopolitan cultures depend upon vast codes of supplementation, traffic codes, graphic signs, and, most of all, texts—what Choay calls open systems.

As she summarizes the historical transition to modernity: "the more the built-up system makes demands on supplementary systems, the more it proves itself obsolete and its former task of information is carried via printing and telecommunications through other systems of information."[7] By the twentieth century, the formerly exclusive landscapes crafted by artists and landscape architects were submerged in discourse and subsumed by their supplementary systems. Landscape, which had emerged in the West as a means of opening a sensual view onto an ancient amalgam of nature and culture, was abstracted into scholarly discourse.

At the same time, over the past half century, the word *landscape* spawned a second, different definition. Within the discipline of geography, landscape was repositioned from the arts to the sciences and became an objective measurement and description of areas or regions.[8] An early pioneer of such approaches was Carl Sauer, who called landscape "an area made up of a distinct association of forms, both physical and cultural."[9] In an empirical spirit, his and other geographical definitions steered clear of painterly mountains and sunsets and removed the word's pejorative aesthetic and moral baggage.[10] They worked instead from direct observation of things at hand, repositioning landscape from something narrowed by archetypes to something that opens up to the world's confounding and expansive reality.

Geographers first associated landscape with the entire surface of the earth, equator to poles, rocky crust to blue atmosphere—everything visible outdoors.[11] This connection of landscape with the earth provoked a need to distinguish it from other empirical sciences. Although geographical landscape studies include biological, geological, and climatic factors, their focus has been on the changes wrought in nature by people—issues of cultivation, development, and building. To be sure, the adjective *cultural* has been greatly important to the field of landscape studies. As Peirce Lewis writes: "By cultural landscape geographers mean the total assemblage of visible things that human beings have done to alter the face of the earth—their shapings of the earth with mines and quarries and dams and jetties; the ubiquitous purposeful manipulation of the earth's vegetative cover in farms, forests, lawns, parks, and gardens; the things humans build on the earth, cities and towns, houses and barns, factories and office buildings; the spaces we create for worship and for play . . . the roads and machines we build to transport objects and ideas."[12]

Another writer to advance the idea of the cultural landscape was J. B. Jackson. Through his journal *Landscape,* founded in 1952, Jackson described landscape as a purposefully transformative activity, "a space deliberately created to speed up or slow down the process of nature."[13] But unlike many geographers, who did not care to ruminate about the greater meaning of freeway

ramps or right-angled grids, Jackson heard a mythic rumbling in all seeming
artifice. Akin to art, language, or religion, he argued that the most ordinary
landscapes were "the infrastructure or background for our collective existence."[14] Jackson's judgment that there was no landscape unrevealing of deep
collective intentions underscored the importance of common or ordinary objects for memory.[15] Similarly, another geographer, D. W. Meinig, remarks that
landscape "is a common word which is increasingly used to encompass an ensemble of ordinary features which constitute an extraordinarily rich exhibit of
the course and character of our society."[16] The ordinary landscape encom-
passes those aspects of the environment ignored by the stylistic focus of the
arts and architectural disciplines.[17]

Unlike landscape painting or garden design, the geographical landscape
has no opposite or inferior partner. It is inclusive and hybrid, strained by size
and scale, stained by mixtures and boundary crossings, and sedimented by relentless change. It is a way of seeing the land in complex chords and massive
dimensions. Included are monuments and malls, museums and theme parks,
cemeteries and tract homes. But as landscape expands to this confusing array
of form and space, how does it convey meaning?

Despite their empirical bent, many cultural geographers have sought to
understand how lasting cultural practices implanted themselves within landscapes and shaped the history of those spaces. Jackson was interested in how
certain megastructures influenced landscape development over time: natural
boundaries and property lines, roads and transportation networks, patterns of
habitation as well as public meeting places and marketplaces, monuments in
the form of graveyards.[18] Wilbur Zelinsky analyzed the lasting impact of the
federal government on the American landscape. He noticed resemblances in
building types, differences between jurisdictional boundaries, and the impacts
of governmental programs like the Works Progress Administration of the
1930s on physical terrain.[19] David Lowenthal approached landscape as a seat
of communal values expressed in specific objects: "nature as fundamental heritage, environment as the setting of human action, sense of place as local difference and ancestral roots."[20]

But do such approaches implant memory onto the landscape in too uni-
form a way? And is not the reception of landscape as important as its production, the current inhabitants as important in determining the temporal angles
of meaning as the original constructors? Taking up such questions, some recent writers have noted that advanced studies in archival and visual analysis
often leave out the visceral and immediate dimensions of popular perception.[21]
Others have emphasized the discontinuities of landscape form in specific
places and discussed the importance of inhabitants (and their class, race,

ethnicity, and gender) in the reception of that form.[22] The reverberations of memory in landscape cannot be the same for all people. For instance, the divisive role of race in American history means that parallel, superimposed, and confrontational memories emerge from the same landscape.[23] In a pluralistic society, would it be desirable for landscape to be a continuous surface of meaning that all people perceive and read similarly?

Today, the meanings attributed to landscapes are confrontational and changeable. Lush green suburban lawns suggest people who have made it, but also people who have no sense of water conservation or the ecological damage done by exotic plant species. An equestrian statue at the end of a palm-lined boulevard provokes sharply different interpretations of national identity, memories of oppression or omission mingling with those of triumph and inclusion. Graffiti-scarred warehouses announce many things: the menacing presence of gangs, an arresting collage contributed by outlaw artists, adolescent doodles on an urban scale, or offensive grime. Skyscraper skylines no longer just point out the power of architectural height and the glory of new design; they also represent blocked views, overly shaded parks and streets, and the noxious domination and homogeneity of corporate culture.

Not only individuals contribute to the visual cacophony of the everyday landscape. The everyday landscape is tied to multibillion-dollar industries. Product advertisements shroud metropolitan geographies, painting short invitations to pleasure through consumption. Points of high voltage sear the eyes: giant billboards showing off movie stars, skinny towers capped by logos, bright lights, moving lights, moving images. Increasingly, landscape is indistinguishable from mediascape. Road and screen entangle. Sensation and memory trace back to physical places and virtual experiences, things seen slowly in the flesh and things seen flashing at a distance. What happens to landscape in a world of "third generation photocopies of original mythic practices"?[24] What happens when landscape liquefies petrochemically and electronically?

Learning from Car Commercials

As I have discussed, exceptionality divides the artistic landscape from the geographical landscape. Painting and garden design call up perfect worlds, an aesthetic encounter determined by tranquility and taste. The quality of any artistic landscape emerges in light of its distance from the hubbub of day-to-day life and commerce. By contrast, geographers are stuck on the world as it is, its vast scale, its commercial character, and its stretches of unremarkable appearance. Everything is included. The perceptual experience is less aesthetic than phenomenological, and by turns banal or overpowering. In both artistic and geographic arenas, however, landscape consists primarily of objects and places, whether they constitute the whole visible surface of the planet or a careful representation of certain outstanding features.

At this point, I would like to argue that as the countryside flashes by at seventy miles per hour or twenty-four frames per second, yet a third definition of landscape rears its forms, spaces, and perceptual characteristics. Beginning on a mass scale with rail travel during the 1830s, and continuing in the twentieth century via automobiles and airplanes, our contact with the earth and sky, buildings and landscapes, is channeled within steel and glass vehicles, confined and controlled spaces capable of incredible speed and range.

The moving landscape may be differentiated from artistic and geographical landscapes by the manner of its framing. Artists fit the landscapes of paintings or vistas into tightly composed viewing frames, rectangles that freeze the world in a beautiful instant. Geographers remove the frame and freely range over a landscape both extensive and unfocused. In the moving landscape, technology structures the frame through which landscape is experienced. Because of its mobility, technology encourages us to visualize landscape shooting out from every direction, crushing against our field of vision, and suddenly vanishing with a turn or click.

Hordes of images and spaces dominate the technological perception of moving landscape. In *On the Road,* Jack Kerouac describes the road blazing new paths of perception: "'Whooee!' yelled Dean. 'Here we go!' And he hunched over the wheel and gunned her; he was back in his element, everybody could see that. We were all delighted, we all realized we were leaving confusion and nonsense behind and performing our one and noble function of the time, move. And we moved! We flashed past the mysterious white signs in the night somewhere in New Jersey that say SOUTH (with an arrow) and WEST (with an arrow) and took the south one. New Orleans. It burned in our brains."[25] Similarly, modern technologies of representation—from the photographic camera to film, television, and computers—orchestrate the experience of landscape within screens and monitors that reconfigure the perception of space and time. For the filmmaker Maya Deren, "[t]he camera can create dance, movement and action which transcend geography and take place anywhere and everywhere; it can also . . . be the mediating mind turned inward upon the idea of movement, and this idea, being an abstraction, takes place nowhere or, as it were, in the very center of space."[26] Contemporary landscape has become an iridescent field of images in movement, an experience derailed into optical whimsy for some, and for others a compelling rerouting of memory and imagination.

A potent experience of the moving landscape takes place in car commer-

cials on television. In the nineteenth and twentieth centuries, painting, photography, railroads, and automobiles opened up (physically and visually) vast
landscapes for tourism. Nowadays, the same practice occurs on television. A
website, "discovermoab.com," recommends scenic driving tours along the
Colorado River in Utah that pass Castle Rock, a fingerlike spire where several
memorable car commercials were filmed in the 1970s. Another site, "Fantas-
tic Roads," recommends the Oak Creek Canyon drive on 89A between
Flagstaff and Sedona, Arizona, largely on the basis of the automobile commercials filmed there. Watching a car wind expertly around the twisting roads
and ocean views on Bolinas Ridge north of San Francisco and then burst out
toward the horizon, turning the background into a blur of blue-green color
and motion, its metal sheen reflecting those colors, one might get the idea that
today's landscape comes, for the choosing, in all spaces and durations.

Already by the mid-1980s, as Paul Rutherford writes, certain ingredients
became essential for a car commercial, "a rugged landscape (to show nippy
handling), a rugged driver (who displays himself), a famous old rock track (a
bit of Steppenwolf), a sudden landscape (to demonstrate the brakes nicely)."[27]
Of late, commercials for flatbed trucks and sport utility vehicles use these elements and more to invoke a vision of the ordinary sublime. The weighty SUVs
are driven with a capital *D,* over puddles, ruts, and even across small rivers,
atop large rocks and alongside treacherous dirt roads built onto the sides of
mountains, reaching destinations that are humanly and mechanically impossible in the real world. Viewers partake of the illusion that regular people can
conquer extraordinary landscapes, drive literally up and over mountains, and
possess views of canyons and mountains that nobody has witnessed before.
All in the lap of luxury. For instance, in a Grand Cherokee commercial of a few
years ago, a drive up a steep road ends up at a mountaintop canvas mansion.
A personal valet welcomes the driver home before the garage door is unzipped.
Unlike the age of exploring, where discomfort and death were bywords, comfort accompanies today's automotive landscape voyeur every camera jump cut
of the way. No matter that "the SUV proves to be the ideal vehicle not for
bombing around the open countryside but for the essentially opposite purpose
of sitting in traffic," as Louis Menand writes. "Perched high above the baking
asphalt, six CDs in the changer and a video playing in the back seat, laptop
plugged into the dashboard, cell phone in continual operation, entire families
creep along the slow-moving conveyor belts that America's highways have become, cool and serene, in what amounts to a den on wheels."[28]

On television, of course, we hardly ever see the SUV or car in traffic. Instead, rapid editing, multiple film speeds, flash frames (with no image), and
landscape associations create a sensation of speed-as-comfort. A commercial

for the Hyundai Santa Fe, in which three temporalities of motion are used, illustrates the automobile's conquest of landscape. Early on, tracking behind the SUV on a straight road, the film suddenly speeds up to give the impression of the car bolting out across the landscape like a rocket. Later, as a contrast, the camera takes a slow-motion curvilinear pan of the Santa Fe as it proceeds along the same road. By presenting the passage over the landscape in multiple expressions of time, the contrast of static landscape and moving vehicle hammers home the car's desirability.

BMW expresses the speed of its Z3 roadster through furious editing. In the approximately twenty-second-long commercial, over eighty different shots careen forward, a great many lasting less than a quarter of a second. The sense of speed that emerges from rapid cutting is increased by the large variety of shots: acute close-ups of all parts of the car, the tires, trunk, sides, gearshift, and windshield; tracking views of the road at high speeds, from the car and from other vehicles including a helicopter; shots of the side of the road, the car racing by, the driver's head. Once, the camera zooms in on the convertible as it hurtles forward, doubling the sense of speed. Another time, it zooms away from the car as it vanishes around a curve. All the while, the car makes its way over a stretch of road in a glacial landscape. The constantly changing backgrounds of spiky evergreen trees, jagged peaks, and ice fields enhance the precipitous sensations of camera cuts and vehicular movement. At the end, a voice celebrates the Z3 roadster: "[I]t satisfies more than your need for motion. It satisfies your need for emotion." The announcer might have added the word devotion. For in this journey to the high peaks of nature and technology, a return to earthbound existence might require divine intervention.

Such techniques construct a landscape divorced from on-site perception in either an artistic or a geographical sense. We watch, as David Miles argues, what amounts to a cubist landscape, where "alternations between close-ups and extreme long shots destroy any sense of separation between television viewer and the image on the screen; telephoto zooms flatten Renaissance perspectival space; and angled in-motion studio-cam shots turn deep panoramas into sliding flat surfaces."[29] The exceptional and ordinary qualities of landscape dissolve within this fluid technological assemblage, as abstract art meets teenage adventure. On the road on the screen, viewers look less at seemingly real places than at the bona fide unfolding of a lifestyle.

The swift experience of landscape as lifestyle often emerges by association. Following old television preludes like ABC's *Wide World of Sports* as much as the hipster-atmosphere ads of Nike and other athletic shoe companies, several car commercials lead up to an image of the vehicle with shots that showcase snow skiing, ocean surfing, or river kayaking. The ensuing car shots carry overtones of reckless, exciting sport. Even when the car stands motionless, it looks as if it is just waiting to burst out of the gate.

Speed also comes in slow packages. Before the compulsory rapid-fire shot sequence, the new Q by Infiniti is depicted by a static camera in several striking architectural landscapes. First, a detailed shot shows rain falling on a small part of the hood. Then, heavier raindrops splatter onto the car, seen in a side view in front of the thick stone walls of a castle. The following shot looks downward at an acute angle at the car parked on a street. The frame is taken up with the wet textures of the angular planes of street, sidewalk, plaza surface, and crosswalk. Finally, after a picture of steam rising from a soaked iron vent, we see the Infiniti parked in the most remarkable architectural space of all. The level medium shot of the side of the car shows steam rising from a vent and cascading over the car's profile. The background is a contemporary hard-edged plaza surrounded by concrete sculptural buildings. The progression from old cityscape to postmodern plaza establishes a sense of temporal movement that begins to unveil vehicular movement. Atmospheric effects further bring out a threat of speed. Throughout the sequence, the sensuous textures of building and street surfaces play off the attractiveness of the car's own surfaces. Against the still automotive and building surfaces, flowing rain, steam, running schoolgirls, and angular camera compositions produce settings packed with drama and potential. The concluding sequence of the Infiniti in motion looks all the more rapid after the coiled tension and luscious materiality of the still shots. The calm history and beauty of great urban landscapes, we are told, constitute the prelude to life's inevitable rush out onto the roads.

The perception of speed brings with it a sense of spatial collapse. A commercial for the Acura 260 divides into two parts expressive of speed and the merger of dissimilar places. The initial sequence of shots establishes the car's journey along a coastal environment: in the first, the car whizzes by a static camera positioned alongside a curvy road with a view of a small town in the background; in the second, an aerial shot, the car crosses a bridge over a glistening sea. The next two shots accelerate: a close-up of the driver's hand shifting into a higher gear and an extreme close-up of the tachometer (which measures the speed of the motor) rising from four to six. The subsequent tracking of the car from a moving camera at road level confirms a sensation of speedy movement over asphalt. The driving sequence concludes with a rear shot of the car reaching a red wooden shack, immediately followed by a pulled-back static aerial view of the small building set within its picturesque harbor environs. This shot then dissolves into a downward view of a bowl of thick clam chowder being stirred. The camera cuts to the driver, seated at a counter in the small restaurant, who says, "Sure doesn't taste this good in New York." A shot reverse to the proprietor who asks him, in a distinctly Maine accent, if he is on vacation. After a pause, the driver responds, "No, lunch."

This classic marketing message sells not just a car, but hope. To the tune of swing jazz, the speed and ease of handling of the Acura 260 makes a brief excursion over beautiful landscapes desirable, if not entirely possible. The insertion of a view of a sign welcoming you to Maine midway through the twenty-second commercial confirms the utter implausibility—did the driver take local coastal roads all the way from New York to Maine?—of this mid-afternoon excursion. Landscape becomes a continuous state of bliss and beauty connecting disparate places, the implied great city of New York, which we never see, and the small village in Maine. Like a painting, this automotive landscape arrays disparate places in a compact environment. It thus has only illusory extent. If such travel were possible, the localized differences of place would cease to exist.

The depiction of landscape as an all-extensive yet highly compressed space rockets ahead in a commercial for the Honda Odyssey, a family minivan. Six shots, each lasting a couple of seconds, establish a long auto journey across the breadth of the United States. From a variety of angles, heights, and distances the camera records the Odyssey smoothly driving: past the Washington Monument and Lincoln Memorial under a red sky; over a great steel truss bridge; across flat midwestern farm fields; over the Mississippi River on the MacArthur Bridge in clear view of the Gateway Arch of St. Louis; up a pass into the heart of the snow country of the Rockies; and, finally, through a stretch of red desert, presumably somewhere in Utah. After over two thousand miles, the camera cuts to a near view of the family in the minivan. A small child asks the father with a whiny voice and expression, "Are we there yet?" As the father answers no, the camera looks at him from behind, and beyond through the windshield, a bank of clouds. It is as if the minivan drives toward heaven. No wonder then that the child, instead of complaining further, responds, "Good." An immediate cut shows him sitting quite contentedly in the middle seat surrounded by his toys. While seven shots are devoted to the landscapes of the journey, nine depict the environment of the Odyssey. The spaciousness of the entire country equates with that of the vehicle. There is no reason for the journey to end since the car has found the groove between its comfortable size and large windows for viewing landscape. The last shot of the Odyssey driving off into the desert distance promises an endless journey, a collapse of the landscape distant and proximate into an escape in the comfy lap of movement.

Of all landscapes, deserts figure most prominently in automobile commercials. Not only are there no large trees or other midsized forms that could obstruct the view or compete for attention, but the spatial grandeur of the desert provides a superb setting to showcase the moving car, truck, motor-cycle, or SUV. Earlier, the same factors led to the use of deserts as the landscape of choice for westerns. *Stagecoach* (1939), *Red River* (1948), *The Searchers* (1956), and *Once upon a Time in the West* (1968) all begin in barren deserts that are then used to display horses, cowboys, and the primal violent encounters of the frontier. "The apparent emptiness" of the desert, writes Jane Tompkins, "makes the land desirable not only as a space to be filled but also as a stage on which to perform and as a territory to master."[30] For Madison Avenue, the desert landscape is apparently more than ever a mythical tabula rasa upon which to showcase products and stimulate popular desire.

Automobile commercials present their products as the speedy foreground to a variable yet always spectacular background. They describe a dreamlike organic relationship to landscape premised on beauty, access, and a shrinkage of distance. But because of the brevity of the commercials and the large number of shots, pictures of existing landscape transform into building blocks of a visual realm absent any continuities of space or time. Moreover, as a result of rapid-sequence editing from a very large set of vantage points, the viewer assumes a universal yet implicated gaze. In the close-range shots near or from the vehicle, the viewer takes on the identity of driver or passenger and gazes at her or himself. And because the series of quick shots amount to incomplete glances rather than a digestible gaze, the viewer will presumably want more of the car and more of the landscape.[31] Unlike composed paintings and gardens, moving landscapes always sets the stage for something to come.

Incredibly, that something can also be an anti-aesthetic of everyday landscape. A few years ago a famous commercial for the Volkswagen Golf was set to the tunes of "Da Da Da" by the eighties German band Trio. A couple of Gen Xers cruise aimlessly around Los Angeles, regarding with studied indifference the subdivisions and strip malls of suburbia. The climax of the ad occurs when they pick up an abandoned easy chair, load it into the back seat, and then quickly discard it because of its stench. But they are soon off again sort of contentedly cruising around their lumpen roads. The automaker's message for the car: "It fits your life or the complete lack thereof." Nothing and nowhere and whatever, apparently, are for sale.

The moving landscapes of car commercials are prominent pieces of a much larger visual diet of desire and consumption. These wider experiences of landscape take place in "off-sites"—on a tour bus or airplane, a movie screen, one of the many rooms in private homes that contain televisions or computers. They can be carefully planned itineraries—the package tour, the PBS documentary, a set of PDF files—where one does not delve deeply, but, then again, less time is wasted, and unpleasant experiences are less likely to occur. Or they can be experiences as repetitive as television clicking or freeway commuting.

Unlike old master paintings, whose illusions of the Roman Campagna paved the way for the creation of extraordinary landscapes in the real world, today's moving landscapes do not extend momentarily the space of a portentous idea. Moving landscapes are not illusions or temporary diversions, since they progressively occupy a greater time-share in people's lives than any real world experiences. For instance, television is not a window onto a greater reality. It is the nexus of that reality—the setting that Americans, on average, engage for twenty-eight hours a week. Likewise, the shifting view out of the windows and mirrors of an automobile is now as normative a perceptual condition as Albertian perspective. For increasing numbers of people accustomed to moving landscapes, especially the young, settings experienced on foot or on-site feel slow, poorly produced, and ironically less real. Many of us prefer living loud and fast in the "illusion."

The moving landscape differs as well from the ordinary landscape. It is not a place where we all live, work, and interact, a world whose vastness is embroidered in the random, the routine, and the reckless. The moving landscape is foremost a produced zone, a sequined thoroughfare advertising choice yet often leading to subordination. On a screen or in a vehicle, in their own private space, remarkable numbers of people experience the same landscape, the same soulful Arizona backdrop on the same channel or from the same minivan. The moving landscape they engage is a setup, filled to the brim with marketing savvy, dominated by commodities, and flavored with the tang of stars and celebrities.

The moving landscape is a merger of sorts between artistic landscapes and ordinary landscapes. Born of popular culture, the moving landscape electrifies the ordinary and spins the extraordinary into kitschy overdrive. As car commercials make obvious, technology enables the moving landscape's special-effects aesthetics: the televisual tympany of commonplace automobiles hurtling toward gargantuan boulders; amphetamine-laced cameras tracking out while lenses zoom in; extreme close-ups of flashing metal alternating with medium shots of a normal family lurching into long shots of red canyons. Technology constitutes the moving landscape's subject and object, its means and item of viewing.

From art to geography to technology, from scene to site to sightseeing, the relationship of landscape to monument changes. In the moving landscape, monuments are no longer just exceptional places or artworks: the sphere jutting out of the center of a space, the secluded garden of antique desire. Nor are monuments subsumed into the scale of geography, their size translated into bridges, big boxes, or boundary lines, their sanctity lost in a sea of individual acts and purchases. The monument makes a surprising comeback in the moving landscape. Despite the entropy of television, the Internet, and global transit networks, the great artistic monuments of the past are getting a new lease on life. Through flickering glass, they live again and again in the throes of tourism and entertainment. As a result, artistic monuments share viewing time with natural monuments, popular monuments, underground monuments, the monuments of spectacle, sex, and violence. In the moving landscape, the exceptional broadens to geographic scope and the word *monument* takes on the historical scope of technology.

Past Present

Nowadays, the past is more often in sight than on site. It can be a historical spectacle on the silver screen, a theme park ride through a reconstructed ancient village, a website that boils down as it bubbles out, or a visit to an actual site managed by the National Parks Service, yet viewed primarily from automotive windows and vista points. The past has a long half-life of reruns, revisions, and repackagings, what amount to technological mediations of its perceptual means—from artifacts to books to photographs to cinema to tourism to video games to television to artifacts, and so on. The inexhaustible breadth of the moving landscape means that more and more of the past is preserved and perceived. It also means that all pieces of the past are more quickly than ever passed over for the next visual course. We no longer struggle lifetimes to recover the past. After centuries of digging, writing, recording, and editing, the past perceives with us.

We are accelerating at machine speed into a past that is no longer historical, no longer tied to an age distanced from our own, and no longer understandable as the direct ancestor of our moment. Whereas the landscapes of extraordinary pictures and ordinary geographies encase and uncover the past within them, moving landscapes customize the past as technological perception. The nineteenth-century linear conception of history has become transformed into the equivalent of a Mandelbrot set, a mathematical form that yields infinite complexity as it is perceived in higher degrees of resolution. The more we look into the past, the more different, multiple, and artificial our memories become. Each moving engagement with the past pieces together different visual elements, a past composed of a cast of constantly changing characters and settings yet familiar plots. Moreover, there is less and less time for any of these pasts to work their wonders on the present. The frenetic transformations of capital, technology, and fashion construct an almost instantaneous obsolescence for any present object or event. The past is not as much a longing for a time gone as anticipation for a time about to go by. "With acceleration," says Paul Virilio, "there is no more here and there, only the mental confusion of near and far, present and future, real and unreal—a mix of history, stories, and the hallucinatory utopia of communication technologies."[32] Because sensory saturation robs the past of its aura and its otherness, the past is ever-present.

The moving landscape is a kind of commoner's Grand Tour, supersonic digitized travel through any and all older cultures with neither starting point nor destination. Like the Enlightenment Grand Tour, today's Grand Tour is preoccupied with rare sightings—the battle scenes of Stalingrad or Normandy in surround sound and image, a contorted gaze from a helicopter onto the terraces of Machu Picchu. This contemporary go round is obviously no longer a diversion of the gentry. The remote panoramas and rituals once seen by a few wealthy individuals are increasingly commonplace. In developed countries, they are the main event of the masses. In fact, the sites and spectacle of time past are so accessible and reproducible that they have become the constant companion to the present and subsumed by its presence. As Marc Augé describes our current mentality: "Everything proceeds as if space had been trapped by time, as if there were no history other than the last forty-eight hours of news, as if each individual history were drawing its motives, its words and images, from the inexhaustible stock of an unending history in the present."[33]

One might say that in one sense we have returned to the days before contrasts between exceptional monuments and ordinary barrens, when most aspects of the landscape were the storehouses and generators of collective memory, where the past could become present at any moment. The great difference today is that the moving landscape has combined object and memory and in the process become a substitute for each. Traditional memory combated loss by reactivating a vanished substantial presence and interceding between life and death. Technological memory, by contrast, is all about gain, bathing us in the noisiness of recovery and reproduction. We have molded much of history and geography into a continuous field of visual artifice with enormous transformative capabilities, and we are becoming our own re-creations. It is like the world of plastic described by Roland Barthes as "the first magical substance which consents to be prosaic. . . . [F]or the first time, artifice aims at something common, not rare. And as an immediate consequence, the age-old function of nature is modified: it is no longer the Idea, the pure Substance to be regained or imitated: an artificial matter, more bountiful than all the natural deposits, is about to replace her, and to determine the very invention of forms."[34] Media reproduction might be that artificial substance with regard to memory of the past. As such, the moving landscape is not a choice between the imaginative expansiveness of the ideal and the grounded limitations of the real, between the prospect of a *bel paesaggio* and a stranger's path through skid row. In the commercial for the Volkswagen Golf, a most ordinary landscape levitates into a state of intrigue. Transgression of codes has become normative behavior. Through such plastic reversibility, car commercials demonstrate that perception itself—on the road, on the screen—has become the horizon of landscape. In its constant penetrations of a fanning periphery, the moving landscape makes irrelevant prior temporal dualisms of possession and loss, remembering and forgetting. And paradoxically, because velocity has no vanishing point, the experience of the constantly moving landscape can seem downright motionless.

In conclusion, I would like to offer some thoughts on the stillness inherent in the moving landscape, the sights just offscreen or passed by on the roadside. These are places within the space-flux of the moving landscape. In the essay "Entropy and the New Monuments" (1966), Robert Smithson wrote: "Instead of causing us to remember the past like the old monuments, the new monuments seem to cause us to forget the future . . . They are not built for the ages, but rather against the ages. They are involved in a systematic reduction of time down to fractions of seconds, rather than in representing the long spaces of centuries. Both past and future are placed into an objective present. This kind of time has little or no space; it is stationary and without movement, it is going nowhere."[35] Smithson was referring to the works of sculptors like Dan Flavin, Robert Morris, and Donald Judd. But his argument was drawn from artworks that emerged from ordinary landscapes, a hyperprosaism that created art from vapidity and dullness. Mechanized society and its tracks of obsolescence had somehow pushed artists toward a geological/astrophysical conception of time.

In the same essay, Smithson also recognized a parallel tendency, which he labeled hyperopulence. Artists like Peter Hutchinson went to the movies to see nature, but the nature they saw was every bit as idealized as any Renaissance landscape painting or garden. The difference was that mediatopia had replaced utopia, what was once marginal now occupying the site of the ideal. In the movie theater, contemporary society relives over and over again primal nightmares, the popularized memories of our human past in the guise of westerns or horror flicks. The extraordinary landscape is now "the slippery bubbling ooze from the movie 'The Blob,' a low-budget mysticism which keeps [us] in a perpetual trance."[36] Seen from an artistic vantage point, the moving landscapes of the roadside and the cinema disclose the future on its rusting edge and blur the usual and unusual into the boring and terrifying. They allow us to live in a technological present moment blown so far out and so far back that it is our collective memory.

NOTES

1. Françoise Choay, "Urbanism and Semiology," in *The City and the Sign: An Introduction to Urban Semiotics,* ed. M. Gottdiener and Alexandros Lagopoulos (New York: Columbia University Press, 1986), 165. More recently, Choay has authored *The Invention of the Historic Monument* (New York: Cambridge University Press, 2001).

2. Howard Morphy, "Landscape and the Reproduction of the Ancestral Past," in *The Anthropology of Landscape: Perspectives on Place and Space,* ed. Eric Hirsch and Michael O'Hanlon (Oxford: Oxford University Press, 1995), 188.

3. Susanne Küchler, "Landscape as Memory: The Mapping of Process and Its Representation in a Melanesian Society," in *Landscape: Politics and Perspectives,* ed. Barbara Bender (Providence, R.I.: Berg, 1993), 86, 103–4.

4. Gina Crandell, *Nature Pictorialized: The View in Landscape History* (Baltimore: Johns Hopkins University Press, 1993), 11–12.

5. John Dixon Hunt and Peter Willis, eds., *The Genius of Place: The English Landscape Garden, 1620–1820,* (New York: Harper & Row, 1975), 8–13.

6. Ever since the eighteenth century (and probably earlier, through depictions of hell), myths of Arcadia have included the wild as well as the cultivated, exhilaration and adventure alternating with bucolic rest. See Simon Schama, *Landscape and Memory* (New York: Alfred A. Knopf, 1995).

7. Choay, "Urbanism and Semiology," 167–68.

8. On the differences between artistic and geographical approaches, see Denis Cosgrove, *Social Formation and Symbolic Landscape* (Madison: University of Wisconsin Press, 1984), 13–38.

9. Carl Sauer, "The Morphology of Landscape" (1925), in *Land and Life: A Selection from the Writings of Carl Ortwin Sauer,* ed. John Leighly (Berkeley: University of California Press, 1965), 321.

10. A historiography of the concept within the field of geography is provided in Peirce Lewis, "Learning from Looking: Geographic and Other Writing about the American Cultural Landscape," *American Quarterly* 35 (1983): 242–61.

11. Peirce Lewis, "Axioms for Reading the Landscape," in *The Interpretation of Ordinary Landscapes,* ed. D. W. Meinig (Oxford: Oxford University Press, 1979), 12. The exclusion of interior space has much to do with the exclusion of natural climatic factors and the creation of a formal realm that is almost wholly artificial.

12. Peirce Lewis, "Common Landscapes as Historic Documents," in *History from Things: Essays on Material Culture,* ed. Steven Lubar and W. David Kingery (Washington, D.C.: Smithsonian Institution Press, 1993), 115–16.

13. J. B. Jackson, *Discovering the Vernacular Landscape* (New Haven: Yale University Press, 1984), 7.

14. Ibid., 8.

15. See, for instance, the essay by Fred Kniffen, "Louisiana House Types," in *Readings in Cultural Geography,* ed. Philip Wagner and Marvin Mikesell (Chicago: University of Chicago Press, 1962), 157–69.

16. Meinig, *Interpretation of Ordinary Landscapes,* 2.

17. Christopher Tunnard and Boris Pushkarev, *Man-Made America: Chaos or Control?* (New Haven: Yale University Press, 1963), 1.

18. J. B. Jackson, "The Public Landscape," in *Landscapes: Selected Writings of J. B. Jackson,* ed. Ervin Zube (Amherst: University of Massachusetts Press, 1970), 153–58.

19. Wilbur Zelinsky, "The Imprint of Central Authority," in *The Making of the American Landscape,* ed. Michael Conzen (Boston: Unwin Hyman, 1990), 311–34.

20. David Lowenthal, "European Landscape Transformations: The Rural Residue," in *Understanding Ordinary Landscapes,* ed. Paul Groth and Todd Bressi (New Haven: Yale University Press, 1997), 184.

21. Dell Upton, "Seen, Unseen, and Scene," in Groth and Bressi, *Understanding Ordinary Landscapes,* 176.

22. Dolores Hayden, "Urban Landscape History: The Sense of Place and the Politics of Space" in Groth and Bressi, *Understanding Ordinary Landscapes,* 117–21.

23. See Craig Barton, ed., *Sites of Memory: Perspectives on Architecture and Race* (New York: Princeton Architectural Press, 2001).

24. Geoffrey O'Brien, *The Phantom Empire* (New York: Norton, 1993), 71.

25. Jack Kerouac, *On the Road* (New York: Viking, 1957), 111.

26. Maya Deren, "Chamber Films," *Filmwise* 2 (1961): 38–39.

27. Paul Rutherford, *The New Icons? The Art of Television Advertising* (Toronto: University of Toronto Press, 1994), 161.

28. Louis Menand, "Alone Together," *New Yorker,* July 2, 2001, 21.

29. David Miles, "Up Close and in Motion: Volvo Invents Cubist Television," *Journal of Film and Video* 46 (winter 1995): 39–40.

30. Jane Tompkins, *West of Everything: The Inner Life of Westerns* (Oxford: Oxford University Press, 1992), 74.

31. Andrew Higson, "The Landscapes of Television," *Landscape Research* 12, no. 3 (1987): 11.

32. Paul Virilio, *The Art of the Motor,* trans. Julie Rose (Minneapolis: University of Minnesota Press, 1995), 35.

33. Marc Augé, *Non-Places: Introduction to an Anthropology of Supermodernity,* trans. John Howe (London: Verso, 1995), 104–5.

34. Roland Barthes, "Plastic," *Perspecta* 24 (1988): 93.

35. Robert Smithson, "Entropy and the New Monuments" (1966), in *Robert Smithson: The Collected Writings,* ed. Jack Flam (Berkeley: University of California Press, 1996), 11.

36. Ibid., 16.

PART II

Time

Monuments and memory are made by and of time, but in widely varying ways. The admonishment "Never forget" seeks to pull future time into the present, while Alois Riegl's terse definition of a monument makes its survival through past time the only definite criterion. The Holocaust-related watchword exemplifies what Riegl called "the intentional monument," a monument by virtue of its framers' intentions. He devised his own criterion of "sixty years" to cover the category of "unintentional" monuments as well, objects that become monuments when historical value eventually accrues to them, or simply by virtue of their age.[1] Similarly Henri Bergson, Pierre Nora, Walter Benjamin, and especially Marcel Proust understood memory to be either voluntary or involuntary.[2] They characterized voluntary memory as conscious, learned, and thus social and public, and involuntary memory as driven by forces deep within the individual and thus more personal and private. The essays in part 2 examine ways in which temporal rhetoric shapes monuments and memorial practice.

Wu Hung's essay on the towers in Beijing that once told time by drumbeat elaborates on the simple dichotomy of voluntary and involuntary, intentional and unintentional, to show how the very articulation of time is at the heart of power relations and thus a constituting element of the monument. The interplay between the visual and the aural, the intentional and the unintentional, marks these towers, which represented the public display by which political authority needs to control time. Time telling, distinct from time keeping, which was kept secret, was symbolized visually by day—through two towers in the busiest commercial district—and aurally by night. The difference between the two intentional monuments and day-to-day

103

experiences of them is evidenced by the rhetoric surrounding the towers: governmental rhetoric concerned the visual, daytime, imagery, while public rhetoric centered on the nocturnal sound of the towers. The daily experience of the monument monumentalized the sound, regulating lives, whereas the visual monument referred to power only, and, in the present time, with the drums silenced, refers only to the power of the past.

Private individuals, like governments, also wish to control time. They wish to stop it, to recapture lost time and those lost with it. Margaret Olin's chapter concerns this poignant aspect of memory's entailment with time. Roland Barthes wished to experience again a relationship destroyed by death. To do so he searched public and private photographs, and—guided by a distinction between voluntary interest and involuntary memories—turned a faded family photograph into a monument of time past. He also left his own traces to suggest the futility of the endeavor. The transformation of photographs into monuments eternalizes memory not only for individuals, however; its consequences extend to communication on the Internet and to the writing of history, especially art history. All of these seek to revive the past and bring it into the present.

Jonathan Bordo also stresses the presentness of memory, this time on a social level. The Canadian whale-killing ritual seeks to keep the past present by reclaiming memory for the past's living witnesses. While we may think of commemoration as entailing the instruction of a nonexpert public in formal history, Bordo uses the term "keeping place" to suggest a concept of memory in which the past is not kept in the past and taught, but revived and lived. A keeping place is a monument that demands living witnesses in an effort to keep the past in the present, as opposed to a museum, where "keepers" keep the past isolated behind glass. Culturally specific custodian witnesses claim memory for their own. Keeping places can leave the place itself, its monument, invisible. The whale hunt discussed by Bordo arose from involuntary memory, not pragmatic social memory. The reenactment was performed not to instruct about the past but to cope with its memory.

Much poetry has been written about the vanity of rulers who built ("intentional") monuments to keep future generations in awe of their great works and mighty power, only to have them molder—at best—into picturesque, meaningless ruins.[3] Julia Bryan-Wilson's essay shows that while the vanity of such monuments may be subdued in the case of a marker warning against a nuclear waste dump, the ambitious folly of seeking to build a monument to speak to future generations abides. Indeed, the most extreme example of the "intentional" monument may be the warning monument at a nuclear waste site that will rise in 2030 to address and protect future generations for ten thousand years. The discourse surrounding this monument, however, has to grapple with an uncanny self-consciousness about historical pitfalls that threaten such intentions. It engages the rhetoric of past ambitious gestures, along with the modernist myth of the universal language and the contemporary rhetoric of tourism. To create this antimonument, it seeks to critique all of these languages and to investigate the social structures around monuments that in the past have kept them alive or allowed them to decay. Yet, as Bryan-Wilson's essay shows, it is almost impossible to avoid the pitfalls of monumental rhetoric in its obstinate stand against time.

The essays in this section, while focused on time, also engage central issues in the other sections. Time does not separate easily from space; hence travel plays into these essays. The travel involved in colonialism plays an important role in the essays by Wu and Bordo: the European clock tower intervened in Chinese time telling first as the gift of visitors from the West. Later, however, Western "visitors" forcibly replaced the drum towers with a clock tower. In his essay, Bordo traces his own position as a traveler-witness and that of two other travelers, Franz Boas and A. Y. Jackson, witnesses to and instigators of the disaster commemorated: the introduction, by colonial powers, of commercial whaling and its demise. The reenactment of the whale killing was not a tourist attraction. Roland Barthes, enjoying at home a portfolio of photographs from the other side of the Atlantic, certainly participated in a kind of armchair tourism. Several of the photographs he used from New York may have reminded him of his recent visit to that city. In contrast, however, one of the greater challenges facing the monument of warning posted at the nuclear waste dump will be to keep the site from becoming a goal for tourists.

In spite of the intentions of the designers of the nuclear waste warning monument, time inevitably does destroy. And indeed, all of these essays about time engage, as a consequence, the topic of destruction. None of the monuments described successfully stopped, controlled, or retrieved time. Instead their histories involve death and loss of memories. The form of temporal control represented by the Chinese towers was destroyed when the beating of the drums was silenced. The destruction of local time through universal time exemplifies the modernist replacement of the local with the universal (which, in this case, means Western colonialism). Death was the beginning of Roland Barthes's search for his mother through photographs. The death of the whale marked the attempt to revive the memory of the whale-hunting economy, itself a destructive event. The nuclear waste monument chronicled by Bryan-Wilson itself threatens death to its beholders. It is fitting that destruction, now of monuments themselves, is the subject of part 3. There the issues of grief, of forcible destruction of the local by the "universal," present in these essays, take center stage.

NOTES

1. "Der moderne Denkmalkultus, Sein Wesen und seine Entstehung" was first published to accompany the draft for a law. It was republished in Riegl's collected essays, *Gesammelte Aufsätze,* ed. Karl M. Swoboda (Vienna: Benno Filser, 1929), 144–93; translated as "The Modern Cult of Monuments: Its Character and Its Origin," by Kurt W. Forster and Diane Ghirardo, in *Oppositions* 25 (1982): 21–51.

2. Walter Benjamin, "The Image of Proust," in *Illuminations: Essays and Reflections,* ed. Hannah Arendt (New York: Schocken Books, 1968), 214. See also the essay by Jonathan Bordo, below.

3. The most famous of them being "Ozymandias" (1817) by Percy Bysshe Shelley.

5

Monumentality of Time:
Giant Clocks, the Drum Tower, the Clock Tower

WU HUNG

This essay investigates two essential problems in regulating and presenting time. The first concerns the relationship between time keeping and time telling; the second, the places and instruments that facilitated these two practices. I will focus on the period in Chinese history when the notion of public time was closely associated with the idea of monumentality—when giant clocks were created to legitimate political authority and when time was announced to a populace from imposing buildings in the center of a city. Whether concealed inside the palace or exposed to the public, these clocks and buildings brought order to the country and helped construct different social spaces and identities.

The three types of mechanical/architectural constructions studied in this essay—the traditional drum tower (often accompanied by a bell tower), the Western-style clock tower, and giant clocks—point to divergent systems of technology, spatial conception, and political power. Oversized chronographs were routinely commissioned by Chinese emperors as symbols of political control over a unified time/space. Sometimes installed in the throne hall, such clocks complemented the drum tower in a marketplace to define twin centers in a traditional Chinese capital. Because of its governmental affiliation and public role, the drum tower was instrumental in maintaining imperial dominance as well as in shaping a community; it derived its monumentality from both its architecture and its sound; its meaning is explicated in both official inscriptions and private memoirs. When the drum tower fell silent and was replaced by the clock tower around the early twentieth century, these events signified the appearance of a new kind of monumentality pertaining to a crucial shift in China's historical temporality from a traditional empire to a modern nation-state.

Time Keeping and Time Telling in Traditional China

People who connect public time telling to Big Ben outside the Houses of Parliament in London will have trouble distinguishing *time telling* from *time keeping,* because in that case a single clock, which moves and sounds automatically, performs both roles. But in the ancient Chinese system, two sets of equipment were employed in separate places for these two purposes. *Time keeping* relied on horology and astronomy, which allowed the government to regulate seasons, months, days, and hours. In his *Science and Civilization in China,* Joseph Needham emphasizes over and over the political significance of time keeping to a Chinese emperor.[1] Hellmut Wilhelm considers ancient Chinese astronomy and horology a secret science of priest-kings.[2] *Time telling,* on the other hand, conveyed a standardized official time to a large population. The principal instrument for this purpose was a drum tower (sometimes accompanied by a bell tower). A drum tower was not a "clock" because it did not compute time and did not record the passage of time. It came alive only at designated moments, when it amplified signals from an official clock and transmitted these signals to the public. What a drum tower presented to the public, therefore, was not a continuous, even, and unidirectional movement of time, but an official *schedule* of projected operations and recurring events.[3]

Time keeping and time telling therefore both provided important means for exercising political control, but the former helped control knowledge while the latter helped control a populace. The locations of these two types of control also differed: time keeping, as a secret science, was practiced in the sealed imperial domain; time telling was by nature "public" and had to be exercised in an open social space. These two locations, as well as the two kinds of political control they implied, were further related to different ideas and traditions of monumentality in ancient China.

As I have explained elsewhere, no monumental architecture was pursued in prehistorical and early historical China; the Chinese works that had a social and political significance comparable with that of the colossal monuments found in other early civilizations (hence "monumentality" in a general sense)[4] belonged to a special class of objects known as *liqi,* or "ritual paraphernalia." These objects—ceremonial jade carvings and bronze sacrificial vessels—always utilized the most advanced techniques available at the time and "squandered" an excessive amount of human labor. Though some had exaggerated sizes, they remained portable and maintained typological connections with their utilitarian prototypes. They were called "heavy objects" (*zhongqi*) for their political and psychological importance, not for their physical appearance and actual weight. Never intending to dominate public view, they were sacred properties of lineage temples, accessible only by the lineage members on special ritual occasions. Underlying this art/architectural tradition was a political tenet that power could be maintained only by keeping it secret.[5] This tradition never disappeared even after architectural monuments gained increasing popularity toward and during the imperial era: lofty buildings and colossal statues were now constructed to celebrate an enduring political or religious institution, and mountain-like tumuli immortalized individual rulers.[6] Consequently, throughout China's imperial history from the third century B.C. to the early twentieth century A.D., two traditions of symbolic art and architecture, one concealing power and the other displaying it, worked together to construct an increasingly complex social and political space.

Once we connect time keeping and time telling to this art/architectural context, we can study more closely the spatial concepts related to these two practices, as well as the structures and equipment created for them. Time keeping consistently served to define the centrality of political power, and instruments made for this purpose readily fell into the category of *liqi.* For three thousand years, Chinese political theory held that harmony between time and space was the foundation of rulership over a unified country. This idea was already firmly established in the *Book of Documents* (*Shang shu*), one of the Confucian classics written during the second and first millennia B.C. The book begins with the "Canon of Yao" ("Yao dian"), which records that Yao, a legendary sage emperor in the time of Great Harmony, established a system that allowed him "to compute and delineate the sun, moon and stars, and the celestial markers, and so to deliver respectfully the seasons to be observed by people."[7] In this system, time was conceived from and framed within the "four ends" of the world, and the mythological emperor could thereby define his position at the center of this temporal/spatial structure known as China.[8]

The triangular relationship between time, space, and political authority gained a more complex and dynamic form around the third century B.C. The new pattern, called "monthly observances" (*yueling*), was translated into the architecture of Bright Hall (Mingtang), perhaps the most complex imperial

ritual building ever attempted in ancient China (fig. 5.1A).⁹ On top of the
structure was an astronomical observatory called the Room of Communicat-
ing with Heaven (Tongtianwu). On the hall's main floor, twelve chambers
along the four sides corresponded to the twelve months, surrounding the central chamber that stood for the middle of a year (fig. 5.1B). It was the emperor
who linked these static spaces into a temporal/spatial continuum: he would
begin his year in the first room at the northeast corner (where the *yang* ether
rose) and move clockwise through the hall. Each month he would dwell in the
proper room, dress in the proper color, eat the proper food, listen to the proper
music, sacrifice to the proper deities, and attend to the proper affairs of state.
It was understood that his synchronous movement with heaven and earth
would secure harmony between his rule and the universe. Conversely, by turning himself into the moving hand of a huge clock, the emperor could complete
the symbolism of the ritual building as an embodiment of the cosmic order.

With such significance, the Bright Hall and related ritual structures became a logical place to house new types of clocks designed to tabulate detailed
temporal divisions. It is therefore no coincidence that the earliest "mechanical
clock" recorded in Chinese history—a seventh-century machine known as the
"twelve double-hour wheel" (*Shi'er chenche*) and designed by an artisan from
Haizhou in south China—served exactly this role. This invention was presented to Wu Zhao in 692. Instead of utilizing it for any practical purposes,
Wu, the only female emperor in Chinese history, installed it in a Celestial Hall
(Tiantang) next to her Bright Hall to symbolize her mandate from heaven.¹⁰

This Tang case exemplifies a long tradition in ancient China, in which various kinds of advanced chronographs, including some extremely complex hydraulic clocks, were invented under imperial patronage to serve the symbolic
role of legitimating political authority. The most ingenious example of such a
clock was completed by Su Song in 1088 (fig. 5.2).¹¹ Powered by an enormous
water wheel, this forty-foot-high "monumental" clock reproduced the movements of the "three luminaries"—sun, moon, and stars—which were crucial
to calendrical calculation and astrological divination. Along the movements of
the celestial bodies, little manikins revolved in measured pace to show the
hours, the quarters (*ke,* each of which equaled fourteen minutes twenty-four
seconds), and the night watches.¹² Su Song's experiments were followed by
those of Guo Shoujing, who served in the Mongol court of Kublai Khan in the
thirteenth century. The clepsydra he created in 1262, according to the *History
of the Yuan Dynasty* (*Yuan shi*), was itself a metal-framed building that reached
more than seventy feet in height and was given the name Precious Mountain
Pavilion (Baoshan lou). Embellished with images of the sun, the moon, and
dragons that could open their mouths and roll their eyes, it was also equipped

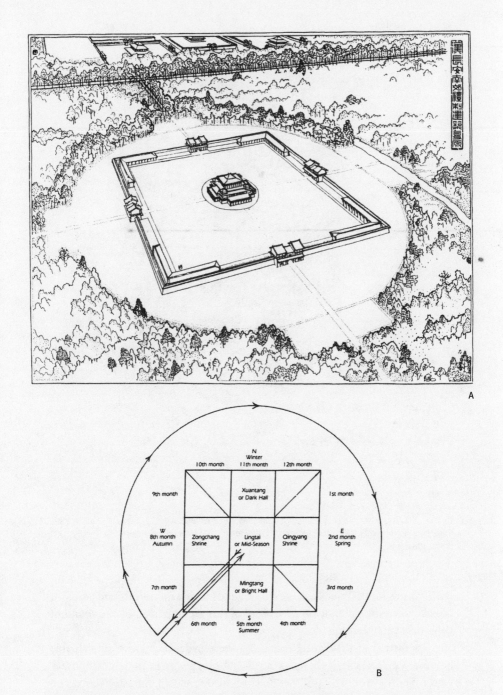

Fig. 5.1. (A) Reconstruction plan of Bright Hall, constructed by Wang Mang in 3 A.D. near Xi'an in present-day Shaanxi province. (B) Twelve rooms of Bright Hall and the imperial positions during the twelve months.

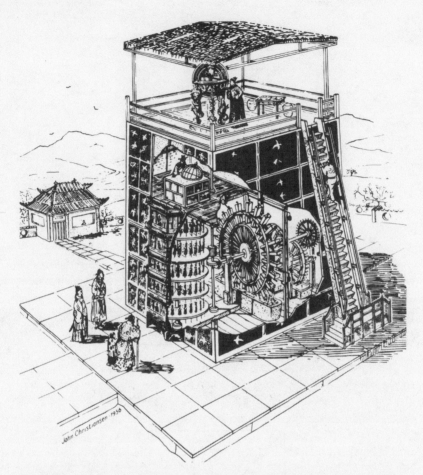

Fig. 5.2. Reconstruction plan of Su Song's astronomical clock tower, Kaifeng, c. 1088. Drawing by John Christiansen, from Joseph Needham, *Science in Traditional China* (Cambridge: Harvard University Press, 1981), fig. 5.

with various kinds of jacks, some shaped like moving immortals and animals, others indicating the time on tablets, all of this accompanied by the sound of bells, drums, and gongs.[13]

For historians of science, records of these hydraulic clocks are valuable because they document the most advanced timepieces in the contemporary world. But for art historians, these records also reveal an unmistakable desire for visual spectacle. With their extraordinary size, automatons, and ornate decoration, these machines were designed more like cosmic theaters than like purely scientific instruments. One wonders what lay behind this desire and why these clocks had to be so enormous and spectacular. The answer must be that their significance lay not only in their practical function as chronographs and cosmological models, and not even in their political symbolism of securing the harmony between heaven and man. Rather, the combination of their exaggerated size, technical sophistication, and visual ingenuity made them the most convincing proof of the extraordinariness of their imperial patrons, who alone could possess these intriguing and imposing objects.

Indeed, we find this relationship between giant clocks and political authority throughout China's imperial era. Even when the Jesuits introduced European mechanical clocks to China in the seventeenth and eighteenth centuries, the new instruments were readily absorbed into an old tradition: a huge Western-style clock was made and installed next to the Chinese emperor's throne. A visitor to the Forbidden City today can still find this clock in one of the throne halls called Jiaotai Dian or the Hall of Union. The hall realized its significance as the nexus of imperial power by displaying two groups of objects. The first group consisted of the emperor's twenty-five official seals in golden boxes. The second group included two enormous clocks flanking the throne: a traditional hydraulic clock to the left of the throne and a Western-style mechanical clock to the right (fig. 5.3). These two timepieces were placed here for symbolic, not practical, reasons. As we have found in the "Canon of Yao" and the Bright Hall, here the idea is once again that through controlling the knowledge of time, the emperor could internalize the intrinsic movement of the universe. He could therefore rule the world without using force. This is why in this hall two large characters hanging above the throne read "Nonaction"—an ancient political philosophy now facilitated by Western science.

More than eighteen feet tall, the Western-style clock in the Hall of Union was represented by a woodblock image in an imperial publication entitled *Huangchao liqi tushi* (Illustrated regulations for ritual paraphernalia of the Imperial Qing dynasty) (fig. 5.4). Assigned by the emperor to update and standardize court ceremonial equipment, a special commission started working on the book in 1759 and published it seven years later. The authors labeled the clock a "self-sounding bell" (*ziming zhong*) and carefully registered its impressive size (one *zhang* six *chi* and six *cun*). The book thus certifies this clock, and by extension identifies all giant clocks commissioned and owned by earlier emperors, as a special category of *liqi*.

Compared with the abundant discussions of the techniques and philosophies of time keeping in ancient Chinese texts, records of public time telling are scarce and nonspecific. This contrast is itself highly significant: unlike time keeping, time telling in traditional China involved little technical innovation

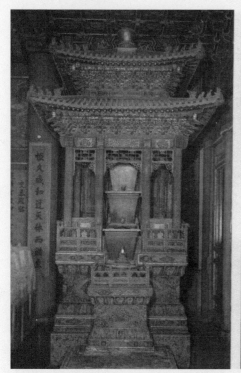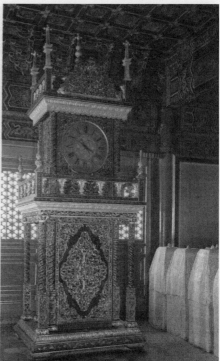

Fig. 5.3. The clepsydra and mechanical clock in the Hall of Union in the Forbidden City, Beijing, eighteenth century.

or philosophical contemplation. The earliest record of this activity—a two-sentence-long statement found in a late-second-century text written by the Confucian scholar Cai Yong—already sums up the basic technique, schedule, and function of public time telling for the next seventeen hundred years: "When the night clepsydra runs out, the drum is beaten and people get up. When the day clepsydra runs out, the bell is struck and people go to rest."[14] What did change over the next seventeen hundred years mainly concerned the placement of the drums and bells: buildings that housed these instruments and their locations in a city. The central players in this development were therefore two architectural structures—the drum tower and the bell tower—which demonstrated their monumentality with their towering image, central location, sophisticated architectural forms, and public function.

Cai Yong's statement implies that by the third century, drum towers and bell towers had been constructed in or near residential areas to announce time to the residents. A newly excavated second-century tomb mural supports this record with visual evidence: it depicts a tower soaring over a residential com-

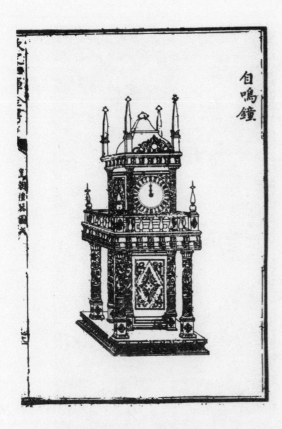

自鳴鐘

Fig. 5.4. "Self-sounding Bell." In *Huangchao liqi tushi* (Illustrated regulations for ritual paraphernalia of the Imperial Qing dynasty), 1766. Reprint, Taipei: Shangwu yinshuguan, 1976, *juan* 3, 78a.

pound, probably a walled village or town; the only object visible in the tower is a large, red drum (fig. 5.5).[15] In early imperial China, time was also announced at marketplaces, usually built around an administrative center called a "market pavilion" (*shi lou*). Both traditions continued into the post-Han period. We are told, for example, that a famous marketplace in Luoyang during the Western Jin (263–317) was dominated by a two-story building on top of a tall terrace: "A drum was hung in the building. When it sounded, the market was closed. There was also a bell. When it was struck, the sound was heard within fifty Chinese miles."[16]

It was probably only during the Tang, however, that a centralized system of public time telling was established in a major city such as the capital, Chang'an. We know this not only because this system was recorded for the first time in official documents as well as in contemporary travelogues,[17] but also because the establishment of this system was closely related to the culmination of an urban design based on walled residential units called *li* or *fang*, both meaning "wards." To be sure, politicians and administrators had recognized

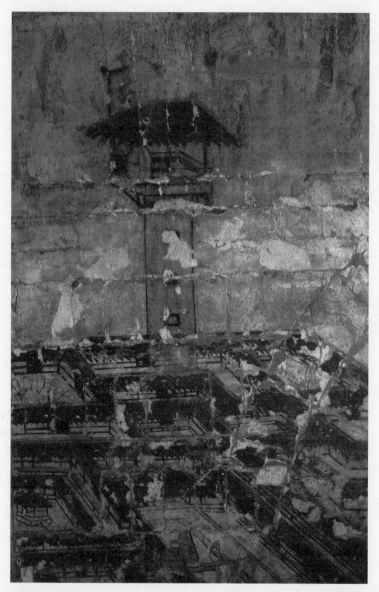

Fig. 5.5. Representation of an eastern Han drum tower. Mural in a tomb at Anping, Hebei province, 176 A.D.

long before the Tang the role of public time telling in safeguarding a village or town.[18] But this idea was applied to an entire city only from the Tang. The largest metropolis in the contemporary world, Chang'an was a planned city laid out on a square grid in nearly perfect symmetry (fig. 5.6A). Its outer walls, made of pounded earth about ten to fifteen feet thick and thirty-five feet tall, extended over five miles north to south and nearly six miles east to west. An "imperial city" stood at the center of the north end of this large rectangle, facing the adjacent "administrative city" to the south. As many as 108 residential wards were neatly arranged on the east, south, and west sides of the palaces and government offices. Each ward was rectangular, with the four sides corresponding to the four cardinal directions. Each side had a gate, which was closed at dusk and opened at dawn. What dictated the opening and closing of these gates were sound signals from the imperial city.[19]

Because an independent drum tower still did not exist, such signals were sent out from the southern gate of the imperial city, called Chengtian men or the Gate of Inheriting from Heaven. Before 636, the drums above this gate sounded each day at dusk and dawn. Following the drumbeats, official guards on horseback shouted out on the streets, telling people to close or open their ward gates. In 636, a reform was initiated by Ma Zhou (601–48), president of the Secretariat of Emperor Taizong: drums were to be installed on every street throughout the capital to amplify the signals from the imperial city; the official guards were to concentrate their duties on night patrols. The result of these measures is recorded in the *New History of Tang:*

> At sunset, the drums were beaten eight hundred times and the gates were closed. From the second night watch, mounted soldiers employed by the officers in charge of policing the streets made the rounds and shouted out the watches, while the military patrols made their rounds in silence. At the fifth watch, the drums within the Palace were beaten, and then the drums in all the streets were beaten so as to let the noise be heard everywhere; then all the gates of the wards and markets were opened.[20]

The specific function of this system was to facilitate the nightly curfew.[21] But in a more general sense, it fully realized the government's supervision of public time telling in a Chinese city. Although drums and bells at marketplaces and in Buddhist temples still sounded at regular hours, their roles remained specific and local.[22] The government-sanctioned drumbeats at morning and evening, on the other hand, controlled the entire capital and its residents by transmitting time signals from the palace to every street. This control was diligently practiced throughout most of the Tang. During the following Song dy-

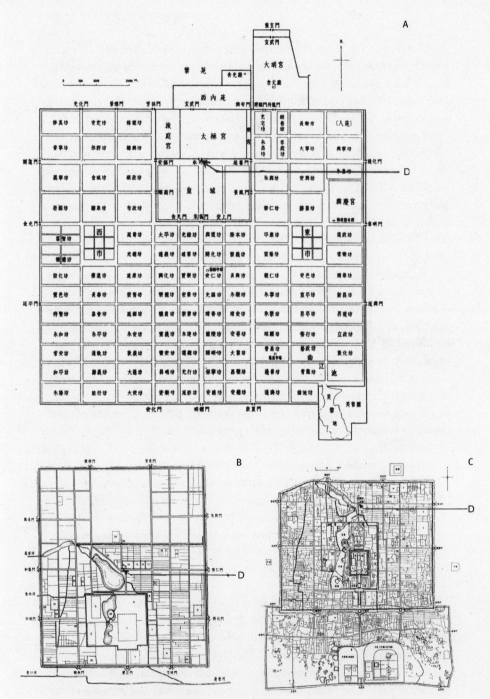

Fig. 5.6. Position of the drum tower *(D)* in three historical capitals. *(A)* Chang'an, Tang dynasty; *(B)* Dadu, Yuan dynasty; *(C)* Beijing, Ming and Qing dynasties.

nasty, however, the ward system gradually declined and finally collapsed; more and more houses and shops in the capital had their gates directly open to the streets; and there emerged a burgeoning nightlife unseen in previous Chinese history.[23] Consequently, both the night curfew and the "street drums" were abolished; local temples now carried out the role of announcing dawn and dusk.

This Song legacy, however, was again broken by the subsequent Yuan dynasty, which followed initiatives made by the Jin to revitalize the Tang system of centralized time telling. Founded by Jurchens in the early twelfth century, the Jin soon became a major military power in north China and seized the northern Song capital Kaifeng in 1126. Architectural projects pursued by Jin rulers, both in this conquered city (renamed the regime's Southern Capital) and in the main capital Zhongdu in present-day Beijing, reveal a conscious return to Tang urban design. Most tellingly, in Zhongdu, a drum tower and a bell tower flanked the southern gate of the imperial city. A night curfew was reestablished, and time signals were sent out from these two three-story buildings at dusk and dawn. The Jin, however, did not stop at revitalizing the Tang practices, but went further to relocate the two towers from inside the palace to outside it. This was done in the Jin's Southern Capital Kaifeng: a drum tower and a bell tower were built near the Zhaoqian Bridge south of the palace, near the city's main commercial district and at a spot where the city's major land and water traffic routes met.[24]

The drum towers in Zhongdu and Kaifeng were known as the Martial Towers (Wu lou), while the accompanying bell towers were called the Civilian Towers (Wen lou). Both names were adopted by the Yuan dynasty, whose drum tower and bell tower also stood in the center of the capital amidst a multitude of shops and residences (fig. 5.6B). There is little doubt that the Yuan followed the Jin system of public time telling and the corresponding urban architectural design. When Marco Polo traveled to Dadu, the capital of the Yuan in present-day Beijing, he found that the drums and the bell on the two towers were sounded every evening to announce the start of the curfew. Only under very extenuating circumstances was anyone allowed to travel on the streets. Cavalry troops, thirty to forty strong, patrolled the city to arrest anyone violating the law; offenders were beaten with a rod.[25]

The central location of the drum tower and bell tower in Yuan Dadu provided a blueprint for structuring contemporary and later Chinese cities: even today, a considerable number of old cities and towns still retain their drum towers and/or bell towers at the central crossroads.[26] The same pattern was adopted by the designers of Ming-Qing Beijing, who substituted newer structures for the Yuan towers (fig. 5.6C). On the other hand, although Beijing's drum tower and bell tower were rebuilt several times and grew taller and taller, the methods used in these buildings to keep time remained old-fashioned and

even degenerated. During the Yuan and Ming, officials stationed here continued to use an old Song clepsydra to determine the moments to strike the drums
and the bell. This clepsydra was lost some time during the Ming; the Qing used
"incense clocks" for the purpose. This type of timekeeper was made by com-
pressing powdered incense in metal templates to form elaborate traceries often resembling characters on a Chinese seal. When burned, the incense would
follow the trail, passing markings that indicated a measurement of time, often
periods of the night watches.[27] It was this kind of rudimentary device that was
employed in Beijing's drum tower and bell tower to regulate public time telling
during the last three hundred years of China's dynastic history. Unlike the
clocks installed next to the emperor's throne, these two towers had nothing to
do with state-of-the-art horology. Instead—as I will show in the following section—their power lay in their silent images and invisible sound, two split features that connected the towers to divergent social spheres in the capital.

Beijing's Drum Tower and Bell Tower

Historians of Chinese architecture are used to studying traditional Beijing
from its two-dimensional layout (the maps in fig. 5.6 exemplify this interest).
As a result, an important feature of this city has escaped most discussions of
its design: during the five and a half centuries of the Ming and Qing dynasties
(1368–1911), the drum tower and the bell tower were the two tallest structures standing on Beijing's central axis, exceeding the emperor's primary
throne hall, the Hall of Supreme Harmony, by more than twenty meters. But
the real difference between the towers and the throne hall was still not their
height but their visibility: while the Hall of Supreme Harmony was concealed
inside the layers of walls of the Forbidden City, the drum tower and the bell
tower were exposed to public view. In fact, among all imperial buildings in
Ming-Qing Beijing, these two towers were the only ones that can be called
"public monuments." Even today, their towering appearance above the surrounding commercial and residential buildings generates a strong impression
of architectural monumentality.

The drum tower and the bell tower are the subject of a wide range of literary works, including official documents, commemorative inscriptions, government archives, travelogues, memoirs, and folktales. Checking this literature,
however, we find that private memoirs and local stories say little about the
buildings' magnificent architectural imagery, but are animated by a strong sen-
sitivity to sound—the beating of the twenty-four drums and an enormous bell
installed above the towers.[28] In contrast, official documents and inscriptions
rarely mention the sound but are mostly concerned with the towers' cosmo-

logical significance and political symbolism.[29] We wonder why there is such a difference and what this difference means. The easiest but perhaps most reliable answer is that the official documents were issued by people who built the towers to practice their control over public time telling, but the memoirs and folktales were created by people whose everyday lives were directly affected by the sound issuing from the towers. The official documents often announce the intention of the towers associated with the towers' visual presentation; the memoirs and folktales often reveal the reception of the towers associated with the towers' audio presentation. The different content and focuses of these two kinds of literature indicate two contrasting aspects of the towers' meaning.

The only description of the rhythmic sound of the drums that I have been able to find, for example, comes from a private memoir written by a Beijing resident, which reports a popular saying in old Beijing: "Eighteen fast beats, eighteen slow beats, and there are yet another eighteen beats that are neither fast nor slow."[30] A well-known Beijing folktale, on the other hand, was inspired by the sound of the bell, which was considered peculiar.[31] It relates that when the Yongle emperor ordered a new bell to be cast in the early fifteenth century, the foundry master failed repeatedly to obtain a perfect casting. The emperor was furious and threatened to punish the incompetent man. The foundry master's daughter heard about this. To save her father's life, she jumped into the huge mold when the molten metal was poured into it, thus making herself a permanent part of the bell. Her father made a desperate clutch at her, but only caught hold of one of her shoes. This time the bell was perfectly cast. But to the ears of Beijing's residents, it ever since gave forth the sound "Xie!"—the sound of the Chinese word for "shoe"—as if the girl kept looking for her missing personal belonging whenever the bell was struck.

I have started this discussion of the two towers with these remembrances and stories, not with emperors' edicts or government documents, because this unofficial literature preserves a vanished aspect of the towers that easily eludes a historical study: these two buildings, though physically intact, are now completely silent; to a modern observer, their meaning seems entirely to depend upon their form and decoration. In other words, with their audible aspect gone, their visual aspect has become the most obvious evidence for their historical significance. It is true that we, as art historians or architectural historians, can happily observe and analyze the architectural features of the towers, and can also reconstruct their histories based on archives that record their repeated construction and restoration. But in such research we run the danger of allying ourselves with the patrons and designers of the towers—our emphases on the buildings' architectural design and intended symbolism seem to echo theirs too closely. What is absent in these emphases is how the towers—

and more specifically the sound issuing from their balconies—actually worked and what they evoked.

We are reminded of this absence when we realize that the towers are now soundless and hence lifeless. This reflection leads me to propose a twofold methodology to guide my discussion of the drum tower and the bell tower. First, to understand their historical monumentality we cannot rely on their physical properties and archival records alone, but must also try to resurrect—to "listen to"—their vanished sound, and to imagine the social interactions and spatial transformations activated by such sound. Second, our only method to resurrect this vanished sound is to activate the memories of the "historical listeners"—memories of ordinary Beijingers that we have discovered in personal memoirs and folktales. It is difficult to find a better metaphor for remembrance than a vanished sound recalled. But the sound from the drum tower and the bell tower was special and indeed monumental—a sound that dictated millions of people's daily lives for several hundred years.

First constructed in 1272 by Kublai Khan in Dadu, the drum tower has since been reconstructed and repaired many times.[32] Its current form and location basically preserve those of the early Ming drum tower, commissioned by the Yongle emperor before he moved his court to this northern city in 1421. A magnificent wooden-framed structure, it is 46.7 meters high and covers an area of seven thousand square meters, painted entirely vermilion except for the green roof tiles and the bluish decorative bands below the repeated eaves (fig. 5.7). The lower story of the tower, actually a tall base of the entire structure reinforced by thick brick walls, raises the upper story to 30 meters above ground, from where one may look down and find traditional Beijing under one's feet. The single enormous room on the upper story originally housed twenty-four drums, each with a round drumhead 1.5 meters in diameter and mounted with cattle skin. Now all the original drums save one have disappeared; so have the bronze clepsydra and other chronographs that imperial officials used to determine the time to beat the drums.

The bell tower stands a short distance north of the drum tower (fig. 5.7). The history of this second tower can also be traced back to the early Ming—Kublai Khan's bell tower was located slightly to the east and is now untraceable. Unlike the drum tower that remains a timber-framed building, the bell tower was turned into a brick and stone structure in 1745—a decision made by the Qianlong emperor of the Qing dynasty after the original wooden bell tower was destroyed by fire. The same emperor also erected a large stone stele in front of the building and inscribed on the stele a long text that he composed to commemorate the "renewed harmony between heaven and earth" achieved

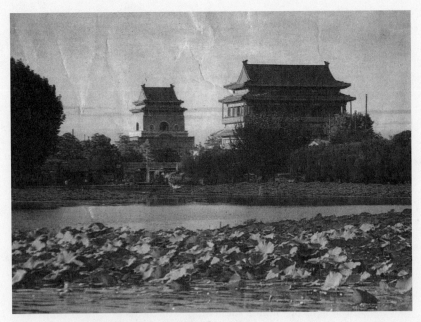

Fig. 5.7. The drum tower and bell tower in Beijing.

by rebuilding the tower. It is possible that Qianlong—a ruler famous for his penchant for art connoisseurship—redesigned the bell tower also for aesthetic and symbolic reasons: the new building has a sober and elegant look that both contradicts and complements the flamboyant drum tower. The drum tower is voluminous and powerful; the bell tower is slender and elegant. Its height of 47.9 meters—even greater than the drum tower's—attests to an unmistakable attempt to achieve verticality. The drum tower is *yang* and masculine; the bell tower is *yin* and feminine.

Like the drum tower, the bell tower is also a two-level building whose first story also serves as a tall base. An enormous bronze bell—5.5 meters tall and 6.3 tons in weight—is hung inside an open vault in the center of the upper story. No door was installed around the vault to block the sound of the bell. As for the drum tower, although there are doors built all around the upper story, they were open wide when the drums were beaten on regular hours, so the sound of the drums could reach every corner of the city.

Here is the schedule for beating the drums and the bell: every day at the *wu* hour, beginning about 7 P.M., the twenty-four drums, followed by the bronze bell, were struck. The rhythmic sound was divided into sections of various paces. As summarized in the popular saying cited earlier, each sequence started with 18 fast beats, was followed by 18 slow beats, and then concluded with 18 medium-paced beats. This sequence was repeated to make a total of 108 beats. Responding to the sound from the two towers, imperial guards stationed at the nine gates of Beijing's Inner City struck the chimes or bell installed in each of the gate towers.[33] With this joint call, all the gates of the inner city were closed one by one, local police shut the "street gates," and people also locked their doors. The same performance of the drums and the bell was repeated at the *yin* hour, about 5 A.M., the next morning: the night was officially over and it was the time for the city to wake up. So with another round of the joint striking of drums and bells, the city gates slowly swung open; markets started to receive customers; and high-ranking officials departed to attend court meetings. Between these two moments—that is, between 7 P.M. in the evening and 5 A.M. in the early morning—the bell tower kept silent and only the drum tower announced the nightly hours.

This schedule seems strange to a modern observer: the drums and bell thundered only at night, and announced time to Beijing's residents only when they were supposed to stay home and sleep. To understand this seemingly bizarre custom is to understand the *working* of the two towers and, indeed, a predominant system of public time telling in premodern China. I have surveyed the history of this system in the previous section; Beijing's example discussed here allows us to summarize two basic roles of this system. First, the joint striking of the drums and bell controlled urban spaces and activities by activating Beijing's gates—not only the main city gates but also all other gates throughout the imperial capital. One type of gate, no longer seen in present-day Beijing, was the "street gate." Numbering 1,219, these gates divided the city's traffic routes into short, isolatable sections. Several members of the British Macartney mission of 1793 mentioned this device in their reports and memoirs. The earl of Macartney himself wrote: "At night all the streets are shut up by *barricadoes* at each end and a guard is constantly patrolling between them."[34] The unified actions of Beijing's gates implied a daily transformation of the city's spatial structure: when all the gates were closed in response to the evening striking of the drums and the bell, not only was the walled city isolated from the outside, but all the walled spaces within the city—palaces, offices, markets, temples, and private homes—turned themselves into enclosed and dissociated units.[35] Roads and streets became empty and ceased to connect the city's various sectors into a dynamic whole.

Traditional Beijing thus underwent a ritualized dormancy on a daily basis, and each period of its inactivity was framed and reinforced by the joint sound of the drums and bell. This primary role of public time telling, to mark the beginning and end of the nightly curfew, was complemented by the second role of public time telling, to punctuate each night into five equal divisions for the night watches—a role performed by the drum tower alone. The joint striking of the drums and bell at dusk was known as *ding geng,* meaning literally "the beginning of the night watch." The following bi-hourly beatings of the drums then marked "the first night watch" (*chu geng*), the "second night watch" (*er geng*), and so on till the bell joined the drums again to announce the beginning of the next day at the "fifth night watch" (*wu geng*). Between *ding geng* and *wu geng,* municipal night watchmen, equipped with long poles with iron hooks on top, patrolled the streets in groups of two or three.[36]

Unlike public bells in medieval Europe, which were "drivers of actions" and "goads to effective, productive labor,"[37] therefore, the Chinese drum tower and bell tower ensured peace through the long night. This particular function of the towers raises questions about the role of their architectural imagery. I have mentioned that the drum tower and the bell tower were the two tallest buildings standing on Beijing's central axis during the Ming and Qing dynasties. Their striking visual images, however, did little to reinforce their public function of telling time. In fact, since these two buildings sent out their sound only from dusk to dawn, their sound and their architectural image were to a large extent mutually exclusive: they were *heard* at night and *seen* during the day. During the day, their imposing but silent presence realized the political control of the time. From the point of view of the imperial authority, the towers could realize such control because they focused public perception and brought about a sense of unification and standardization.

This particular role for the monumentality of the towers is clearly stated by the Qianlong emperor, in a text that he ordered inscribed on a stele erected in front of the bell tower in 1747:

> My divine capital is as broad as an ocean, and it possesses all sorts of goods. Its run-through avenues intersect with streets and lanes, and a large, well-off population dwells there. But when things multiply the opinions become diverse. Unless an instrument is created to unify people's minds, synchronization of dawn and dusk cannot be achieved. The effectiveness of such an instrument is determined by its physical size. This is why this tower must be constructed as a multileveled building of unusual height: only in this way can its solemn image be seen near and far. Moreover, the drum tower and the bell tower will form a pair, guarding the Forbidden City to the rear.[38]

The last sentence in this quotation refers to the position of the two towers relative to the imperial court. Ming-Qing Beijing consisted of a number of subcities—the Outer City, the Inner City, the Imperial City, and the Forbidden City (see fig. 5.6C). Nested deep inside layers of walled rectangles, the Forbidden City was the personal domain of the Son of Heaven. The next subcity, the Imperial City, protected the Forbidden City and contained imperial parks, armories, and residences of royal relatives, high ministers, and powerful eunuchs. With thick walls and guarded gates, these two cities in central Beijing blocked off more than two-thirds of the east-west traffic routes within the Inner City. To travel from the east part of the city to the west part, an ordinary Beijing resident had to make a considerable effort, either circling around Di'anmen, the Gate of Earthly Peace that marked the north end of the Imperial City, or taking a detour behind Qianmen, the Front Gate of the Inner City. If he took the first route, he would pass by the drum tower, through streets lined with large and small shops.

This hypothetical journey helps explicate two important implications of the location of the drum tower and the bell tower, which further signify the buildings' social identity and political symbolism. First, unlike all other imperial structures in Beijing, these two towers stood outside the royal domain and were accessible to anyone who lived in or traveled to the city. Second, the area centered on these two towers was one of the busiest commercial districts in the city. Many records of old Beijing describe at length the many restaurants and shops one could find here. The authors of these records also unanimously emphasize the attraction of this area to people of different professions and social classes. While the artificial lakes southwest of the towers offered educated people quiet places for literary gatherings and relaxation, teahouses and open-air performances attracted commoners, women, and children.

It is important to realize that the identity of the drum tower and the bell tower as a center of Beijing's urban popular culture was already implied in the city's symbolic structure. By locating these two buildings outside Di'anmen, the designer of Beijing consciously associated them with the element *di* or "earth" as opposed to *tian* or "heaven." As mentioned earlier, Di'anmen, or the Gate of Earthly Peace, was the north or rear gate of the Imperial City; the south and front gate of the Imperial City was the famous Tiananmen or the Gate of Heavenly Peace. These two gates constituted a pair pertaining to the *yin-yang* opposition: the area outside Di'anmen was a public space populated by the subjects of imperial rule, while Tiananmen symbolized the emperor as the master of the whole population. As a designated center of Beijing's public life, the drum tower and the bell tower both counterbalanced the Forbidden City and were subordinated to it. The political dominance of the Forbidden City over these two towers was most acutely expressed by locating the towers at the northern end of Beijing's central axis. The symbolic center of this axis was a series of throne halls inside the Forbidden City; the two towers were therefore understood as a far-reaching projection of imperial power from the throne halls into the public domain.

It is at this juncture that we arrive at a more complete understanding of the relationship between the two towers and the imperial clocks in the Forbidden City, a relationship which determined their different forms of monumentality. I have mentioned that two huge clocks, one a traditional hydraulic clock and the other a Western mechanical clock, flanked the emperor's throne in the Hall of Union. We have also observed tensions as well as connections between the towers and these clocks. On the one hand, the towers and the clocks were distinguished by their locations, accessibility, visibility, and different kinds of technical sophistication (horology versus architecture). On the other hand, they belonged to a single symbolic system and actually constituted this system. While the clocks in the emperor's private domain signified the imperial control over time keeping, the towers manifested this control over public time telling by amplifying the clocks' size and sound. Because the two towers sounded only at night, they undertook a daily transformation from silent architectural monuments to what may be called "auditory monuments." As architectural monuments they derived their political symbolism from their juxtaposition with the Imperial City and Forbidden City; as "auditory monuments" they dominated the rest of Beijing with invisible sound signals.

Coda: The Clock Tower

For centuries, the sound of the drums and the bell dictated to Beijing's residents when to work, rest, open the city gates, or retreat into individual courtyard compounds: this was the schedule of a community in a tightly walled city. What the sound signified was an eternal repetition recognized as time itself. The history it commemorated had no event and occasion, date or name. The memory it evoked, using Pierre Nora's words, was "an integrated memory— all-powerful, sweeping, un-self-conscious, and inherently present-minded—a memory without a past that eternally recycles a heritage, relegating ancestral yesterdays to the undifferentiated time of heroes, inceptions, and myth."[39]

This way of telling and knowing time in Beijing was finally challenged by two changes in public time telling, both brought about by foreign military and economic invasions. First, the old drum tower was silenced. During the 1900 invasion to suppress the Boxer Rebellion, soldiers of the Eight-Power Allied Forces (sent by Britain, France, the United States, Japan, Germany, Italy, Austria, and Russia) occupied the tower and slashed the leather drumheads with bayonets.[40] After the Republic of China was founded, the building was renamed Realizing Humiliation Tower (Mingchi Lou), and a Center for Common Education in the Capital (Jingzhao Tongsu Jiaoyu Zhongxin) was established on its lower level.[41] The tower thus acquired the identity of a witness to the "crimes of foreign devils" and a major national humiliation. This change in the building's significance was intimately related to China's transformation from an ancient empire to a modern nation-state. As part of this transformation, the drum tower joined some other architectural sites to arouse people's consciousness of the calamities befalling their country.[42] The silence forced upon the old tower thus made it a "modern" monument: not only did it serve a contemporary political agenda, but its changing monumentality implied the uprooting of its traditional "integrated memory" by a historical narrative based on events and happenings.[43]

Second, around the same period, time was announced in Beijing by mechanical clocks installed on Western-style public buildings.[44] Mostly attached to banks, custom houses, railway stations, schools, and government buildings, these clock towers provided the most concrete and convincing evidence for the superiority of Western science, education, and social and political systems. It would be wrong to think that these structures "replaced" the drum Tower and bell tower because they never actually constituted a practical system of public time telling. A study of their locations reveals that clock towers in Beijing were not built in residential areas. Rather, they typically appeared in places that were rich in symbolism and associated with political and economic authorities. Most tellingly, three prominent clock towers, one belonging to Beijing's first railway station and the others standing above two powerful banks, were constructed on three sides of Tiananmen Square (fig. 5.8). Displaying their intimidating height and advanced chronographs, these towers not only surrounded the most prominent political space in traditional China but also overpowered it. To the city's residents, however, these startling public symbols of modernity did little to change their daily life.

Themselves intruders in an old Chinese city, clock towers in Beijing were tangible references to an alien system of time and space. They transcended the city's boundaries and connected Beijing to a huge colonial network marked by a chain of clock towers in London, Singapore, Shanghai, and Hong Kong. This social network realized the Enlightenment design of a universal scheme of time and space. Indeed, if in 1600 the Chinese saw the first Western mechanical clocks and world maps as curiosities, in 1900 they found themselves governed by such clocks and maps, which had reassigned their country—the Central Kingdom—to quite a different place in a global time-space legitimated by *science*.

What distinguished the monumentality of these clock towers from that of the imperial clocks and the drum tower, therefore, was a new *technology* which, according to Robert M. Adams, should always be thought of as a *social-technical system*: "What underlies and sustains technological systems is partly institutional and partly technical, partly rooted in material capabilities and

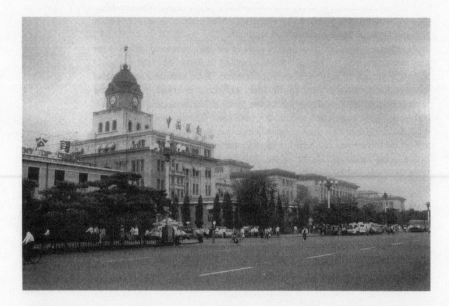

Fig. 5.8. The Japanese Dadong Bank (now the Bank of China) with its Western-style clock tower near Tiananmen Square. Photograph by Wu Hung.

possibilities and partly in human associations, values, and goals."[45] The traditional, parallel systems of time keeping and time telling became obsolete when a public clock moved and struck by itself. This fascinating, automatic timepiece freed time keeping from imperial control. It also changed the nature of public time telling altogether: instead of issuing an official timetable, it presented an "objective" time that was believed to be homogeneous and universal. The silent remains of the drum tower (renamed Realizing Humiliation Tower), however, inevitably problematized this significance of the clock tower: in establishing its "universal" monumentality, it had to destroy that of the local.

NOTES

1. Joseph Needham, *Science and Civilization in China,* vol. 3 (London: Cambridge University Press, 1959), 189.

2. Hellmut Wilhelm, *Chinas Geschichte; zehn einführende Vorträge* (Beijing: Vetch, 1942), 16.

3. One definition of *schedule* is "a tabular statement of times of projected operations, recurring events, arriving and departing trains, etc., a timetable." *Webster's New Collegiate Dictionary,* 7th ed.

4. See Wu Hung, *Monumentality in Early Chinese Art and Architecture* (Stanford: Stanford University Press, 1989), 1–4.

5. Ibid., 4–24; also Wu Hung, "Tiananmen Square: A Political History of Monuments," *Representations* 35 (summer 1991): 86–88.

6. For the appearance of architectural monuments in China, see Wu Hung, *Monumentality*, 99–115.

7. For an English translation of this text with the original Chinese text, see James Legge, *The Chinese Classics,* vol. 3, *The Shoo King* (Oxford: Clarendon Press, 1871), 15–27. The passage cited here is translated by Joseph Needham, *Science and Civilization in China,* 3:188. Although traditional Confucians attributed this text to Yao himself, modern scholars believe that it was probably written around the fifth or sixth century B.C.

8. For an excellent study of the relationship between time, space, and political power based on excavated divinatory inscriptions, see David N. Keightley, *The Ancestral Landscape: Time, Space, and Community in Late Shang China (ca. 1200–1045 B.C.)* (Berkeley: Center for Chinese Studies, University of California at Berkeley, 2000).

9. For a discussion of this architectural form and its symbolism, see Wu Hung, *Monumentality,* 176–87.

10. Li Fang, *Taiping guangji* (Wide gleanings of the Taiping era) (Taipei: Xinxing shuju, 1969), *juan* 226, 4a (2:880). Translation by Antonio Forte, *Mingtang and Buddhist Utopia in the History of the Astronomical Clock: The Tower, Statue, and Armillary Sphere Constructed by Empress Wu* (Rome: Istituto Italiano per il Medio ed Estremo Oriente, Paris: Ecole française d'extrême-orient, 1988), 109.

11. This clock has been carefully studied by Joseph Needham and his collaborators in *Heavenly Clockwork: The Great Astronomical Clocks of Medieval China,* 2d ed. (Cambridge: Cambridge University Press, 1986).

12. David S. Landes, *Revolution in Time* (Cambridge: Harvard University Press, 1983), 17–18. Landes has also noted the function of such hydraulic clocks as cosmological models; see p. 29.

13. Song Lian, *Yuan shi* (History of the Yuan dynasty), *juan* 48, 7a–b. See Catherine Pagani, *"Eastern Magnificence and European Ingenuity": Clocks of Late Imperial China* (Ann Arbor: University of Michigan Press, 2001), 13–14.

14. Cai Yong, *Du duan,* in *Yang ke Cai zhonglang ji jiaokanji,* comp. Xu Han (Ji'nan: Qi Lu shushe, 1985), 86.

15. For a description of this image and the tomb containing it, see Wu Hung, "The Origins of Chinese Painting," in Richard M. Barnhart et al., *Three Thousand Years of Chinese Painting* (New Haven: Yale University Press, 1997), 31–33.

16. Yang Xuanzhi, *Luoyang qielan ji* (A record of Buddhist monasteries in Luoyang) (Shanghai: Guji chubanshe, 1958), 75.

17. Sulaiman al-Tajir, an Arab traveler of the mid-ninth century, reported that a Tang city had ten drums over city gates which officials beat at regular hours. See Needham et al., *Heavenly Clockwork,* 93 n. 1.

18. For example, we read in the third-century B.C. text *Guangzi:* "Set up strong points and close off [the approaches to villages] with barricades. Let there be but a single road [leading into each village], and let [people] leave or enter only one at a time. Let the village gates be watched and careful attention paid to keys and locks. The keys shall be kept by the village commandant, and a gatekeeper shall be appointed to open and close the gates at the proper time." W. Allyn Rickett, trans., *Guangzi,* vol. 1 (Princeton: Princeton University Press, 1985), 104.

19. There are numerous books and articles discussing the "ward" system of Chang'an. For a recent publication, see Victor C. Xiong, *Sui-Tang Chang'an: A Study in the Urban His-

tory of Medieval China (Ann Arbor: Center for Chinese Studies, University of Michigan, 2000), 208–13.

20. Translation from Etienne Balazs, *Chinese Civilization and Bureaucracy,* trans. A. F. Wright (New Haven: Yale University Press, 1964), 69.

21. According to the *Tang Code,* a book which provides the fullest documentation of medieval legislation, "Moving about the streets after the drum has sounded to close the gates and before the drum has sounded to open them is a violation of curfew." Wallace Johnson, *The T'ang Code,* vol. 2, *Specific Articles* (Princeton: Princeton University Press, 1997), 469–70.

22. Tang dynasty Chang'an had two official markets in the east and west sections of the city. Following an old tradition, the markets opened for business at midday after a three-hundred-stroke beating of drums, and closed before dusk with a three-hundred-stroke beating of gongs. See Xiong, *Sui-Tang Chang'an,* 173–74. For a brief introduction to time telling conducted in Buddhist temples, see Yu Tao, *Zhongguo guzhong shihua* (A narrative history of ancient Chinese bells) (Beijing: Zhongguo luyou chubanshe, 1999), 138–41.

23. See Katô Shigeshi, "On the Development and Prosperity of Cities and City Life during the Song Period" (in Japanese), in idem, *Studies in Chinese Economic History* (in Japanese), 2 vols. (Tokyo: Toyo Bunko, 1952–53), 1:299–346. Yang Kuan, *Zhongguo gudai ducheng zhidushi yanjiu* (Shanghai: Guji chubanshe, 1993), 248–426.

24. Yang Huan, *Bian gugong ji* (Records of old places in Kaifeng), cited in Yang Kuan, *Zhongguo gudai ducheng zhidushi yanjiu,* 450.

25. Marco Polo, *The Travels,* trans. Ronald Latham (Harmondsworth: Penguin, 1958), 220–21; also see 130.

26. These cities and towns include Xi'an in Shaanxi, Liaocheng in Shandong, Xuanhua in Hebei Tower; Taigu, Jiexiu, and Pingyao in Shanxi, Jiuquan and Wuwei in Gansu. See Xiao Mo, ed., *Zhongguo jianzhu yishushi* (A history of the art of Chinese architecture), 2 vols. (Beijing: Wenwu chubanshe, 1999), 2:695–97.

27. When the Jesuit Gabriel Magalhaens visited China in the seventeenth century, he observed that incense clocks bore "five marks to distinguish the five parts of the Watch or Night." See Needham, *Science and Civilization in China,* 3:330.

28. A different account is that there were twenty-five drums, including one large drum and twenty-four smaller ones; the latter symbolized the twenty-four divisions of a year. See Luo Zhewen, "Beijing Zhonglou, Gulou" (Beijing's drum tower and bell tower), in Research Association of Shishahai in Beijing, *Jinghua shengdi Shishahai* [Shishahai: a famous spot in Beijing], (Beijing: Beijing chubanshe, 1993), 139–49.

29. As I will discuss later in this essay, one official document written by the Qianlong emperor does refers to the sound of the bell. But the language used in this description is flowery and stereotyped. Instead of conveying a listener's real experience, it endows the sound of the bell with a finite political symbolism. This text is inscribed on a stone stele, which the emperor established in commemorating the rebuilding of the bell tower during this reign.

30. Jin Lin, "Beijing Zhonggulou wenwu zaiji" (Miscellaneous records of things related to the drum tower and the bell tower), in Editorial Committee, *Wenshi ziliao xuanbian* (Selected archival materials on modern Chinese history), no. 36, p. 213.

31. One early source of this story is the late Qing publication *Yanjing fanggu lu* (Searching for ancient sites in Beijing) by Zhang Jiangcai, reprinted in *Jing Jin fengtu congshu* (Books on local customs of Beijing and Tianjin) (Taipei: Guting shuwu, 1969), 79. This story has been told and retold many times, and has been elaborated into modern versions of "folk literature" (*minjian wenxue*). For a modern version, see Jin Shoushen, ed., *Beijing de chuanshuo* (Legends of Beijing) (Beijing: Tongsu wenyi chubanshe, 1957), 40–44.

32. The building was destroyed by fire even before the Yuan dynasty perished, and was rebuilt by Emperor Chengzong in 1297. It was reconstructed in early Ming and early Qing, respectively; and was extensively repaired in 1800, 1894, and 1984.

33. It is said that except for Chongwen Men, which had a bell in its gate-tower, all other gates used a chimelike instrument called a *dian* to ring the hours. See Hu Yuyuan, ed., *Yandu tangu* (Talking about the old days of Beijing) (Beijing: Yanshan chubanshe, 1996), 40, 75.

34. George Macartney, *An Embassy to China; Being the Journal Kept by Lord Macartney during His Embassy to the Emperor Ch'ien-lung, 1793–1794*, ed. J. L. Cranmer Byng (Hamden, Conn.: Archon, 1963), 158. Other members of the mission, including George Staunton, Jone Barrow, and Aeneas Anderson, made similar reports. See Alison Dray-Novey, "Spatial Order and Police in Imperial Beijing," *Journal of Asian Studies* 52, no. 4 (1993): 894.

35. Because of the system of nightly curfew, public theaters located mainly in Beijing's outer city during the Qing dynasty staged performances only during the day, making sure that visitors from the inner city could return home before the gates closed.

36. See Jin Lin, "Beijing Zhonggulou wenwu zaiji," 213. For a detailed study of the roles of police and security measures in traditional Beijing, see Dray-Novey, "Spatial Order and Police in Imperial Beijing," 885–922.

37. Landes, *Revolution in Time*, 69.

38. This stele still stands in front of the bell tower in Beijing.

39. Pierre Nora, ed., *Realms of Memory: The Construction of the French Past*, trans. Arthur Goldhammer, 3 vols. (New York: Columbia University Press, 1996–98), 1:3.

40. It is unclear which foreign nationality was responsible for this destruction. Contemporary Chinese authors blame either Russian or Japanese soldiers for this crime. Since evidence is given in neither case, such claims may instead reflect the changing relationship between China and these foreign countries.

41. This was accomplished in 1924 and 1925 by Xue Dubi, the mayor of Beijing at the time. See Jin Lin, "Beijing Zhonggulou fenwu zaiji," 214.

42. Not coincidentally, the famous ruins of the Yuanmingyuan Garden, left from the destruction of the joint forces of the British and French armies in 1860, also attracted wide public attention from the early twentieth century, before they finally became not just a particular war ruin but a nationalist monument.

43. The meaning of the drum tower as a war ruin and a nationalist monument, however, largely vanished after the establishment of the People's Republic of China. For about three decades from the 1950s to the 1980s, the tower was used as the site of a Workers' Cultural Palace. It began to draw wider attention in the 1990s when its upper level was reopened to the public. Since then, the building has been renovated and a new set of drums has been made. But these are silent replicas created to showcase a perished past for the sake of a burgeoning business—the tower has become a major tourist attraction in Beijing and its lower level now houses a large gift shop.

44. Clock towers first appeared in Beijing in the eighteenth century; but the early examples were commissioned by Qing emperors for private purposes. One of them was located inside the imperial Summer Palace outside Beijing and had no public function at all. Another example, a temporary Western-style building with a clock on it, was made on the occasion of the birthday of the Qianlong emperor's mother, as depicted in a painting that represents the birthday celebration, now housed in Beijing's Palace Museum.

45. Robert M. Adams, *Paths of Fire: An Anthropologist's Inquiry into Western Technology* (Princeton: Princeton University Press, 1996), 23.

6

The Winter Garden and Virtual Heaven

MARGARET OLIN

> Earlier Societies managed so that memory, the substitute for life, was eternal and
> that at least the thing which spoke Death should itself be immortal: this was the
> Monument. But by making the (mortal) Photograph into the general and some-
> how natural witness of "What has been," modern society has renounced the Mon-
> ument. A paradox: the same century invented History and Photography.
>
> Roland Barthes, *La chambre claire*

Touching Photographs

This essay is an allegory of looking: close looking of the sort art historians do. When we look, we search through our "monuments" for
the abundant details where, it is said, Aby Warburg thought *"der
liebe Gott"* could be found.[1] Art historians find many of these details
in photographic reproductions, and analyze them with reference to
the memory of other reproductions. Taking the two forms of looking,
art history and photography, together, and taking seriously the term
"monument," which art historians use to identify their objects of
study, the present essay imagines art history as a memorial, if not a
mourning, practice, and asks whether the nature of the contact between viewers and communities of remembered photographs informs

the way in which art historians conceive photographs in the *lieux de memoire* of their practice.[2]

In the 1950s, well before Pierre Nora began his ambitious project to investigate France's *"lieux de memoire,"* Roland Barthes published monthly "Mythologies," which investigated everyday myths supporting community identity: the Tour de France, the Eiffel Tower, the French menu.[3] Among these mythic forms, photography came to stand out, for example, in Barthes's 1964 essay "Rhetoric of the Image," which investigated an ad for packaged pastas and sauces.[4] The name of the company, Panzani, evoked Italianicity, as did the colors, red pepper, green tomatoes, of the Italian flag. A string bag with these vegetables tumbling out of it, along with packages of pasta and cans of sauce, brought to mind the experience of shopping in an open air market and cultural associations of still lives and cornucopias. But the fact that the ad was photographed, rather than drawn or painted, made these cultural and national associations seem to flow directly from the objects themselves.

This effect is due to the way photography represents its object: "[A]lthough the Panzani poster is full of 'symbols,' there nonetheless remains in the photograph a kind of natural *being-there* of objects, insofar as the literal message is sufficient: nature seems to produce the represented scene quite spontaneously."[5] The term "indexical" is often used to denote the naturalness Barthes ascribes to the photograph. As opposed to an "icon," which represents its object through similarity, an index represents its object through contact: it points at its object, or it is itself a trace of, or mark made by, that object. A thumbprint is an index. Because the item had to be there for an indexical representation of it to exist, an index is often regarded as inherently more persuasive than an icon, although not by C. S. Peirce, from whose complex analysis of logic these terms are roughly excerpted.[6] In relation to photography, similarity generally means visual resemblance: a photographed portrait, like a painted one, is an icon. Yet it is also an index. A photograph is like an icon with a seal of approval, or, as Barthes calls it elsewhere, a "certificate of presence."[7] Because the pasta had to be there to be photographed, we feel as though we are looking at it directly, not through a representational medium. The connotation of Italianicity gets a free ride on indexicality; it seems to be in the photograph along with the green peppers. Indexicality gives the myth—that one can get Italianicity and freshness out of a can—its persuasive force.

Barthes's interest in photography continued and became the subject of his last book, *La chambre claire: Note sur la photographie,* published in 1979, fifteen years after "The Rhetoric of the Image."[8] Like the earlier discussion of photography, *La chambre claire* accepts photography's indexical nature. The photograph and its referent adhere to one another, are co-natural.[9] From this premise, however, the book moves in a different, more agonized direction. Since the person (and here it is most often people, and never pasta, who are the subject) must really have been there for a photograph to have been taken, the photograph is a trace, a remnant, of the person who was there. The trace is tactile, like a footprint, or perhaps more accurately like a navel. Barthes's metaphors are both cosmic, but he gives them a natal feature by comparing the rays to an umbilical cord. As in medieval visual theories, these rays seem to extend from the subject of the photograph, to the sensitive plate, to the finished portrait, and end by literally touching (nourishing?) the photograph's viewer.[10] Because of this communication between the past and the present, a photograph has a memorial element, and relates directly to death, even if the person in question is alive still. Instead of the index that seemed to guarantee the myth, *La chambre claire* dwells on the "that has been" of the photograph and draws out the consequences of this touching quality of photographic mourning.[11]

Barthes lays out his theory in two parts. The first is a theory of photographic reception, the second an outpouring of grief for his recently deceased mother on the basis of a photograph of her when she was five years old. The division may suggest a separation between mind and emotion, the scholarly versus the personal. Both parts are, however, personal. In the first part, Barthes bases his theory of photography on his search for photographs that "exist" for him. To explain the ways that photographs can "exist," he uses two Latin terms: *studium* and *punctum*. The *studium* denotes the field of its cultural or educational possibilities: the interest requires the "rational intermediary of an ethical and political culture."[12] This unitary "field" is pierced by the second element, the *punctum*, which breaks out of the cultural field and into the personal. It "shoots out of it like an arrow, and pierces me."[13] The *studium* is the "field" and the *punctum* is that which pierces the field.

The punctum, Barthes observes, is often a detail. And this detail calls for(th) some close looking. As an example, Barthes illustrates a photographic portrait by the Harlem photographer James Van Der Zee. Thematically, Van Der Zee is close to the heart of *La chambre claire*. He is known for his *Harlem Book of the Dead* (1978), newly published when Roland Barthes visited New York in November 1978.[14] The book consists of mortuary photographs that Van Der Zee made in the 1920s, when his photographic practice flourished. If the recently bereaved Barthes saw it, he may have been struck, and perhaps horrified, by the photographer's pictures of his own mother, both alive and after her death.[15]

To illustrate his notion of the punctum, however, Barthes uses not a photograph from the book of the dead but a portrait of a family that was alive when Van Der Zee photographed them in his studio in 1926 (fig. 6.1). Barthes

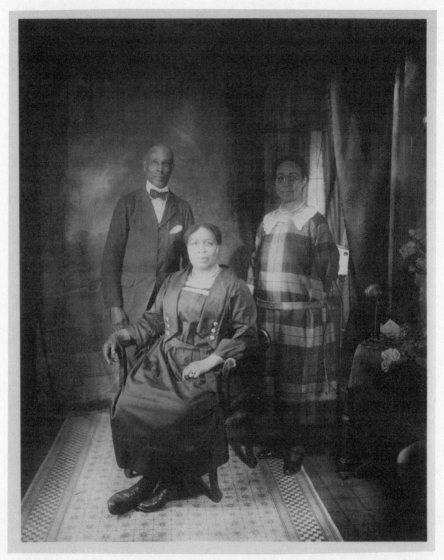

Fig. 6.1. James Van Der Zee, Family Portrait, 1926. Photograph by James Van Der Zee. Copyright Donna Mussenden Van Der Zee.

describes the portrait's studium in the following language: it enunciates "respectability, family life, conformism, Sunday best, an effort of social advancement in order to assume the White Man's attributes (an effort touching by reason of its naïveté)."[16] The cultural field of this studium could have been literature of or about the "New Negro," or the writings of W. E. B. Du Bois and others, who exhorted Negroes to emulate whites to be accepted by them.[17] Van Der Zee himself was engaged as an official photographer of Marcus Garvey's Universal Negro Improvement Association.[18] The "Sunday best" might actually have been borrowed best, since Van Der Zee kept fashionable clothes on hand for clients whose imaginations outdistanced their means.[19] These observations indicate directions for further investigations of this studium.

Actually, Barthes adapted these not very studious remarks from the caption of the photograph in a special issue of *Le Nouvel Observateur*, on photography, the source for many of the photographs for *La chambre claire*.[20] The caption tries to do justice to the family's identity: "visibly American, and clearly something else." The family is "desirous of giving itself an image conforming to the marks of prosperity of the American Way of Life. The visages are serene, transfigured. No unattractive quality can hold out against the hands of James Van Der Zee." At that time, according to the caption, "black is beautiful" was not a cry of defiance and despair.[21]

Yet Barthes's judgment of their "naïveté" is no less problematic for its possibly having been shared by an editor of a French literary journal. Are the sitters naive to think that the acquisition of "Sunday best" and jewelry will make them like whites, or are they naive to think that whites will treat them better if they acquire such things? But which attributes does he mean? Why *"attributs du Blanc,"* rather than attributes of the middle class, entry to which a portrait by Van Der Zee may have certified? Are there attributes that are more properly theirs and that they could display if they were less touchingly naive? What "imaginaire" (image system or repertoire, to use Barthes's expression) would they have created for themselves had they chosen to construct their visual identities without the resources of Van Der Zee's studio?[22] Why does he call the identity of these people into question? Do they misidentify themselves? What are they "by nature?" This puzzles me because Barthes earlier deconstructed myths that white people held of black people, who were no more "touchingly naive" than whites.[23] Moreover, that Barthes finds the identification with whites not only interesting but "touching" suggests that the studium conveys feeling just as does the punctum.

It touches, but it does not "point" (prick), unlike the punctum, specifically "the belt worn low by the sister (or daughter)—the 'solacing Mammy'—whose arms are crossed behind her back like a schoolgirl, and above all her *strapped pumps* (Mary Janes—why does this dated fashion touch me? I mean: to what date does it refer me?). This particular *punctum* arouses great sympathy in me, almost a kind of tenderness."[24] This punctum is actually two details: first one, then another. But later a third detail comes to him, and this work by Van Der Zee serves to point out another quality of the punctum: it illustrates the way in which (like the experience of a romantic poet, although Barthes does not make this connection) the true significance can often be specified only later, when the image, no longer there, has "*worked* within me."[25] Without the photograph to distract him, he realizes that the punctum in Van Der Zee's portrait is not a pair of shoes or a belt, but a necklace.

> I realized that the real *punctum* was the necklace she was wearing; for (no doubt) it was this same necklace (a slender ribbon of braided gold) which I had seen worn by someone in my own family, and which, once she died, remained shut up in a family box of old jewelry. . . . I had just realized that however immediate and incisive it was, the *punctum* could accommodate a certain latency (but never any scrutiny).[26]

Never any scrutiny indeed. The reason that Barthes can recognize this punctum only in the absence of the picture itself is that the detail he picks out, the slender ribbon of braided gold, is not there. The lady wears a string of pearls, as does her seated relative. Most readers do not notice Barthes's "mistake," since the Van Der Zee photograph is several pages away by the time Barthes recognizes the punctum. Possibly for this reason, few writers have commented on it, and those who do merely puzzle over it, remarking that it is, after all, personal, or chalking it up to the reproduction, where "it looks white and rather thick."[27]

In fact, such a necklace appears, but in a different photograph, reproduced in *Roland Barthes par Roland Barthes* (fig. 6.2). This mistaken detail, then, not the real one, led Barthes to the center of pain in the photograph and to the time of the "strapped pumps," which really are in the image. Indeed, Barthes's aunt Alice occupied the same place as Van Der Zee's "solacing mammy" in the family picture, or at least in the picture of the family, and it is no doubt the composition of the photograph, not the pumps or the necklace on a real person, that enabled him to make the identification. The necklace worn by Aunt Alice in the family portrait Barthes reproduces in *Roland Barthes par Roland Barthes* is quite possibly the "slender ribbon" Barthes had in mind. Presumably, Barthes recognized the family constellation, even though to do it he had to move the detail, the punctum, and never acknowledged the true connecting link between these women, their place in a photographic composition.

Like a scientist or scholar who misses the forest while searching for a particular tree, Barthes—or rather Barthes's first-person narrator—failed to see the composition of the whole while trying to decide on the decisive detail. This failure illustrates aspects of the punctum that he does not mention: the punc-

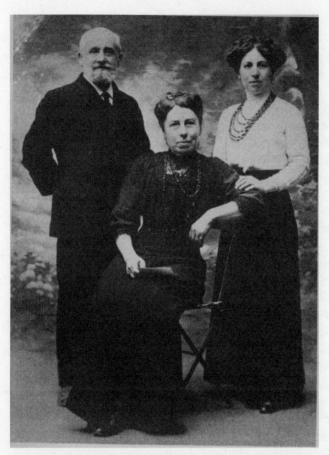

Fig. 6.2. Berthe and Léon Barthes and their daughter Alice. From *Roland Barthes par Roland Barthes* (1975), 2d ed. (Paris: Seuil, 1995).

tum may be the composition; the punctum may be forgotten; the punctum may be in a different photograph. The example illuminates an important aspect of memory: the deception at its heart, its ability to embroider and change, to be displaced like the details of a Freudian dream interpretation.[28] Not just the memory of whatever incident or person the punctum reminds one of, but memory of the photograph, the spur to memory, itself can enact this displacement. But the mistaken memory opens the possibility of comprehension. When Barthes's memory replaced the pearls with the necklace that should have been there, the aunt who occupied the "solacing mammy's" place magically appeared. This braided gold necklace was, perhaps, the punctum of Barthes's family photograph. Poignantly, he recognized the necklace he had seen his aunt wear, and that lay after her death inside a "family box," a dark chamber or *camera obscura*, rather than the light chamber of Barthes title, *La chambre claire*.[29] But perhaps Van Der Zee's portrait merely reminded him of having seen the photograph of his aunt's family, and even the jewelry shut up in the family box had itself lived, for Barthes, only in a photograph. Art Spiegelman wrote: "Snapshots illuminate my past like flares in the darkness. . . . Although often they only help me remember having seen the photos before!"[30]

Could Barthes's "mistake" about the punctum illuminate his mistake (surely it was one) about the naïveté of the sitters in the studium? It turns out that the touching naïveté he sees in the portrait, the respectable family life, indeed covers up the dreary life of a woman who, in her utter respectability, is utterly pitiable. But it is not the black family in Harlem whose naïveté is exposed. It is that of a white family in France, Barthes's family. "This sister of my father never married, lived as an old maid near her mother and it always distressed me to think of the sadness of her provincial life."[31] And whether or not the black family identified with white attributes, certainly Barthes identified his own family with the black family's attributes: with their touchingly naive, and mistaken, self-identification. But what is touching in another family is wounding in one's own. Did Barthes understand these reversals, did he know that the necklace was not there? Surely the narrator's parenthetical remark, that the punctum will not bear any scrutiny, slyly warns us not to turn back to look.

Barthes identifies a second source of punctum, described as "the lacerating emphasis of the *noeme* ('that has been')," the pure representation of the passage of time.[32] Any photograph has an about-to-die, already-dead, quality, even if the subject is not dead—yet, and although not all will have this effect as forcefully as the portrait by Alexander Gardner of a soon-to-be-executed, would-be assassin.[33] Barthes centers his argument on a more personal photograph, which arouses intense pain: a photograph of his mother taken when she was a small child. He found it while sorting photographs after her death, in search of one in which he could do more than recognize her, in which he would find "the truth of the face I had loved."[34] He found several pictures, some more characteristic than others, but one finally gave him what he was looking for. He christened it the "Winter Garden Photograph," because it was taken in a greenhouse:

> My mother was five at the time, her brother seven. He was leaning against the bridge railing, along which he had extended one arm; she, shorter than he, was standing a little back, facing the camera; you could tell that the photographer had said, 'Step forward a little so we can see you'; she was holding one finger in the other hand, as children often do, in an awkward gesture.[35]

It was a pale, yellowed photograph; his mother's face, unclear, was in danger of disappearing altogether. Yet it was revealing. It showed "a figure of a sovereign *innocence*, . . . In this little girl's image I saw the kindness which had formed her being immediately and forever, without her having inherited it from anyone."[36] Unlike the other photographs he discusses, he chooses not to reproduce this picture in his book, ostensibly because it would mean nothing to his readers.

But probably because no "Winter Garden Photograph" exists, or perhaps only the one of Kafka at the age of six, described, with its palm trees and Kafka's soulful eyes, as well as an oversized hat like that of the grandfather in "La Souche," by Walter Benjamin in his essay "A Short History of Photography."[37] This essay was translated in *Le Nouvel Observateur* and illustrated not with the photograph of Kafka but with several other photographs, including Van Der Zee's portrait of a family.[38] The resemblance between the described, but not reproduced, Winter Garden Photograph and "La Souche" has barely been remarked (fig. 6.3). As with the pearls that were exchanged for a slender

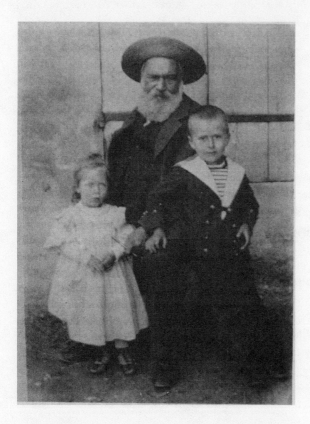

Fig. 6.3. "La Souche." From Roland Barthes, *La chambre claire: Notes sur la photographie* (Paris: Gallimard / Seuil, coll. Cahiers du cinéma, 1980).

ribbon, the distance between the description and the reproduction of the photograph may have disguised the resemblance for some, although here it is the photograph rather than the description that is delayed. The resemblance between the two photographs has not completely escaped notice, even from the beginning. It has puzzled some readers, one of whom wonders why the Winter Garden Photograph was so much more powerful than this one, while another mistakes "La Souche" for a portrait of Barthes's father.[39] Yet, when Diana Knight finally raised in print the likelihood that "La Souche" is the Winter Garden Photograph, few readers were willing to follow this twist of the plot.[40]

The connection, however, was easy to miss, because Barthes's tendency, here as elsewhere, is to distract our attention, emphasizing his mother's look of sovereign innocence as the picture's distinguishing mark. Other details he mentions, however, are more telling, for example, the "awkward gesture" of his mother's, "holding one finger in the other hand, as children often do." How often do children make that gesture after all? Perhaps every day, although looking through several generations of my own family photographs I failed to find any examples of it. Assuming there really was a "Winter Garden Photograph," then Barthes's mother presumably made that gesture more than once. That would make a minimum of three such gestures in Roland Barthes's family album, two by Barthes's mother, and one by Barthes himself as a small child (fig. 6.4).

Perhaps here, as supposedly in the portrait by James Van Der Zee, the punctum is a detail. In the Winter Garden Photograph, Roland Barthes discovered not his mother, or not only his mother, but also himself, himself as a child, specifically as a child known from photographs. A chain of photographs leads Barthes, like an art historian moving from image to image in search of something, to the unexpected discovery of himself as his own mother, just as he was his mother's mother while he cared for her during her last illness.[41] He is also Aunt Alice. How different was this woman, who never married but lived alone near her mother all her life, from Barthes himself, who lived alone with his mother until her death, two years before his own? In *La chambre claire* he wrote that in certain photographs he had his "father's sister's look."[42] They have been compared, by Diana Knight, the perceptive observer of many of the anomalies of Barthes's favorite photographs: "[B]etween them [they] incarnate the termination of the paternal line."[43] But what struck Barthes was her loneliness, not her lack of progeny. "The father's sister: she was alone all her life," reads the caption of a portrait of Alice in *Roland Barthes* (fig. 6.5).[44] Did the formal portrait of Alice with her parents cover up the sadness exposed in her childhood portrait? The portrait of Barthes as a young boy also sparks an insight into *"l'irréductible"* in himself: "in the child, I read quite openly the dark underside of myself," an original darkness that inhabits the man as well.[45]

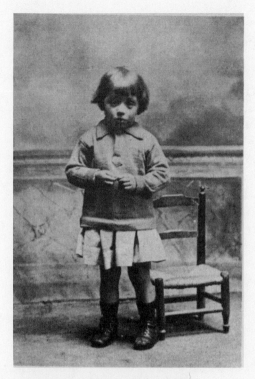

Fig. 6.4. Roland Barthes as a small child. From *Roland Barthes par Roland Barthes* (1975), 2d ed. (Paris: Seuil, 1995).

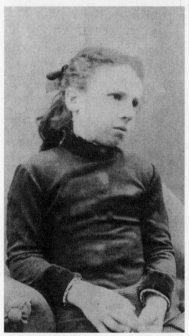

Fig. 6.5. Alice Barthes as a child. From *Roland Barthes par Roland Barthes* (1975), 2d ed. (Paris: Seuil, 1995).

Barthes and his aunt were very different from Barthes's mother, whose luminous portrait concealed no dark underside; but the essence of all three is revealed in their childhood portraits. The memories to which these photographs led were at least in part memories of other photos, links in a chain of visual signifiers that never quite reach the living beings themselves.

Certainly there could have been a Winter Garden Photograph; perhaps, whenever his mother and her brother posed, they automatically took the same positions, she nestling one finger in her other hand, standing back a bit, he coming forward, leaning on and extending his hand on whatever was handy, railing or knee. They posed the same way wherever they were: at the end of a wooden bridge or at the end of a life; among the branches and palms of a flourishing winter garden, or around and between their grandfather, in the bare dirt of a garden in winter, with no trees except themselves, two offshoots of the *souche* (stock of tree, founder of a family), as Barthes calls the old man. But even if the Winter Garden Photograph was always in that chamber of light where an unclouded vision could have seen it at any moment, what needed to be hidden, unlike Poe's purloined letter, was not the photograph but its meaning.[46] The reader must be discouraged from wondering how this banal photograph could have inflicted such a wound, and the children must be placed in a winter garden by themselves, not in the distracting company of this old man. "What relation can there be between my mother and her grandfather," he wrote, concerning this photograph, "so formidable, so monumental, so Hugolian, so much the incarnation of the inhuman distance of the Stock?"[47] Indeed, if "La Souche" is the Winter Garden Photograph, then not only did the fabrication of the Winter Garden translate his mother's photograph to suit Barthes's metaphor of a bright room, it removed the inconvenient grandfather at the same time. The braided gold necklace should have been there; the old man should not. Man and necklace are present but absent. The punctum is the detail that is not there, or that one wishes were not there. Absence, in this book about loss, is presence. Like Sartre's mental image in *L'imaginaire,* to which *La chambre claire* is dedicated, the punctum is "a certain way an object has of being absent within its very presence," or perhaps present within its absence.[48] The punctum's Lacanian counterpoint is the gaze that traps the eye.[49]

If the punctum is displaced, like an alibi, then the detail that is not there, the "that has been," never was. And neither was the indexical power of the photograph. The fact that something was before the camera when the photograph was taken is no longer the source of the photograph's power. Its power lies elsewhere, in a "performative index," an "index of identification." The narrator of *La chambre claire* performs, rather than argues, the meeting in the winter garden, because he, like many an art historian, was caught up in the rhetoric of proof and existence, the truth, defined as originality, of his mother's face. He was looking for what a photograph is "in itself."[50] But he did not want an "in itself," and he did not want "truth." He wanted a relation. He tried to use photography to satisfy his desire to possess or commune with his mother, to absorb her into himself and preserve her there through identifying with her. Photography is a winter garden, like a *"chambre claire"* that lets in light in the winter and keeps alive artificially that which should have died.

Angels Online

Raymond Williams suggested that the original function of photographs was to keep families in contact as economic necessities scattered them across the globe.[51] He could have added that they kept families in contact after death. Technologies cannot disrupt social purposes, he wrote, any more than they can bring them into being. Rather, new technologies arise to satisfy the same purpose. One such technology, the Internet, where people come together and make contact with images, is ideal for mourning.

In the fall of 1996, I ran across a reference to an Internet site pertaining to the murder of Israeli prime minister Yitzhak Rabin, which had occurred the previous year. I logged on wondering what to expect (the Internet was new to me), and was confronted with a photograph of Rabin and the message "click here to light a candle."[52] I did not click, so I do not know what would have happened. But the following year I tried my luck with another recently deceased hero and typed the phrase "Princess Diana" into Yahoo. Out of quite a long list of "hits," I clicked on two that looked to be both interactive and unofficial. They looked unofficial because of their bad spelling; I do not recall what made them look interactive.

The first was billed as the "(Unauthorized) Princess Diana Page." "Read and post condolences," it said.[53] On a black background, the word "Diana," in script (her signature?) dissolved into a picture of a rose. Signatures are indexical, since they are made by the hand of the person they symbolize (even though this one was digital). Below the rose/signature were the dates 1961–1997 and a link to "read the letters." This was followed by a text that read, "The page closed to new letters at 2200 GMT (6pm EDT) on 9/6/97. A representative sampling of letters will remain for viewing indefinately [*sic*]. Your response has been overwhelming. I am honored that you have entrusted your words to me. Thank you. 0052477." The only clue, besides this number, to the person to whom so many entrusted their response was the logo of the commercial domain: Microsoft Internet Explorer. This was one of many such unauthorized pages, several with links to Elton John's song "Candle in the Wind," in memory of the princess, and to the monarchy's official website (anyone can have a "link" with royalty) to which they promised to forward letters. These pages all had in common their sponsorship by private individuals, their international contributors, and, as I mentioned, their bad spelling.

The letters had something else in common: their mode of address. They were in several different languages and from many more different countries. But few of them addressed Diana's family or other mourners. Whatever the language, most of the writers addressed Diana directly: "Your death hit me like a bomb," begins the letter from Ana, 18, Portugal.[54] The letter from Melissa, in Portland, Oregon, suggests the problematic of the indexicality of photographic relations. It begins: "I barely even knew you, pictures were the only time you crossed my mind." Melissa knew Diana, if only barely, through pictures. Now that she is gone she can write to her. Others were not satisfied with words and tried to send flowers. The text under the rose reads: "Many of you sent picture attachments of flowers and other remembrances. The first I received last (8/31) Sunday morning came from Carl Perreault, of Hull, Quebec, Canada. Please think of this rose as representing your personal contribution."

I returned to the Diana memorial sites in early 2001, expecting to find them gone. But in fact, the ones I had seen shortly after her death were just the beginning of a flood. Indeed, many sites keep people in touch with deceased celebrities. At this writing, there are still places to go on the Internet if you wish to let poet Allen Ginsberg know how his poetry has affected your life, for example, and perhaps show him your own latest poems.[55] But cyberspace is not the equivalent of a constellation in heaven, reserved only for heroes. Even in 1997, my search for cyberspace memorials yielded more than twenty sites where anyone with a modem could rest eternal, many more if one includes memorials for deceased pets, including, "tamagochi" virtual pets, which were popular at the time. By August 2001, a search on Google yielded three hundred or more sites. Internet florists on memorial sites warn net surfers that they will deliver virtual flowers only to their own clients, and some have discontinued the service.[56]

My search for everyday memorials confirmed that there is a place called cyberspace, and when we die we can go there. The site "Dearly departed" advertises: "Your loved ones deserve to be remembered, give them a permanent place on the Internet; free service." "Eternal Monuments" calls itself "Your loved one's final resting place in Cyberspace." In "Virtual Heaven, an eternal site," I read, "Our heartfelt sympathies go out to all the friends, relatives and acquaintances of those dearly departed who now exist solely within these un-charted realms of Cyberspace."[57] The constantly repeated, and, given the tran-sitory nature of the Worldwide Web, overoptimistic word *eternal* resonates not only with euphemistic descriptions of death as "eternal rest" but also with Barthes's notion of photography's entailment with time.

People talk to deceased loved ones online. One message in "Virtual Heaven" reads in part: "Hi mom and dad. Remember dad I said one day I would get a computer? I did, but I never thought that I could write you in heaven. . . . Maybe this will help, that I can talk to you this way. love Gail."[58] Not all messages are loving. One message on "Dearly Departed" blames poor dead dad for everything bad that ever happened to the family. The son says he does not miss his dad, but if Dad were not missed, at least as a target for chil-dren to vent their anger, he would not rest in cyberspace.

Several sites offer the possibility of making a site for oneself to be acti-vated in due course. "Links" can unite departed ones with other departed ones in cyberspace, their photographs arranged at the bottom of the page, while counters keep track of the number of contacts made. Anyone with the means and know-how can construct such a memorial page including photographs and links. Angels Online (http://www.angelsonline.com), however, offers a free site that is nearly as good. In 1997, a site on Angels on Line contained flowers, the deceased's picture, and places for loved ones to send messages, such as "we miss you, mom." A picture of her grandson on the webpage came with the comment: "Every time I look at him, I see you."[59] The chain of iden-tification goes on, photograph touching photograph, and being touching at the same time. As overoptimistic as it may be to call these sites "eternal," most of them, including the one just mentioned, were still there more than five years later, and family members continued to write letters to mom in her guestbook.

Sending a baby's snapshot to a deceased grandparent in cyberspace, like sending a rose to a dead princess, is a real act, even if the rose, and the snap-shot, are "attachments" and the deceased a digital photograph. These poignant gestures indicate that the claim to personal contact or possession is as impor-tant as, and can replace, the claim to truth. We need truth because we care about the nature of our contact with it. The "link," not accuracy, is the most important thing about cyberspace. On the Internet, photographs bypass the indexicality of proof and go directly to indexical relations of all kinds. If, in-stead of dying in an accident soon after publishing *La chambre claire* in 1980, Roland Barthes had lived to see the Internet revolution, he would have been able to send the Winter Garden Photograph (if there is one) to cyberspace and place a shortcut to his mother's site on his desktop.

Art History Is a Winter Garden

It is unlikely that Barthes would have done such a thing, but his contact with the photos laid out on his desk was as important as the contact of any mourner with a photo in virtual heaven. Does an art historian, however, following her own path from one image to another, live in, and connect with, this community of images? When at the outset I suggested that my reflections on Barthes's misidentifications and virtual memorials constituted an allegory of looking, I meant that the art historical gaze is a memorial.

Art history, like memorial looking, involves assembling a community of images, often literally. In 1930, Adolph Goldschmidt used several pages of his assessment of the state of the discipline to discuss the impact and importance of photograph collections.[60] He meant black and white photographs, but similar advice now pertains just as often to slides or downloaded jpegs. Laying these images out on light tables, dark wooden desks, or screens, linking them in cyberspace, the art historian establishes communication with the visual past. The activity resembles that of a mourner paging through boxes of old photographs. Is the aim different? To want to understand an image *en soi,* as Barthes asks of his mother, and of photography, is to want to know what it is outside of oneself, not in relation to oneself. Thus Barthes finds what his mother was "in herself" only by finding out what she was before he was born. Following this originary, or genetic, notion of history, one finds the truth by turning to the origin, the little girl.[61] Barthes does not ask what historical circumstances helped form her; he wants to know what she was all along.

Art history is a monumental practice not because the historian may be in mourning for a lost monument. While perusing an advertisement for spaghetti, one is not generally in mourning for pasta. One might well, however, be searching for an essence to incorporate within oneself. A child, like a vegetable, cannot disguise its essence for Barthes in *La chambre claire.* Similarly, it was once thought that art history was consciously informed by monumental constructions rather than memorial practices. A monumental art history examines the monument and the historical circumstances that made it, and which it must continue to represent, as though what Alois Riegl called the *gewollte,* or intended, monument had succeeded in impressing on posterity its own agenda and all art historical objects were such *gewollte* monuments.[62] But when the "Winter Garden Photograph" was taken, Barthes's mother did not know she was to become, and to become known as, his mother, just as the painting *The Company of Captain Franz Banning Cock and Lieutenant Willem van Ruytenburgh* did not know that it was to become Rembrandt's *Night Watch* and would have to be placed behind bullet-proof glass. The little girl's intention, and that of her parents or the photographer, had little to do with Barthes's encounter with her photograph. Hers was an "unintended" (*ungewollte*) monument.

In the passage used as our epigraph, Barthes sees the photograph as the monument's replacement. But if Barthes thought photographs were exempt from the art historian's practice of turning everything he or she studies into a monument, he was wrong. Given that in art historical terminology a monument is that which the historian studies, the historian makes the monument in choosing it and foregrounds his or her own relation to that object of study by means of the same act, just as, by a similar chain of events, Barthes made his mother's photograph into a monument. The project of linking history and memory, of understanding the relation of the historian to her/his memory, foregrounds a relationship that places its stamp on history, even if the historian is unaware of the fact. Does the historian aim "at calming the dead who still haunt the present and at offering them scriptural tombs," as Michel Certeau suggests, making history a monumental practice that terminates the relation between past and present?[63] Or does the historian, who after all spends a great deal of time visiting tombs, wish to forge a connection to the past, to keep it in living memory, beyond all probability, nurturing its continuing relevance to the present? What indeed is the point of historical or memorial practices unless what we remember has to do with ourselves? Memorial practices seek to fold the remembered into the community of the living, or to fold the community of the living into the remembered.

The photograph resists inclusion, however, according to Barthes, who described it as "that which excludes me." Indeed, although Barthes envisions Van Der Zee's sitters as seeking acceptance, it is Barthes himself who seeks admission to their portrait. In the end, Barthes has indeed entered Van Der Zee's portrait through a necklace; for if Barthes identifies with Alice, and identifies Alice with the lady in the Van Der Zee portrait, then in a cross-gender, cross-Atlantic, interracial identification, Barthes too identifies with the lady in the portrait. That same necklace, however, drives away the people who were already there. In fact, the act of approaching images to form a community invites all the same mistakes that one makes when one tries to bring people together in order to develop a community. Differences are forgotten; misidentifications are made; we project ourselves into other people and get too close to look at them.

Another form of community building, also from cyberspace, may suggest a model for photographic communities. I have mentioned communities of individual families on the Internet, but wider communities also gather there. One such site, which "mourns" and "constructs" an entire country, closely resembles the art historian's traffic with images (fig. 6.6). This site, "akakurdistan.com,"

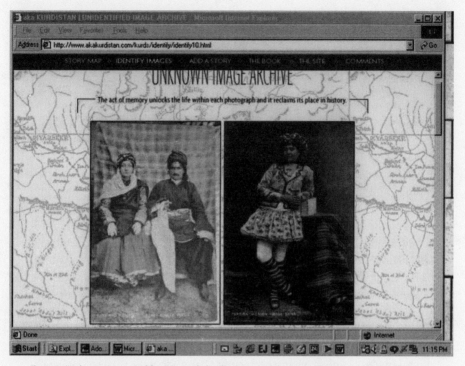

Fig. 6.6. "Unknown Image Archive." From akakurdistan. Copyright Susan Meiselas and Picture Projects.

which is centered on historical photos, has been increasingly complex over the past several years. Artists post photo essays, people "identify," and argue over, historical pictures. While it once attracted primarily "cybergraffitti-ists" who wander from site to site to heckle and deposit random expletives, as of 2001 the now-well-policed guest book was active and often combative. There was little attempt to adjudicate the origin of the photographs. "Identifications" conflicted, came from friends and enemies, represented several sides of the political spectrum, and expressed differing notions of Kurdish nationality. "Identification" in the sense of labeling these photographs almost faded into the background, but identification in another sense was fostered. When I wrote this essay, even more evanescent gatherings of photographs were appearing on walls in New York City, where the pain of the destruction of the World Trade Center was raw. Images came together to be mourned and to share information. A close but temporary bond occurred between photographs and mourners. A community forms around an image, like a pearl around a grain of sand in an oyster. But the community is not necessarily a pearl. The image is the pearl, and the community is made of shifting sands.

The art historian tries to avoid the mistakes made by the community that forms and reforms about an image. We need to get the necklace right, and our disciplinary apparatus is there to ensure we do. *La chambre claire*'s appeal to art historians is in part its affirmation of the personal and subjective over the objective demands of the discipline. Barthes's "mistaken" identifications are liberating. Our specialized skills cannot eliminate all errors. I have pointed out several by good critics in the course of my argument and surely made more of my own. The skills themselves, with their policing of borders, come out of the same colonizing social impulses that govern some of the mistakes. Barthes's desire to identify with the marginalized is not an unknowable subjective choice; it is informed by myths of margin and center, the same ones that, until recently, kept Van Der Zee outside the art historical canon.[64]

If the historian shifts her focus from the indexical origin of the representation, to the indexical quality of the relation between the image, other images, and their viewers, she can reenfold the seemingly subjective element of community that the disciplinary apparatus would have her block out, and can make use of her mistakes, as Barthes did his. The relationships made among photographs become not comparative but communal. Groupings of such memorials, like the ties between Warburg's lovingly observed details (made in the pursuit, it seems, of "truth" and not "God"), are no longer merely arguments but communities of which historians are members.[65]

The historian wishes not to bury the past but to forge a connection to the past, to keep it alive—in living memory—beyond all probability, nurturing its continuing relevance to the present. Art history, like photography, is a winter garden that keeps artificially alive visual beings from the past, placing them in contact with one another, photograph to photograph, and with the historian. An art historian, following her own path from one image to another, lives in, and connects with, her community of images, tending art history's winter garden, restoring these visual beings to life and placing them in contact with one another, with the historian, and with her readers. Whatever reality there is resides only in the encounter with the historian, with its future, its children.

NOTES

I am grateful to audiences in Amsterdam, Houston, Los Angeles, and Williamstown and to students in my seminars at the School of the Art Institute over the last ten years for invaluable contributions to this essay.

1. Ernst Robert Curtius, quoted by William S. Heckscher, "The Genesis of Iconology," in *Stil und Überlieferung in der Kunst des Abendlandes,* Akten des 21. Internationalen Kongresses für Kunstgeschichte in Bonn 1964 (Berlin: Gebr. Mann, 1967), 3:244 n. 10.

2. The term *"lieux de mémoire"* comes from Pierre Nora, ed., *Les lieux de mémoire* (1989–92), translated as *Realms of Memory: The Construction of the French Past,* trans. Arthur Goldhammer, 3 vols. (New York: Columbia University Press, 1996–98). The essays discuss repositories of memory in modern French culture.

3. Most were originally published in *Les Lettres Nouvelles,* beginning in 1953, and collected in Roland Barthes, *Mythologies* (Paris: Seuil, 1957). A smaller number were translated in Roland Barthes, *Mythologies* (1957), trans. Annette Lavers (New York: Hill and Wang, 1972).

4. Roland Barthes, "Rhetoric of the Image" (1964), in Roland Barthes, *The Responsibility of Forms: Critical Essays on Music, Art, and Representation,* trans. Richard Howard (New York: Hill and Wang, 1985), 21–40.

5. Ibid., 34.

6. See C. S. Peirce, "Logic as Semiotic: The Theory of Signs," in *Philosophical Writings of Peirce,* ed. Justus Buchler (New York: Dover, 1955), 98–119; Michael Leja, "Peirce, Visuality, and Art," *Representations* 72 (2000): 97–122. Barthes's terms "metaphor" and "metonymy" mean roughly what is designated by the terms "icon" and "index." For the use of Peirce, see Rosalind Krauss, "Notes on the Index," *The Originality of the Avant-Garde and Other Modernist Myths* (Cambridge: MIT Press, 1985), 196–219. More recently, Carol Armstrong described the photograph as "first and foremost an indexical sign—that is, an image that is chemically and optically caused by the things in the world to which it refers." Carol Armstrong, *Scenes in a Library: Reading the Photograph in the Book, 1843–1975* (Cambridge: MIT Press, 1998), 2.

7. Roland Barthes, *La chambre claire: Notes sur la photographie* (Paris: Gallimard/ Seuil, coll. Cahiers du cinéma, 1980), 135; translated as *Camera Lucida: Notes on Photography,* trans. Ron Howard (New York: Noonday Press, 1981), 87. I will cite both editions (henceforth abbreviated *CL,* pages references to the French edition follow).

8. On Barthes's interest in photography, see especially, besides sources mentioned below, Jean Delord, *Roland Barthes et la photographie* (Paris: Créatis, 1981); Nancy M. Shawcross, *Roland Barthes on Photography: The Critical Tradition in Perspective* (Gainesville: University Press of Florida, 1997); and essays in Jean-Michel Rabaté, ed., *Writing the Image after Roland Barthes* (Philadelphia: University of Pennsylvania Press, 1997).

9. *CL,* 6, 76/18, 119.

10. *CL,* 80–81/126. The medieval theory of visual rays involved the controversy between intromission (Barthes's assumption) and extramission. David C. Lindberg, *Theories of Vision from Al-Kindi to Kepler* (Chicago: University of Chicago Press, 1976), 61–85. On haptic rhetoric in *La chambre claire,* see Kenneth Scott Calhoon, "Personal Effects: Rilke, Barthes, and the Matter of Photography," *Modern Language Notes* 113, no. 3 (1998): 612–34, esp. 612–18.

11. *CL,* 77/120–21. The French edition refers to this essence, in Latin, as the *"interfuit,"* and in French, as the *"Ça-a-été."*

12. *CL,* 26/48.

13. *CL,* 26/49.

14. James Van Der Zee, Owen Dodson, and Camille Billops, *The Harlem Book of the Dead* (Dobbs Ferry, N.Y.: Morgan & Morgan, 1978); Louis-Jean Calvet, *Roland Barthes: A Biography,* trans. Sarah Wykes (Bloomington: Indiana University Press, 1994), 233.

15. Van Der Zee, Dodson, and Billops, *The Harlem Book of the Dead,* illustrations on pp. 10, 13.

16. *CL,* 43/73.

17. See Henry Louis Gates Jr., "The Face and Voice of Blackness," in *Facing History: The Black Image in American Art, 1710–1940* (San Francisco: Bedford Arts; Washington, D.C.: Corcoran Gallery of Art, 1990), xxix–xlvi; and Gates, "The Trope of a New Negro and the Reconstruction of the Image of the Black," *Representations* (fall 1988): 129–55. See also Melville J. Herskovits, "The Negro's Americanism," in *The New Negro*, ed. Alain Locke (1925; Atheneum, New York, 1969), 353–60; and other essays in this important collection.

18. Roger C. Birt, "A Life in American Photography," in *VanDerZee: Photographer, 1886–1983*, ed. Deborah Willis-Braithwaite (New York: Harry N. Abrams, 1998), 46–48.

19. Ibid., 44–45.

20. Barthes lists his photographic sources in the French edition only. Barthes, *La chambre claire*, 187.

21. [Robert Delpire?], in *Le Nouvel Observateur*, Special Photo 2 (1977): 19.

22. The concept of an *"Imaginaire"* (translated "Image repertoire") appears in *CL*, 11/25, and Barthes, *Roland Barthes par Roland Barthes* (1975), 2d ed. (Paris: Seuil, 1995), 98–99. In the English translation *"Imaginaire"* is rendered "Image System." Barthes, *Roland Barthes by Roland Barthes*, trans. Richard Howard (New York: Hill and Wang, 1977), 105. Hereafter the English edition of this work will be cited, with references to the French edition following. The concept echoes ideas in Jean-Paul Sartre, *L'Imaginaire: psychologie-phénoménologique de l'imagination* (Paris: Gallimard, 1940), translated as *The Psychology of Imagination* (New York: Philosophical Library, 1948). Barthes dedicates *La chambre claire* "In Homage To *L'Imaginaire*" by Jean-Paul Sartre."

23. For example, "Bichon and the Blacks," in *The Eiffel Tower and Other Mythologies*, trans. Richard Howard (New York: Hill and Wang, 1979), 35–38. The essay appeared in the French edition of *Mythologies*.

24. *CL*, 43/73–74, original emphasis.

25. *CL*, 53/87, italics in the English translation only.

26. *CL*, 53/87–88.

27. Derek Attridge, "Roland Barthes's Obtuse, Sharp Meaning and the Responsibilities of Commentary," in Rabaté, *Writing the Image after Roland Barthes*, 88 n. 4. He adds: "This discrepancy is of no account, however; even if we did see what Barthes describes, we would remain impervious to the *punctum*'s laceration." Diane Knight refers to "the supposed retrospective punctum of her necklace." Knight, *Barthes and Utopia: Space, Travel, Writing* (Oxford: Clarendon Press, 1997), 263.

28. Sigmund Freud, *The Standard Edition of the Complete Works of Sigmund Freud*, vol. 4, *The Interpretation of Dreams* (1899), trans. James Strachey (London: Hogarth Press, 1953), 277–309.

29. *CL*, 106/164.

30. Art Spiegelman, "Mein Kampf (My Struggle)," in *The Familial Gaze*, ed. Marianne Hirsch (Hanover, N.H.: University Press of New England, 1999), 100.

31. *CL* 53/88, translation slightly revised.

32. *CL* 96/148.

33. *CL* 96/148–50.

34. *CL* 67/106.

35. *CL* 67–69/106.

36. *CL* 69/107.

37. Walter Benjamin, "Kleine Geschichte der Photographie" (1931), in *Gesammelte Schriften*, ed. Rolf Tiedemann and Hermann Schweppenhäuser (Frankfurt a.M.: Suhrkamp,

1977), 2.1:375; translated as "A Short History of Photography," trans. P. Patton, in *Classic Essays on Photography,* ed. Alan Trachtenberg (New Haven, Conn.: Leete's Island Books, 1980), 206.

38. Walter Benjamin, "Les Analphabètes de l'avenir," *Le Nouvel Observateur,* Special Photo 2 (1977): 16. In this translation, the background is definitively described as that of a winter garden, unlike Benjamin's original German. Kafka's portrait, illustrated in Liliane Weissberg, "Circulating Images: Notes on the Photographic Exchange," in Rabaté, *Writing the Image after Roland Barthes,* 111, shows him beside a potted plant. She does not relate this image to the Winter Garden Photograph.

39. Carol Armstrong, "From Clementina to Käsebier: The Photographic Attainment of the 'Lady Amateur'" *October* 91 (2000): 106; and Ralph Sarkonak, "Roland Barthes and the Spectre of Photography," *L'Esprit Createur* 22, no. 1 (spring 1982): 56–57. Weissberg assumes that "The Stock" is "open to speculation: it may represent the author's family and it may not." Weissberg, "Circulating Images," 113.

40. Knight raises the issue in *Barthes and Utopia,* 265–66. For a hesitant response to Knight's "suggestion," see Attridge, "Roland Barthes's Obtuse, Sharp Meaning," 86 and 89 n. 9.

41. CL 72/112.

42. CL 103/161.

43. Knight, *Barthes and Utopia,* 264.

44. Barthes, *Roland Barthes by Roland Barthes,* 14/20.

45. Ibid., 22/28. In the English edition, a change in spacing makes the caption for this photograph appear to belong to a different photograph.

46. Diana Knight refers to Poe in relation to the Winter Garden Photograph, *Barthes and Utopia,* 266. Barthes used the Poe story as a parable relating to the concealment of meaning. Daniel Ferrer, "Genetic Criticism in the Wake of Barthes," in Rabaté, *Writing the Image after Roland Barthes,* 225.

47. CL, 105/163–64, translation slightly amended.

48. Sartre, *Psychology of Imagination,* 104.

49. Margaret Iversen brings out Lacanian elements in Barthes, including the relation to Lacan's discussion of the gaze. Margaret Iversen, "What Is a Photograph?" *Art History* 17 (1994): 450–63. See also Jacques Lacan, *The Four Fundamental Concepts of Psycho-Analysis,* ed. Jacques-Alain Miller, trans. Alan Sheridan (New York: W. W. Norton, 1977), 65–119.

50. CL, 3/13.

51. Raymond Williams, *Television: Technology and Cultural Form* (Hanover, N.H.: University Press of New England, 1992), 16–17.

52. A Yitzhak Rabin Condolence Page (www.jcn18.com/rabinpg.htm) was still up more than two years after he was murdered (November 4, 1997), but no longer existed in 2001.

53. http://members.aol.com/douglasb52/index.html, no longer in existence.

54. She also includes a postscript to "William," Diana's son.

55. See the following Ginsberg memorial sites, with links: http://www.naropa.edu/ginsberg.html, http://www.levity.com/corduroy/ginsberg/remember.htm

56. World Gardens, which still exists at http://www.worldgardens.com/, offered virtual flowers in 1997, but has since discontinued the option.

57. www.cyberspace.com/~ais/vbmain.html, run by AIC Corp. The owners of this site now request the eulogy in writing, along with a ten-dollar donation to cover costs. "Dearly departed" remains free.

58. http://www.cyberspace.com/~ais/heaven/m&d.html, no longer in existence.

59. As of August 2002, this site could be accessed at the following web address: www.angelsonline.com/pages/etawney/index.htm.

60. Adolph Goldschmidt, "Kunstgeschichte," in *Aus Fünfzig Jahren deutscher Wissenschaft. Die Entwicklung ihrer Fachgebiete in Einzeldarstellungen,* ed. Gustav Abb (Berlin: De Gruyter, 1930), 192–97.

61. On Barthes and genetic criticism, see Daniel Ferrer, "Genetic Criticism," in Rabaté, *Writing the Image after Roland Barthes,* 218.

62. Alois Riegl, *Gesammelte Aufsätze,* ed. Karl M. Swoboda (Vienna: Benno Filser, 1929), 144, 172–73. On Riegl's theory of monuments, see Margaret Olin, *Forms of Representation in Alois Riegl's Theory of Art* (University Park: Pennsylvania State University Press, 1992), 175–80.

63. Michel Certeau, *The Writing of History,* trans. Tom Conley (New York: Columbia University, 1988), 2.

64. On Van Der Zee scholarship, see Birt, "Life in American Photography," 71–73.

65. Fritz Saxl quoted Warburg as saying, "Truth lies buried in the detail," according to Heckscher, who thought Flaubert coined the phrase. Significantly, Curtius identified the crucial element as the links between the details. Heckscher, "Genesis of Iconology," 244 n. 10.

7

The Keeping Place
(Arising from an Incident on the Land)

JONATHAN BORDO

On July 20, 1998, Inuit of Pangnirtung killed a single bowhead whale off the waters of Kekerton Island in Cumberland Sound, eastern Baffin Island. Including the long three-week duration of the wait, the chase and kill, the dismemberment, the feast and the sharing of the gift, the hunt lasted about six weeks. The hunt was a herald of the political autonomy achieved by Inuit of the eastern Arctic with the creation of Nunavut as a new territory in the Canadian federation. Territorial status gives Inuit a constitutionally elected parliament and political rights and administrative powers comparable to those exercised by provinces in Canada or states in the United States. These include control over education, welfare, and natural resources. Territorial status gives Inuit territorial integrity over a vast tract of land and water, including full hunting rights. Inuit have a right of return to their ancestral lands. To indicate just how momentous the transformation is, consider that the vast expanse of territory comprises approximately 350,000 square kilometers of land (fig. 7.1).[1]

Retrospectively, the whale hunt might be thought of as Pangnirtung's symbolic contribution to this unprecedented creation of a new and democratically constituted state; however, there was something very local and intimate about it that might resist such an easy political

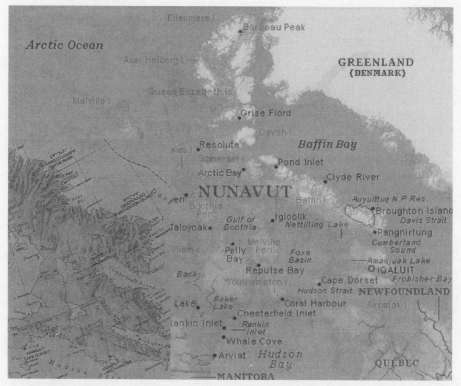

Fig. 7.1. Map of Nunavut with Tinijjuarvik (Cumberland Sound Inset). Nunavut Implementation Commission, 1995.

incorporation. The whale hunt was an event in living memory. This essay explores the special way that this event was a site of memory. I advance this articulation in two parts. In the first part, I begin with an account of my presence at the event, arising from my pursuit of landscape-art-related inquiry. I then describe three picturing practices that span the more than one hundred years of Inuit-European contact. In the second part I introduce the notion of a keeping place in order to suggest why the whale hunt eludes the commemorative expectations of Western practices of memory.

Travel Circumstances

Northern Hospitality

I was invited to attend the whale hunt because of my previous visits to Pangnirtung as part of my university teaching and writing on landscape art. "Landscape" is a rather charged and mystified word. It remains to this day, not just in Canada and Australia but in many other parts of the world, haunted by colonialist agendas that fuse the aesthetics of picturing and the legitimation of captured and territorially reconstituted lands. The critique of landscape has exercised my thought and that of other scholars over the past decade.[2]

Not landscape painting in general, not the study of a genre in art history, but rather a particular landscape image has been the object of my inquiry. The "Group of Seven" were Canadian painters, mostly from Toronto, who formed a school of landscape painting largely active in the epoch between the two world wars. The topic of the wilderness organized their landscape painting project. Its visual articulation was the principal object of their picturing practice, a symbolic contribution to the formation of the imaginary community of the emerging nation-state called Canada (fig. 7.2).[3]

To be sure, Tom Thomson and the Group of Seven did not invent the wilderness as a visual topic. The so-called Hudson River School was its most impor-

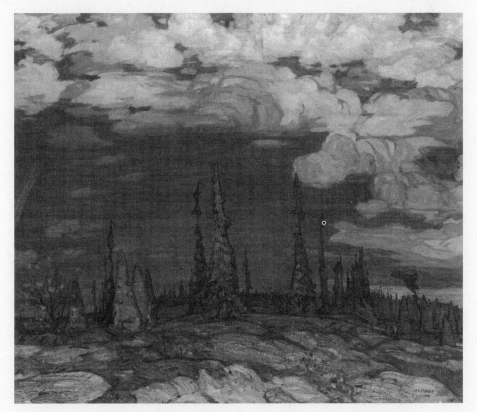

Fig. 7.2. A. Y. Jackson, *Terre Sauvage*, 1913. National Gallery of Canada, Ottawa. Reproduced by permission of the Estate of Naomi Jackson Groves.

tant, impressive, and influential cultural predecessor. This school bequeathed a visual legacy of spectacular imperial grandeur, translating an American claim to manifest destiny into aesthetic theology.[4]

At the end of the Great War, when the United States had already leapt into cosmopolitan modernism, Canada was just entering into a modernist-tinged, expressivist, and northern symbolic landscape painting project. One significant difference between the Canadian articulation of the topic of wilderness, emerging from World War I, and the pre–Civil War American version was the almost systematic and relentless way that the Group of Seven pursued the *idea* of wilderness as a state or condition bereft of human presence. The Canadian discourse of wilderness sought to extinguish the subject, while the visual discourse of American wilderness adhered to the constraints of the Kantian idea of nature. In the American discourse, "wilderness" was nature in its most pristine and untouched state, but that discourse never advanced the suppression of the specular witness.[5] Even when American transcendentalist discourse raised ontological questions concerning the viability of human existence and dwelling, the positing of a specular witness was never challenged. The American landscape is always witnessed (fig. 7.3).

The Group of Seven took the extinguishment of the subject as the premise for its visual articulation of the wilderness. For Tom Thomson and the Group of Seven, picturing wilderness is marked by a sustained effort to enun-

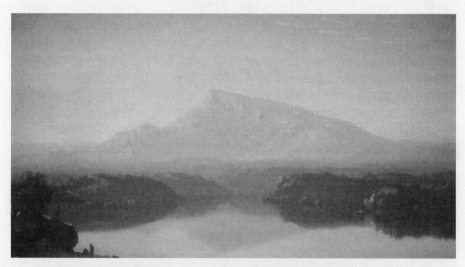

Fig. 7.3. Sanford Robinson Gifford (American, 1823–1880), *The Wilderness,* 1860, oil on canvas, 30 × 54-5/16 inches (976.2 × 138 cm), Toledo Museum of Art. Purchased with funds from the Florence Scott Libbey Bequest in Memory of her Father, Maurice A. Scott, 1951.403. Reproduced by permission of the Toledo Museum of Art.

ciate visually a metaphysical statement. In its paradoxical ambition to cross the threshold from witnessed to unwitnessed landscape, the Group of Seven systematically deleted figural traces of human presence. For this reason the nonhuman figure of a solitary tree as a spectral stand-in serves both as a paradigm and an icon for this early-twentieth-century Canadian landscape project.[6] The wilderness is thus a deliberate sign for human absence, and it aspires, however paradoxically, to be a landscape without a witness.

My inquiry into this landscape picture brought me north, eventually to be a witness to a whale hunt in Arctic waters. I was invited to travel north to behold "tundra" because a colleague treated my account of the Group of Seven's wilderness as a symbolics bounded by northern forest, which he contrasted to treeless landscape: taiga versus tundra. He contrasted my problematized arboreal wilderness marked by the erasure of human presence and its figural substitution by a solitary northern tree to the wilderness of tundra, which Inuit mark with the symbolic stone man—the Inukshuk, which means literally stone shaped as a human being.

What is an Inukshuk?

An Inukshuk contributes to a labyrinth, a great land weir for trapping and corralling herds of caribou, a network of cairns or markers on the land for Inuit out on the land. Because they are erected on tundra, an environment without trees, they are both traps set by hunters and cairns for travelers to get bearings and to gauge distance. They are also food depots, temporary dwellings, and rest stops on the peripeteia of the hunt. They may also be grave sites. The Inukshuk is thus "ready found" to be "readymade." All these tasks condense into the totemic figure of human beings in stone, arms stretched out declaring *This is a human being* or *Here there are human beings* or *Human beings are present on the land*. The word for human being in Inuktitut is *inuk*. What starts with a cosmological assertion unfolds a repertoire of pragmatic dispositions and tasks.[7]

This human effigy of piled up rocks is a declaration of hospitality. The landscape picture of the Group of Seven with its symbolics of wilderness enunciates a double absence. First, there is the absence constituted by the visual sign of the wilderness, the image as sign of human absence. Second, there is the absence that arises from the denegational logic of picturing itself: picturing wedges itself into a space-time continuum and creates a gap that allows it to interpellate and reorganize the world. Space-module-like, picturing is a displace, a condominium for travel.[8] The picture inserts itself into the world, dislocating without necessarily making any other ontological claim for itself except that it is a picture. The picture destabilizes just what the Inukshuk lays claim to as a ground. The picture in its relation to locality is not ground but *ab-grund* in

Heidegger's terms—a clearing. The Euro-Canadian landscape picture of wilderness interrupts the hospitality of the Inukshuk (figs. 7.4 and 7.5).[9]

Picture Lessons from Pangnirtung

In my own northern peripatetic reflection upon landscape as a picture, I was preceded by two travelers to Pangnirtung and its vicinity, each of whom carried distinctive and influential picturing practices. The Canadian landscape artist A. Y. Jackson traveled north in the summer of 1927 "in pursuit of the great arctic landscape," making a brief stopover in Pangnirtung in late August. Forty years earlier, in 1883, a youthful Franz Boas had passed through Pangnirtung in quest of a pure ethnographic object—"the Eskimo." Their journals provide important insights into their motivations for visiting.[10] The journals also provide invaluable insights into their practices of picturing.

> **A.Y. Jackson, Journal Entry, Monday, August 22, 1927**
> We prepared for a big day, and woke up to find rain and fog. Made some pencil drawings of Eskimo dwelling and then went up the hill back of the settlement and wandered around most of the day in the drizzle. Rich foregrounds—moss and lichens and big boulders, but above us the curtain of fog shutting everything off. . . . Well, we kept going in the drizzle, dined on some Bess Housser chocolate and returned empty-handed to the police post and had supper. All the Eskimos went out to the steamer and saw a movie show down in the coal hold. They whooped when they saw themselves, taken on a previous trip, and at Felix the Cat and at some flappers in bathing suits on the beach in Vancouver; it makes me realize right away the value of simplicity. Well, there is only Lake Harbour now, in which to find the great arctic landscape.

This is A. Y. Jackson's only entry for his brief and thwarted visit to Pangnirtung. In the Arctic there is no special place to be on the land in order to be *in* the landscape to look at it. A traveler does not leave the town, climb up past the pasturage, the cow dung and the tree line, vertically to ascend to the alpine meadow to stake out the prospect, guided by the familiar Burkean markers. Instead, a traveler to the Arctic is immersed in its environment upon arrival. Jackson was right there in "the great arctic landscape" that he sought and that persistently seems to have eluded him.

Two unrelenting disturbances blocked Jackson from discovering the

Fig. 7.4. (opposite, top) Tom Thomson, *The Jack Pine,* 1916–17. National Gallery of Canada, Ottawa.

Fig. 7.5. (opposite, bottom) Inukshuk on the land, July 1997. Photograph by Jonathan Bordo.

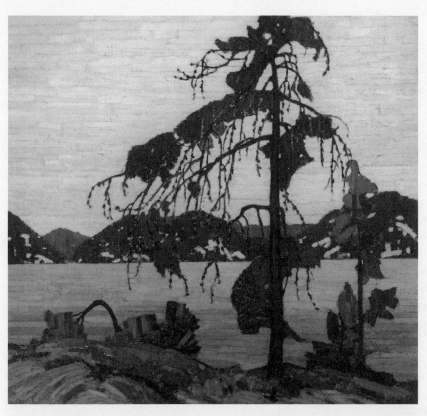

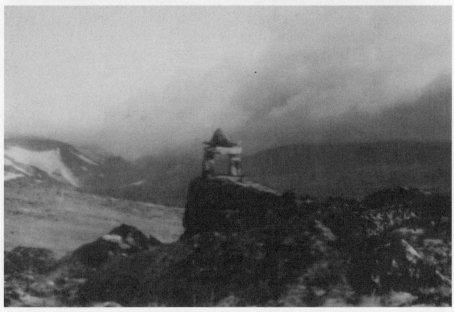

object of his pursuit — the weather and Inuit. In this entry as elsewhere, he gives a "ranger report" of the fauna and flora that he encounters. Intoning the proper names of fauna and flora contributed to Jackson's way of designating the possible color combinations of a field palette. His denominations of the flora and fauna move in and out of reports about the weather. The weather thwarts him from leaving his quarters on the ship to get out on the land. The weather forces him prematurely to interrupt his forays on the land and return mostly picture-poor to the ship. Even though he is there in a dwindling season of midnight sun, Jackson's excursions seem to be coordinated to a twelve-hour cycle. Even though there is light almost twenty-four hours a day, there is never enough time or light or the right kind of light for him. "Weather" blocks him from his pursuit. It is overcast; it is raining; it is too damp; the fog has set in.

Jackson's complaints about the weather have their own interest, particularly when one considers that Inuit seem not to have a single noun for our word *landscape* to betoken an expectation invested as an inherent quality of the external real that marks a spot as having something "picturesque" about it—having face: *prosopopeia*.[11] Inuit themselves seem to lack such a picturesque expectation. Inuktitut seems to have no single, binding substantive for "landscape." This might seem curious because Inuktitut is a language that is able to render thickly, quickly, and accurately phenomenological descriptions of the minutest modal changes in the environment: in the quality of the water brought on by changes in the winds or in the light; in the gradations of the clouds and snow; in qualities of the scat of caribou; and in the minute division of the seasons.[12] The word for all of these transformations in Inuktitut is *sila* meaning "weather."

> **A. Y. Jackson, Journal Entry, Sunday, August 28, 1927**
> We got ashore, and it seemed so strange to have sunlight I could not find anything to do. We went tearing all over the place. I have been looking for something that I visualized—it exists around here, but I did not discover it. An arctic landscape, no place in particular, a generalized landscape. . . . I got on a big hill that looked over miles of hills and lakes, and, of course, made a punk sketch.

The last landscape entry of his journal recording a perfect day prompts him to recall his reason for being up there in his painterly profession as a landscape artist. The Arctic landscape that he pursued had to conform to "a generalized landscape" that would be "no place in particular." Acting within the rule of his picturing practice, he was already in possession of that which would allow him to judge success and failure. Jackson had the equipment and the opportunity but not the occasion—Arctic weather blocked his pursuit of the image.

Jackson also knew what to exclude from his picture to realize the image. Wilderness as "a generalized landscape" image required the deletion of human presence.

A. Y. Jackson, Journal Entry, Tuesday, August 9, 1927

Low down fog shutting off everything over a hundred feet up. We went ashore in the motor boat. Swarms of birds, sea pigeon, gulls and a kind of wicked looking cuss, gull shaped but black and with his legs trailing behind in flight. New job: archeology. Nothing to sketch so we dug out some old igloos. The guy whose house I picked must have been part Scotch, he left so little. Whale bone and walrus ribs were scattered all over the place. There are remains of ingloos [sic]everywhere it was possible to hunt and get shelter, all the way to the north of Ellesmere.

The Inuit presence was everywhere, "all the way to the north of Ellesmere," wherever "it was possible to hunt and get shelter." In this regard, consider that the closest approximation to the word *wilderness* in Inuktitut is *inuilaq,* which translates literally as a place with no Inuit; since Inuit are the humans; it is thus a place without humans![13] Present but absent, Inuit had already been excluded from the picture a priori. If "bad" weather in Jackson's National Weather Bureau notion of weather was the first hindrance to his finding the general landscape, the local inhabitants themselves were the second hindrance. Since Jackson's general image was "no place in particular," nobody at all, not nobody in particular, was his maxim for picturing wilderness; and Inuit were not an exception to this rule. Indeed, to picture in accordance with his rule, his gaze had to pass through Inuit presence in order to feign it away. Thus to apply methodically his picturing gaze, he routinely swept away the incidences of Inuit, whether it was the delicate paths he walked, the bones of animals, the shelters, the skeletal remains, or of course Inukshuks! In those sentences of his journal that record forays in pursuit of landscape, there are no notes of their presence. In these non-landscape-related entries, Jackson describes their constant and overbearing presence.

Perhaps because Jackson could not resolve his image, he came to be overwhelmed by Inuit, suffocated by their presence. He met Inuit in white spaces and he suppressed them from the one space he controlled, the picture space. Thwarted in his landscape mission, he found himself falling into the enviable (for most other travelers to the north) enterprise of collecting and recording the artifacts and detritus of Inuit presence. This is "archeology" for Jackson.

> **A. Y. Jackson Journal Entry, Wednesday, August 31, 1927**
> [L]ying in crevices. A few Eskimos living in tents. They are the vanishing race, too much contact with white people is the end of them.

Inopportune weather compels him to acknowledge the existence and presence of Inuit. The picturing practice sets in motion a string of binary oppositions. What it needs, it cannot have—good weather. Inuit, excluded from the gaze of the picture in order to image "pristine" wilderness, rise up psychologically to overwhelm him. How else to explain the disdain, the grudging attitudes, and even racist-tinged outbursts against Inuit that come to appear in the latter entries, culminating in his declaring them a "vanishing race"?

Jackson's outburst is provoked by sightseeing. The whites are gathered on the steamer's deck to watch the sky. The Inuit are down in the ship's hold watching movies. How could Inuit not be watching the aurora borealis? Inuit have failed the landscape test. Instead of watching the northern lights up on the deck, they are watching Felix the Cat in the ship's hold:

> **A. Y. Jackson, Journal Entry, Wednesday, August 31, 1927**
> the aurora made great spirals in the sky the Eskimos were down in the hold seeing the movie show.

One might say that a picturing practice channels a "will to absence" into a matter of method. Jackson's discontent with the productivity of his picturing practice unfetters that will to absence—he goes from wishing Inuit not to be in the picture to wishing Inuit not to be. The fragile lattice of Jackson's split view collapses toward the end of his visit. *Willing absence* moves from method to angry outburst. It was time for Jackson to leave.[14]

Jackson's visit took place a few years after the collapse of the whale industry. The impoverished conditions of Inuit life that he observed at Pangnirtung were consequent upon the collapse of the whale economy, causing Inuit to take refuge at Pangnirtung.[15]

While Jackson seemed to will the vanishing of aboriginal presence in pursuit of a sovereign national image, Franz Boas forty years before set as his ambition to discover and preserve the remaining vestiges of an authentic Eskimo form of life as a pure and untainted ethnographic object. The construction of an objective picture of Inuit as a pure ethnographic object before they vanished motivated Boas to travel to the Arctic and stay over winter in 1883–84. It was his first field excursion in pursuit of an ambitious geographical program. Boas sought to bring the Inuit form of life within the physical and environmental determinations of geographical representation. His recently published journals and letters from his sojourn in Cumberland Sound consist of two manuscripts, one a journal that he addressed to his fiancée and the other the minutes of his daily research practice.[16] Befriended by James Mutch, the factor of the Scottish whaling station, Boas secured rooms in its cramped quarters. He devoted each day to measuring tides, collecting physical specimens and cultural artifacts, and taking bearings for the construction of a Mercator map of Cumberland Sound. He also meticulously gathered Inuit place-names for this map.[17] The place-name for this area in Inuktitut is Tinijjuarvik.

Consider Boas's practice to be the second picture lesson from Pangnirtung. Whereas Jackson's picture was subjective and expressivist, Boas's was objective and empirical in keeping with the scientific world picture.

Boas was witness to a disaster that he recorded faithfully, not as a disaster but as an ethnography of an endangered form of life. Like many others of that generation including Baldwin Spencer, he believed that he was preserving the record of a vanishing form of life. The European advent in the waters of Tinijjuarvik/Cumberland Sound was, as many have written, a disaster for the Inuit that almost led to their collective destruction. The Inuit were vulnerable to the diseases that the Europeans brought, and the powerful magnet of attraction of the whaling station prompted a sudden and dramatic demographic shift into the sedentary confines at Kekerton that left them dependent, and often destitute—a classic toxic case of Alfred Crosby's ecological imperialism.[18] To take an example, Boas notes in his journals the deaths of over twenty Inuit from diphtheria and pneumonia that he personally witnessed:

Franz Boas, Journal Entry, October 26, 1883

[N]ow fortunately I have finished setting up my meteorological instruments and hope to be able to get a decent run of readings at least until I leave Kekkerton. On the day before we arrived here, I was called to see a sick woman, who probably had pneumonia. I was expected to help the poor woman but could do nothing. They sat there the whole day and "ankuted" (lit. *anguqtuq* = exorcised) while the woman sat, her body uncovered in a cold tupik and the wind and the weather blew in her face. I wanted to ensure that she at least wrapped herself up, but there could be no thought of that since her belief in the angekoks (angakkuq = shaman) is stronger than anything else. She died yesterday and I feel really miserable that I was unable to help.[19]

From Boas's obvious inability to satisfy Inuit that he had powers equal to or greater than that of a shaman, vouchsafed by his "Herr Dr." status, he soon found himself treated not as a healer but as a scapegoat. That he might indeed be the carrier of European diseases seems not to have occurred to Boas, if the journals and letters are to be counted as evidence. Boas was so absorbed in constructing his scientific picture of an emerging ethnographic object that he called "the Eskimo" that he never became aware of the consequences of his practical participation with and dependency upon Inuit at the whaling station. Inuit at Kekerton were simultaneously both his material conveyances and the objects of his emerging ethnographic practice. Boas seems never to have considered himself either an epistemological disturbance to the objectivity of his inquiry or a social disturbance to the Inuit he intended to study. In his pursuit of an ethnographically untainted object, Boas did not have a single ethnographic encounter that was not carried along and infected by the communication belt of the whaling station. On the one hand, the whaling station was the communication channel; on the other hand, from a communications point of view, Boas was the Serrean parasite who contributed to the channel while becoming an obstacle to communication. In part he was an obstacle because he never considered his theory to be necessarily in a situation of mediation. Boas's insistence on an objective epistemological stance prevented such recognition. While the aesthetic stance of Jackson feigned away the indigenous presence as a disturbance to the picture, the objective specular stance of Boas affirmed an indigenous presence as an object of pure inquiry by denying the material and existential presence of the inquiring subject, Franz Boas. One might say that the picturing practices of Boas and Jackson are two sides of the same world picture.

Boas's journals and letters provide the intimate and touching details of life at Kekerton. They show how the sustained contact, an enthralling attraction, was a near fatal misadventure for the Inuit. The way the disaster of this sustained Inuit-white contact is reflected in the picturing practices of Inuit themselves is the third picture lesson from Pangnirtung. The men of the Hunters and Trappers Association at Pangnirtung who organized the July 1998 hunt never spoke about the whaling era as a disaster, at least to my knowledge,[20] and yet the threads lead back to this era and not to a time prior to the arrival of the whalers as the justification for the hunt.

First, the need to recall the period of the whaling was declared simply and eloquently by the elder Aksayuk Eduangat, the last living Inuit to have participated in whaling before its close in 1923 and the very same Eduangat who viewed the Boas map one hundred years later in 1984. Eduangat, in his narration in the film *Remember,* says: "Come see how we used to hunt the great whale from the deep, how we worked for Qadlunnat and how we lived off the land after the whalers left, the old ways are dying, we shall remember."[21]

The end to the old ways was brought about by the contact between the Inuit and the whalers. The film, made by the Inuit Broadcasting Corporation, recalls not the old ways *before* the whaling but the "old ways" *of* the whaling era and the threat to Inuit ways *after* the whaling ended. Eduangat narrates that epoch without calling it a "disaster." When he says as a speech act, *"We shall remember"*—an injunction to remember cast in the future—the site of memory of the whale hunt is already being prepared for an event still to take place and that will take place not so long after his death in July 1998. The expanse under the place-name "Kekerton" was clan lands before and even during the epoch of the whalers; the clan lands became a whaling station; because it was a whaling station, it attracted visitors. Thus it was not coincidental that the families who actively participated in the hunt of July 1998 played a major part in the whaling. It may well have been that Aksayuk Eduangat encountered Jackson as a youth, may have been down in the ship's hold watching Felix the Cat to Jackson's chagrin. Jackson's visit took place after the collapse of the whaling in Cumberland Sound and the retreat of the Inuit in destitution to Pangnirtung, where another white settlement around the Hudson Bay Company and the Anglican church had taken hold. Aksayuk Eduangat's testimony brings into the present as an oral narrative the era of Franz Boas and connects the whaling era to the new era of an emerging Canadian colonial presence. Eduangat's life is a bridge between Boas and Jackson. Thus it is significant that Aksayuk Eduangat had the occasion to examine the map that Franz Boas constructed of Cumberland Sound in 1883. Indeed the epoch of European whaling in the waters of Cumberland Sound is the main subject of the dialectically presented displays at the Angmarlik Center, a center named after the most renowned Inuit whaler in the employ of the Scots, who is buried in the Scottish cemetery at Kekerton. The legends accompanying these displays not only present the history of the contact between Inuit and whalers but speak about it as if this was when "history" began; with the coming of the whalers, an era called "history" commenced. One might say that Inuit history began in 1843 and what Inuit would mean by that is that a European mode of timekeeping was absorbed into Inuit narrative practices and not the other way around. That these events were a "disaster" is an interpretation that arises when Inuit historicize themselves. It is one version of the story. From one point of view, the history is ritual mimetic, from another, it is chronological. Both are contained in Eduangat's narrative as well as his act of turning Boas's map into a document of contemporary Inuit culture (fig. 7.6).

The disaster as a leitmotif of commemoration is poignantly and remark-

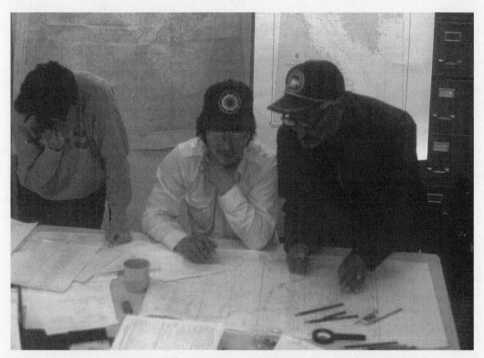

Fig. 7.6. Aksayuk Eduangat and Alan Angmarlik studying Franz Boas's map and other materials, Pangnirtung, August 1984. Photo courtesy of Ludger Müller-Wille, Montreal.

ably indicated in the way that contemporary Inuit artists at Pangnirtung render animals in their prints. The prints contain their own history of white-Inuit relations going back to the mid-nineteenth century. They carry their own account of the disaster. In my initial viewings of the collection of prints at the Pangnirtung Print Shop in the summer of 1997, I noted with uneasy premonition that animals on the endangered list—whales, husky dogs, seals—received the most loving, lyrical, and vivacious visual renderings. Each of these animal species, upon which the Inuit have been most dependent for their sustenance, either has been eliminated (as in the case of the whale and the husky dog) or is endangered (as in the case of seals). Indeed each animal kind might be taken generically to represent an epoch in the era of coloniality from 1840 to 1998.[22] These images evidence the loss of their animals commencing in the first epoch of the colonial era with the destruction of the bowhead whale. Inuit imaging of their animals might be taken as an allegory of the disaster, whose threatening actuality only occasionally breaks the lyrical and placid surface of the images themselves. The images are afterimages.

The picturing practices of Boas and Jackson were infused with the belief that a picture was adequate to carry the freight of the world. Each man considered the picture to be the ground and reason for his travel. Inuit picturing practice acquired from the whites may be votive, ritual-mimetic, and totemic but it is not "foundational" in the world-picture sense in the same way as Boas's and Jackson's are. Indeed printmaking is a rather ad hoc and recent medium that arose with the postwar creation of settlements. The prints provided a conveyance for expressing their attachment to their animals. It is not mimetic in the Platonic sense of "an essential copy"[23] but carries affiliation and attachment, akin to tattoos, decals, and transfers. Contemporary Inuit practices of representation are pictures freed of the world picture.

These three practices of picturing offer a clue to understanding the significance of the Pangnirtung whale hunt. The picturing practice of the prints remembers by keeping the animals alive as images, just as the filmic presence of the recently deceased elder Aksayuk Eduanagat is considered as a living presence calling upon his community to remember the era of whaling. To observe this transformation, I briefly return to Boas's map and the recent Inuit history of it. This map may have been the first ethnographic map of its kind to use exclusively indigenous place-names. A remarkable linkage in the transmission belt of living memory took place in the summer of 1984 when Ludger Müller-Wille showed a copy of the map to Aksayuk Eduangat, one hundred years after Boas's visit to Tinijjuarvik. For Eduangat and other elders at Pangnirtung to see the map full of Inuit place-names, place-names that they could check against their memory, must have been an extraordinary event. Maps change hands and purposes. In this rare case, a map is returned and in returning becomes itself a contribution to contemporary aboriginal history.

The film, the prints and the map are living images, documents, and *events* in contemporary Inuit history.[24]

Site-as-Event

Volonté de Mémoire

Pierre Nora, the director of the encyclopedic *Lieux de mémoire*,[25] has the ambition to inaugurate a new practice of memory through the constitution of a new object that he calls a *lieu de mémoire*. He seeks to articulate this new practice of memory by distinguishing it from the usual and familiar sites of memory (monuments, documents in archives, art works in galleries, traces in museums, texts in libraries) and the modern practices of memory that support these sites. For Nora a *lieu de mémoire* is fueled by what he calls a *volonté de mémoire*. The combination of words making up this term recalls Rousseau and Bergson. Evoking Rousseau's *volonté générale,* it suggests a memory that is a corporate, civil, and social obligation. Evoking Bergson's *mémoire volontaire,* it suggests a kind of memory that is intentional, conscious, collective, habitual, and willful. In short, *volonté de mémoire* betokens a memory secured by memorization. Bergson contrasted such memory disparagingly to what he called *mémoire involontaire,* true memory that is unwilled, occasional, uncontrollable, and individual. Perhaps Nora emphasizes the voluntarist and deliberate aspect of social memory because he feels so strongly that the national patrimony of France is being forgotten. Nora's premonition of France sliding into collective amnesia is abetted by the fact that professional and scientific practices of memory continue to fill the archives, libraries, museums, and other myriad repositories of France with the artifacts of that very patrimony.[26] It is almost as if for Nora there were an implicit negative correlation between the excess of the state's investment in official and public memory and a societal dearth of genuine remembrance. Nora develops a semiotic approach to memory by arguing for a distinction between memory and history, where "history" comes to be the shorthand for objective and scientific historiographical practices, most notably scientific historiography, archaeology, and art history. For Nora a *lieu de mémoire* must be animated by an ongoing and active *volonté de mémoire.* His requirement is present, contemporary, and active. The present active tense of the new practice calls for living witnesses who are the agents of this practice. The need for living witnesses to orient the temporality so that the past is brought into the present, made present, distinguishes the new practice of memory from archaeology, scientific historiography, and art history. A scientific practice of memory establishes its specific epistemological objects by delineating its own specific temporal field. Within its domain, it offers artifactual evidences of the past that serve as tokens for the memory it writes. These artifacts are thus evidential tokens of the past, memory-objects or *memes,* as if to say that to know them counts as recalling the past.

Such epistemologically grounded preservation is at the core of modern practices of memory. *To keep the past in the past* is what marks their orientation. They require the nonexpert community to appreciate the past by studying the products of historiographical memory. By learning about these objects, attested to belong irretrievably to the past, a nonexpert public shares in this memory. Looking at an object behind some glass might well recall the past. Such directed looking would be like committing that object to memory. To look at it is to confirm its previously established epistemological value as a fact. History demands that a nonexpert public memorize its facts as social memory lest we repeat the past.

Nora's notion of *volonté de mémoire* provides a countervailing criterion because it allows him to break with the preservationist rule of modern objective practices of memory to keep the past in the past. The presentist, revivalist, and contemporary orientation of Nora's program for a new practice of memory reveals itself in the following passage where he explains why sites of great antiquity have no significant bearing on his project:

> What makes certain prehistoric, geographical or archeological sites ex-
> alted sites often excludes them from being sites of memory because of the ab-
> solute absence of a will to memory which is compensated by the crushing
> weight that they bear as holding temporality, knowledge, the dream and hu-
> man memory.[27]

From this point of view, archaeology might be thought of as a practice bereft of a *volonté de mémoire* because the locals themselves are extinct, bereft of what might be called living witnesses. The archaeological site, at least in its theoretical rigor, proposes a longer, deeper, and ruptural notion of historical time, outside living memory. It posits a "deep past" before the historical past—"prehistory." The temporal slot into which archaeology makes its theoretical insertion, to constitute its site, is methodologically on the other side of the threshold between the historical past and the deep past. Archaeology posits, at least as an ideal limit, an absolute divide between traces of extinct human descendants and descendants who continue to exist as living witnesses. The archaeological site ought to be without such inheritance, as if it belonged to prehistory without relevant human succession. Archaeological sites are from a methodological point of view dormant. Archaeology's role arises faute de mieux in the absence of such custodians or living witnesses. Archaeological sites should be without inheritance.

It could be said that archaeology performs a proxy role of representing no longer living witnesses, in the name of a more abstract human constituency— race, nation, humanity itself. Indeed, the very way that archaeology makes a theoretical insertion might well require the site to be declared dormant, bereft of living memory. In this way it might even, and often does, substitute itself for and preempt living witnesses. Perhaps for this reason above all else, archaeological practice has, for Nora, a diminished *volonté de mémoire*. For this reason, archaeological sites and many rock art sites belonging to the deep past or even the historical past seem not to count for Nora either as primary sites of memory or as norms for regulating his notion of a *lieu de mémoire*.

To curate a "site" as a locale of memory means to bring it within the regimen of a practice of memory. The site is not synonymous with the locale; *site* refers to whatever agendas (religious, scientific, ideological) are brought to a "spot" to make it a locale of memory. Thus a locale of memory can have many, even conflicting sites at the same time (consider the intractable and conflict-ridden ones—Temple Mount/Noble Sanctuary, the Plains of Abraham). Nora seeks to dislodge historical practices of memory whose apostolic functions are to preserve the locales as sites of the past and to redirect them so that they require living witnesses. The whale hunt of July 1998, the event at the locale of Kekerton, seems to meet to the highest degree Nora's criterion that the *volonté de mémoire* mark a *lieu de mémoire*.

Let me call a site of memory that in principle gives dominance to living witnesses a "keeping place" and thus distinguish it from all those depositories of memory where preservation takes precedence over recollection—museums, galleries, archives, and so on. It was in the 1980s that the "keeping place" emerged as a distinct site of memory in Canada and Australia when the Kow Swamp Pleistocene burials were disposed of by the Echucha people of Victoria, Australia, after having been retrieved from a construction site and saved by archaeologists. Instead of establishing a joint custodianship where preservation could coexist alongside and in support of ritual curatorship by local indigenous people who claimed these remains to be theirs, the Echucha people dumped the Kow Swamp burials into the river, condemning the archaeologists for having desecrated their burial site. The archaeologist D. J. Mulvaney articulated the notion of the keeping place as the potential institutional depository to hold such precious, sensitive, and living stores. He adopted the term "keeping place" in order to bridge the apparent unresolvable contradictions in the situation:

> The prudent compromise over Kow Swamps, which kept future options open, and did not place the burden of reaching a final solution upon a small community, would have been to place them in a ritual center under absolute community custodianship. There are precedents in Australia for such Keeping Places. A suitably designed underground vault, entry to which is controlled (or denied) by the community, simulates the burial process.[28]

Mulvaney thus posits a keeping place as a *new* site of memory distinct from the typical modern depositories such as museums, galleries, and archives in that living custodians are the dominant keepers of these precious and sensitive things. "Keeping place" as a designation opens the possibility for a division between a *heritage* or generalized legacy and a *lieu de mémoire* requiring interested, engaged, and culturally specific custodian-witnesses. Indeed, there are many such sites of contested curatorship in Australia and Canada and doubtless elsewhere. Such sites are marked by a continuing contestation over custodianship between a hegemonic state-sanctioned practice of memory that acts as if there are no living witnesses and practices of memory that acknowledge living witnesses who claim these traces to be theirs to curate.

Kekerton is truly a keeping place or at least a part of one. The jurisdiction over the site and the access to it are completely in the hands of Inuit. Kekerton Island and the whaling station are part of an archipelago of locales throughout Tinijjuarvik that are administered by an Inuit-run ritual center at Pangnirtung called the Angmarlik Center. The center holds a variety of objects that have special mnemonic value—baleine, narwhal tusks, carvings, photographs. It also presents as displays a dialectical history of local Inuit culture. The Center consists of an elders room, objects behind glass, some diacritical displays, the town library, a video room, and bound volumes of photographs placed on a table before a picture window that faces out onto the fjord. The heart of the center is without doubt the elders room with comfortable chairs and tables and a tea kettle. Instituted to accommodate elders, it invites rumination and storytelling. On the wall to one side are photographs going back to the whaling era. There is a grouping of photographs of the elder Aksayuk Eduangat, including his citation for the Order of Canada. The center also performs other roles. In order to visit Kekerton Island or for that matter to purchase a fishing license and charter a boat, a visitor makes arrangements through the center. In this respect the Angmarlik Center performs the role of gatekeeper between insiders and visitors. I came to appreciate the fact that so much of what I considered to be cultural activity, ranging from the acquisition of carvings and prints to hiring a boat to go out to Kekerton, was part of the extended subsistence economy of Pangnirtung.

Until the whale hunt of July 1998, very few Inuit of Pangnirtung had ever visited Kekerton. Very few Inuit have prints in their homes, and virtually all of the soapstone carving leaves the community. The whale hunt was an event that took place at a locale that is itself a node in a vast and disparate keeping place whose focus or epicenter was for the month of July at the former whaling station at Kekerton Island. Aksayuk Eduangat's injunction to remember, captured in the film *Remember* referred to earlier, may be considered a premonition or even the initiating moment of the very *volonté de mémoire* that Nora speaks about. Eduangat's injunction to remember recalled the history of Inuit-white contact.[29] The film picks up the chain of memory that links the heyday of whaling to the elder's room at the center and brings it into the present.

The ruin of the whaling station is a node, a station in a vast relay of memory that spreads over Inuit lands of Tinijjuarvik. The keeping place is both material and fixed, immaterial and indefinite. The *event* is the site of memory.

Does site of memory translate Nora's term *lieu de mémoire*? Can an event be a *lieu* for Nora? Can Nora admit a practice of memory that ritually slaughters a whale as a mimetic reenactment as the *lieu de mémoire*?

WB in the Arctic

We have come to isolate the keeping place as a special kind of *lieu de mémoire*. Not every site of memory is a keeping place. Keeping places are episodic, ephemeral, and unstable; they are subject to relapses and rebirths just as they might not appear to be specially marked or institutionally framed. They may contain nothing "valuable" at all—valuable in the sense that museums and safety deposit boxes carry valuables. Keeping places can suddenly flare up. For those who are untrained or uninitiated, they may be without prospect. At their most fragile (and powerful) they are held together neither by institutional structures nor by writing as a "descriptive binder." They might be passed on by word of mouth over generations. Since the role of the keeping place is to keep the invisible invisible, keeping places may contrast with modern practices of memory where exhibition is a necessary condition for securing the artifactual deposition.[30]

A ritual act of killing is out of place at a modern heritage site. For the modern commemorating space to hold memory, it must keep the past in the past. The whale hunt seems to have cut through our armature of recollective practices—heritage, history, trauma, and so on. What began with an affront to the post-European digestive system—killing a whale and eating its flesh "raw"—continued by tampering with our very codes of commemoration. The whale hunt left no "significant" artifacts for deposition, and it did not take place in a space marked out semiotically for retrospective reflection. Kekerton does not meet the criteria for an iconic site as set forth by Nora, who speaks of a *lieu de mémoire* as an exalted icon, what he calls a *templum*.[31] It was an event that could not be repeated even though the event itself was a ritual-mimetic repetition. Pierre Nora's mnemonic ambitions seem to have official monuments as their goal. The whale hunt at Pangnirtung released modalities of remembrance; it arose from the *mémoire involontaire* even though it had to be organized under the jurisdiction of the federal government of Canada. Indeed, the event itself was conducted under the close watch of the Department of Oceans and Fisheries. Revisiting Bergson, the whale hunt triggered the *mémoire involontaire*. It broke through the frame of Bergson's second memory of pragmatic social habituation.[32]

The event was a repetition and yet would be unrepeatable even if a Noraesque memory project turned Kekerton into an official heritage site with costume dress, fiddlers, and a shot of alcohol on Fridays. The paradox of its being an "unrepeatable" repetition leads to a formulation of its last and most probing contestation. The whale hunt injected mimesis into memory. In the second chapter of *Matière et mémoire,* Bergson has nothing to say about mimetic repetition in his critique of memory as social habituation. The repetition that concerns him is rule-governed habituation that treats memorization as if it were recollection. The mimesis of a ritual act or for that matter the repetitions of play, art, or ritual are not of much concern to Bergson. They are not included in his two poles of memory, perhaps because cultual and artistic repetition fall in between his protostructuralist opposition between the *mémoire involontaire* and the *mémoire volontaire.* To elucidate briefly this point, I return for the last time to Aksayuk Eduagat and his injunction that the Inuit of Pangnirtung remember the advent of the whalers. The hunt reenacted their advent. His act of remembering was filmed and the film itself, in its indexical realness,[33] brought back to life the beloved, deceased elder. The film is a nonrepresentational mimesis. The film is the past itself speaking. Eduangat is brought back to life. The past is speaking memory in the present. As Barthes has taught, it brings back the dead, only not back fully to life. The whale hunt eucharistically recovers the past. How else could the chain of memory be enacted if not through a mimesis or through an act that can be understood only by having recourse to the concept of mimesis? The difference between a mimetic enactment that is unrepeatable and an enactment that can be endlessly repeated places the whale hunt within the domain of Bergson's *mémoire involontaire* and not Nora's *volonté de mémoire.*

Kekerton was inevitably the locale of memory because it was the locus of a disaster. Inuit families closest to the whalers returned to the ground zero of the disaster, the delirious vortex of the misadventure that endangered their very survival. All these forces gathered together into a single act that returned, almost like a repetition compulsion, in order to launch a project into the future. Is this *acting out* or *working through*? But does not Freud's analytic antinomy *acting out/working through* presuppose the disaster to be named as an incident as such? Is not the psychoanalytic periodization of the soul into archaic, historical (preconscious), and contemporary (conscious) strata a writing of occidental historiography onto the body? Its inscription onto the body allows the disaster to be read from the body. More generally does not the very grammar of social memory construe remembering as a deliberate and definite haloing, making commemoration a "meta-act" initiated by a declaration of the act as an act of remembering? It names itself as such—"The Plains of Abraham," "The Battle of the Wilderness," "The Somme," "The Shoah." By declaring itself through the linkage of the proper name to the toponym, remembering temporally and spatially, the act of remembering lifts itself out of the continuum of time, imposing "homogeneous, empty time" in Benjamin's formulation as the ruling temporality. Is this not the way Western historiography constitutes a locale of memory? Is this not why indigenous cultures charge that what Western society considers history is forgetting?

This Inuit practice of commemoration did not require some distinct act of turning back and naming the past as a disaster. Rather the commemorative event sought to put all the toxic strands to use at the locale as fuel for the event. One can proceed almost arithmetically to add into the "site" at the Kekerton locale all the significant figures and events that compose Inuit history, including missionaries, administrators, friendly and unfriendly visitors (Green Peace was expected). Each element in this boat-like conveyance added ballast to the event. The event was the site of memory at Kekerton. In W. J. T. Mitchell's whimsically exact and telling phrase, "A keeping place is a taking place."[34]

The whale hunt goes back to the beginning of the era of Canadian coloniality to recall the threat to the Inuit way of life as a threat to the animals upon which they were dependent, a threat directed at the ecological heart of their relationship with animals. The whale hunt was an annunciation. It heralded a new era with the creation of the state of Nunavut, bringing to an end the era of coloniality that began with the coming of the whalers and the traders in the first part of the nineteenth century. A painful history was absorbed into the present by the whale hunt as its site of memory, which returns us to the oldest meaning of the word *site: syte* is pain. *Syte* is the locus where incidence and incident converge as feeling. The event sought to absorb the memory of the pain and move off from it.

Over the time that I spent at Pangnirtung, the recipient of their hospitality, only one thing was asked of me individually and as a teacher, to participate by my presence and the presence of the students in the whale hunt of July 1998.[35] I was no less the carrier of landscape as a world picture than my illustrious predecessors, Franz Boas and A. Y. Jackson. Mine was a deconstructed picture, but that fact did not lessen the weight of its carriage. *Nachträglich* is the German word for such carrying; it suggests a burden, a grudge, a remittance, but also the role of being a bridge, a temporal mediator between the past and the present. The loss of an object does not lessen the burden. The wilderness picture might have carried me there, but it ran out in the way that reasons often run out, leaving me to be present there throughout the event, holding onto a picture whose spell had been broken. Unlike Boas and Jackson, I found myself compelled by my circumstances into a mediating role for theory and all the vulnerabilities that the recognition of such an epistemologically diminished justification for travel entails. Stripped of these distances, and forced to

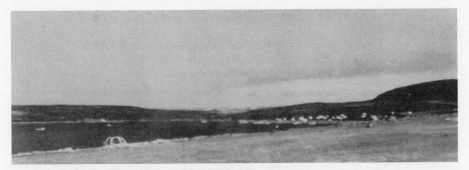

Fig. 7.7. Kekerton Island, July 1998. Photograph by Jonathan Bordo.

accept a weakened agency, I found myself unable to use the specular distance of theory to evade a responsibility in a vernacular situation arising from my awareness of my dependency and my marginal place somewhere precariously in its midst. I fell into inarticulacy, and I came to be a witness at the point where theory ran out into inarticulacy. This writing itself arises from an anxiety, a very *Qallunut* need to reciprocate that invitation by offering a delayed gesture of vicarious participation in a recollective process. This writing is an effort after several years to recall and articulate the hospitality that was offered to me as an invitation when Billy Eduangat phoned me from Pangnirtung back in the winter of 1998.

The Pangnirtung whale hunt of July 1998 brushed history against the grain (fig. 7.7).

NOTES

Special thanks to so many persons in Nunavut for their hospitality over the three summers that I spent up north: Billy Eduangat and his family, Thomassie Alikatutuk, Roy and Annie Bowkett, Steve Kanoloosie, Jaco Eshuluktuk, Simione Keenainak, Leesie Karpik, Louie Mik, and indeed the community of Pangnirtung. Andrew Tagak and Andrew junior took care of me in Iqaluit. Thanks to Harold Coward, Paul Duro, Mandy Martin, Ian McLachlan, Tom Mitchell, Keith Moxey, Ludger Müller-Wille, D. J. and Jean Mulvaney, Doreen Small, Jesper Svenbro, and Andrew Wernick, each of whom helped to advance the discourse of this essay. I am indebted to Margaret Olin and Robert Nelson for having intellectually engaged me in their locales of memory project. The research and writing for this project were greatly facilitated by a Trent Sabbatical Research Grant for the academic year 2000–2001. The essay is dedicated to the memory of Sam Brooks.

1. See Jens Dahl, Jack Hicks, and Peter Jull, eds., *Nunavut: Inuit Regain Control of Their Lands and Their Lives,* IWGIA document no.102 (Copenhagen, 2000).

2. See W. J. T. Mitchell, ed., *Landscape and Power,* 2d ed. (Chicago: University of Chicago Press, 2002); Paul Carter, *The Lie of the Land* (London: Faber, 1996); Nicholas

Thomas, ed., *Double Vision: Art Histories and Colonial Histories in the Pacific* (Cambridge: Cambridge University Press, 1999).

3. See Jonathan Bordo, "The Jack Pine: Wilderness Sublime or the Erasure of Aboriginal Presence from the Landscape," *Journal of Canadian Studies* 27 (winter 1992–93): 98–128; Jonathan Bordo, "Terra Nullius of the Wilderness," *International Journal of Canadian Studies* 15 (spring 1997): 13–36; Roald Nasgaard, *The Mystic North* (Toronto: University of Toronto Press/Art Gallery of Ontario, 1984); Charles C. Hill, *The Group of Seven: Art for a Nation* (Toronto: McClelland & Stewart/National Gallery of Canada, 1995).

4. See for example Angela Miller, *The Empire of the Eye* (Ithaca: Cornell University Press, 1993); John K. Howat, ed., *American Paradise: The World of the Hudson River School* (New York: Metropolitan Museum of Art, 1987); Elizabeth Johns, Andrew Sayers, and Elizabeth Kornhauser, *New Worlds from Old: Nineteenth Century Australian and American Landscapes* (Canberra: National Gallery of Australia,1998).

5. See Jonathan Bordo, "Picture and Witness at the Site of the Wilderness," *Critical Inquiry* 26, no. 2 (winter 2000), esp. 229–34; "Terra Nullius of the Wilderness," esp. 25–32.

6. See Bordo, "Jack Pine," 108–15; for the solitary tree as a phantom, see Bordo, "Picture and Witness," esp. 243–44.

7. Based upon conversations with Andrew Tagak and a paper that he wrote for a cultural studies course that he took with me in 1997–98. The mistakes in its elaboration are mine.

8. See Bordo, "Picture and Witness," esp. 238–43; also Louis Marin, *To Destroy Painting* (Chicago: University of Chicago Press, 1995), 45–64.

9. Concerning picturing and extinguishment and how the route to the general image had of necessity to suppress indigenous presence, see Bordo, "Picture and Witness," esp. the first two sections; see also W. J. T. Mitchell, "Holy Landscape: Israel, Palestine, and the American Wilderness," *Critical Inquiry* 26, no. 2 (winter 2000), esp. 211–13, and Edward Said, "Invention, Memory and Place," *Critical Inquiry* 26, no. 2 (winter 2000). All three essays are republished in Mitchell, *Landscape and Power.* See also Saree Makdisi, *Romantic Imperialism* (New York: Cambridge University Press, 1998), chap. 1.

10. *Franz Boas among the Inuit: Journals and Letters,* ed. and introduced by Ludger Müller-Wille, trans. William Barr (Toronto: University of Toronto Press, 1998); A. Y. Jackson, *The Arctic 1927* (Moonbeam, Ont.: Penumbra Press, 1982).

11. See for example J. Hillis Miller, *Topographies* (Stanford: Stanford University Press, 1995), 50–54.

12. See Hugh Brody, *Living Arctic* (Vancouver: Douglas and McIntyre, 1987), particularly chap. 9.

13. Alex Spalding and Thomas Kusugaq, *Inuktitut: A Multi-Dialectical Outline Dictionary,* (Iqaluit, 1998), 26.

14. Jackson would revisit the Arctic after the Second World War in a different and much more open frame of mind.

15. Marc Stevenson, *Inuit, Whalers and Cultural Persistence* (Oxford: Oxford University Press, 1997). It also coincided with the state's efforts to suppress the potlatch in West Coast aboriginal communities. See Christopher Bracken, *The Potlatch Papers* (Chicago: University of Chicago Press, 1998); Douglas Cole and Ira Chaikin, *The Law against the Potlatch* (Vancouver: Douglas and MacIntyre, 1990).

16. *Franz Boas among the Inuit of Baffin Island, 1883–84,* ed. and introduced by Ludger Müller-Wille (Toronto: University of Toronto Press, 1999), 128.

17. See Ludger Müller-Wille and Linna Weber Müller-Wille, "Inuit Geographical Knowledge a Hundred Years Apart: Place Names in [Cumberland Sound] in the 1880s and 1980s,"

in *New Directions for Inuit Studies,* ed. Pamela Stern and Lisa Stevenson (Lincoln: University of Nebraska Press, forthcoming).

18. Alfred Crosby, *Ecological Imperialism* (New York: Cambridge University Press, 1996), and Tom Griffiths and Libby Robbin, eds., *Ecology and Empire* (Melbourne: Melbourne University Press, 1997).

19. *Franz Boas among the Inuit: Journals and Letters,* 128.

20. The description of the whaling epoch as a disaster cropped up in ordinary conversation with Louee Mik and other women, and the story of this difference in the representation of recent Inuit history is still to be written.

21. *Remember,* Inuit Broadcasting Corporation, Iqaluit.

22. George Wenzel, *Animal Rights, Human Rights* (Toronto: University of Toronto Press, 1991). See also Shelagh S. Grant, *Sovereignty or Security?* (Vancouver: University of British Columbia Press, 1994), and Peter Kulchyski and Frank James Tester, *Tammarniit—Mistakes: Inuit Relocation in the Eastern Arctic, 1939–63* (Vancouver: University of British Columbia Press, 1996).

23. Norman Bryson, *Vision and Painting* (New Haven: Yale University Press, 1983), 13–35. For example, Martin Heidegger, "The Age of the World Picture," in *The Question concerning Technology* (New York: Harper & Row, 1977), 115–54. In my "Witness in the Errings of Contemporary Art," in *The Rhetoric of the Frame: Essays on the Boundaries of the Artwork,* ed. Paul Duro (Cambridge: Cambridge University Press, 1996), I develop an argument of the posit of the witness as a necessary accompaniment of the modern world picture. See especially 190–201. Ferdinand Hallyn, *The Poetic Structure of the World* (New York: Zone, 1990); Louis Marin, *To Destroy Painting* (Chicago: University of Chicago Press, 1995); W. J. T. Mitchell, *Picture Theory* (Chicago: University of Chicago Press, 1996). For modern mapping as a picture, see John Gillies, "Posed Spaces: Framing in the Age of the World Picture," in Duro, *Rhetoric of the Frame,* 24–43. For an authoritative account of early modern scientific practice as a world picture, see E. J. Dijksterhuis, *The Mechanization of the World Picture* (Oxford: Oxford University Press, 1960).

24. The film was screened in the Parks Canada Building to a full house on a Saturday in July 1998. There were also other circumstances, including the abortive whale hunt in Repulse Bay. See Helle Høgh, "Bowhead Whale Hunting in Nunavut," in Dahl, Hicks, and Jull, *Nunavut,* 196–205.

25. Pierre Nora, ed., *Lieux de mémoire,* 3 vols. (Paris: Gallimard, 1997).

26. Ibid., 1:30–32.

27. Ibid., 1:39.

28. D. J. Mulvaney, "Past Regained, Future Lost: The Kow Swamp Pleistocene Burials," *Antiquity* 65, no. 246 (March 1991): 19.

29. Michael Taussig, *Mimesis and Alterity* (New York: Routledge, 1992).

30. See my "Witness in the Errings of Contemporary Art," 197–202. Tom Griffiths, *Hunters and Collectors* (Cambridge: Cambridge University Press, 1998); D. J. Mulvaney, *Encounters in Place: Outsiders and Aboriginal Australian, 1606–1985* (Brisbane: University of Queensland Press, 1989); Sarah Clift, "Heritage and Its Gift of Transmission," M.A. thesis, Trent University, Peterborough, Ont., 1997.

31. Nora, *Lieux de mémoire,* 1:43.

32. Henri Bergson, *Matière et mémoire* (Paris: P.U.F., 1968), 92.

33. Roland Barthes, *La chambre claire: Notes sur la photographie* (Paris: Gallimard/Seuil, coll. Cahiers du cinéma, 1980); see also Margaret Olin, "Lanzmann's Shoah and the Topography of the Holocaust Film," *Representations* 57 (winter 1997): 1–23, and my

"Phantoms," in Alan Cohen, *On European Ground* (Chicago: University of Chicago Press, 2001).

34. A remark arising from his lecture entitled "Country Matters," given to the Centre for Theory, Culture and Politics, Catharine Parr Traill College, Trent University, September 27, 2002.

35. Jaco Evic, the co-captain of the hunt, was the last able Inuit to have hunted a bowhead whale in 1944. See his first-person narrative "Bowhead Whale Hunt at Qikitan Nunavut, July 1998," *Inuktitut* 85 (1999): 44–66. For an eyewitness report on the duration of the whale hunt at Kekerton in July 1998, see David Laurence Dunne, "The Bowhead Whale Hunt at Kekerton, Nunavut Territory (July 1998)," M.A. thesis, Trent University, Peterborough Ont., 2002.

Building a Marker of Nuclear Warning

JULIA BRYAN-WILSON

These structures mark an area used to bury radioactive wastes.

This place was chosen to put this dangerous material far away from people.

Do not drill here.

Do not dig here.

Do not do anything with the rocks or water in this area.

Do not destroy this marker.

This marking system has been designed to last 10,000 years.

Proposed text to be inscribed on stone monoliths

at the Waste Isolation Pilot Plant nuclear waste storage facility

On March 26, 1999, New Mexico's Waste Isolation Pilot Plant began storing used nuclear fuel and high-level radioactive transuranic waste from the U.S. nuclear weapons industry. Located in a rural area twenty-six miles east of Carlsbad, New Mexico, the Waste Isolation Pilot Plant, known as WIPP, is the only receptacle for transuranic waste in the United States, receiving shipments from more than twenty nuclear weapons plants around the country.[1] The waste, including sludge from spent nuclear fuel as well as gloves, hats, rags, and other radioactively contaminated tools, is packed into fifty-five-gallon steel drums, then neatly stacked in cavernous chambers nearly half a mile underground. In the year 2030, when the storage facility reaches its maximum capacity after receiving more than thirty-seven thousand shipments, it will be permanently sealed. At that time, the transportation facilities and maintenance buildings now planted over the deep storage site will be shut down and dismantled, and its 850,000 barrels of radioactive waste are meant to sit undisturbed in perpetuity, embedded within the underground salt-rock formations of this arid southwest landscape.

Transuranic waste includes plutonium and neptunium, which are heavier elements than uranium and much more dangerous. These elements are lethal even if inhaled in minuscule doses and have astounding longevity: neptunium's half-life is approximately two million years. In addition, plutonium is a highly mobile particle which can leak into groundwater, be absorbed into underwater crevices, or form a high-pressure gas that can seep corrosive energies out onto the surface of the earth. Because these materials retain their toxic potential so far into the future, WIPP has taken extra precautions to ensure their inaccessibility and has assured critics that the salt walls will slowly creep inward, surrounding the barrels on all sides to create an impenetrable seal.

This is the first and only permanent deep geologic waste dump in the world, the single site where radioactive matter—which will continue to be lethal for over 200,000 years—is to be housed, secure, forever. Of course, forever is a long time, and the entire area could one day be flooded with water as it was centuries ago, or earthquakes could rock the region and disrupt the salt beds. Predicting what the earth will do for the next few hundred millennia necessitates the calculation of geologic, climatologic, seismic, volcanic, tectonic, and hydrologic probabilities.[2] The U.S. Department of Energy believes (and has promised, in its many reports to Congress during the twenty-year process of approval/construction of WIPP) that this site is geologically stable: there is negligible risk of earthquakes, volcanoes, or other breachable openings.[3] Only human intervention, WIPP claims, could cause these matters to leach out from their engineered graveyard. Thus the Environmental Protection Agency's regulation 40 CFR Part 191 has mandated that the WIPP site maximize impenetrability against human encroachment for the next ten thousand years.[4]

Guessing what the earth might do in the next ten thousand years is one thing; guessing what *humans* will do over the next five hundred generations is its own special problem. The WIPP builders must account for the possibility of human intrusion into the underground chambers—drilling, mining, or excavating—until the year 12,030 A.D. The EPA, in an attempt to forecast how future populations will interact with this storage facility, has ordered a highly visible marker to be placed over the dump, decreeing that "disposal sites shall be designated by the most permanent markers, records, and other passive institutional controls practicable to indicate the dangers of wastes and their locations."[5]

To prevent future generations from digging, inhabiting, or planting this poisoned terrain, a government-appointed team of anthropologists, linguists, archaeologists, and engineers is currently involved in fabricating a warning marker to be constructed over the vault once it is sealed in 2030.[6] In a Department of Energy–sponsored workshop that took place in 1991, this team sketched out a series of preliminary designs and schematic plans for a marker. These plans form the basis for my investigation here. The team intends for the marker to survive the next ten millennia while continually broadcasting its message of danger with no slippage or decay of meaning. Here the stakes of "reading the visible" are urgent and bodily—genetic damage or death awaits those who misunderstand. How can existing iconographies convey this threat long past the projected decline of current semiotic systems? The marker must transmit its warning information to any and all future societies, whether illiterate or unthinkably technologically advanced.

Unable to predict how visual clues will be understood in the future, and certain that current languages will have long since faded into the arcane, the designers of the marker, referred to in official government documents as the Marker Panel, attempt to forge an architecture which will *permanently* signify the presence of danger. As the report states: "[A] major premise of our work is that the physical form of the entire WIPP and each of its structures can be communicated through a universal, 'natural language' of forms."[7] This statement, with its totalizing pursuit of the universal, seems open to all kinds of academic derision, as it is made in the wake of decades-old debates about cultural specificity and the "period eye."[8] Yet the Marker Panel takes this belief as their starting point and addresses the charge of developing a "universal language of forms" seriously, as if it were, indeed, a matter of life and death.

The panel put forth several options, all of which are currently under review: one will be chosen and built in approximately thirty years at the cost of millions of dollars.[9] Sandia National Laboratory's three-hundred-page report *Expert Judgment on Markers to Deter Inadvertent Human Intrusion into High Level Waste Sites* emphasizes that the scale of this marker will be "colossal . . . equivalent to the pyramid complexes of Egypt."[10] The simple placement of a low earthen wall around the boundary of the site (almost sixteen square miles) would require the excavation of twelve million cubic meters of earth: a gargantuan task involving incredible financial expenditure and labor power.[11]

Thus this hazardous dump will sprout above it one of the biggest construction projects in history, and it will loom over the dry, scrubby landscape to be visible not only from a great distance but also, according to some plans, from space.

To speculate about how such a monumental topos will be deciphered in the centuries to come, the designers mined the past, locating historical icons of threat to find effective symbols of caution and repulsion. Seeking lessons about the mechanics of monumentality, the WIPP team studied archaeological evidence such as Stonehenge, the Great Wall of China, the Egyptian pyramids, and Peru's Nazca lines for design ideas. None of the historical precedents studied by the panel were devoted to devalued sites; the WIPP marker is unique because it will designate not a site of worship or worth but one of toxic, deadly garbage. Looking at highly guarded sacred sites and taboo regions, the panel concluded that the most permanent, visible, and durable marker would follow what they refer to as the Stonehenge model. Stonehenge, of course, does not prevent access to its site; rather, it has become a tourist mecca, and its power to draw thousands of visitors each year stands in sharp contradiction to the fundamentally prophylactic charge of the WIPP marker. Disregarding this major flaw in logic, the panel decrees that the marker will consist of megaliths from thirty to seventy feet in height, constructed of local, common, and valueless materials.[12] The preferred designs also emphasize a high level of redundancy; multiple monoliths increase the probability that some will remain if others are destroyed, damaged, or removed.

Many of the proposed marker designs utilize similar visible codes. "Landscape of Thorns" (fig. 8.1) consists of towering fields of jagged stone spikes littered on the land where the waste is buried.[13] However, if the marker were only a vertical masonry monument, it would risk being read as honorific or commemorative; thus in "Landscape of Thorns" the danger is meant to be conveyed via an anti-artistic, anti-elegant, archaic style that belies both its careful investment in technology and the highly engineered waste dump beneath it. The thicket of thorns leans precariously, implying or threatening imminent catastrophe. Each rough, uneven stone, made of local basalt or granite, will weigh sixty tons or more, thus minimizing the likelihood that they will get carted off and used for other projects. Supplementing these megaliths will be a million buried glass or ceramic objects emblazoned with warnings seeding the entire area. These are but one element of an organized environment of signs, which includes a message kiosk, capsules scattered throughout the site, a buried information center, and an archive located elsewhere with detailed maps and scientific materials in many languages.

"Skull and Crossbones Used for Earthworks, at Closure and after 500 Years" follows a recommendation from Carl Sagan, the most illustrious expert

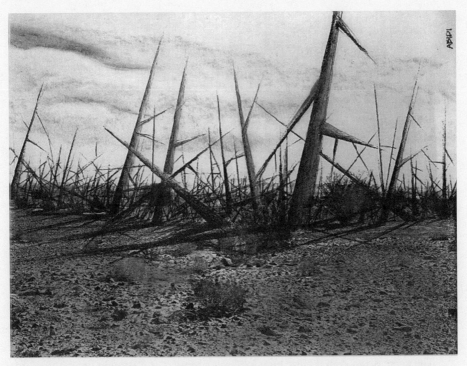

Fig. 8.1. "Landscape of Thorns, view 1." Concept by Michael Brill. Art by Safdar Abidi. Courtesy Estate of Michael Brill.

consulted.[14] Two drawings in *Expert Judgment* show a large earthen skull-and-crossbones laid atop the waste storage area. One drawing shows it when first built, its hollow face rendered with neat lines; the other shows it five hundred years later, irrevocably disintegrated. Because it lies low to the ground and relies on a certain coherence of shape, it is subject to a far more rapid deterioration than the already-ruined look of the "Landscape of Thorns," whose sinister ruggedness would only increase with time. The forecasted decay of the formerly crisp outline well beyond the point of readability led the designers to veto the idea, for there will be no upkeep of these grounds after 2030 when the dump closes. (The EPA stipulates that the WIPP marker must signify on its own, passively, with no guards or maintenance staff.)[15] "Skull and Crossbones" encapsulates many of the marker features the panel ultimately abandoned: a design which hugs, rather than juts from, the ground; a projected softening of form; and a reliance on an arbitrary sign that, although widely used today, has no inherent relation to the idea of radioactivity or danger. Despite Sagan's confident assertion that it is the "one tried and true . . . transcultural symbol with unmistakable meaning,"[16] in today's lexicon the skull and crossbones could as easily signify "pirates" as "poison."

Ultimately, a giant Mr. Yuk face in the desert or its equivalent was deemed insufficient given the malignant potency of nearly six million cubic feet of nuclear waste.[17] The urgent message the panelists want to sound across the next five hundred generations—"KEEP OUT!"—is a speech act they hope is so powerful that it will continue to resonate despite the unforeseen evolution of both visual and verbal languages. The panel undertakes a semiotic task, then, which is no less than the permanent cementing of the signifier to the signified. In order to execute this task (an impossible post-Saussurian maneuver), the panel has recourse to the cultural symbolism of Carl Jung, operating from a logic of archetypes infused with an almost psychic, rather than cognitive, meaning. Struggling to come up with an ensemble of such symbols, the panel looks to what it sees as the "uncoded" sign systems of the human body.

The panel researched previous, more literal precedents for the "universalism" of the human figure, such as NASA's 1971 Pioneer spacecraft with its plaque of two naked humans, the man waving a greeting,[18] and the more comprehensive 1977 Voyager space capsule meant to introduce aliens to the human race.[19] (In fact, astronomer Frank Drake of UC–Santa Cruz was on the team that designed the Voyager spacecraft as well as the WIPP Marker Panel.) The panel decided that basic human physiognomy is one element of iconography unlikely to change and that physical gestures of repulsion and disgust are "cross-culturally unambiguous."[20] One proposed warning sign twins a crude sketch of Edvard Munch's *The Scream* with a drawing of a nauseated man from an anthropological textbook on facial features depicting the registration of disgust.[21] Assuming a transparent and inert meaning for these faces, and with no consideration for how these faces might be very specifically raced, gendered, or otherwise freighted with meanings that might complicate the intended message, the committee relies on bodily gestures to provide the most basic level of information: the distressed expressions on the warning plaque indicate that something man-made, and dangerous, lurks beneath. For the panel, these faces have a fixed signification that transmits the idea of threat with a crystalline purity. Wresting Munch's face from its painted context, they equate this art historical element with a diagram, hardening its interpretive ambiguity in an effort to turn art into science. However, these message plaques do not reach the level of imposing size deemed necessary, so the panel proposed incorporating them within more specialized message centers and inscribing them onto a series of megaliths. For the linchpin of this constellation of symbols—the central, stabilizing component that gives the warning system meaning—is the above-ground marker: it is this area that does the heaviest work to either deter or attract visitors. The huge spikes, as well as the agonizing faces, are what will, it is hoped, refuse all curious eyes and bodies both from a distance and up close.

While massive earthen works have materially survived for several millennia and are found all over the world, their precise meaning or function often remains a matter of conjecture to us today; but the designers of the marker push for a foreboding, and physically colossal, plan, insisting that such a marker will be resistant to decay both from the natural elements and from the inevitable mutation of current symbology. The designers fantasize about something that can persist through any political, economic, or ecological change— and hence, they deduce, a certain amount of spectacularity is required. As one panelist put it, "[A] marker system should be chosen that instills awe, pride, and admiration, as it is these feelings that motivate people to maintain ancient markers, monuments, and buildings."[22] Since any physical barrier erected could be eventually breached, the panel focuses instead on psychological, fear-instilling obstacles that express prohibition and inhibit interest.

In the "Black Hole" sketches (fig. 8.2), the area above the storage site is covered with dark, irregularly cracked and jagged asphalt. Here the designers marshal what they see as the inherent ugliness of the landscape itself as a de-

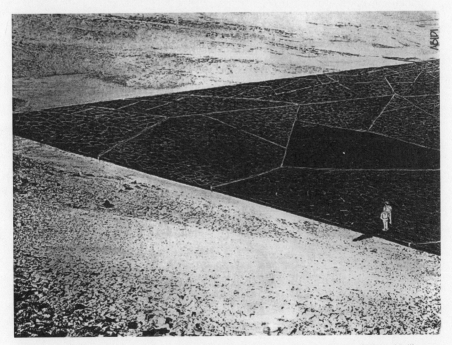

Fig. 8.2. "Black Hole." Concept by Michael Brill. Art by Safdar Abidi. Courtesy Estate of Michael Brill.

terrent. This proposal turns the hot desert into a patchwork black parking lot—surely a repellent structure if there ever was one. Its description reads: "[T]he heat of this black slab will generate substantial thermal movement. It should have thick expansion joints in a pattern that is irregular, like a crazy-quilt, like the cracks in parched land. And the surface of the slab should un-dulate, so as to shed sand in patterns in the direction of the wind."[23] While the black asphalt is at once a visual sign of danger, its sheer scale and radiant heat become a corporeal threat as well, as anyone attempting to cross it bakes on its hot surface.

The designs self-consciously avoid centering the monument or creating perfect forms employing Greek standards of proportion, not wanting to indi-cate that treasures can be found underneath. Instead, the panel plans to spread the entire contaminated plot with rubble ("Rubble Landscape"), blackened stones ("Forbidding Blocks"), or spikes poking through an uninhabitable grid ("Spikes in Grid"). A self-conscious primitivizing is effected, featuring irregu-lar geometries, rough-hewn edges, an eschewing of craftsmanship, and a de-nial of technological sophistication. The panel attempts to create a primordial response, a powerful place charged with somatically felt, rather than under-stood, meaning—triggering notions of a void, abyss, or, as the openly Jung-influenced report puts it, "fear of the beast."[24]

However, the panel recognizes that while the marker should be visually compelling, it should avoid the fate of previous dramatic emblems of deter-rence, which have been ignored or dismissed only to later become destination points for inquisitive tourists. The tombs of Egyptian rulers, while still visible today, were repeatedly raided despite sentinels and elaborate warnings. This is a paradoxical charge: the marker must be monumental but not too monu-mental, visible yet repulsive to sight, incredible and legible, but not so loaded with specialized information that it will be too complicated for an illiterate wanderer to understand. In the preferred designs, erosion over time will only enhance the marker's aesthetic of desolation, reinforcing the message and heightening its capacity to warn. In "Spike Field" (fig. 8.3), shown here as a preliminary, not-to-scale, computer-generated plan, the concept of tilting thorns is pared down to simple, irregularly spaced obelisks interspersed with message kiosks and a dividing wall. "Spike Field" creates a landscape threat-ened by megaliths which bespeak intentional and labored effort. The jutting rocks, however, asymmetrically thrusting up through the man-made grid, re-sist any notion of ideal beauty and are meant to deny visual interest. Spikes are placed on a mesa of black concrete blocks which soak up the desert sun and concentrate it, making it impossible to plant on or drive machinery into the ra-dioactive area. Ghostly visitors wander through the forest of granite into cozy

SPIKE FIELD

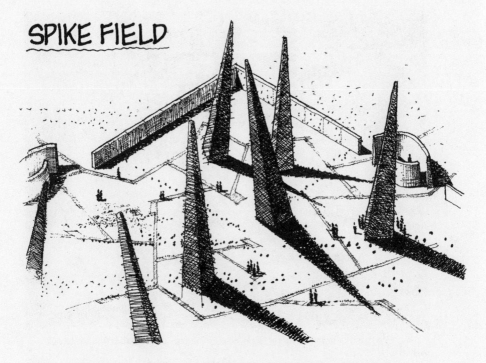

Fig. 8.3. "Spike Field, view 1." Concept and art by Michael Brill. Courtesy Estate of Michael Brill.

concrete message kiosks, where Munch's *The Scream*—once again recruited to register universal horror—is to be chiseled along with cautions in six different languages.

"Menacing Earthworks" (fig. 8.4) is the panel's most favored design. It consists of lightning-shaped crooked stones, each fifty feet high, radiating from a flat center. In the middle is the remnant of a decayed concrete building—the current WIPP administration office, left to rot. The stones are meant to press in uncomfortably on the viewer, limiting her vantage points and leaving her disoriented: "Walking through it, the massive earthworks crowd in on you, dwarfing you, cutting off your sight to the horizon, a loss of connection to any sense of place."[25] Rather than erecting a warning grid with clear sight lines and points of entry and exit, the designers prefer eliciting a haptic response from the viewer, who is integrated into, and viscerally repelled by, the structure. "Menacing Earthworks" has an overpowering presence which belittles and subsumes the viewer, who is meant to walk among the stones rather than survey them from above. There is a disconnect between the visual images shown here and the written description of the design, indicating two dis-

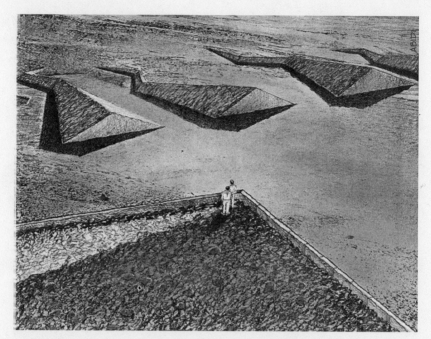

Fig. 8.4. "Menacing Earthworks." Concept by Michael Brill. Art by Safdar Abidi. Courtesy Estate of Michael Brill.

crepant perspectives. These two figures standing on the earthwork, it seems, are not representations of the viewer who perambulates in confusion on the ground and ultimately flees, but rather indicate the position of the designers themselves. They stand on top of the tall rocks like tourists from the past surveying the future ruins. These diagrammatic means synthesize the received language of postcard vistas and scenic views, betraying their perceived confidence in their own inoculation against its hazards.

The use of the second person—"the massive earthworks crowd in on you"—transports the reader far into the future after the marker is built, while the grammar simultaneously insists on the present tense. The pressing of future and present together is one hallmark of the entire WIPP marker project, as the team is occasionally caught between tenses as it figures out whom (and when) it is addressing. Carl Sagan's idea, however ludicrous, in fact has a certain logic with regard to this time trouble; for the skull-and-crossbones is, to some extent, legible to us now, and hence might be decipherable in the future by archaeologists. Designs such as "Spike Field," however, have no contextual meaning in the present, rest upon no supporting interpretive framework, and hence are that much more blind to the future.

"Menacing Earthworks" shows a clear, if unintentional, affinity with the ruinous aesthetic found in much land art. It is clear that the tropes of monumental earthworks bear upon the WIPP team; indeed, James Turrell and others are mentioned in the Sandia report.[26] One compelling comparison might be Michael Heizer's desert *Double Negative* (1969–70), which displaced a quarter of a million tons of rock in Nevada in an oblique conversation with the nuclear bombs dropped nearby at the Nevada Test Site.[27] However, crucial to the tenets of earthworks is entropic pull, the drive toward obliteration with time, and WIPP mimes their designs for precisely the opposite purpose.[28] Whereas Robert Smithson's works crumble toward extinction in pursuit of his idea of entropy, the marker is motored by a quest for inherent, eternally stable form and meaning. It is this dream of positivism that leads the panel to a denial of art, which is repeatedly referred to within the report as "arbitrary" and "ambiguous." Despite this, the visual details of many earthworks and the proposed nuclear marker are surprisingly similar; in fact, a cautionary appendix in the report fears that the WIPP marker will be seen merely as the supreme example of this late-twentieth-century "school of outdoor sculpture."[29]

While looking to art history and its range of interpretive tools would certainly be useful in the context of designing the marker, the report rejects the contributions made by art historians in understanding how visual imagery is read differently across time. Hence still-unresolved questions of intentionality surrounding the interpretation of the paintings at Lascaux,[30] for instance, are ignored in favor of a scientific argument that the WIPP marker can and will transmit its complex meaning through time: "[F]uture, more advanced scientists would have fewer problems interpreting pictographs, symbols and scripts purposely designed for transparency of interpretation."[31] There was a suggestion of an open artist's competition, but panelist and scientific illustrator Jon Lomberg protested that "I'd die before I'd let the art world come anywhere near this." He further cautions:

> The art world in places like New York is anti-scientific, anti-representational, and seems to favor more detached and (to me) nihilistic statements. . . . [T]hey are likely to end up picking a giant inflatable hamburger to mark the site.[32]

This comment ignores the nihilism inherent in a field of spikes meant to keep bodies off a highly lethal nuclear waste dump. (And, unlike Mr. Lomberg, I would be very curious to see what Claes Oldenburg—someone who understands the absurd precepts of monumentality—might conjure for this project.)[33] Reminiscent of the opposition between Fredrick Hart's conservative Vietnam veterans' sculpture and Maya Lin's "antirepresentational" (and thus,

by Lomberg's account, "detached" and "nihilistic") memorial,[34] this gratu-
itous insult aimed at Oldenburg betrays WIPP's ultimate anti-art functionality
and positions it ideologically against the earth art to which it bears a surface
resemblance.

The planning of the WIPP marker follows on the heels of a tremendous
period of monument design and construction. The past several decades have
seen an explosion of documents, proposals, and groundbreakings, along with
a blossoming of studies and critical assessments that challenge the conceptual
bases of monumentality. A common critique of traditional monuments is that
their allegorical forms bury memory and ossify the past, that they glorify
destruction with elegant bronzes, consolidating the place of tragedy rather
than activating a more diffuse and hence self-reflective decentering. Andreas
Huyssen notes that "monumental" has become a negative word; monuments
are seen as ethically and politically suspect, or more simply, just bad taste.[35]
The WIPP marker has drawn one lesson from criticisms of conventional monuments: it should not be pretty. As the panel notes, even the durable pyramids
were looted for their fine sheath of marble: better to steer clear of magnificence
lest the marker inspire cultic worship or fascination.

Interestingly, these worries—that the marker might be inspiring or visually pleasurable, and hence entice rather than dissuade visitors—also came up
in connection with the Holocaust countermonuments which have recently
sprung up throughout Europe and the United States.[36] Countermonuments often de-emphasize loveliness, aiming instead for roughness, quietness, and in-
trospection. And indeed, with the WIPP proposal's emphasis on uncertainty,
dispersal, and denial of beauty, it would seem that the marker has certain
affinities with Holocaust memorials. However, with its ambitions to show
brute strength and inspire awe, the team seems to find fascistic aesthetics even
more timeless than beauty. The organized, permanent environment of monoliths, messages, and sound (in some designs, wind wails through specially can-
tilevered stone chambers) creates a totalitarian *Gesamtkunstwerk* that has
more in common with Albert Speer's visions of building Nazi Germany so that
its ruins would remain glorious for posterity than with eloquent works such as
Esther and Jochem Gerz's *Monument against Fascism* (1986–93). The Gerzes'
memorial consists of a column that gradually sinks into the ground as its soft
surface is scribbled upon by passersby, its literal disappearance allegorically
presaging the slow decline of collective memory itself. This is a far cry from the
heavy, overwhelming megaliths of the WIPP marker, which will bear down
upon future viewers in the New Mexico desert for ten thousand years with a
wish to transcend language in order to convey a horror that will be "more felt
than understood."[37]

The WIPP team, with its drive toward monumentality, dismisses the possibility that the marker might simply be ignored or erased and emphatically overloads the designs with hugeness in order to maintain the high pitch of its rhetorical address. As Robert Musil has noted, monuments fall easily toward the invisible.[38] How naturalized into the landscape might these stone spikes become in one hundred years, much less ten thousand? The marker's deliberate archaism could merely confuse future audiences as to its moment of production. Rather than speaking to its precise era of conception, the marker muddles its own temporal context: for the benefit of the future, it is made to look as if it is from the past.

One distinctive aspect of the WIPP marker is its true inseparability from its site—its hyperbolically indexical relation to the landscape. It must be located directly on top of the buried waste, declaring that *here* is the locus of danger. (Interestingly, the French National Agency for Radioactive Waste Management contradicts the U.S. findings, recommending that radioactive waste markers should be 10–20 kilometers away from the actual site as a distracting measure.) Thus fixed in space, it conforms to Rosalind Krauss's logic of the monument as that which is site-specific, declaratively placed.[39] At least two fundamental units of meaning need to be communicated by the marker: first, the location of the site, and second, its danger. The panel's working assumption, following the EPA's charge, is that *knowledge alone* of the radioactive toxicity will be sufficient deterrence. The Department of Energy, in insisting on building an expensive marker for WIPP, aims to consolidate all nuclear fears onto this one spot, creating for the future a definitive map of where danger lies. The emphasis on a singular site disregards the many other radioactive landscapes that still bear the traces of nuclear activity. Why lavish attention on *this* site when others have been wasted by radioactivity? For instance, at the Savannah River site in South Carolina, 135 gallons of spent nuclear fuel were poured into shallow holes drilled into the earth. At this deadly place, the holes were simply filled with dirt, plugged with concrete, and marked by a small plaque. And just a few miles from New Mexico's WIPP, a nuclear test blast entitled Project Gnome went awry in 1961, spewing radionuclides over the exploded landscape. There a granite slab marker was erected to ward off trespassers. Written on a copper plaque, green from oxidation, is the warning THIS SITE WILL REMAIN DANGEROUS FOR 24,000 YEARS.[40] The raised lettering is corroded almost to the point of illegibility, and cattle have rubbed against it for the past thirty years, nudging it several meters from its original site. I point to these sites, two of many examples in the long history of nuclear disaster, to demonstrate the U.S. government's Janus-faced attitude toward radioactivity: the present dangers of nuclear waste, which continues to be manufactured, are

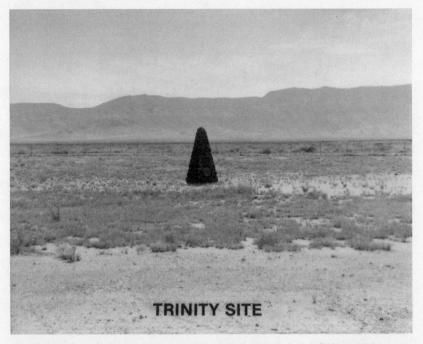

Fig. 8.5. Peter Goin, "Trinity Site," 1991. From Peter Goin, *Nuclear Landscapes* (Baltimore: Johns Hopkins University Press, 1991), 29. Photograph courtesy of Peter Goin. Reprinted by permission of The Johns Hopkins University Press.

downplayed while billions are spent to warn the future about one small portion of the U.S. radioactive remains.

These markers are not the only concrete reminders of the imprint left by decades of nuclear activity in the American West. "Trinity Site, 1991" by photographer Peter Goin (fig. 8.5) documents a stone stele that commemorates the first atomic blast, detonated in 1945. This, too, is New Mexico, and Goin's photograph, with its straightforward documentary style, seeks by force of sheer banality to make this monument strange. Goin wants to render the damage done to the southwestern land, yet the desert's eerie palette of colors and dusty surfaces already look devastated.[41] The marker, centered in the image and at some distance from the camera's lens, is presented to us matter-of-factly, and its radioactive energy is made known only by the caption. So unassuming that it risks being entirely overlooked, this is a monument made ironic. One of a series of Goin's "nuclear landscapes," "Trinity Site" utilizes the conventions of bald photojournalistic "objectivity" as a part of its strategic political point. In the face of governmental secrecy, these works act as alternative archives, keeping precise records of who and what has been damaged.

Patrick Nagatani's 1989 "Trinitite, Ground Zero" (fig. 8.6), made in collaboration with Andrée Tracey, is a photo of the same stone marker, but it is made stagily and explicitly toxic. Chunks of dayglow green rock rain from a threatening sky as an atomic worker absurdly shields himself with an umbrella. Nagatani denaturalizes the landscape by using photomontage to try to make perceptible the lingering radioactivity. In sharp contrast to Goin's almost military precision, Nagatani's collaged works are fantasyscapes where hidden truths can be visualized. Both Nagatani and Goin are part of a loose confederation of artists who are committed to documenting the nuclear age—others include Carole Gallagher, Paul Shambroom, Richard Misrach, and Robert del Tredici. Working since the early 1980s, artists and activists such as these photographers have set out to record the human and environmental costs of the nuclear age, fighting to document what is in fact highly resistant to imaging. Because radioactivity's damage is wreaked over decades, and even passed on to future generations, it is very difficult to capture it in the brief, instantaneous flash of the camera. It is high irony that with the WIPP marker, the state has

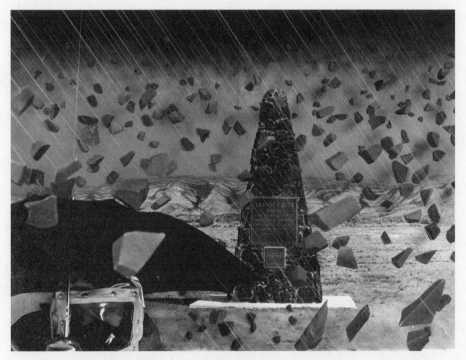

Fig. 8.6. Patrick Nagatani in collaboration with Andrée Tracey, "Trinitite, Ground Zero," 1988–89. From Patrick Nagatani, *Nuclear Enchantment* (Albuquerque: University of New Mexico Press, 1991), plate 1. Courtesy Patrick Nagatani.

set out to do what many could not, which is to make visible, confirm, and authenticate the threat of radiation.[42]

The Waste Isolation Pilot Plant marker is a remarkable instance of a state-ordained attempt to control the future of information, an expensive effort to manipulate, even custom-design tomorrow. While origins or beginnings are critical for myths of the nation, it seems just as critical to understand how the nation ideologically plots for the far, far future. What kinds of institutions are being set into place by the United States with this project? A different WIPP panel has suggested the creation of a nuclear priesthood whose purpose would be to maintain and safeguard information about the site, or the invention of an epic oral poem that might ignite the imagination of the public and be passed down through the generations. Or the construction of a parliamentary body called the House of Future Affairs whose duty would be to reproduce and manage the warning system. Or the enlistment of a corporation to create a lovable cartoon character—their suggestion was "Mickey Nuke"—who would perpetually enchant and forever caution children about the dangers of WIPP.[43] Turning the most deadly site in the United States into an absurdly banal image of commercial cheer fits in well with the studied nonchalance so characteristic of official attitudes toward nuclear harm—from the early "Atoms for Peace" campaign in the 1950s to today's indifference toward the devastation caused by nuclear power. The ostensible end of the cold war and our increasing distance from the catastrophes of the nuclear age such as Chernobyl have led to a general relaxation about this particular threat.[44] In Missouri, a former nuclear production site—still laced with radioactivity—has been revamped as a family-oriented museum.[45] The fundamental premise of WIPP is consonant with this new comfort level with nuclear power: the harm has not yet happened, is very remote, and is completely avoidable.

Monuments usually have specific functions: to uphold a current regime, explain or educate, pay homage. In all of these roles, they actively create memory. The WIPP marker, to be sure, is not precisely a monument, but it does strategically wield the tropes of monumentality. The design of the WIPP marker thus tells us much about the status of monument making in the late twentieth century. Monuments can be erected to act as testaments, to offer proof in the form of relics of destruction. The WIPP marker, perversely, is a relic not of destruction but of its very potentiality, as misunderstanding or disobeying its warning might be fatal. If its mission to deter fails, it will be nothing more than a crypt for the deaths that will occur after the waste site is breached. The monumental marker will become instead a memorial, a future cemetery.

Often, monumental architecture buttresses national origins; the WIPP marker acts as a limit case that searches for an endpoint or terminus. This is how the government imagines itself on fast-forward and addresses itself to the future—a future of subjects psychologically cowed by sheer masses of heavy stone. It is a type of deferred imminence that we are unaccustomed to examining: not the sudden blast of nuclear apocalypse but a protracted, steady, inevitable poisoning. What are our paradigms for futurity? We have words for the structures of our relationship to the past: nostalgia, amnesia, sentimentality, history. But what words do we have for the future besides anticipation or dread—prophecy?

Time itself is a decaying force; it erodes meanings and messages in the same way that radioactive particles break down. In order to stick in the annals of collective history despite this incessant erosion, memory needs to have a specific address; Pierre Nora calls it the "will to remember."[46] Here is that address pulled to its breaking point: the audience is everyone—everyone today, everyone tomorrow, everyone forever. The marker's very universality renders it vulnerable to inconsequence and semiotic impenetrability. This is something the panelists have ignored: the felicity of the speech act, the context of its reception, and the way its meaning is shaped and conditioned by narrative circumstances.[47] Sandia Laboratories and the Department of Energy agree that questions of cosmological legibility and extreme duration are best put to scientists—those who trade in probabilities, statistics, and distant time spans that to most humanities scholars seem unimaginable, verging on science fiction. Yet the longevity of the marker, and its semiotic coherence long into the future, are complexly implicated within the realm of the visual. To untangle the proposals for the WIPP marker is also to ask questions about how monuments regard the future: Do they view the future as continuous with the present? How will their contextual address shift, destabilize, or collapse?

In the WIPP marker, seemingly disconnected terrains come to occupy the same map: waste management, governmental land use, nuclear politics, and the visual specifics of monumental architecture. Investigating the centuries-long legacy of nuclear waste is of special urgency in the aftermath of September 11, 2001, given George W. Bush's plans to increase the use of nuclear power for the nation's energy problems, his enthusiasm for missile buildup, and his deployment of nuclear fears to galvanize support for a war against Iraq.[48] The plans for this eternal marker tell us much about our construction of the future and how we read it. They contest profound beliefs about the stability of visual imagery, delving into prophetic realms usually associated with religion, magic, or science. Indeed, the very provisional nature of this marker is what makes it so interesting, for these plans necessarily beg several salutary questions. How can the future itself be a site of study, and what will trying to divine it tell us about history? How sufficient are our means for making and preserving memory?

WIPP produces a speculative viewership within both rhetorical and real spaces. One could say that the marker commemorates something that has not yet happened in order to erase that which has, building a huge marker to rivet our gaze away from the Savannah River Site in South Carolina or the Nevada Test Site. The plans for inscribing cultural memory at WIPP demonstrate the state's refusal to admit a contaminated present. It is for precisely all the reasons that critics of monuments decry them—they solidify history and locate it too precisely—that WIPP, under the guise of a "marker," so desperately wants a monument.

The questions that WIPP raises about the persistence of information and memory loss are strikingly relevant for art history: all images regard the future, it just depends on how far out we draw the timeline. All monuments must account for the fraught dream of embedding a deep history within them. "This place is a message and part of a system of messages. Pay attention to it! . . . We considered ourselves a powerful culture. This place is not a place of honor. No highly esteemed deed is commemorated here. Nothing is valued here. . . . What is here was dangerous and repulsive to us."[49] So reads the inscription on a towering monument planned by the U.S. government to mark the site of the country's only deep geological radioactive waste dump. The instabilities of visual signs over time, inherent to the challenge of art history, are here discarded, as the engineers who build the marker are sure of progress and a clean concrete signifier. For them, the future is not uncertain but unfolds according to laws, equations, and calculations. Theirs is a future of ever-improving technology, one without apocalypse, deterioration, or regression: this is what Walter Benjamin calls "homogeneous, empty time."[50] The WIPP marker aspires to be a solid center point of time, an obdurate witness that casts an impassive eye on the centuries as they unfold. In his "Theses on the Philosophy of History," Benjamin writes a chilling vision of the angel of history, with the storm of progress caught in its wings. It flies with its face turned away from the future, with catastrophic wreckage piling at its feet. In the WIPP marker is built a new, stone angel of nuclear history, and it too is propelled into the future while it is determined only to look back. And the horrible waste keeps heaping underneath it.

NOTES

1. There are other radioactive waste storage facilities located in Oak Ridge, Tennessee; Rocky Flats, Colorado; and Savannah River, South Carolina, but WIPP is the only storage site meant to hold radioactive wastes forever. Sites such as Rocky Flats were built as temporary solutions to the country's nuclear waste problems, and it is still unknown if the materials there will be reused or will need to be removed and buried elsewhere. For a trenchant look at the

waste disposal crisis in the United States, see Valerie L. Kuletz, *The Tainted Desert: Environmental and Social Ruin in the American West* (New York: Routledge, 1998).

2. These nonhuman disruptions were studied in great detail before the opening of the site. See, for example, Peter Davies, *Variable Density Groundwater Flow and Paleohydrology in the WIPP Region, Southeastern New Mexico* (Denver: U.S. Department of Energy, 1989); Stephen Richey, *Geologic and Hydrologic Data for the Ruster Formation Near the WIPP* (Denver: U.S. Department of Energy, 1989); and Allan Sanford, *Seismicity in the Area of the Waste Isolation Pilot Plant,* Sandia National Laboratories SAND80-7096, 1980. These and other DOE reports are in the public domain.

3. WIPP was built and is overseen by Sandia National Laboratories under contract from the Department of Energy. Environmental activists contend that WIPP's design creates a significant potential for contaminating the area's groundwater, and these debates delayed the opening of WIPP for almost twenty years. The first legislative mandate for a defense transuranic waste storage site was passed in 1979; the facility itself was begun then, but it then languished owing to court battles until 1999, when it began receiving waste. The most comprehensive account of the history of WIPP is Chuck McCutcheon's *Nuclear Reactions: The Politics of Opening a Radioactive Waste Disposal Site* (Albuquerque: University of New Mexico Press, 2002).

4. The site will remain radioactive past 12,030, but feasibility studies led the EPA to opt for this date as one in which the most significant risks will be sufficiently reduced.

5. Assurance Requirements, EPA, 40 CFR 191.14c, 1985, quoted in Kathleen M. Trauth, Stephen C. Hora, and Robert V. Guzowski, *Expert Judgment on Markers to Deter Inadvertent Human Intrusion into the Waste Isolation Pilot Plant* (Albuquerque: Sandia National Laboratories, 1993, contract DE-AC04-94AL85000), F-19. This document includes all the drawing and plans referred to here.

6. The panel consisted of thirteen members, representatives of the following disciplines: materials science, architecture, environmental design, anthropology, linguistics, archaeology, astronomy, communications, geomorphology, scientific illustration, and semiotics. The panel was broken into two teams, who developed their proposals independently of each other. Their final recommendations had remarkable overlap, and thus I refer to the panel as a whole rather than distinguishing between the two component teams, although I quote team members by name when I refer to their personal statements. There was, however, one significant difference in the two approaches which deserves mentioning. Team A was far more sympathetic toward artistic modes of communication than was Team B, which perhaps accounts for the wonderfully rendered drawings conceived by Team A member Michael Brill and drawn by Safdar Abidi. Before his death in 2002, Brill was very generous with sharing his designs with me, and I thank Sue Weidemann Brill for granting permission to reprint them. The personal statements printed in *Expert Judgment* are often thoughtful musings on memory, nuclear hazards, and strategies of markings, particularly Frederick Newmeyer's—moments of wisdom that, I hasten to add, were minimized in the bulk of the final governmental report.

7. *Expert Judgment,* F-39.

8. Michael Baxandall's widely influential notion of the "period eye" was elaborated in his *Painting and Experience in Fifteenth Century Italy* (Oxford: Oxford University Press, 1972). Indeed, most current art historical methodologies, including social art history and semiotic theories of visual culture, take as foundational the disputation of stable, transhistorical interpretations of objects and images.

9. The Marker Panel recommendations have been passed along to the Westinghouse Corporation, which will be responsible for the final marker design and construction when the vaults are sealed in 2030.

10. *Expert Judgment,* F-24-25.

11. Ibid., F-142.

12. Ibid., F-95.

13. These drawings illustrate only a small corner of the total area to be covered.

14. A sketch is reproduced in *Expert Judgment,* G-13; owing to space considerations, I was unable to reproduce it here.

15. "After installation, passive markers should remain operational without further human attention." Ibid., A-3.

16. Sagan declined to join the Marker Panel owing to scheduling conflicts, but sent in a letter urging the use of the skull and crossbones. Letter printed in ibid., G-88.

17. "We decided against simple 'Keep Out' messages with scary faces. Museums and private collections abound with such guardian figures removed from burial sites." Ibid., F-34.

18. Laurie Anderson has commented on the ambiguity of this drawing in her 1979 performance *Americans on the Move:* "Do you think they will think his hand is permanently attached that way? Or do you think they will read our signs?" Reprinted in *October* 8 (spring 1979): 45–57. Craig Owens sees the man's raised hand as an image of sexual difference. To the aliens who might read these signs, it could appear that on our planet only men speak, while women are still and silent. "The Discourse of Others: Feminists and Postmodernism," in *Beyond Recognition: Representation, Power, and Culture* (Berkeley: University of California Press, 1992), 166–90.

19. This capsule was designed to give a rudimentary knowledge of human languages and included images, texts, and sound recordings.

20. *Expert Judgment,* F-43.

21. Ibid., F-115.

22. Ibid., F-152.

23. Ibid., F-58.

24. Ibid., F-42.

25. Ibid., F-58.

26. Ibid., F-135.

27. For work on the use of the West as a nuclear ground zero, see Bruce Hevly and John M. Findlay, eds., *The Atomic West* (Seattle: University of Washington Press, 1998).

28. See Smithson's "Entropy and the New Monuments," *Artforum* (June 1966), reprinted in *Robert Smithson: The Collected Writings,* ed. Jack Flam (Berkeley: University of California Press, 1996), 10–23.

29. Jon Lomberg's statement, *Expert Judgment,* G-85.

30. The cave paintings from Lascaux, dating to around 15,000 B.C., are late in the Paleolithic era; some date back to 23,000 B.C. The issue of archaeological "intentionality" is taken up by Whitney Davis in *Replications: Archaeology, Art History, Psychoanalysis* (University Park: Pennsylvania State University Press, 1996).

31. *Expert Judgment,* G-65.

32. Ibid., G-85-86.

33. In 2001, the Marjorie Barrick Museum at the University of Nevada–Las Vegas, held an open competition inviting artists to design universal warning signs for the nuclear waste dump scheduled to open at Yucca Mountain, Nevada. The winning entry proposed planting the entire mountain with genetically modified, self-replicating, cobalt blue cactuses.

34. For an extensive discussion of these contrasting visions of public memorials, see Marita Sturken's *Tangled Memories: The Vietnam War, the AIDS Epidemic, and the Politics of Remembering* (Berkeley: University of California Press, 1997).

35. Andreas Huyssen, "Monumental Seduction," in *Acts of Memory: Cultural Recall in the Present,* ed. Mieke Bal, Jonathon Crewe, and Leo Spitzer (Hanover: University Press of New England, 1999), 191–207.

36. See James Young, *The Art of Memory: Holocaust Memorials in History* (Munich: Prestel-Verlag, 1994), and *The Texture of Memory* (New Haven: Yale University Press, 1993).

37. *Expert Judgment,* F-41.

38. Robert Musil, "Nachlass zu Lebzeiten," in *Gesammelte Werke,* ed. Adolf Frisé (Reinbek: Rowohlt, 1978), 2:506–9.

39. Rosalind Krauss, "Sculpture in the Expanded Field" (1978), in *The Originality of the Avant-Garde and Other Modernist Myths* (Cambridge: MIT Press, 1988), 276–90.

40. This site was explored and documented by Gregory Benford in his *Deep Time: How Humanity Communicates across Millennia* (New York: Perennial, 1999).

41. I have argued elsewhere that the Department of Energy chooses sites such as Nevada and New Mexico because they already look postnuclear; "Zero Visibility: Picturing Nuclear Test Sites and the Landscape of Disaster," presented at "The Coercive Image," graduate art history conference, University of Southern California, 1999.

42. After tens of millions of dollars spent on legal fees defending the government from lawsuits that insisted that bomb making caused genetic damage, leukemia, immune suppression, cancer, and early death, in August 2001 payment finally began for the families of these radiation workers, many of whom died decades ago from cancer. See Michael Janofsky, "Nuclear Cleanup Workers Exposed to Radiation," *New York Times,* December 8, 2000, A4; Matthew Wald, "U.S. Acknowledges Radiation Killed Weapons Workers," *New York Times,* January 29, 2000, A1; Michael Flynn, "A Debt Long Overdue," *Bulletin of the Atomic Scientists* (July/August 2001): 39–49; "Payments to Begin for Arms Workers Ill from Radiation," *New York Times,* July 30, 2001, A12.

43. These possibilities were considered by four expert commissions that were convened simply to spin out scenarios for the future; they met separately from the Marker Panel. See *Expert Judgment on Inadvertent Human Intrusion into the Waste Isolation Pilot Plant,* Sandia Report, SAND90-3062, 1993, and the follow-up *Effectiveness of Passive Institutional Controls in Reducing Inadvertent Human Intrusion into the Waste Isolation Pilot Plant for Use in Performance Assessments,* WIPP/CAO-96-3168, 1996. The panel built models of probability which account for changes in population, environment, war, and disease. Some scenarios point to religious cults digging up the site in search of higher meaning, or a society of prisons where prisoners mine the site since they are incapable of understanding the dangers. The only scenario in which the warning is effectively communicated is one in which in the distant future, a "Disney-sponsored WIPP World has become a major tourist attraction. Mickey Nuke is a fictional character that survives many generations. As long as he survives, the warnings about WIPP survive." The utterly grim sense that capitalism, spectacle, and cartoon knowledge are our best possible hope is perhaps indicative of a general failure of imagination, as Fredric Jameson puts it, with regard to alternate political systems. One scenario sees a "feminist world" as soon as 2191 (if only!) where "women dominate society partially through the selection of girl babies. Twentieth-century science is discredited as male arrogance. Warnings about repository are dismissed as another example of muddled masculine thinking." This misguided scenario sees patriarchy as somehow less durable than capitalism, and curiously understands antirationalism as the basis for feminism.

44. Despite the current (2003) U.S. administration's hypocritical hand-wringing about weapons of mass destruction, the frenzy of concern about nuclear arms has waned since the Reagan era. The mid-eighties in particular saw activists and scholars alike focused with special intensity on the apocalyptic threats of nuclear energy and weapons. In 1984, a special issue of the journal *Diacritics* entitled "Nuclear Criticism" suggested that "the nuclear" was so

basic to collective understandings of contemporary culture that it would be the next great academic interdisciplinary field. *Diacritics* 14, no. 2 (summer 1984). For a brilliant take on why this did not happen, see Peter Coviello's "Apocalypse from Now On," in *Queer Frontiers: Millennial Geographies, Genders, and Generations,* ed. Joseph Boone et al. (Madison: University of Wisconsin Press, 2000), 39–63.

45. See Stephanie Simon, "From Atomic Dump to Tourist Draw," *Los Angeles Times,* August 13, 2002, A1, 8.

46. Pierre Nora, "Between Memory and History: *Les Lieux de Mémoire,*" *Representations* 26 (spring 1989): 7–25. The marker might seem to be the ideal example of Nora's delineation between artificial histories and the "true" memories they supplant, but his binary is troubled when it comes to such an organized, yet utterly untested, effort to tailor future responses. Those steeped in recent debates about distinctions between collective versus public memory might quibble with my loose application of these terms, but the extreme temporal dislocations caused by discussing an unbuilt marker that will function as a visible generator of memory well into the future has led me, by necessity, to a certain simplification of terminology.

47. In different contexts, both J. L. Austin and Mikhail Bakhtin have argued for the social embeddedness of signification. See Austin's *How to Do Things with Words* (Cambridge: Harvard University Press, 1962), and Bakhtin's *The Dialogic Imagination: Four Essays,* ed. Valim Liapunov, trans. Michael Holquist and Caryl Emerson (Austin: University of Texas Press, 1981).

48. With this renewed interest in nuclear power comes new questions about how and where to store nuclear waste; battles rage in Congress over which states will house these materials, with some desperate to keep dumps out, and some, usually in very impoverished areas, eager for the jobs they might create. Meanwhile, waste languishes in inadequate storage facilities. See Matthew Wald, "A Shift in Strategy for Radioactive Waste in Nevada," *New York Times,* July 31, 2001, D1, 2.

49. *Expert Judgment,* F-49.

50. Walter Benjamin, "Theses on the Philosophy of History," in *Illuminations: Essays and Reflections,* ed. Hannah Arendt, trans. Harry Zohn (New York: Schocken Books, 1968), 253–64.

PART III

Destruction / Reconstruction

Monuments are mortal. In fact, a monument often becomes so powerfully symbolic that someone acquires a vested interest in destroying it. This potential for destruction or defacement may be the most meaningful aspect of the monument's existence as an object. Consequently, when monumental discourse turns iconoclastic, it engages the objecthood of the monument at its core.

Because of its direct engagement with the monument's material existence, the discourse of iconoclasm would seem to come closer than any other monumental discourse to older art historical paradigms. The essays in this section, however, do not enact received art historical methodology. Instead, they examine destruction and deformation in themselves as discourses that play a role in the making and unmaking of monuments. Threats to destroy or alter monuments, destructive parodies, and actual destruction are all integral to monumental and memorial discourses, as are the signs of destruction themselves. Sometimes an object becomes a monument only when it is destroyed or altered. In one sense, however, traditional art historical discourse is highly relevant to iconoclasm. As we shall see, iconoclastic discourse engages directly the professions—art history, criticism, museum curatorship, and archaeology—which are involved in preservation. The essays in this section begin to suggest the range and complexity of discourses and institutions engaged by iconoclasm.

The monuments Jaś Elsner discusses in his essay on forms of iconoclasm—alteration in ancient Rome and the changes in the architectural plan of Tom's Quad, Oxford—are, to speak in deconstructive terms, "under erasure." That is, their former meanings are erased, yet the signs of erasure are visible, becoming themselves a form of communication. When these signs of destruction are present, obliteration is an act of preservation and memorialization. Elsner explores the message of erasure from the transmitting to the receiving end, examining how rededication of buildings, recutting of sculptures, and the changes in design of a quadrangle in progress may have been understood by the Roman, and British, public. Further, Elsner expands the notion of iconoclasm to include "instant ritual desecration," such as the rearrangement of seating when formerly Catholic churches become Protestant, so that the congregation no longer faces east. All of these changes are visible reminders of the forgotten, or repressed, showing its greatness, and consequently the even greater power of that which has obliterated it.

Tapati Guha-Thakurta's essay about the controversy between Hindus and Muslims at Ayodya, which culminated in the destruction of a sixteenth-century mosque and the ongoing construction of a Hindu temple to replace it, similarly engages a destruction that preserves the memory of what it has destroyed. The mosque itself had come to stand as a sign for a—possibly apocryphal— destroyed Hindu temple that it replaced. The invention of the previous act of iconoclasm against the temple justified the perpetration of a new one, the destruction of the mosque.

Yet the incident also reveals the relevance of scholarship to the passions and beliefs that motivate iconoclasm. During the controversy, the disciplinary rhetoric of archaeology was mobilized to sponsor the historical positions on both sides. Archaeology, however, which was drawn into the controversy as an objective, academic authority, actually has its own interests at stake. The use of archaeological rhetoric to sponsor iconoclasm was a threat to institutionalized archaeology, for which even the proof of the existence of a prior Hindu temple could not have justified the destruction of the mosque. Iconoclasm, therefore, threatens not only the monument but the professional discipline as well. In fact the professionals see themselves as owners of the sites. When threatened by demolition, a work can acquire a new monumental significance as a national archaeological treasure, a distinction on which the professional disciplines thrive. The professionals consider no one else competent to make decisions about such monuments, including the communities—Hindu or Muslim—surrounding the sites. The locals are destructive, whether they pilfer the stones, destroy relics, or seek restorations without the benefit of the professional. The professional is the only preservationist. Yet scientific archaeology destroys the integrity of the monument as well, by dispersing it into "strata." As opposed to a "keeping place," the archaeological community is committed to a pedagogically controlled approach to memory that is not always successful in keeping the monument in existence.

Richard Wittman's essay also pits professional against competing local interests. The destruction of the decorations in Amiens Cathedral took place at the beginning of the movement whereby imagined communities, made up of people personally unacquainted with one another, replaced local communities.[1] The marks of the local community in Amiens were effaced in favor of the emptiness that accorded with the aesthetic dictates of current architectural treatises favoring a classical style. In this case, that which was to develop into the professional institution, architectural criticism, was used to sanction the act of iconoclasm, by extolling aesthetic clarity and plainness. The destruction of the decoration, however, was not purely aesthetic. The treatises represented a dispersed reading public, rather than a local face-to-face one. Destruction of the decoration according to their dictates was a coded way of destroying this face-to-face community in favor of an abstract conceptual public. Aesthetic beholding requires distance, which is impossible for locals to achieve, disinterestedness breeding iconoclasm. As in modern warfare, it is much easier to kill something distanced and remote. This form of warfare need not kill people. An equally effective way to destroy a community is to destroy a monument that symbolically represents it.

There is little room for iconoclasm within the realm of the modern museum, at least for recognized monuments. There, iconoclasm itself is mostly symbolic, taking the form of installations and photographs that comment on existing monuments and seem to alter their nature. Ruth Philips writes about interventions in Canadian monuments made in order to forefront the native peoples marginalized in the great monuments. One such intervention involves viewing public "icons" from different (postcolonial) perspectives; another is a "repainting" of Benjamin West's famous painting *The Death of General Wolfe* to highlight a marginalized Native American; another is the making and remaking of a museum courtyard containing a memorial, by a white European, to "extinct" native peoples. The courtyard containing the memorial was redesigned in accordance with changing notions of memory: the redesign modified the memorial by changing its context, in order to retrieve native populations, very much alive, from their supposed extinction, and to make a statement about who controls memory. Through their countercuratorial projects the artists responsible challenge the hegemonious character of history and its claim to professionalism. Without recutting the stone, they alter the way monuments, and their communities, are seen.

NOTE

1. Benedict Anderson, *Imagined Communities: Reflections on the Origin and Spread of Nationalism.* (London: Verso, 1983), traced this phenomenon.

Iconoclasm and the Preservation of Memory

JAŚ ELSNER

Introduction: Memory and the Materiality of Monuments

Can we say that memory inheres in the materiality of a monument?
We normally understand memory as belonging to the realm of mentality—subject to the affect and nostalgia of patrons, spectators, and
consumers, not to speak of artists and builders.[1] Yet much anthropological work has served recently to undermine the overpositive distinction between the objective and the subjective in the relations of
art and memory.[2] To adapt some propositions of Walter Melion and
Susanne Küchler, memory not only enables the transmission of images but is itself enabled by such transmission and—moreover—the
making (and altering and destroying) of art is itself a mode of memory.[3] While historians have sought to emphasise social memory including bodily practices and rituals as well as textual forms of remembering,[4] anthropologists have worked with the place of memory
in the making and uses of objects within given cultural systems.[5] Neither of these disciplines has given close attention to the forms of objects, which is the traditional domain of art history. To return to the
preoccupations of my opening question (and accepting the place of
images in social memory and in a cultural system, where they both

construct and are constructed by memory): Is there nonetheless nothing specific to their formal nature as material objects (made, altered, partially or wholly destroyed over time) which may allow monuments to function in a manner special to their material nature as spurs to memory in given cultural contexts?

My concerns here are sparked because—despite all the discussion of the semiotics of images in the last twenty years—very little attention has been given to the ways objects themselves, as material forms, may signify through a specifically material semiotics.[6] There has been lamentably little theoretical interest in how particular classes of objects—miniatures, for example, or models—function and create meaning by virtue of their specific material differences from and yet resemblances to other classes of objects (especially those they appear to replicate).[7] Indeed most theoretical work in art history today does not perhaps sufficiently acknowledge the potential differences between the functionings of a linguistically based semiotics, of semiotics as a culturally based system of communication, and of a more directly object-based semiotics. This may be a reaction to an earlier period of formalism which might be branded as essentialist—at least in its strongest versions (such as those espoused over almost a century by the so-called Vienna School).[8] I hold no brief for essentialism; but objects or buildings are made and adapted, damaged and repaired in every culture—and in their material operation as objects (to which very different kinds of cultural responses may be possible) there may be a certain similarity of function. The point is not more essentialist than admitting that language is common to all cultures, and even (if we believe Chomsky) that the impulse to language is inherent in all human beings. I am suggesting that the impulse to embed meaning and some of the visual methods by which meaning may be sparked in spectators are common to monuments across cultural divisions and across history.

I concentrate here on the ways objects have been deliberately deformed and on how such iconoclasm may relate to memory. The act of deformation and the presentation of deliberately altered works of art are specifically formal gestures within a material semiotics. The preserved damaged object, in its own material being, signals both its predamaged state—a different past, with potentially different cultural, political, and social meanings—and its new or altered state. In part, the meaning of the "new" monument is defined by its difference from (that is, by the changes made to) the "old" monument. Like the Roman god Janus, such monuments face in two directions simultaneously. The kinds of meanings one might read out of them vary in different cultures (even in the same culture), depending on how deep are various viewers' grasps of the specific histories being effaced and the specific politics of replacement.

But the space for making a "two-directional" interpretation, for seeing that a deliberate change has occurred and that this has a meaning, is offered by the object through its material form.

Iconoclasm, Memory, and Absence in Roman Art

Monuments have many kinds of memory. There is the commemoration envisaged by the first builder—for instance, the bid for perpetuity implied in the Mausoleum of Halicarnassus, whose name (originally just a genuflection to its entombed dedicatee, Mausolus) became ultimately the term for a whole class of buildings.[9] Such commemoration comes in many forms—from the personal to the collective, from the megalomaniac gesture to the genuine sign of bereavement.[10] There is the kind of memory acquired over time by a monument whose very grandeur becomes a kind of byword. When Constantius, son of Constantine, first built the church of St. Sophia in Constantinople in about 360,[11] he could not have envisaged the architectural masterpiece Justinian established in the same spot. Not could Justinian have predicted that St. Sophia would become a liturgical paradigm for the Orthodox churches of the Byzantine Empire and, in the sixteenth century, an architectural paradigm for the Ottoman mosques of Istanbul in the empire which succeeded Byzantium.[12] My subject here, however, is a third kind of memory associated with monumentality: not the memory of presence with which buildings are most familiarly imbued, but that of absence. Paradoxically, the act of iconoclasm—while apparently a kind of visual defacement that effaces the memory of the destroyed—may nonetheless preserve the memory of the condemned in the very act of obliteration.[13]

We have to place the practice of such iconoclasm within a specific cultural context. Visual commemoration within Roman culture—a society that recognized the imperial presence (and indeed that of other elite figures, civic benefactors, and generals) through the erection of statues and other monuments—belonged to what may be termed a performative mode, even a ritualized process, of embodied remembering.[14] It was effectively a social discourse. One potential gesture—always available within such a discourse and especially when a high symbolic store was set on the erection of an impressive monument—was the act of iconoclasm. Such defacement was not just a performance of forgetting the previously remembered image; it was also a public act of noting the fact that someone grand enough to have once been commemorated was now "forgotten." Such "forgetting" (to use the term as anthropologists have done) is active, purposeful, and collectively performed.[15] To adapt what has been said of the arts of the Malangan of New Ireland, because of the contextualization of Roman public art in the ceremonies of public life, monuments thematized representation and remembering as embodiment. Not only the setting up but also the demolition of public art took on a significance as a general metaphor for the process of recent history.[16]

Consider two models of visual iconoclasm associated with the ancient Roman practice of *damnatio memoriae*, the terminology of which we should remember is modern, despite its apparently legalistic Roman formulation.[17] Nonetheless, the notion of *damnatio* usefully tempers "forgetting" with suggestions of censoring, damning, even continual punishment. Both examples are relief sculptures which decorated public monuments in Rome. In a panel from what was probably once an arch of Marcus Aurelius, now in the Museo Conservatori in Rome, erected after his triumph of 176 A.D. but already dismantled in antiquity (before other panels from the same monument found their way onto the Arch of Constantine in the early fourth century),[18] the Emperor Marcus—a victory hovering over his head—rides through the city of Rome (fig. 9.1).[19] His chariot, pulled by four horses, is adorned with images of Neptune, Rome herself seated in the center, and Minerva, while a lictor and musician personify the grand triumphal procession to which the image alludes. In the background, a temple and triumphal arch figure the urban context of Rome's own buildings which this procession passed. The relief gestures to a historical event, namely, the triumph jointly celebrated by Marcus and his son Commodus in December 176 for their victories over the Sarmatian tribes in the so-called Marcomannic wars,[20] whose battles would subsequently be depicted in the reliefs on the Column of Marcus. Close visual analysis of the panel has shown that the figure of Commodus originally accompanied his father at the front of the chariot. An empty space remains beside Marcus, and the victory's hand—poised to place what was once probably a wreath over the younger emperor's head—now floats in space. Clearly, some time after the fall of Commodus, his image and the victory's wreath were chiseled away, the imperial figure transformed into the steps, bases, and columns of the temple that now hovers awkwardly in the upper center of the visual field—filling with "background" the absent center of the composition.[21] Interestingly, the relief proposed Commodus as the senior emperor (literally) in front of Marcus, which might perhaps point to a post-180 date when Commodus became sole emperor after his father's death. Since the images of Commodus were subjected to a vicious damnatio after his murder in late 192, it is most likely that the changes were made shortly after his death. By mid 193, after a period of instability, Septimius Severus had seized Rome by force and established the Severan dynasty. One means he used for legitimating his rule was to have himself posthumously adopted into the Antonine dynasty, as the son of Marcus

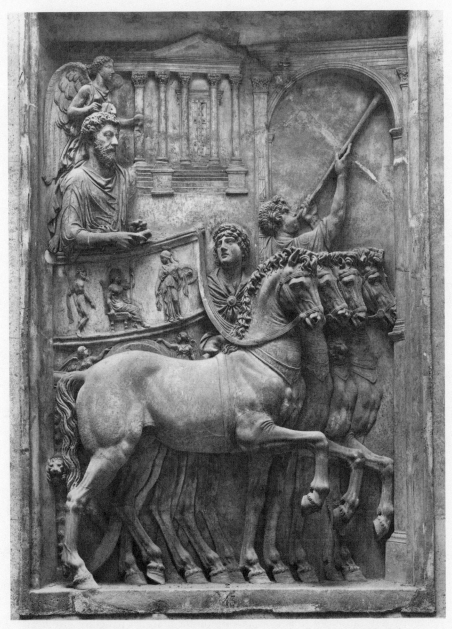

Fig. 9.1. Panel from the lost Arch of Marcus Aurelius in Rome, showing the emperor's triumphal carriage, c. 176–80 A.D. Now in the Museo Conservatori, Rome. Photo: Alinari/Art Resource, New York, 6044.

Aurelius and the brother of Commodus (probably in 195). One presumes that the destruction of Commodan images ended as soon as Severus reversed the damnatio. Certainly by 197, Severus had engineered the deification of his deceased "brother" to accompany their father as a god in the heavens.[22]

About thirty years after this act of recutting, in late 211, Severus's son Caracalla, who ruled jointly with his brother Geta on their father's death in the same year, had his brother murdered. Geta was accused of trying to kill Caracalla, and his images were subjected to a systematic *damnatio memoriae*. Several monuments and numerous inscriptions show evidence of his elimination.[23] One example in Rome is the Gate of the Argentarii, erected by a guild of silversmiths or bankers in 204 with two large frontal reliefs of the Severan family performing sacrifice (figs. 9.2 and 9.3).[24] Originally, one of the two panels on the inner faces of the gate's trabeated bay showed Severus, his wife Julia Domna, and his son Geta, while the other depicted Caracalla, his wife Plautilla, and his father-in-law, Plautianus. Although Plautianus was disgraced and killed as early as 205, Plautilla was murdered by her husband only in 211 or 212. The changes to the gate's sculptures seem part of a single campaign of iconoclasm (probably conducted in 212), when the gate's inscription was carefully transformed to remove any mention of Plautilla and Geta.[25] In the inscription, the bronze letters were replaced in such a way as to airbrush Plautianus, Geta, and Plautilla out of all mention.[26] But in the sculptures, the condemned figures were not recut or turned into background; instead, gaping holes were left indicating where the gouged-out figures had once stood. Had the inscriptions been preserved, they would have been testimony to the visual absence and its condemnatory implications for the named individuals. By effacing all mention of the condemned but leaving the hollows to speak for their loss, the Argentarii panels highlight the public gesture of forgetting. It matters less who has been forgotten (though at the time everyone would have known) than that a public "forgetting" has happened and is perpetually marked in stone.

On the face of it, these two examples speak of two different kinds of iconoclasm. The Marcus panel appears to airbrush Commodus into perpetual oblivion, like a Communist ex-leader in Eastern Europe.[27] The relief's recutting is a creative act of forgetting. By contrast, the Argentarii reliefs (though not the gate's inscriptions) seem to preserve the memory of the eliminated as condemned even in the act of their eradication. The gouged hollows and clumsy restoration (of Julia Domna's arm in the east-pier panel for instance) grace the finished sculpture for eternity. Semiotically, they signal not just that someone's memory has been annihilated but that we must note and remember that the forgotten are forgotten. Neither instance of iconoclasm is unique in the Roman context. Other public examples of Geta's portrait (for example a

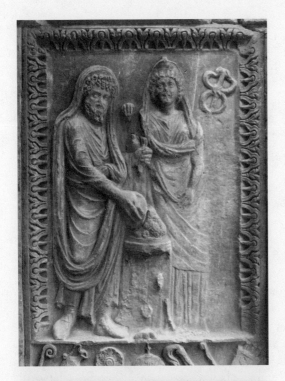

Fig. 9.2. Panel A from the Gate of the Argentarii in the Forum Boarium, Rome, showing Septimius Severus and Julia Domna performing libation, 204 A.D. Still in situ. Photo: DAI Rome, 70.993.

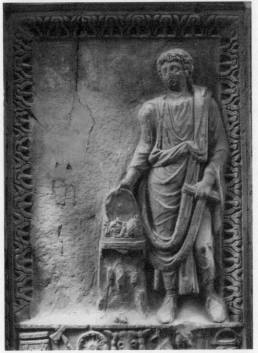

Fig. 9.3. Panel B from the Gate of the Argentarii in the Forum Boarium, Rome, showing the young Caracalla performing libation, 204 A.D. Still in situ. Photo: DAI Rome, 70.1000.

painted tondo from Egypt and the reliefs of an arch erected by Severus in Lep-
cis Magna in Africa—both showing dynastic compositions of Severus, his
wife, and sons) are marked with the same gaping destruction, the same commemoration of a condemnation to be remembered.[28] Other emperors subjected to damnatio beside Commodus had their features transformed in an apparently parallel attempt to forget they had ever existed. A famous example
from a comparable public monument in Rome (what exactly it was we shall
perhaps never know) is the Cancellaria relief now in the Vatican in which the
features of the condemned Domitian were recarved with those of his elderly
successor Nerva after the former's fall in 96 A.D.[29]

However, we should resist the assumption that recutting in the form of
airbrushing was itself unequivocally an act of forgetting.[30] The Cancellaria
Nerva, his head too small for his body and stiffly attached, in the context of
viewers' recent memories of what the relief looked like, might well have constituted a contemporary comment on Domitian rather than (or as well as) a
deliberate attempt to forget him. In the case of the triumph of Commodus and
Marcus, the arch which supported the image would have been a conspicuous
landmark, associated with a famous triumphal festival that emphasised father
and son. Whatever specific changes were inflicted on the reliefs (at least one
other panel still surviving from this arch was substantially recut to remove all
evidence of Commodus,[31] and the inscription was surely rewritten), the monument as a whole cannot instantly have come to signify a world in which Commodus never was. Given his murder, the political instability that followed, and
the removal of his statues and other images, the one presence towering over all
the evocations of this and other transformed monuments of the time was the
memory of the newly absent Commodus. In effect, damnatio of the airbrushing sort was at best a stab at effacing long-term memory: in the short term, it
cannot have helped anyone to forget.

Given the evidence for the recycling, recutting, and reuse of statues throughout the history of the Roman Empire,[32] we may suppose that Roman viewers
were visually sensitive not only to what was now before their eyes (after an act
of recutting) but also to what was once there. The Colossus of Nero—whose
identity our sources tell us was transformed more than once to that of the sun
god, each time from being the statue of Nero—suggests that the condemned
original referent was never forgotten despite initial damnatio and repeated re-
effacement.[33] The double significance of a Caligula recut as Augustus (for example) opened more than one interpretative option for any viewer who
troubled to think what the image might mean. It is significant in the Arch of
Constantine that some aspects of the positive implications of its reused reliefs
dating from the eras of Trajan, Hadrian, and Marcus Aurelius, in which the

imperial heads were replaced by that of Constantine, remained in play in viewers' responses.[34]

All these monuments had a public presence within the life of the city. These were images that both evoked the public life of Rome and were a conspicuous part of it. It is against the collective memory of the local citizenry, which in part constitutes the stage upon which the rituals of public life are enacted, that these acts of iconoclasm resonate. Although the direct assault may be upon a piece of stone, what is deliberately violated in the logic of iconoclasm is the assumption that the world will continue as it normally is and should be. The memory of damnatio is written into the monuments in their social significance amidst a collectivity of viewers. Semiotically, that which was the normative flow of image production and reception is halted and reversed—whether the sign of reversal is itself elided (as in the Conservatori triumph panel) or explicitly signaled (by the blank spaces of the Argentarii libations). That act of reversal is very public, and its major resonance is within what one might call the liturgical or normative daily use of monuments. If we move from decorations of buildings to their forms and structures, the point is more effective still.[35]

Famously, Hadrian's Pantheon in Rome—an entirely new building on a revolutionary design—retained the old inscription that recorded the dedication of its demolished predecessor, the Pantheon of Agrippa.[36] Hadrian's rebuilding was the opposite of iconoclastic. It sheltered behind an already venerable text—using the fig leaf of an ancient inscription to proclaim Hadrian's modesty in monumental tones of pious genuflection louder than any panegyric. Here the memory of Agrippa is spectacularly used as a counterpoint to the citizenry's knowledge of the city's recent rebuilding program under Hadrian.[37] Yet the absence of an inscription bespeaking Hadrian meant that in the long term the memory of his role would be forgotten, until the modern archaeology of brick stamps revived the knowledge of his building panache and proved conclusively a Hadrianic rather than Agrippan genesis for the current building.[38] Several centuries later in about 608, in an act which simultaneously ensured the great building's preservation and iconoclastically trampled on its ancient divine heritage, the Christian emperor Phocas and Pope Boniface IV cleared the Pantheon of "pagan filth" and rededicated it as

> a church to the holy and always Virgin Mary and all the martyrs, so the commemoration of all the saints hereafter should take place where not the gods but the demons once were worshipped.[39]

The moves, in the early history of the Pantheon, of rebuilding but preserving a dedication and preserving a building but radically revising its dedication and use are formidable plays with the memory as well as the architecture of a venerable monument. At stake is precisely the significance of memory in a prestigious monumental landmark. Hadrian rehouses Agrippa's gods in a manner more suited to the times. He (loudly) seeks no acknowledgment of his munificence, but only the pious preservation of Agrippa's memory as initiator of the original temple. Since Agrippa's temple had itself been rebuilt under Domitian in the eighties (after a fire), it is conceivable that Hadrian was restoring Agrippa's name as an act of inscriptional damnatio toward Domitian (the hated tyrant overthrown by his own dynasty of Nerva and Trajan). Boniface and Phocas, meanwhile, damn the gods of Agrippa and Hadrian to the hell they deserve in the Christian dispensation, but preserve the memory of all the gods in their dedication of the new church to all the martyrs and all the saints. In its Christian dispensation, every liturgical service in what remains Hadrian's great church in the city of Rome is thus simultaneously an acclamation of the company of heaven and an act of trampling on the idolatrous demon worship of paganism which the Christian liturgy replaces. In condemning the pagan gods, Christians retain their memory—vibrantly, actively, and ritually through the repeated use for nonpagan purposes of a building from whose façade Agrippa's name was never removed.

The Pantheon is unusual among ancient buildings in signaling so clearly how usage and rededication (rather than simply destruction) could serve an iconoclastic purpose. The "iconoclasm" rendered here was not principally material (though the old temple's furnishings and decorations were altered) but rather a repeated liturgical gesture that looked back toward, and affirmed the rejection of, a despised pagan past. Similarly, the Parthenon's millennium of worshipping a Virgin goddess was followed by a near millennium dedicated to the Virgin Mother of God, before the Ottomans put a mosque within its still sacred precincts in 1460, ironically repeating the Christians' rejection of paganism with their own damnatio of Christianity.[40] But the appropriation of buildings to a new calling and the simultaneous trampling (rather than forgetting) of their earlier state were common in antiquity. The basilica built by Maxentius around 307 A.D. at the eastern end of the Forum was appropriated by Constantine when he conquered the city in 312 and subjected his defeated rival to damnatio. Recent excavation contradicts the view that the Constantinian takeover involved any substantial architectural changes.[41] But the colossal image of Constantine, found in 1486 inside the basilica's ruins and now in the courtyard of the Palazzo Conservatori, appears to be a reworked version of Maxentius—too large perhaps to remove from the finished building but certainly susceptible to rededication.[42]

It is difficult to trace the implications of this kind of transformation in reception by the Roman populace. That it occurred within an established system (that is, the Roman principate with its culture of invoking damnatio on a deposed predecessor) rather than at a point where cultural systems are themselves transformed (as when the Pantheon and Parthenon changed from temples to churches) makes its impact much more problematic to assess. But the point is that these changes were not radically different in kind. They belonged to a long discourse of iconoclasm as the spatial and visual mark of change, whether political or religious. And this discourse of iconoclasm was itself dependent on the ancient cultural system of using buildings and statues to signal approbation and power. The mark made by iconoclasm was both a sign of the new and equally an erasure of the old that called explicit attention to what was erased and the fact that it was erased. What is difficult to explore in antiquity, given the parlous state of the surviving evidence, is the ways that a building's functions may have emphasized the iconoclastic transformation we have been examining. To test this issue, it may serve to move from antiquity to some more recent examples within the Christian dispensation.

Iconoclasm, Memory, and Absence in the Reformation

Let us look at changes in the articulation of buildings within a continuing Christian cultural frame rather than at a point of radical disruption of frames. The first impression of Tom Quad in Christ Church is of one of Oxford's grandest quadrangles (figs. 9.4–9.6). But a brief inspection gives rise to a sense of oddity, incompleteness. The buildings entirely enclose the quad all around, but they are set on a raised base, about three feet high, which forms a wide and comfortable pavement encircling the central space (now consisting of paths, lawns, and a pond). This is not a raised platform with a straight edge, but is regularly abutted by bases sticking out into the main court which appear to serve no useful function. The buildings are decorated on their lower story with what seems a blind Gothic arcade going all the way around the court, although its upright pilasters and even at one point its arch are occasionally knocked out by doors or windows.[43] This arcade seems very odd—insufficiently emphasized or related to the windows or doorways to be a "design feature" and yet apparently without any structural purpose. Only when one looks at the capitals that complete the pilasters, from which the arcade's arches rise, does one see that they are also bosses carrying the remains of a vault that would have arched over the paved platform to turn it into a cloister. Each corner of the quad has a more elaborate double pilaster with internal tracery that looks as if it would have been continued in the vaulting of what would have been the cloister's four corners.

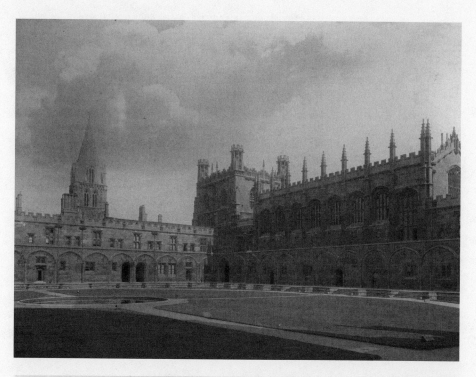

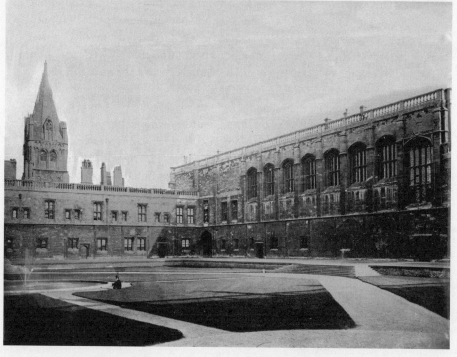

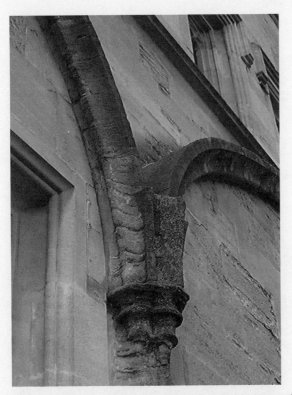

Fig. 9.4. (opposite, top) Tom Quad, Christ Church, Oxford, looking southeast. This is a relatively recent photograph showing the college as it now is, after the works of the last quarter of the nineteenth century. Photo: Christ Church Archives. By kind permission of the Governing Body of Christ Church, Oxford.

Fig. 9.5. (opposite, bottom) Tom Quad, Christ Church, Oxford, looking southeast. This photograph, taken by Taunt about 1850, shows the college before the works of Bodley and Symms after 1875. Among the differences is the absence of the southeast tower, of crenellations and pinnacles on the dining hall to the south, and of all "butresses" along the paved platform around the interior. While one can see the faint marks of the missing cloister arches along the sides (especially on the south wall below the hall), the nineteenth-century works strongly reemphasized these (as in fig. 9.4). Photo: Christ Church Archives. By kind permission of the Governing Body of Christ Church, Oxford.

Fig. 9.6. (above) Tom Quad, Christ Church, Oxford. Detail of a capital originally for the springing of the projected cloister vault. Southeast corner of the Quad, on the east side. Photograph by Tony Brett and Jaś Elsner.

Tom Quad in Christ Church was laid out between 1525 and 1529 as part of the construction of Cardinal Wolsey's college at Oxford (the last college founded before the English Reformation) under the title of Cardinal College.[44] When Wolsey fell from power in 1529 and his college was suppressed, his architects had laid the foundations of the whole court up to about seven feet and constructed the south range (including the hall) and roughly half each of the eastern and western sides.[45] The plans envisaged by Wolsey's builders—who were the royal masons, Henry Redman and John Lubbyns (the best money could buy)[46]—involved a great cloister around the quad on the model of Wolsey's old college, Magdalen. Today, the bosses from which the cloister's outer vaults were to spring on the inner walls of the quad remain in place, a perpetual reminder of what might have been.[47] When Henry VIII refounded the college as Christ Church in 1546, the new foundation somewhat extended the eastern range beyond where it had stopped in 1529, but the north side and part of the west were left open, with Wolsey's foundations for what was to have been his grandiloquent chapel along the north side effectively a track for townspeople and cattle between east and west.[48] Only in the 1660s, after the Restoration of Charles II, was the northern side of the quad completed. Yet despite being about a century and a half later than the rest, the north side was completed to look just like the rest—arcade, pilasters, and springing cloister vaults included. In 1876, in a fit of pseudo-archaeological "accuracy," the buttress bases around the platform were added, in effect exacerbating the sense of loss by more clearly registering the pre-Reformation plan (compare the 1850 and 1960s photographs, figs. 9.4 and 9.5).[49]

What is obvious is that Tom Quad remains an unfinished testament to Wolsey's original plans. The great foundations for the cloister and the interior walls of the quadrangle would not be as they now are had a plan not been aborted. This way of materially marking and adapting space not only signals change and a new vision but also actively commemorates what was once planned but never completed. The final product, like the altered Arch of Marcus and the Gate of the Argentarii, certainly faces in two ways. These changes of plan had more than one meaning as history unfolded. By suppressing Cardinal College and abandoning Wolsey's works in 1529, Henry VIII signaled the fall of a once-loved minister. In this dispensation, the cloister stood unbuilt, the quad's incompleteness gesturing to the modern *damnatio* of an all too worldly prelate. By 1546, when the buildings were reappropriated for Christ Church, Henry—once the Defender of the Catholic Faith—had broken with the Church of Rome. The cloister—unfinished but its foundations never dismantled—stood for something larger than the fall of Wolsey. With the break from Rome had come the dissolution of the monasteries, a wholesale process of appropriation and ruin that had left most of the nation's sacred institutions depredated and partially destroyed. Like all these ruins, the cloister of Tom Quad spoke—with the eloquence of grand foundations abandoned—about the finality of England's break with Rome.[50] But what was ruined was not merely the architecture or the "idolatrous" pictures. A traditional life of liturgical action (extremely rich in pre-Reformation England)[51] and centuries of piety were overturned and readjusted by the dismantlement of the artifacts at which devotion had been directed. The end of a projected cloister was the end of a monastic way of life. It proposed a new learning (in the context of an Oxford College) whose Protestant principles would have none of the Roman Catholic foundations that less than twenty years before were envisaged by Wolsey. In the last years of the seventeenth century, when the quad was finally completed amidst a politics of royal Restoration and then the displacement of the last Roman Catholic king, James II, one might argue that the quad's implicit Protestantism spoke loud. Today, as the issue of a transformed plan and an unfinished courtyard becomes obscure to most visitors, the quad gestures to the more modern themes of elite education, old buildings, and pretty theme-park culture. Its monumentality can still speak to memories of religious and cultural upheaval, but our memories (like those which knew that Hadrian had really built the Pantheon) have changed.

The phenomenon of Tom Quad is by no means unique among the lands touched by Protestant Reform in continental Europe. One thinks readily of the whitewashed Dutch churches painted repeatedly by Pieter Saenredam (1597–1665),[52] often with figures (such as dogs) and activities (for instance, the graffiti that include the artist's signature in the London National Gallery's 1644 panel of the Bauerkerk, Utrecht [fig. 9.7)[53] that would have been anathema to a Roman Catholic sensibility. The painter's usual focus on Gothic (that is to say, pre-Reformed) holy spaces, whitewashed to remove the idolatry of wall paintings, cleared of all the portable bric-a-brac of altars, retables, and devotional panel paintings and filled with what might be called anti-rituals (such as people playing with dogs),[54] gestures toward iconoclastic desecration just as much as does the unbuilt cloister at Christ Church. Alongside a reformed architecture, developed in a clandestine manner by the evangelical Sebastiano Serlio in sixteenth-century Venice and Fontainebleau,[55] and the creation of a Calvinist code for an actual Protestant architecture (itself described as an "aesthetics of subversion"),[56] went the explicit preservation of Catholic places of liturgy rearranged so that the sites of pre-Reformed rite were trampled. Churches throughout the Netherlands, for example, were denuded of their Catholic images and whitewashed (as Saenredam so potently records) and then brilliantly insulted (from the viewpoint of Catholics!) by having their interiors reshaped into a reformed liturgical space. Whereas in the Catholic rite all devotion was directed to the east—as is embedded in the material form of the basilica church plan, with its longitudinal thrust eastward and its focus at the apse—the Protestants turned their benches toward the preacher and pointedly turned their backs on the east.[57] No believer (on either the Reformed or the Catholic side) could have been insensitive to the memory of a centuries' old tradition

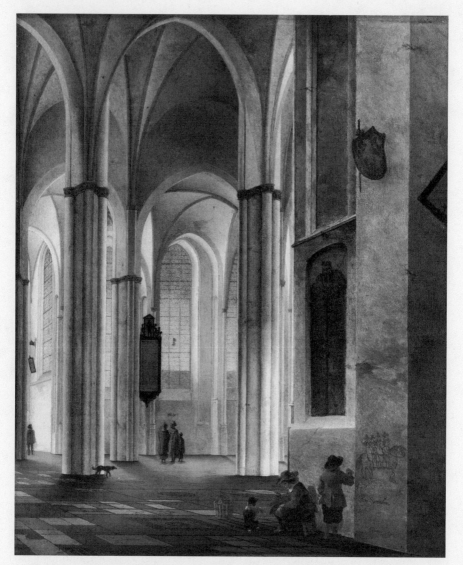

Fig. 9.7. Pieter Saenredam (1597–1665), *The Bauerkerk, Utrecht,* oil on oak, 60.1 × 50.1 cm., 1644. Now in the National Gallery, London (NG 1896). Photo: National Gallery.

inscribed in architectural space and to the very specific spatial signals of rejection. This is not iconoclasm in the literal sense of demolition, but rather it repeats a constant ritual desecration of the memory of pre-Reformed liturgy— a memory preserved in and by space, and enhanced (if only to be derided) in the ways that space has been adapted.

As with Tom Quad or the Pantheon in its Christian incarnation, the re-arrangement of charged spaces (a subject hardly explored within art history, even in the copious literature of art and Reform in the Low Countries) was a *damnatio memoriae* of old ritual through the assertions of new ritual. But the *damnatio* was also enacted through the potent combination of preserving the architectural space in its original arrangement and then specifically altering the focus of behavior within it. The apse remains the apse in a Dutch Gothic church (like the Oude Kerk in Amsterdam), but the orientation of action and the specific denial of sanctity to the place where the high altar once stood turn a space like the apse into an empty shell. Whether the viewer's response to such emptiness is to revel in an idolatry disrupted or to mourn for a liturgy lost, the key issue is that memory remains inscribed in monumentality (and deliberately so), however much the building has been transformed.

Concluding Thoughts: Memory and Affect in the Recarved Image

I began with some intentionally provocative remarks about transhistoricism (at least on the level of artistic forms) in the phenomena of alteration, demolition, and monumental memory.[58] Let us conclude by reversing this. Picture the con-quering heroes of Europe in 1945—Churchill, Stalin, Roosevelt (the last, al-ready dead, now saint as well as hero). Imagine that in the shattered civic spaces of the continent the statues of the defeated tyrant, far from being pulled down, were simply recarved; his hated features replaced with theirs. The very possi-bility is unthinkable. The hatred of Hitler then, like that of Stalin later (which manifested itself after 1989 in the demolition of his statues in formerly Com-munist Eastern Europe), necessitated total demolition. Hitler was so detested a figure that his use (even in the form of recycled damnatio) would have served as an insult to those who might have taken his place on the statue's podium. On a less ideological and more pragmatic level, there was no technological need to reuse old bronze or marble in this way. Statues can easily be manufactured anew. Yet such recutting was precisely the strategy of the Roman world. Our surviving Caligulas, for example, include beheaded statues of the young tyrant, cast into rivers or buried on his fall; but they include also portrait heads re-shaped as his uncle Claudius (who succeeded him) and some turned into his ancestor Augustus, the greatest of his predecessors.[59] The memory of the con-demned remains in the telltale marks upon the stone. Under Constantine, such recarving served not only the negative function of replacing the fallen tyrant— in the case, for instance, of the colossal image from the basilica of Maxentius— but also the positive purpose of casting the new emperor into the bodies once occupied by Trajan, Hadrian, and Marcus Aurelius on the Arch of Constantine. In these cases, albeit in more or less subtle ways, my point is that the memory of the figure condemned (even the memory of his forgetting) is preserved.

Our reluctance to countenance today a visual strategy once considered utterly normal is more than a sign of radical changes in attitudes about how memory may be appropriately treated within the Western visual tradition. In a cultural context where few would confuse a representation with its prototype, or a portrait photograph with the actual person portrayed, there is nonetheless a visceral and very premodern repugnance about tainting Churchill's image with Hitler's. Perhaps it is because in modern popular culture more people than we like to admit still stick pins into the pictures of their enemies (and especially their former lovers). In antiquity, by contrast, the relations of image and prototype were much less distinctly separable, not just in the case of sacred images but also in that of portraits of emperors.[60] This very inseparability is what made *damnatio memoriae* so powerful as a destructive tool. Yet, despite it, there appears to have been no problem about the recycling of the hated and officially forgotten in the guise of the current and officially approved. While part of the explanation for antiquity's promiscuity with changing heads lies in practical matters of cost and workmanship which are not problems today, modernity's resistance to such artistic activity is strongly (perhaps viscerally) ideological. Yet, in a funny way, modernity's refusal to conduct itself like the Roman past signals not only difference in attitudes to monumental commemoration, but also surprising similarities in the subtle arena of imputing affect and even imputing the power of the prototype to what seems only an image worked in stone, wood, or metal.[61]

NOTES

My particular thanks are due to the editors for their insightful critique and to Keith Thomas for his kind comments.

1. On memory as *evoked* by objects, see, e.g., M. Kwint, "Introduction: The Physical Past," in *Material Memories: Design and Evocation*, ed. M. Kwint, C. Breward, J. Aynsley (Oxford: Berg, 1999), 1–16, esp. 2–5.

2. S. Küchler, "Making Skins: *Malangan* and the Idea of Kinship in Northern New Ireland," in *Anthropology, Art and Aesthetics*, ed. J. Coote and A. Shelton (Oxford: Oxford University Press, 1992), 94–112; idem, "Landscape as Memory: The Mapping of Process and Its Representation in a Melanesian Society," in *Landscape: Politics and Perspectives*, ed. B. Bender (Oxford: Berg, 1993), 85–106; A. Gell, *Art and Agency: An Anthropological Theory* (Oxford: Oxford University Press, 1998), 223–28, 233–38.

3. W. Melion and S. Küchler, "Introduction," in *Images of Memory: On Remembering and Representation*, ed. S. Küchler and W. Melion (Washington D.C.: Smithsonian Institution Press, 1991), 1–46, esp. 2–3 and 7.

4. P. Connerton, *How Societies Remember* (Cambridge: Cambridge University Press, 1989), esp. 4 and 74 on inscribed or textual and performative or embodied remembering (with critique in D. Battaglia, "The Body in the Gift: Memory and Forgetting in Sabarl Mortuary Exchange," *American Ethnologist* 19 [1992]: 3–18, esp. 3) and 6–40 on social memory; also see J. Fentress and C. Wickham, *Social Memory* (Oxford: Blackwell, 1992). The historical literature on memory is vast; recent appraisals include K. L. Klein, "On the Emergence of *Memory* in Historical Discourse," *Representations* 69 (2000): 127–50; P. Geary, "The Historical Material of Memory," in *Art, Memory and the Family in Renaissance Florence,* ed. G. Ciappelli and P. Rubin (Cambridge: Cambridge University Press, 2000), 17–25.

5. S. Küchler, "Malangan: Art and Memory in a Melanesian Society," *Man* 22 (1987): 238–55; idem, "Malangan-Objects, Sacrifice and the Production of Memory," *American Ethnologist* 15 (1988): 625–37; Battaglia, "Body in the Gift."

6. A call to a material-based semiotics can be found in M. Gottdiener, *Postmodern Semiotics: Material Culture and the Forms of Postmodern Life* (Oxford: Blackwell, 1995).

7. The exception (from a literary theorist rather than an art historian) is S. Stewart, *On Longing: Narratives of the Miniature, the Gigantic, the Souvenir, the Collection* (Durham, N.C.: Duke University Press, 1993).

8. E.g., C. Wood, ed., *The Vienna School Reader: Politics and Historical Method in the 1930s* (New York: Zone, 2000).

9. On the mausoleum, see G. Waywell, "The Mausoleum at Halicarnassus," in *The Seven Wonders of the Ancient World,* ed. P. Clayton and M. Price (London: Routledge, 1988), 100–123, with bibliography at 173; on the imperial Roman tradition it inspired, see P. Davies, *Death and the Emperor: Roman Imperial Funerary Monuments from Augustus to Marcus Aurelius* (Cambridge: Cambridge University Press, 2000).

10. On monuments and public mourning, see J. Winter, *Sites of Memory, Sites of Mourning: The Great War in European Cultural History* (Cambridge: Cambridge University Press, 1995), 78–116; M. Rowlands, "Remembering to Forget: Sublimation as Sacrifice in War Memorials," in *The Art of Forgetting,* ed. A. Forty and S. Küchler (Oxford: Berg, 1999), 129–45; A. King, "Remembering and Forgetting in the Public Memorials of the Great War," ibid., 147–69. On personal mourning, see, e.g., M. Pointon, "Materialising Mourning: Hair, Jewellery and the Body," in Kwint et al., *Material Memories,* 39–57.

11. R. Mainstone, *Hagia Sophia* (London: Thames & Hudson, 1988), 9, 129–33.

12. On Ottoman St. Sophia, see M. Ahunbay and Z. Ahunbay, "Structural Influence of Hagia Sophia on Ottoman Mosque Architecture," in *Hagia Sophia: From the Age of Justinian to the Present,* ed. R. Mark and A. Çakmak (Cambridge: Cambridge University Press, 1992), 179–94; G. Necipoğlu, "The Life of an Imperial Monument: Hagia Sophia after Byzantium," ibid., 195–225.

13. Cf. C. W. Hedrick Jr., *History and Silence: The Purge and Rehabilitation of Memory in Late Antiquity* (Austin: University of Texas Press, 2000), xi–xii, 100, 109–10 (statue bases as monuments to "forgetting"), 113–26; A. Wharton, "Erasure: Eliminating the Space of Late Antique Judaism," in *From Dura to Sepphoris: Studies in Jewish Art and Society in Late Antiquity,* ed. L. I. Levine and Z. Weiss, *Journal of Roman Archaeology,* supp. 40 (Portsmouth, R.I., 2000), 195–214, esp. 195–96 and 208–12 (modern effacements of ancient objects).

14. For a discussion of embodied remembering, see Battaglia, "Body in Gift," 3–4; Küchler, "Landscape as Memory," 91–92. On statues in Roman society, see P. Stewart, "Statues in Roman Society," Ph.D. diss., University of Cambridge, 1998. On the imperial image, see K. Hopkins, *Conquerors and Slaves* (Cambridge: Cambridge University Press, 1978), 147–242.

15. Battaglia, "Body in Gift," 5, 12–14; Küchler, "Making Skins," 103.

16. I paraphrase Küchler, "Landscape as Memory," 91–92.

17. F. Vittinghoff, *Der Staatsfeind in der römischen Kaiserzeit,* Neue deutsche Faschungen, Abteilung alte Geschichte 2 (Berlin, 1936); Hedrick, *History and Silence,* 91–94, 113–26. On material culture, see P. Stewart, "The Destruction of Statues in Late Antiquity," in *Constructing Identities in Late Antiquity,* ed. R. Miles (London: Routledge, 1999), 159–89; S. Carey, "'*In Memoriam (Perpetuam) Neronis': 'Damnatio Memoriae'* and Nero's Colossus," *Apollo* 152 (July 2000): 20–31.

18. On the Arch of Marcus, see S. De Maria, *Gli archi onorari di Roma e dell'Italia Romana* (Rome: L'Erma di Bretschneider, 1988), 303–5; M. Torelli, "Arcus Marci Aurelii," in *Lexicon Topographicum Urbis Romae,* ed. E. M. Steinby, vol. 1 (Rome: Quasar, 1993), 98–99.

19. I. S. Ryberg, *The Panel Reliefs of Marcus Aurelius* (New York: Archaeological Institute of America, 1967), 15–20; E. Angelicoussis, "The Panel Reliefs of Marcus Aurelius," *Römische Mitteilungen* 91 (1984): 141–205, esp. 152–54; G. M. Koeppel, "Die historische Reliefs der römischen Kaiserzeit IV," *Bonner Jahrbücher* 186 (1986): 1–90, esp. 9–11 and 50–52.

20. Commodus, then fifteen years old, took his first state office as consul in January 177, immediately after the triumph: see A. Birley, *Marcus Aurelius* (London: Eyre & Spottiswoode, 1966), 269–70.

21. The recutting was first pointed out by M. Wegner, "Bemerkungen zu den Ehrendenkmälern des Marcus Aurelius," *Archäologische Anzeiger* (1938): 155–95, esp. 160–64.

22. A. Birley, *Septimius Severus: The African Emperor* (New Haven: Yale University Press, 1989), 117 ("adoption" by Marcus), 127 (deification of Commodus).

23. E. Varner, "Tyranny and Transformation of the Roman Visual Landscape," *From Caligula to Constantine: Tyranny and Transformation in Roman Portraiture,* exhibition catalogue (Atlanta: Michael C. Carlos Museum, 2000), 9–26, esp. 18–19 with bibliography.

24. D. Haynes and P. Hirst, *Porta Argentariorum* (London: Macmillan, 1939), 17–27; M. Pallottino, *L'Arco degli Argentarii* (Rome: Danesi, 1946), esp. 73–92; F. Ghedini, *Giulia Domna tra Oriente e Occidente* (Rome: L'Erma di Bretschneider, 1984), 27–53.

25. See Haynes and Hirst, *Porta Argentariorum,* 2–6 (though they believe Plautianus's name was removed in 205 and the space left blank until the other changes of 211–12); Pallottino, *L'Arco degli Argentarii,* 37–38; H. Flower, "*Damnatio Memoriae* and Epigraphy," in Varner, *From Caligula to Constantine,* 58–69, esp. 65–66.

26. On epigraphy in public culture including collective memory, see A. Petrucci, *Public Lettering: Script, Power and Culture* (Chicago: University of Chicago Press, 1993). This is weak on the destruction of inscriptions, however.

27. Hedrick, *History and Silence,* 109, drawing on M. Kundera, *The Book of Laughter and Forgetting* (New York: Knopf, 1980), 3.

28. Varner, *From Caligula to Constantine,* 18–19 with bibliography.

29. F. Magi, *I rilievi flavi della Cancellaria* (Rome: Pontificia Academia Romana, 1945), esp. 60–69; G. M. Koeppel, "Die historische Reliefs der römischen Kaiserzeit II," *Bonner Jahrbücher* 184 (1984): 1–65, esp. 29–34.

30. Hedrick, *History and Silence,* xi–xii, 89–130.

31. This is the Liberalitas panel now on the north attic story of the Arch of Constantine: see Angelicoussis, "Panel Reliefs of Marcus Aurelius," 154–58; Koeppel, "Die historische Reliefs der römischen Kaiserzeit IV," 72–75.

32. H. Blanck, *Wiederwendung alter Statuen als Ehrendenkmäler bei Griechen und Römern* (Rome: L'Erma di Bretschneider, 1969); J.-P. Rollin, *Untersuchungen zu Rechtsfragen römischer Bildnisse* (Bonn: Habelt, 1979); D. Kinney, "Spolia, Damnatio and Renovatio Memoriae," *Memoirs of the American Academy at Rome* 42 (1997): 117–48.

33. Carey, "'*In Memoriam (Perpetuam) Neronis,*'" esp. 24 and 28, with bibliography at n. 9.

34. H. P. L'Orange and A. von Gerkan, *Die spätantike Bildschmuck des Konstantinsbogens* (Berlin: de Gruyter, 1939), esp. 162, 190–91; J. Elsner, "From the Culture of *Spolia* to the Cult of Relics: The Arch of Constantine and the Genesis of Late Antique Forms," *Papers of the British School at Rome* 68 (2000): 149–84, esp. 172–75. For an alternative view (that recutting strongly implies the obliteration of memory), see Kinney "Spolia, Damnatio and Renovatio Memoriae," 142–46.

35. On damnatio and architectural space, see P. Davies, "'What Worse Than Nero, What Better Than His Baths?': '*Damnatio Memoriae*' and Roman Architecture," in Varner, *From Caligula to Constantine,* 27–44.

36. K. De Fine Licht, *The Rotunda in Rome* (Copenhagen: Gyldendel, 1968); W. L. Mac-Donald, *The Pantheon: Design, Meaning and Progeny* (London: Lane, 1976); A. Ziolkowski in *Lexicon Topographicum Urbis Romae,* ed. E. M. Steinby, vol. 4 (Rome: Quasar, 1999), 54–61; M. Wilson-Jones, *Principles of Roman Architecture* (New Haven: Yale University Press, 2000), 177–212.

37. M. T. Boatwright, *Hadrian and the City of Rome* (Princeton: Princeton University Press, 1987), 33–73.

38. The fundamental work was done by Herbert Bloch in the 1930s: De Fine Licht, *Rotunda in Rome,* 186–90.

39. John the Deacon, *Chronicon Venetum* 8.20, in *Monumenta Germaniae Historica* 7 (1846). See also *Liber Pontificalis* under Boniface IV, ed. Louis Duchesne (Paris, 1886–1957), 1:317). On parallel Christian appropriations in the east, see B. Ward-Perkins, "Re-using the Architectural Legacy of the Past: *Entre ideologie et pragmatisme,*" in *The Idea and Ideal of the Town between Late Antiquity and the Middle Ages,* ed. G. P. Brogiolo and B. Ward-Perkins (Leiden: Brill, 1999), 225–44, esp. 233–40. On adapting pagan temple to Christian church, see F. W. Deichmann, "Frühchristliche Kirchen in antiken Heiligentum," *Jahrbuch des deutschen archäologischen Instituts* 54 (1939): 105–36.

40. On the Parthenon as church (like the Pantheon, which was made into a church c. 600 A.D.), compare F. W. Deichmann, "Die Basilika im Parthenon," *Athenische Mitteilungen* 63, no. 4 (1938/39), 127–39, with Ward-Perkins, "Re-using the Architectural Legacy of the Past," 235–40. On the Parthenon as mosque, see M. Korres, "The Parthenon from Antiquity to the Nineteenth Century," in *The Parthenon and Its Impact in Modern Times,* ed. P. Tournikiotis (Athens: Melissa, 1994), 137–61, esp. 150–55.

41. The northern apse appears to be late fourth or early fifth century, rather than Constantinian, while the entrance and staircase on the south side seem original to the building: see F. Coarelli, "Basilica Constantiniana, Basilica Nova," in *Lexicon Topographicum Urbis Romae,* ed. E. M. Steinby, vol. 1 (Rome: Quasar, 1993), 170–73; O. Hekster, "The City of Rome in Late Imperial Ideology: The Tetrarchs, Maxentius and Constantine," in *Mediterraneo Antico* 2 (1999): 717–748, esp.725–26 and 737–39.

42. Varner, *From Caligula to Constantine,* 14, with bibliography at n. 50.

43. Two doors on the south side, one going under the great hall, two on the east side, and one window at the southwest corner of the west side.

44. On Wolsey and Oxford, see C. Cross, "Oxford and the Tudor State, 1509–1558," in *The History of the University of Oxford,* ed. J. McConica, vol. 3, *The Collegiate University* (Oxford: Oxford University Press, 1986), 117–49, esp. 120–24.

45. On Cardinal College, see J. G. Milne and J. H. Harvey, "The Building of Cardinal College," *Oxoniensia* 8/9 (1943/44): 137–53; J. Newman, "The Physical Setting: New Building and Adaptation," in McConica, *History of the University of Oxford,* 3:611–15.

46. On the royal masons, see J. G. Harvey, "The Building Works and Architects of Cardinal Wolsey," *Journal of the British Archaeological Association* 8 (1943): 50–60.

47. *The Royal Commission on Historical Monuments (England): An Inventory of the Historical Monuments in the City of Oxford* (London: H.M. Stationery Office, 1939), 30–33; J. Sherwood and N. Pevsner, *The Buildings of England: Oxfordshire* (London: Penguin, 1974), 109–13.

48. W. G. Hiscock, *A Christ Church Miscellany* (Oxford: Oxford University Press, 1946), 198–200.

49. See the Quadrangle Committee reports to the Christ Church Governing Body (GB papers xv.c.1, fols. 116 and 118) and GB minutes for May 24, 1876 (i.B.2, p. 189); see also B. Law, *Building Oxford's Heritage: Symm and Company from 1815* (Oxford: Prelude, 1998), 49–51.

50. On the English Reformation, see E. Duffy, *The Stripping of the Altars* (New Haven: Yale University Press, 1992), 379–477. On iconoclasm, see J. Phillips, *The Reformation of Images: Destruction of Art in England, 1535–1660* (Berkeley: University of California Press, 1973); M. Aston, *England's Iconoclasts* (Oxford: Oxford University Press, 1988); idem, "Iconoclasm in England: Official and Clandestine," in *Iconoclasm versus Art and Drama,* ed. C. Davidson and A. Nichols (Kalamazoo, Mich.: Medieval Institute Publications, 1989), 47–91. On ruins in the Reformation, see idem, "English Ruins and English History: The Dissolution and the Sense of the Past," *Journal of the Warburg and Courtauld Institutes* 36 (1973): 231–55.

51. Duffy, *Stripping of the Altars,* 11–368.

52. See G. Schwartz and M. Bok, *Pieter Saenredam: The Painter and His Time* (London: Thames & Hudson, 1990), for life and works.

53. Ibid., 199, fig. 211. On such inscriptions in Dutch painting, see S. Alpers, *The Art of Describing* (Chicago: University of Chicago Press, 1983), 169–221, with 172–80 specifically on Saenredam. The possibility that the activities portrayed in this picture might have had positive meanings for Saenredam's Reformed patrons and viewers (see Schwartz and Bok, *Pieter Saenredam,* 200–204) does not remove the edge of criticism directed against the whitewashed shell of what was once a site of Catholic rite.

54. On iconoclasm as ritual in the Reformation, see M. Aston, "Rites of Destruction by Fire," *Faith and Fire* (London: Hambledon, 1993), 291–314; S. Michalski, *The Reformation and the Visual Arts: The Protestant Images Question in Western and Eastern Europe* (London: Routledge, 1993), 76–79; more generally, see D. Freedberg, *The Power of Images* (Chicago: University of Chicago Press, 1989), 378–428.

55. On Serlio, see M. Tafuri, "Ipotesi sulla religiosità di Sebastiano Serlio," in *Sebastiano Serlio,* ed. C. Thoenes (Milan: Electra, 1989), 57–66; M. Carpo, *La maschera e il modello: Teoria architettonica ed evangelismo nell' "Extraordinario Libro" de Sebastiano Serlio* (Milan: Jaca, 1993). The "Evangelicals" were a Lutheran- and Calvinist-influenced group in France that wished to reform Catholicism from within: see C. Randall, *Building Codes: The Aesthetics of Calvinism in Early Modern Europe* (Philadelphia: University of Pennsylvania Press, 1999), 78–82.

56. See Randall, *Building Codes,* 5–7, 25, on subversion. For Calvinist influence on the visual arts, see P. C. Finney, ed., *Seeing beyond the Word: Visual Arts and the Calvinist Tradition* (Grand Rapids: Eerdmans, 1999).

57. On Protestant liturgical space, see B. Reymond, *L'architecture religieuse des protestants* (Geneva: Labor, 1996), 142–71.

58. This does not mean I would endorse any sort of transhistoricism of response, as appears to be the position of Freedberg, *Power of Images.*

59. A convenient collection is in Varner, *From Caligula to Constantine,* nos. 4–19, pp. 96–125; a full account is in D. Boschung, *Die Bildnisse des Caligula* (Berlin: Mann, 1989).

60. On the imperial image, see K. M. Setton, *Christian Attitudes towards the Emperor in the Fourth century* (New York: Columbia University Press, 1941), 196–211; H. Belting, *Likeness and Presence* (Chicago: University of Chicago Press, 1994), 102–14. On the gods, see R. Gordon, "The Real and the Imaginary: Production and Religion in the Graeco-Roman World," *Art History* 2 (1979): 5–34, esp. 7–8. On conceptual issues, see M. Barasch, *Icon: Studies in the History of an Idea* (New York: New York University Press, 1992), 23–43; J. Elsner, "Image and Ritual: Reflections on the Religious Appreciation of Classical Art," *Classical Quarterly* 46 (1996): 515–31. On the inherence of prototype within image even in some modern responses to art, see D. Freedberg, "Holy Images and Other Images," in *The Art of Interpreting,* ed. S. C. Scott (Philadelphia: Pennsylvania State University Press, 1995), 68–87.

61. On the premodern nature of some of modernity's attitudes, see D. Freedberg, *Iconoclasts and Their Motives* (Maarssen: Schwartz, 1985), 33–35; also Freedberg, *Power of Images,* 32, 276–77, 281, 414.

|||||| 10

Archaeology and the Monument: An Embattled Site of History and Memory in Contemporary India

TAPATI GUHA-THAKURTA

Ayodhya: The Eye of the Storm

During the 1980s, the small temple town of Ayodhya (around six miles from the city of Faizabad in eastern Uttar Pradesh) and a sixteenth-century mosque situated here became the focal point of the most violent of national conflicts. The sacred town has a long-standing mythological association as the birthplace of Lord Rama, an incarnation of Vishnu, the hero of the epic poem *Ramayana*. The mosque, widely referred to as the Babri Masjid, built in 1528 by Mir Baqi, a noble in the Mughal emperor Babur's court, acquired a more recent notoriety as a structure that is said to have been erected after the destruction of an ancient Rama temple that occupied the same site. Recent history has seen the orchestration of virulent claims to the existence of a prior *Ramjanmabhumi mandir* (temple commemorating the place of Rama's birth) at the very site of the *masjid* and a campaign for its reconstruction. These claims, as is well known, have been at the heart of the country's right-wing *Hindutva* politics, asserted by a cluster of militant ultra-Hindu organizations, the most powerful of these being the Rashtriya Swayamsevak Sangh (RSS), the

Vishwa Hindu Parishad (VHP), and the Bajrang Dal, their common electoral face being represented by the Bharatiya Janata Party (BJP).[1] Since 1989–90, activists and volunteers of these organizations have converged around this site with the agenda of "liberating" this true and only birthplace of Rama (fig. 10.1). Liberation, to them, meant nothing short of bringing down the existing structure of the Babri Masjid to make way for the new *Ramjanmabhumi mandir,* the foundation for which had already been ceremonially laid in the adjoining premises in November 1989 (fig. 10.2). It is this agenda which culminated in the demolition of the mosque on December 6, 1992.[2]

No other dispute has aroused as much frenzy, fanaticism, and alarm in independent India as this *Ramjanmabhumi*–Babri Masjid controversy. Its beginnings can be traced back to various points in time, depending on the positions at stake.[3] Historians are generally of the consensus that the contending claims on the site surfaced no earlier than the mid-nineteenth century—and that the first sparks of violence can be traced back to events that occurred between 1853 and 1855, when the Hanumangarhi temple in Ayodhya was occupied by a sect of Muslims under similar allegations that it had supplanted a mosque, provoking a retaliatory takeover by the temple priest of Hanumangarhi of a portion of the Babri Masjid compound.[4] The colonial government's move of fencing off and demarcating separate places of worship for Hindus and Muslims within the premises of the *masjid* met with repeated appeals and contestations from both communities. The present face of the controversy is marked out by events that closely followed on the nation's independence.— The surreptitious installation of an idol of infant Rama inside the mosque on the night of December 22–23, 1949 (claimed ever since as a miraculous manifestation of Rama) led to the new government's decision to lock the disputed premises, barring all worship within it. The motif of the lock came to figure prominently in the agitation launched soon after by the VHP for the recovery of the sacred site for Hindu worship. And it was the government's order for the opening of the locks in February 1986, giving in to the Hindu demands for free access to the shrine, which stands out as the decisive turn—the one treacherous act that turned the tide in favor of the *Ramjanmabhumi* movement. Thereafter the Indian state can be seen as playing a clearly ineffectual and passive, if not an openly complicit, role in the torrent of events and agitations at Ayodhya leading to the debacle of December 1992.

It is not just this scenario of the political mobilization of communal hostilities that has been a source of consternation. An equal cause of anxiety is the manner in which the *Ramjanmabhumi* demands have been presented, repeatedly employing the authority of history and archaeology and their modes of

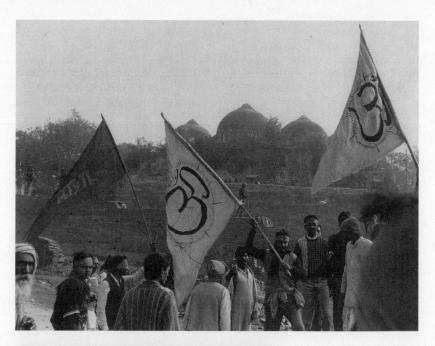

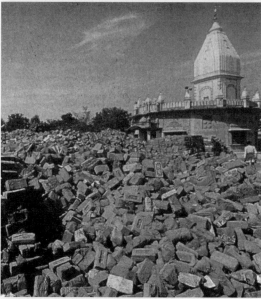

Fig. 10.1. *(top)* The *Ramjanmabhumi* volunteers propagating their cause, with the doomed Babri Masjid in the background, Ayodhya, 1989. Courtesy Anandabazar Patrika library and archive, Calcutta.

Fig. 10.2. *(bottom)* "Consecrated" bricks brought from all over the country and heaped at an adjacent site to the Babri Masjid, as a part of the foundation-laying ceremony (called the Shilanyas) of the proposed Ram temple, held on November 9, 1989. From *Frontline*, vol. 17, no. 13, June 24–July 7, 2000. Reproduced by permission of *Frontline*.

verification. Legend and faith have acquired the armor of historicity, presenting a series of conjectures as undisputed facts. So, the "certainty" that present-day Ayodhya is the historical birthplace of Lord Rama passes into the "certainty" that there was a tenth- or eleventh-century *Vaishnava* temple commemorating the birthplace site, both of these in turn building up to the "hard fact" that this temple was demolished in the sixteenth century to make way for the Babri Masjid. Such invocation of "facts" made it imperative for a camp of left/liberal/secular historians to attack these certainties, to riddle them with doubts and counterfacts, in order to recuperate the fields of history and archaeology from their political misuse.

The intention of this essay is neither to reconstruct the course and politics of this widely written about Ayodhya controversy, nor to test the relative truth of the claims and counterclaims that circulated around the disputed site.[5] My interest lies primarily in the terms and rhetoric of the debate and the wider questions it raises about the status of evidence and the nature of knowledge in disciplines like history and archaeology. Over the past decade, the onus of proving or disproving the remains of a destroyed temple beneath the now-demolished mosque has devolved more and more on the discipline of archaeology, on the elaboration of its excavation methods and analytical techniques. In dealing with the archaeological debate around this disputed site, I have found it necessary to deliberately disengage form from content, rhetoric from evidence. This helps to silhouette the way the discipline, pushed against the wall in this controversy, has staked its scientificity and expertise and has labored to police the boundaries of its professional domain.

Such an emphasis also helps to place the case of Ayodhya in a larger historical frame, where we find similar battles over the custody of monuments unfolding in other spaces and times. In the latter section of the essay, I treat the present debate as a moment steeped in earlier histories, using it as a way of marking disciplinary positions and claims whose genealogies can be traced back to the first archaeological surveys and writings of the late nineteenth century. I ask, for instance, How has archaeology been shifting its grounds on the subject of the historicization of monuments and remains? How are its histories related to other meanings, beliefs, and residual associations that linger around the same sites? And what are the limits that have invariably confounded the staging of "scientific" or "objective" knowledges? The lessons from Ayodhya, I would argue, are less about the abuse of history and archaeology and more about the unresolved contradictions that have trapped the disciplines in their own shells and pitted them against the larger world of public faith and demands.

A Threatened Site, a Threatened Science

Let me begin with the theme of the violation of truth and objective knowledge at Ayodhya. When on December 6, 1992 the *Ramjanmabhumi* volunteers and supporters razed the Babri Masjid, what they destroyed was much more than an old mosque. The mosque, in any case, had been fairly insignificant as a religious or historical structure; but its rubble became the symbol of the utmost violence, the deepest transgressions of religion and history. The day came to be inscribed as one of the blackest days in national history. The frenzied act violated not just Muslim sentiments but also a century-long tradition of historical and archaeological conservation. It trod over the cardinal governmental principle that an old monument, whether it be a living or deserted shrine, even when it belonged to a particular religious community, remained in the last count "the cultural property and heritage of India."[6] The razing of the mosque, then, has been widely derided as a betrayal of the very principles of modernity and a retreat to medieval barbarism and intolerance (fig. 10.3). And the VHP's unrestrained agenda for constructing the Rama temple on this very site is seen today as an open defeat of the republic's laws and principles.[7]

Of the many dangers that these events epitomize, not least have been the perceived threats to the "modern" academic professions of the historian and

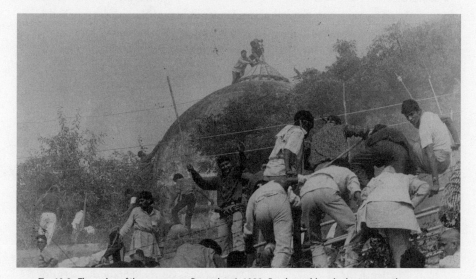

Fig. 10.3. The razing of the mosque on December 6, 1992. *Ramjanmabhumi* volunteers on the rampage on one of the three domes of the Babri Masjid. Courtesy Anandabazar Patrika library and archive, Calcutta.

archaeologist—to the integrity of their investigative methods and the objectivity of their knowledges. Where archaeology is concerned, the debate on the *Ramjanmabhumi*/Babri Masjid has brought on, as seldom before, a defense of the scientificity, specialization, and uniqueness of the disciplinary field. It is this issue—its projections and tensions, its possessions and dispossessions—which I wish to foreground within the body of the debate. From the start, the VHP's demand for a Rama temple rested on the mobilization of a "mass of literary, historical, archaeological and judicial evidence," which it compiled and formally presented to the Government of India in December 1990.[8] Hence arose the urgent need to refute and challenge what was falsely presented as incontrovertible proof: a task taken up in right earnest by the Centre for Historical Studies of Jawaharlal Nehru University, New Delhi, in 1989.[9] The fight, it was stressed by these historians, had to be conducted on the lines laid down by the opponents. The very form of the presentations of the *Ramjanmabhumi* demands, as a historically testifiable thesis, made proof a central element in the debate.

For the VHP, however, the historicity of the figure of Lord Rama or the proof of his birth at the present-day Ayodhya were hardly relevant questions, by "international standards prevalent in this kind of issue"—for, it explained, no one demands evidence for the sacredness of sites like the Dome of the Rock at Jerusalem, and no one questions the Christians' right to the holy site.[10] It set out instead to prove only the following: (1) the long tradition of worship in this town by Ram devotees, (2) the existence of an earlier *Vaishnava* temple at the very spot of the Babri Masjid, (3) the demolition of the temple in 1528 by Mir Baqi, assimilating some of its parts within the mosque that was constructed in its place. The specific archaeological and art historical evidence was only one segment of a large body of documentary evidence which was presented under three heads, "Hindu testimony," "Muslim testimony," and "European accounts." While the first category cited the references to Ayodhya from a vast list of Sanskrit literary, epic, and scriptural texts, the "Muslim" and "European" testimonies compiled quotations from a lineup of writers, from Abul Fazl in the sixteenth century, through nineteenth-century British travelers, surveyors, and gazetteers, to two recent Dutch and Belgian scholars writing on Ayodhya.[11]

Against this array of sources, archaeology was assigned the task of producing the most concrete, on the spot evidence of the material remnants of the temple beneath the mosque. The evidence here has centered on both a scrutiny of the standing structure and a discovery of hidden under-surface traces. The case built itself around what was seen as the obvious architectural incongruity of a series of black schist stone pillars, carved with figural and ornamental motifs, supporting vital parts of the mosque. The stone, structure, and carvings of these pillars were all traced to a regional Hindu temple of roughly the tenth or eleventh century, of the "late Pratihara or Gahadvala style." The case then moved underground to reveal, among other finds, rows of burnt-brick pillar bases (of the same directional alignment as the pillars above), different floor bases (where the topmost mosque floor level could be stratigraphically distinguished from earlier premosque layers), and a variety of Islamic glazed ware sherds, dated between the thirteenth and fifteenth centuries.[12] Later, in 1992, in the course of the demolition of the *masjid,* a team of scholars laid claim to the discovery of a hoard of sandstone sculptures and architectural fragments found deposited in a pit beneath the floor levels: a hoard that was directly identified with a demolished Hindu temple complex at the site.[13] Taken together, the archaeological evidence from Ayodhya—the standing stone pillars, the excavated pillar bases and floor levels, and the hidden deposit of stone sculptures—was offered as "conclusive proof" of the existence of a prior temple, its demolition, and its selective incorporation within the Babri Masjid.

The search for archaeological proof for *Ramjanmabhumi* dates back to a project undertaken between 1975 and 1980 by B. B. Lal (then director general of the Archaeological Survey of India), called "Archaeology of the Ramayana Sites."[14] Yet, even as a renowned professional like B. B. Lal sought to validate archaeologically the mythical past of the *Ramayana* and *Mahabharata,* another colleague in the field, B. P. Sinha, admitted "the inadequacy of archaeology as the only or even a dominant source for the reconstruction of ancient history."[15] If the past yielded little by way of architectural remains or foolproof material traces, it could nonetheless be richly conjured through a collation of other narratives and representations in Indian art and literature. We see throughout this laboriously argued "pro-*Mandir* thesis" a free move back and forth between what was classified as hard material evidence, literary allusions, and persuasive conjectures. Thus, for instance, the evidences from the excavated pillar and floor remnants slide in with the argument that a site as centrally and prominently positioned within the town as the current *masjid* site could never have been left free of a temple by the Hindu kings of Ayodhya.[16] Likewise, detailed listings from records of a history of religious conflict and Hindu efforts to retrieve this *Janmabhumi* site converge with reasons of faith. So, we are reminded, if "for hundreds of years, if not thousands, the Hindus have *believed* this site to be the birthplace of their divine Lord Rama," we "cannot whisk away such long-held pious belief of millions with . . . tons of weighty polemics" or contrary propositions.[17] The argument slips from the invocations of "hard facts" to a recourse to "common-sense" to an ultimate stand on "belief."

It is precisely this style of argument—this unwarranted mix of the divine and the historical, the believed and the proven—which has made much of this pro-*Mandir* thesis quickly contestable. Let us identify some of the main premises of the parallel anti-*Mandir* campaign:

> What is at issue is the attempt to give historicity to what began as a belief. Whereas anyone has a right to his or her beliefs, the same cannot be held for a claim to historicity. Such a claim has to be examined in terms of the evidence, and it has to be discussed by professionals. . . . Historicity . . . cannot be established in a hurry and, furthermore, has always to be viewed in the context of possible doubt. Archaeology is not a magic wand which in a matter of moments conjures up the required evidence.[18]

This statement of the leading historian of ancient India, Romila Thapar, pinpoints the moot issues of the counterposture. The statement sifts out history from belief, objective from motivated scholarship, the properly brewed methods from their "instant" varieties. It marks out also the exclusivity of the professional domain, its singular responsibilities of authenticating the past, and the long gestation of its working methods. Let us add to this the more outraged response of Thapar's archaeologist colleague Shereen Ratnagar, seeking to protect the autonomy of the discipline of archaeology against the philistinism of nonspecialist intruders.

> The professional disgrace that Indian archaeology led itself into concerning Ayodhya is not only because of a diabolical conspiracy. There has been a general unconcern with method and even with the scope of the subject. This has left the field open for the mofussil "neta" [small-town politician] to misappropriate available information, with all attendant vulgarity.[19]

Taken together, these responses provide a full-blown sense of violated knowledge and endangered science.

Returning Ayodhya to Archaeology

This scholarly lobby has found it important to contest, first and foremost, the kind of procedures employed at Ayodhya in search of evidence for a preexisting temple, and to challenge their very status as archaeology. The allegations have operated at different levels. To begin with, they have posed an inconsistency between B. B. Lal's first published reports from his Ayodhya excavations of 1976–77 and the later public declarations of various "new archaeological discoveries" in 1992 as "direct proof" of the *mandir* thesis.[20] They distinguish a "professional" report of an eminent scholar from the later flagrantly "unprofessional" projections that came none the less in the guise of archaeology from a "Historians' Forum."[21] In the context of the "new discoveries" of 1992, the profession confronted with particularly acute consternation this phenomenon of "demolition" or "voodoo" archaeology, in which the leveling of land by the government and the mosque by a frenzied mob magically threw up incontrovertible evidence for scholars.[22] The problem is seen to lie in the way professional archaeologists (those who clearly know better) have attempted to convince a gullible public (those who know no better) that this is "true" archaeology. The reaction has been to both seal off the disciplinary domain from deviants and outsiders, and create a new, "corrected" domain of public knowledge.

The most crucial plank of the archaeological critique has been a questioning of excavation methods and a careful screening of what constitutes evidence in archaeology.[23] The ultimate concern was with distinguishing "finds" from "evidence," with establishing that very few of the finds at Ayodhya could classify as evidence, and with arguing the impossibility of anything like "incontrovertible evidence" in archaeology. Setting out to question each of the reported discoveries, the criticisms have tended to converge around a singular issue, that of "stratigraphic context," the constitutive core of the present-day science of archaeology. For example, an in-depth analysis of the data about the pillar bases, it is alleged,

> immediately reveals the complete ignorance of the stratigraphic context of the concerned finds. . . . But for the casual information that there are two floors, one above the other and separated by a thick layer of debris, nothing has been communicated about the relationship of the floors with the "pillar bases," the various bases with one another, or the glazed pottery with the floors and "pillar bases."[24]

The task is to return every material remnant to its embedded location within the excavated soil strata: for in this stratigraphic reconstruction lies the clue to the relative chronology and interrelationship of different artifacts. It is through such stratigraphic analysis that the conclusions about the pillar bases were overturned with the following counterdeductions: (1) that the various remnants claimed to be vestiges of the pillar bases were not contemporaneous, but belonged to at least five sequential structural phases, (2) that the so-called pillar bases were most probably remnant portions of walls from these different phases, and (3) that, even if these were assumed to be pillar bases, they were constructed of brickbats laid so haphazardly that they seemed incapable of bearing the load of the large stone pillars above. So, it was argued, there was nothing about these finds to suggest even in a circumstantial manner that they were a part of any single structure, leave alone a pillared temple from the eleventh century.[25] The invocation of stratigraphy became all the more pointed with regard to the discovered hoard of stone sculptures. Faulty digging in the course of a land-leveling operation had led inevitably to a confusion of soil layers, a mix-up of sequences, and a complete loss of the stratigraphic context of the objects—thus denuding them of any value as evidence. These stone sculptures were branded as "contaminated" (with modern postdepositional debris)—even if their artistic and iconographic features could be productively analyzed, they remained denuded of "archaeological value."[26] For the latter is grounded centrally in fidelity to stratigraphy and proper excavation procedure. The point was made that present-day archaeology's primary concern is with excavated material rather than with overground standing structures. All "surface material," it was stressed, "is required to be consistent with excavated finds *if it has to qualify as evidence* . . . ; systematically excavated material alone is conclusive."[27] This invalidated the elaborate conclusions drawn around the black stone pillars in the mosque. And it reduced to secondary status much of the iconographic analysis of the material from the suspect "hoard."[28]

In retrospect, this emphasis on stratigraphy can be seen to have been integral to the progressive recasting of archaeology as a "hard" science in post-Independence India. At the cusp of Independence, Sir Mortimer Wheeler (retiring from his post as director general of archaeology in India to head his new Institute of Archaeology in London) provides the most powerful plea for the reform of archaeology in India into an "organised science."[29] The 1930s and 1940s were a time when Western experts in the field began to pointedly address what they saw to be the main problem with Indian archaeology—the lack of proper experience and scientific methodology in the field, compounded by the immense scope for excavation and conservation that the country presented. The subsequent maturing of the scholarly profession in India—its shifts away from the administrative apparatus of the Archaeological Survey to small university enclaves of research—were couched in these parables of a new and autonomous science. We could locate the present consternation about the misuse of archaeological knowledge at Ayodhya within this lineage—each point of contention with the "pro-*Mandir* thesis" becomes also a stand about the advancement of the science, its marked progression from its nineteenth-century concerns, and the separateness of its spheres from those of ancient history or art history. There has been an attempt all along to return the objects uncovered at Ayodhya to this self-enclosed space of archaeology—to remove them from all the extra-archaeological wrangles of the *Ramjanmabhumi* movement. And as each excavated remnant is arduously relocated in its stratigraphic context, the discipline itself retreats into its own ingrown, exclusive sphere of methods and expertise.[30]

The Limits of the Science: The Assault of Mythic Histories

But where, we might well ask, does this leave us vis-à-vis the current Ayodhya dispute? We can keep piling on evidences and refutations; and, on each of the counterpostures, keep hearing out the responses and fresh proofs offered by the *Janmabhumi* protagonists. Each criticism and allegation is matched by a set of reverse charges by the VHP, who have stuck firm to their grounds of historical facticity.[31] On either side, the recourse to the languages of history and archaeology has only exposed a problem whose dimensions clearly lie outside their frame. To put it starkly, one can say that the proof for or against the destroyed temple beneath the mosque stands quite irrelevant to the passions and politics that have been generated around Ayodhya. Still, there is no doing away with the need for proof in a national site that is so "ineluctably engulfed by history." However ineffectual the academic debate, Ayodhya can no longer figure outside history as what Pierre Nora would term a *milieu de mémoire*: it has slipped once and for all outside a people's collective memory into the nation's historical and pedagogical memory.[32]

Let us turn for a moment to the play of historical memory around Ayodhya. While the *Ramjanmabhumi* debate confronts us with a pointed display of archaeological reasoning and expertise, it also brings home a deeper, fundamental tension that resides within the attitude to such historical monuments and relics. The tension stems from an unresolved schism between the archaeological valuation of monuments and their various alternative configurations—whether in popular, collective memory or (as we see in the VHP endeavor) in the nation's freshly manufactured memory. Such disputed sites clearly embrace a whole sphere of beliefs, imaginings, and residual meanings that lie beyond the bounds of scientific knowledge. What is seen as extra-archaeological invariably intrudes on the domain of archaeology to defeat the intricacies of its arguments. There is no way historicity can be completely and safely separated from belief. We see in this debate a constant blurring of boundaries between history and mythology, between fact and faith, despite the attempts of historians and archaeologists at resoldering this cardinal line of divide.

History and its pedagogic accoutrements, we find, have powerfully infiltrated the domain of popular memory at a site like Ayodhya. We see this in the ways and the degrees to which popular legends of Ayodhya as the *Janmasthan* are shot through with the modes of reasoning and forms of dissemination of modern-day histories. In a proliferation of new popular Hindu histories of Ayodhya, what were myths and metaphors stand metamorphosed as true history. These accounts of the past of Ayodhya share with the historical discipline the core claim to the real and comprehensive truth; at the same time, they remain essentially ahistorical in the way the verities of fact are bolstered by the certainties of belief—in the way legends are supported by the scientific apparatus of dates, statistics, and geographical details.[33] Academic historians have increasingly recognized the need to take seriously the many mythological histories of *Ramjanmabhumi* to understand how myth, history, and communal politics "inter-relate in complex ways."[34] They have also realized that "historical consciousness, even fairly organised" is by no means a monopoly of professional historians alone, but exists within a larger public domain.[35] Across both camps, the notion of "popular belief" has remained a crucial nodal point of the dispute, the "popular" figuring both as a means of legitimization of positions and as a prime target of address.

Once again, it was the BJP/VHP/RSS combine that led the way in foregrounding this popular forum: since the 1980s, its case has been forcefully made in a series of popular Hindi histories and pamphlets[36] and in newspaper articles in its mouthpiece, the *Organiser*. The left/secularist lobby counterbid for a lay public audience has been undeniably weaker. It is a weakness embedded, to some degree, in its ingrained refusal to properly acknowledge or engage with the formidable popular front of the *Ramjanmabhumi* movement. Treating the popular phenomenon only as "political manipulation" of the people by a "fascist Hindu right," calling the demolition of the *masjid* and the accompanying violence acts of "vandalism" by a "lumpen-proletariat," the opposition is left either bemoaning the "incomplete secularisation" of Indian culture or blaming the Indian state for not being "aggressively secular."[37] Alternately, it is left trying to retrieve an illusory, uncontaminated domain of popular memory, where Hindus and Muslims coexist in harmonious and symbiotic histories.[38]

This other domain of myth and memory, I would argue, can no longer be distinctly figured as a space "on the outside." Rather, it exists as a nether zone within the invoked fields of history and archaeology—disrupting the proprieties of their methods and procedures, challenging their evidentiary logic, refusing to keep apart "proven fact" from "imagined truths." The professional practitioners of the disciplines have tried to disqualify such knowledge as neither proper history nor archaeology. But selectively assuming their colors, these illegitimate intruders hover at the boundaries of the disciplines, confronting them with their own built-in limits. We can see archaeology as a clear victim of such a process. Repeatedly, we find archaeology dragged out of its self-enclosed scholarly sphere into a larger public stage, where it is made to play out its expertise for a lay and an inevitably inappropriate audience. In the process, we see the corpus of scientific knowledge battling to assert itself vis-à-vis a welter of countermeanings and associations rallied around sacred sites.

It can be argued that archaeology, even when it has been most flamboyantly used in defense of the *Ramjanmabhumi* claims, hardly figures in the main body of the *Hindutva* discourse and the kind of popular Hindu histories of Ayodhya it has nurtured.[39] The "pro-*Mandir* thesis" itself provides a stark example of the way archaeology defeats itself through its own terms. If we were to take a strictly archaeological perspective on this issue, we can well argue that even the "incontrovertible proof" of a destroyed *Vaishnava* temple beneath the Babri Masjid cannot by any means justify the present-day razing of a sixteenth century mosque. For such an action would negate one of archaeology's fundamental constitutive principles, that of historical conservation, enshrined in a series of acts and statutes in colonial and independent India.[40] And because there are temple remains beneath mosques as well as Buddhist remains beneath Hindu edifices throughout India, it would render illegitimate, by the same logic, large numbers of the country's historical monuments that lie in the treasured custody of the Archaeological Survey.

On the other hand, if we take a political or religious perspective on the disputed site, what we meet headlong are a set of convictions and claims that have little to do with excavated finds or their arduous analysis. The issue becomes one of a perceived reversal by Hindus of a historical injustice, of a physical wresting of a long-lost possession: an imagined Rama temple that is the birthright of an equally imagined community of Hindus. And all "histories" of Ayodhya are woven around this one narrative of past dispossessions and present rectitude (figs. 10.4 and 10.5). So the whole history of the temple town of Ayodhya from ancient times comes to center on a single grand monument at the holy site of the *Janmasthan* and the singular relentless struggle of the Hindus to liberate this site from its Muslim appropriators. Everything old here, from the river Saryu to the mute stone artifacts, is made to stand witness to this singular tale of the town's "*raktaranjit itihas*" (a history colored in blood). These narratives keep proliferating, while archaeologists are left wrangling over whether any of the finds in the Ayodhya trenches can classify as conclusive evidence, and while historians have gone to lengths to show that the present-day Ayodhya cannot be equated with the ancient mythical city or that the claimed *Janmabhumi* site was in all probability a place of Buddhist religious establishments.[41] Recovering this objective past of Ayodhya and returning each

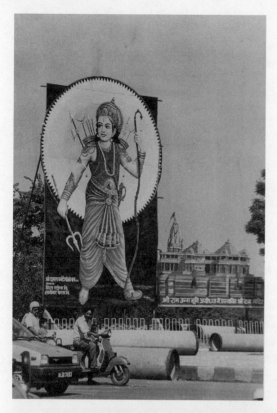

Fig. 10.4. (left) A giant billboard on the streets of New Delhi of the mythological figure of Ram as warrior and crusader, demanding of his devotees that a new temple (as in the model depicted behind him) be erected in his name at Ayodhya, c.1990. Courtesy Anandabazar Patrika library and archive, Calcutta.

Fig. 10.5. (below) Cadres of the most ultra-Hindu militant outfit, the RSS, in their famous "khaki shorts" taking their pledge to construct the temple in front of a poster of the proposed *Ramjanmabhumi* temple, New Delhi, 1992. From *Frontline,* vol. 17, no. 13, June 24–July 7, 2000. Reproduced by permission of *Frontline.*

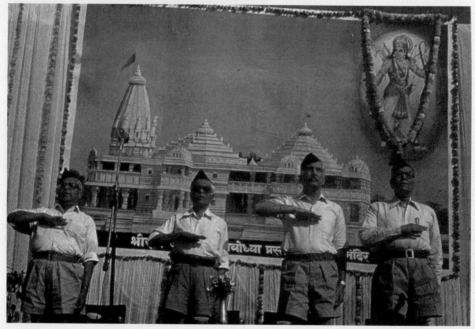

excavated find to its stratigraphic context have failed, clearly, to dislodge these other popular histories or to keep at bay their explosive consequences.

From the Present to the Past: Tracking Earlier Histories

These confrontations and failings of archaeology come to us as part of a long history. Though they were never outlined with such sharpness before, the discipline, ever since its inception in colonial India, has had to contend with similar tensions and oppositions, both within and outside its boundaries. To move from Ayodhya to the positions and practices of archaeology in late nineteenth-century India means going back to a time when the field of knowledge was far less specialized and autonomous, less centered on undersurface remnants, and not tied to the comparative methodologies of the natural sciences. Archaeology featured then as a part of a broad, composite field of antiquarian studies, with its particular focus on the country's vast stock of monumental remains and architectural antiquities. Its spheres closely overlapped with those of art and architectural history, and it had to work closely in tandem with epigraphy and numismatics to uncover a chronology of ancient India.

But there were similar questions being raised within the discipline even then—about what constituted scientific method and procedure, about what made for evidence in the ascription of dates, styles, and influences to structures, or about who had the ultimate authority to adjudicate on these matters. Archaeology's self-positioning in the Ayodhya controversy resonates with the history of these earlier stakes and claims. Right from the outset, the European practitioners in the field had to settle the prime question of who "owned" the country's ancient monuments. It could never be the local rulers or people who had lived for years with these ruins, quite oblivious of their historical value, allowing them to disintegrate, freely pillaging their stones for building purposes. Nor could it be the different religious groups and sects who were battling for control over old sacred sites—for they would only make further infringements on the bodies of these structures or produce domains of counterauthority around them.[42] The issue of ownership and custody could be decided only by a new community of scholars and administrators who alone commanded a proper historicized and archaeological knowledge of these edifices. It required a careful dissociation from this other, traditional sphere of claims, beliefs, and practices for the modern discipline to establish the authority of its knowledge.

But the success of the colonial project also involved a constant process of reengagement with an indigenous public—and it is this process that would invariably trouble the certainties of the scholarly field and split its internal unities. This process involved, on the one hand, a drive to transform and discipline popular perceptions to create a proper public for its archaeological sites and museums. It involved, at the same time, the participation of Indian scholars and experts, the forging of an indigenous professional community which would be imbued with the full rigor of the new discipline and expand its sway into new areas. While this latter agenda was eminently successful, it opened up, nonetheless, various grounds of tension. For although Indian scholarly participation was encouraged in the late nineteenth century, the terms of that participation were often open to contest. And the content of the new modernized Indian knowledges often produced dissenting nationalist positions within the field. The case of the antiquarian scholar Raja Rajendralal Mitra in Bengal in the 1870s—his close involvement with government archaeological programs and his debates with his European peer, James Fergusson, on the origins of stone architecture in India—offers a pointed example.[43] This moment of indigenous intervention is an instructive point from which to survey the mapping-out and the bounding-in of the new discipline. This double agenda of archaeology in colonial India—of both pointedly dissociating itself from native knowledges, and selectively transforming them to mobilize them in its own cause—exposed the kind of contradictions that continue to batter the discipline today. The problem, then, as in the current dispute, lay primarily with the constitution of an effective public forum for the expertise that archaeology engendered. A distinct demarcation of the discipline had to involve a rigid sense of all that it superseded and all that lay outside its "scientific" field.

If the present controversy harks back to earlier episodes in the internal self-constitution of the discipline, it also echoes with themes and approaches that have always obsessed the archaeologist in India. We can extract from the archaeological arguments around the *Ramjanmabhumi* site at least two concerns that have long been fundamental to the disciplinary episteme. Let us take up, first, the recurrent narratives of authenticity and origin, whereby the true identity of a structure comes to rest on the recovery of a presumed primary moment of its coming into being. With all the advancement of excavation and investigation techniques, archaeology remains committed to pushing back the histories of each monument and site to higher and higher moments of antiquity. The deployment of archaeological evidence by the *Ramjanmabhumi* movement provides a stark instance of the way a site comes to be historicized (and sanctified) only through a conjectural history of a preexisting temple, with the standing edifice of the sixteenth-century mosque serving only as a sign of negation of an absent original structure. And each relic recovered from the site—whether pillar bases, floor remnants, or stone sculptures uncovered beneath—assumed meaning only through its place within this lost primary unit of a *Vaishnava* temple. The opposition attempted to crack these constructions by vesting originality squarely on the structure of the mosque, by disproving the possibility of a preceding temple at precisely the same spot, and by diverting attention to the more general traces of the material culture of the town of Ayodhya, which could be dated back to the sixth century B.C. Over the years, the objects of archaeology graduated from monuments to material cultures, from overground edifices to underground remnants of everyday life; but what persisted all along is the quest for oldest histories of a site.

In the late nineteenth century, the search for origins played itself out in the mapping, documenting, and classifying of a vast landscape of architectural ruins.[44] As each building found its slot in an intricate grid of dynastic and religious classifications, the first architectural denominations of "Buddhist", "Hindu," "Jain," or "Mohammedan" rested centrally on the expert's acumen at identifying the "pure" and "primary" structure beneath all subsequent accretions, alterations, or decay. This sifting and recovery of the original—the ultimate target of archaeological intervention—established, in turn, a distinct hierarchy of knowledges concerning these monuments. Thus, in all archaeological monographs of the time, we find a constant privileging of ancient sources over the medieval and modern histories of these monuments.[45] While ancient references (whether gleaned from legends and literature, inscriptions or coins, or travel accounts of Chinese pilgrims) served as a key mode of authentication, the medieval and modern phases registered primarily as a story of depredation and decline. The specter of "medieval ravage" inevitably dovetailed with a more current scenario of "native apathy and neglect": the widespread local destruction of relics and pilferage of stones by the local populace. Together, the two provided the critical backdrop against which modern archaeological scholarship advertised its achievements and underlined the urgency of its own restorative project.

Central to this project was a second core concern of the archaeologist: his fascination with the histories hidden in these monuments, with the stories that stone could tell. They were stories to which only the expert field archaeologist or architectural historian could claim access: but they stood waiting to be told to a larger public to awaken them to the real historical value of these monuments. Over the mid-nineteenth century, India's vast reserve of architectural antiquities assumed utmost primacy as sources for the country's hidden history. Systematically surveyed and classified, these came to be regarded by both British and Indian scholars as the most authentic indices of the past, in the absence of written histories or textual records. If, for Fergusson, the main working method consisted of the decoding of pure architectural evidence (the evidence of style, structure, or design), for his contemporary, Alexander Cunningham, the testimony of architectural style had to be matched and corroborated by the evidence of other material relics, such as coins and inscriptions. As distinguished from Fergusson's architectural scholarship, Cunningham evolved a genre of work that has been termed "text-aided archaeology"; yet his approach too placed a great priority on material remains over and above all ancient textual sources as sources of history.[46] Archaeology in late-nineteenth-century India came to revolve centrally around this theme of the unique testimony of stone— around the solidity and infallibility of this evidence, and the many finely honed methods of extracting it. The theme spread to and permeated the new indigenous endeavors in scientific history and archaeology in Bengal.[47]

The Ayodhya debate stirs up again this vexed theme of stone as the mute but most reliable witness of history, opening up a complex chain of past claims and contestations. It is possible to trace two main trajectories in the way meanings and values are affixed to stone remains. In one, we remain within the scientific confines of proof, restricted to the range of what is verifiable or arguable from the precise remains. Following the lines laid down by nineteenth-century archaeology, the present-day discipline has used all its new technical acumen to hone in on the sheer materiality of the remains. A main source of consternation, as we have seen, was the loose concoction of "facts" by the pro-*Mandir* camp of historians and archaeologists—their style of free conjectures about a Rama temple from what was considered debatable material evidence. The counterstance has been to constantly underscore the limits of archaeological knowledge—to stratigraphically disaggregate the conjectured whole into a set of disembodied traces and fragments, returning each excavated bit to its location within the soil. An imagined monument is thus dispersed and dissolved into geology.[48]

The second trajectory operates in striking contrast to this first approach, often in open violation of its norms. In this case, we see stone structures acquiring a voice, body, and persona of their own as they emerge as oracles of the past, standing as silent witnesses of a history of which they alone bear the traces. The *Ramjanmabhumi* movement, we know, thrives on histories that resist the constraints of hard evidence as they conjure vast epochs and debacles around scattered traces. They also repeatedly transcend the specificities of an individual site and monument to inhabit the entire national space. Thus, the tale of *Ramjanmabhumi* becomes archetypal of innumerable other lost Hindu temples; and the Babri Masjid becomes one among a large list of *dargahs, idgahs* and *masjids,* tabled region by region from all over the country, all of which become witnesses to the same tale of the destruction and appropriation of temples.[49] Again and again, in the VHP rhetoric, we see individual local histories conflated into a collective national saga, and diverse details compressed into the singular trauma of the Muslim ravage of Hindu temples. The

term "Hindu" is conveniently conceived here as a homogenized umbrella category, standing in "for all schools of *Sanatana Dharma*—Buddhism, Jainism,
Shaivism, Shaktism, Vaishnavism and the rest."⁵⁰ Such a configuration serves
to strategically erase other conflicting histories—all instances, say, of violent
intersectarian strife or Shaivite appropriation of Buddhist sites—to perpetu-
ate a single recurring myth of Muslim depredation and to construct India's entire archaeological history around a single Hindu/Muslim polarity.

Such extreme "Hindu" constructions certainly carry the marks of earlier
colonial and nationalist readings of monuments. The first phases of archaeological survey and scholarship in the country were focused primarily on the recovery of India's "ancient" sites. While Buddhist cave temples or *stupa* remains
offered the earliest examples of India's architectural antiquity, the operative
principle of the ancient in the nation's history became loosely that of the pre-
Muslim past. It was a sense in which all the differentiated genres of Buddhist,
Jain, or Hindu styles (with all the subdifferentiations of period and region)
could figure as a composite "ancient" collective vis-à-vis a later medieval Mohammedan architectural heritage. It was also a sense in which the authentication of the true, ancient history of these monuments meant a stripping away of
all medieval traces and their restitution from this later history of damage and
destruction. Thus, we find centuries of earlier mutations and transformations
of Buddhist or Hindu structures receding before the one cathartic blow of
"Muslim ravage"—and all prior additions or appropriations freezing around
a phenomenon of "medieval decline." It is this trope which acquires an unprecedented hardness and manipulative edge in the current *Hindutva* discourse, sliding into a kind of programmatic agenda for the counterappropria-
tion of Muslim sites that the nineteenth-century discipline could never have
condoned.

I would suggest that more than the content of these *Ramjanmabhumi*
claims, it is the style of their invocations which leads us back to some fundamental strains and tensions within the discipline. The problem largely revolves
around the type and scope of history that a stone relic can be made to tell. Archaeological narratives, like all historical reconstructions, have always worked
with large elements of speculation and conjecture; but in each phase, with
each specific subject, the question of what constitutes feasible possibility and
fact has had to be carefully negotiated.⁵¹ The lines of truth in archaeology have
had to be constantly demarcated, not just against falsities and distortions, but
also against the fictional and imaginary. Since the nineteenth century, this exercise has been open to contest at different levels, among different Indian writers engaging with the field of scientific knowledge on their own terms and using its prerogatives to construct narratives that may or may not have been

classifiable as strict history. This opened up some of the most productive tensions within the subject. While it exposed the internal limits of the field—the limits of its evidence and deductions—it also brought it face to face with the possibilities of imagination. The involvement of an indigenous intelligentsia, driven by the new demands for a national history, was needed to extract from archaeological science the tools to test and correct the interpretations the colonial masters attached to their art and architectural history, stretching the possibilities of evidence in ways that could compound the glories of ancient India. It also required a parallel space of writing in the regional languages—particularly a space of literature and fiction—for writers to implicitly ride above the regime of hard facts and indulge the romantic potentials of the histories hidden in stone.[52] Here the truth claims of archaeology coalesced with the romance and thrill of historical tales. It was only through such a give and take—through both a laying of boundaries and their subtle transgression—that archaeological relics could configure within a more affective zone of the nation's collective memory and belief.

The Ayodhya controversy—its uses and abuses of archaeology—returns us to this central dilemma of scientific history. In its heated battle over facts and evidence, we confront in new forms the same struggle and unease of the archaeologists in their role as the interlocutors of "mute stone," or in their status as guardians of the "true" histories these reveal. There remains an unbridged gap between proof and persuasion, between reason and belief, in which all scholarly discourses keep stumbling and dissembling. This hiatus resurrects in turn that old dichotomy between archaeological science and the archaeological imagination. At the same time, we see here the disappearance of the distinction that Pierre Nora construes between "*milieux de mémoire*" and "*lieux des mémoire*," as any possible space of pure or traditional memory dissipates, and both history and belief become the handmaids of a modern-day politicized religious community that calls itself the "Hindu nation."[53]

Neither an active site of worship, nor a valued symbol of India's art and architectural heritage, the doomed Babri Masjid had little on its side—little that could have ensured its survival against the death wishes of those who were determined to replace it with a *mandir*. A decade later, that wave of determination and destruction continues almost unabated. The country's entire apparatus of archaeological protection and legal jurisdiction over historical monuments stands countered by the continued violation of the rule of law at Ayodhya. Even as a Supreme Court injunction and criminal case proceedings hang heavily on the site of the destroyed mosque, the proposed temple construction has continued apace, with its foundations, pillars, and sculptures being fabricated off-site in special workshops across north India (fig. 10.6). New

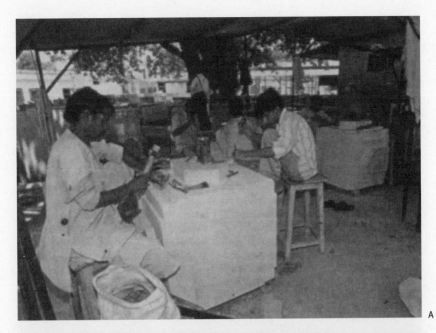

A

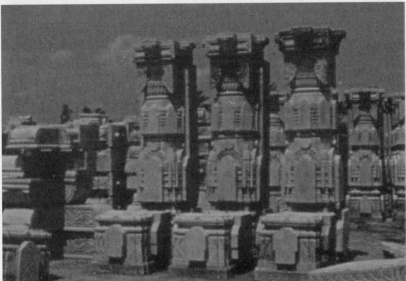

B

Fig. 10.6. The imagined Ram temple now taking concrete shape in workshops in and around Ayodhya, flouting all court orders and injunctions, 2000. *(A)* Artisans carving decorations on stone at a temple construction workshop at a place named Karsevakpuram at Ayodhya. *(B)* Samples of the prefabricated, intricately carved pillars standing at Karsevakpuram at Ayodhya. From *Frontline,* vol. 17, no. 13, June 24–July 7, 2000. Reproduced by permission of *Frontline.*

devastating pogroms of cleansing the Hindu nation have in the meantime erupted, periodically shifting the focus of *Hindutva* activity from Ayodhya to centers like Gujarat, leaving fresh trails of terror and destruction. But the *mandir* continues to rise, invisible but unstoppable, determined to implant itself at the precise site of its prohibition.[54] And Ayodhya, both as a place of rich and multiple pasts and as a sphere of scholarly authority, has it seems been irretrievably forfeited to a besieged public zone of history and memory.

NOTES

An earlier version of this essay, entitled "Archaeology as Evidence: Looking Back from the Ayodhya Debate," was circulated as Occasional Paper no. 159 of the Centre for Studies in Social Sciences, Calcutta, April 1997.

1. On the term *"Hindutva,"* see Tapan Bose, Pradip Datta, Sumit Sarkar, et al., *Khaki Shorts and Saffron Flags,* Tracts for the Times, no. 1 (New Delhi: Orient Longman, 1991), and the essays in Gyanendra Pandey, ed., *Hindus and Others: The Question of Identity in India Today* (New Delhi: Viking, 1993).

2. See Ashis Nandy, Shikha Trivedi, Shail Mayaram, and Achyut Yagnik, *Creating a Nationality: The Ramjanmabhumi Movement and Fear of the Self* (Delhi: Oxford University Press, 1995).

3. The historical background and chronology of the conflict are laid out in Sarvepalli Gopal, ed., *Anatomy of a Confrontation: The Babri Masjid–Ram Janmabhumi Issue* (New Delhi: Viking, 1991).

4. Sushil Srivastava, *The Disputed Mosque: A Historical Inquiry* (New Delhi: Vistaar, 1991), attributes this flare-up of communal animosities to colonial policies and discourses. While the Muslim attack on Hanumangarhi was effectively crushed, the Hindu priests were allowed, from this time onward, to occupy a portion of the *masjid* compound. Under the new arrangements authorized by the British government, the Hindu intrusion could even leave its physical marks within the body of the *masjid* structure—in the *Ram Chabutra* (a canopy) that was constructed in the compound in 1857, and later in a small sanctum of a temple that was telescoped into the existing mosque. The structure was thus transformed over time into a *masjid/mandir* complex.

5. The case for the *Ramjanmabhumi* had one of its earliest full statements in S. P. Gupta's article "Ram Janmabhoomi Controversy: What History and Archaeology Say," *Organiser,* March 29, 1987. On the refutation of these claims, see, especially, the essays in Gopal, *Anatomy of a Confrontation,* particularly, the appendix, "The Archaeological Evidence," pp. 223–32; and D. Mandal, *Ayodhya: Archaeology after Demolition,* Tracts for The Times, no. 5 (New Delhi: Orient Longman, 1993)—henceforth referred to as *AAAD.*

6. This point is strongly argued in K. M. Shrimali's article "The Future of the Past," *Social Scientist* 27, nos. 9–10 (September–October 1998).

7. "The real estate in dispute is not the site on which the Babri Masjid once stood but the constitutional ground on which the Indian republic is built." Mukul Kesavan, "A Coup in Slow Motion," *Telegraph* (Calcutta), April 22, 2001.

8. *Evidence for the Ram Janmabhoomi Mandir,* presented to the Government of India on December 23, 1990, by the VHP.

9. *The Political Abuse of History: Babri Masjid–Ram Janmabhumi Dispute* (New Delhi: Centre for Historical Studies, Jawaharlal Nehru University, 1989; updated version, 1992).

10. *Evidence for the Ram Janmabhoomi Mandir,* 1.

11. Ibid., 2–16.

12. Ibid., 95–98, Annexure 28.

13. *Ramjanmabhumi: New Archaeological Discoveries* (New Delhi: Historian's Forum, 1993).

14. Under what was termed a "national archaeological project," the team excavated Ayodhya over two seasons, concentrating specifically on the areas south and west of the Babri Masjid. The findings were first published in *Indian Archaeology—A Review* (1976–77): 52–53.

15. B. P. Sinha, "Archaeological Evidences of Ram Janmabhoomi," in *Evidence for the Ram Janmabhoomi Mandir,* 99–104.

16. *Evidence for the Ram Janmabhoomi Mandir,* 19.

17. Sinha, "Archaeological Evidences of Ram Janmabhoomi," 103.

18. Romila Thapar, editorial preface, *AAAD,* xiii.

19. Shereen Ratnagar, "Archaeology: In Search of the Impossible," *Economic and Political Weekly,* November 5–12, 1994, 2901.

20. AAAD, pp. 17–18.

21. Gautam Navlakha, "Archaeology: Recovering, Uncovering or Forfeiting the Past?," *Economic and Political Weekly,* November 19, 1994.

22. *AAAD,* xi, 2–3, 17, 42, 49–52.

23. Ibid., 26–55, chap. 2.

24. Ibid., 26–27.

25. Ibid., 39–40.

26. Ibid., 42–45.

27. *AAAD,* 52–54.

28. See, for example, the comment by R. Champakalakshmi, in Gopal, *Anatomy of a Confrontation,* 228–32.

29. R. E. M. Wheeler, "Archaeological Planning in India: Some of the Factors" (1946) and "Archaeological Fieldwork in India: Planning Ahead" (1947), reprinted in *A Source Book of Indian Archaeology,* ed. F. R. Allchin and Dilip K. Chakrabarti (New Delhi: Munshiram, Manoharlal, 1979).

30. This new disciplinary stance in India replicates in many ways the phenomenon of what was termed the "New Archaeology" in the United States and Britain of the 1970s (also termed mainstream "processual archaeology"), which employed the methodology of natural sciences like geology, paleobotany, or ecology and attempted to produce a new "science of the archaeological record." These stances of the New Archaeology came under attack in the 1980s by a new school of "postprocessual" approaches. See, e.g., Ian Hodder, *Reading the Past: Current Approaches to Interpretation in Archaeology* (Cambridge: Cambridge University Press, 1986).

31. The VHP, we find, has constantly returned charges of political manipulation and tampering of evidence against the other camp. There is an allegation, for instance, of later deliberate suppression of "Muslim testimony"—of selective omissions from later reprints of various Persian and Hindi books and manuscripts of all passages referring to "the demolition of the temple at the Janmasthan" (*Evidence for the Ram Janmabhoomi Mandir,* 19–20).

32. Pierre Nora, "Between Memory and History: Les Lieux de Mémoire," *Representations* 26 (spring 1989): 18–20.

33. On this theme, see Gyanendra Pandey, "Modes of History Writing: New Hindu Histories of Ayodhya," *Economic and Political Weekly,* June 18, 1994, 1523–28.

34. Neeladri Bhattacharya, "Myth, History and the Politics of Ranjanmabhumi," in Gopal, *Anatomy of a Confrontation,* 132.

35. Sumit Sarkar, "The Many Worlds of Indian History," *Writing Social History* (Delhi: Oxford University Press, 1997), 2.

36. Some of the best-known and most widely circulated Hindi histories and pamphlets are Pratap Narain Mishra, *Kya Kahati Hai Sarayu Dhara? Sri Ramjanmabhumi ki Kahani* (What does the River Saryu have to say? The story of *Ramjanmabhumi*) (Lucknow, 1986; 2d ed., 1990); Radhey Shyam Shukul, *Sri Ramjanmabhumi: Sachitra Pramanik Itihasa* (An illustrated authentic history) (Ayodhya, 1986); and Ramgopal Pandey, *Ramjanmabhumi ka Raktaranjit Itihasa* (The blood-stained history of *Ramjanmabhumi*) (Ayodhya, n.d.).

37. For a critique of the secularist stand on Ayodhya, I have drawn on an unpublished paper by Vivek Dhareswar, "History and the Politics of Self-Description," 1996.

38. Outside the stranglehold of *Hindutva* discourses and the official secular rhetoric, a body of alternative approaches, most powerfully presented by Ashis Nandy, have attempted to reconstruct the everyday "lived" world of Ayodhya, with its multiple "forms of interweaving of pieties and communities." On such an idealized account of this "other" world of Ayodhya, see Nandy et al., *Creating a Nationality,* 1–6.

39. These popular histories (as shown by Pandey, "Modes of History Writing," 1523–24) are seldom constrained and inhibited by the limited corpus of verifiable facts that archaeology has laid at their disposal. For instance, while archaeological and art historical evidence talks only of a tenth/eleventh-century Vaishnava temple of the late Pratihar style, the imagined *Ramjanmabhumi* temple in the Hindu histories is freely drawn back in time to the first rediscoverer of the site, Vikramaditya, who himself is variously located between the second century B.C. and the fifth century A.D.

40. Archaeology's record of historical conservation in India is, of course, far from foolproof, especially where it has come up against the logic of Hindu nationalist claims. A glaring instance of the defeat of archaeological logic can be found in the years immediately following India's Independence, when invoking a similar history of Islamic iconoclasm (Mahmud of Ghazni's destruction of the Somanatha temple in Gujarat), the state government saw nothing amiss in the demolition of what it described as a "dead and disused" twelfth-century temple at the site to rebuild a new temple there as a "living symbol" of the Hindu nation. Discussed in Richard Davis, "Reconstructions of Somanatha," *Lives of Indian Images* (Princeton: Princeton University Press, 1997).

41. See Srivastava, *Disputed Mosque,* chap. 7.

42. In the first years of the Archaeological Survey of India, this problem surfaced openly around Buddhist attempts to reclaim the sacred site of Bodh-Gaya (the site of Buddha's Enlightenment) in the province of Bihar, which had for centuries been appropriated by a Hindu Shaivite sect. In subsequent years, the colonial government faced one of the severest challenges to its archaeological claims over the main temple at the site, as it sought to mediate between the violent contentions that raged between a neo–World Buddhist movement and the Hindu priests of Bodh-Gaya. I compare and contrast the two cases of Ayodhya and Bodh-Gaya in the last chapter of my book *Monuments, Objects, Histories* (forthcoming, Columbia University Press).

43. On the debate between Rajendralal Mitra and James Fergusson, see my essay "Monuments and Lost Histories: The Archaeological Imagination in the Colonial and Nationalist Imagination," in *Proof and Persuasion: Essays on Authority, Objectivity and Evidence,* ed. E. Lunbeck and S. Marchand (Turnout: Brepols, 1997).

44. Between the 1840s and the 1870s, the surveys and writings of James Fergusson pioneered this work of the documentation, illustration, and classification of Indian architecture, culminating in his comprehensive *History of Indian and Eastern Architecture* (London: John Murray, 1876). In parallel, from 1861, Alexander Cunningham, in his newly created office of Archaeological Surveyor to the government, began to map out through his field excavations a detailed topography of the ancient archaeological sites of upper and central India.

45. Alexander Cunningham, for instance, centrally premised his archaeological investigations on one key ancient source: the travel accounts of the two Chinese Buddhist pilgrims Fa Hien and Hiuen Tsang, who visited India in the fourth and seventh centuries A.D.

46. These priorities of Cunningham are laid out in his early directive of 1848, "Proposed Archaeological Investigation," reprinted in Allchin and Chakrabarti, *Source Book of Indian Archaeology,* 10–11.

47. This is best reflected in the obsessive preoccupation with the "evidence of stone" in the writings of turn-of-the-century Bengali historians and archaeologists like Akshay Kumar Maitreya or Rakhaldas Banerjee.

48. The emphasis on hard scientific method disembodies the artifactual remains to the point where they become abstracted traces of the past, unhinged not only from any imaginable structure but also from any tangible human histories. Thus, for the earliest periods of Indian history, we have "archaeological cultures" and whole periods defined purely through the diagnostic trait of common "artifact-types" labeled as Painted Grey Ware (PGW) or Northern Black Polished Ware (NBP).

49. Sita Ram Goel, "Let the Mute Witnesses Speak," in Arun Shourie, Harsh Narain, Jay Dubashi, Ram Swarup, and Sita Ram Goel, *Hindu Temples: What Happened to Them (A Preliminary Survey)* (New Delhi: Voice of India, 1990), 62–181.

50. Ibid., 62.

51. The issue of permissible conjecture was constantly raised within the archaeological discipline in India. Going back to a statement of 1905, archaeology as a "science . . . risen out of the study of antiquarian odds and ends" was seen to be still principally working with "imagination and hypotheses" (James Burgess, "Sketch of Archaeological Research in India during Half a Century," *Source Book of Indian Archaeology,* 29). Four decades later, in 1949, Mortimer Wheeler emphasized the advancement of the "science" of archaeological fieldwork in independent India that now allowed "the methodological, logical use of *the disciplined imagination* in the evaluation of cause and effect." See "Archaeological Fieldwork in India: Planning Ahead," 44.

52. A wonderful example is the "historical romance" written in 1914 by the Bengali archaeologist Rakhaldas Banerjee, called *Pashaner Katha* (The story of stone), which conjured the nation's history around the reconstructed ruins of an ancient Buddhist *stupa*. Discussed in my essay, "Monuments and Lost Histories"; also in chap. 4 of my forthcoming book, *Monuments, Objects, Histories.*

53. Pierre Nora, "Between Memory and History," 13–14. A site like Ayodhya presents a scenario closely akin to what Nora describes, where, with the virtual disappearance of the practices of "traditional" memory, the "indiscriminate production of archives" has led to a new kind of terror, "historicized memory."

54. A discussion of the changing political configurations within the BJP, VHP and RSS, and between the Central and Uttar Pradesh governments—that has determined the fluctuating intensity of the temple agenda at Ayodhya—is outside the scope of this essay.

Local Memory and National Aesthetics:
Jean Pagès's Early-Eighteenth-Century Description of the "Incomparable" Cathedral of Amiens

RICHARD K. WITTMAN

I

By the year 1700, the relative isolation in which French provincial towns had long existed was rapidly disintegrating. For centuries, public authority had been decentralized, even atomized, and in both city and country local custom had played the preponderant role in everyday life.[1] Physical existence and social identity alike had depended on a thick horizontal weave of small, localized collective bodies—clan, confraternity, guild—which offered a defense against an insecure and often anarchic world. But over the seventeenth century all this had begun to change. Administrative innovations from the royal center overcame some local power structures and rendered others obsolete; state authority was imprinted on the natural order, through government-sponsored road networks, frontier fortresses, canals, and new port cities;[2] the Counter-Reformation Church systematically attacked unsanctioned religious practices on the local level, instituting a more hierarchical, more authoritarian regime; and economic activity turned more and more toward an integrated commodity market, which required of individuals an awareness of events well beyond the spatial orbit of daily life. Printing also played a major role in this process. New periodicals like the *Journal des Savants* and Bayle's *Nouvelles de la République des Lettres* publicized elite literary and intellectual work, while publications associated with the royal academies disseminated learned information and official commentary on art, history, and scientific endeavor. Popular culture too was engulfed by new forms of mass popular imagery and cheap literature, which projected a version of the putatively more rational and civilized mores (and taboos) of the metropolitan elites.[3]

Around 1700, then, a heterogeneous and particularistic society was gradually amalgamating under the pressure of centralization and acculturation. Vertical ties connecting each subject and associative body to an overarching, normative culture were developing at the expense of the old variegated local cultures.[4] Well-informed persons in particular were becoming conscious of their involvement in new collectivities that stood somewhere above and beyond those smaller groups—collectivities that, instead of occupying discrete places in time and space, were dispersed bodies on a vast scale, united only conceptually, within an impersonal sphere of public authority, intellectual discourse, and economic exchange. Ill-defined and nebulous, nonetheless already in the seventeenth century they were being referred to with names like "the public" and "the nation."[5]

I would like to consider here how these transformations affected the understanding of historical monuments. Recent scholarship has had much of interest to say about how historical monuments were pressed into service by the regimes of nineteenth-century France to embody a narrative of national development intended to promote a sense of national unity and identity; and about how such efforts tended to decontextualize monuments and to drain them of their specific (and necessarily local) historical and religious associations.[6] In the present study I shall look at a much earlier stage in this development, one in which the intentions of the actors were perhaps less concrete and the conflicts more ambiguous, but in which similar patterns may be discerned. My analysis will focus on a single document, a three-hundred-page manuscript description of the northern French cathedral of Amiens, written in the form of a fictional dialogue, in 1708 or 1709, by Jean Pagès (1655–1723), a master in the Community of Merchant Mercers in Amiens (figs. 11.1 and 11.2).[7] This remarkable document offers a vivid witness to how a beloved historic monument could appear to an educated provincial who, at this turn of the eighteenth century, was in many ways caught between a local culture of tradition and an emerging national culture. I shall argue that Pagès's text, and the stories it tells, help us trace the deep roots of the patterns which in modern times have tended to govern experience of historical monuments.

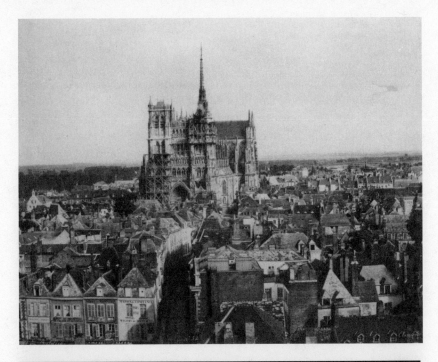

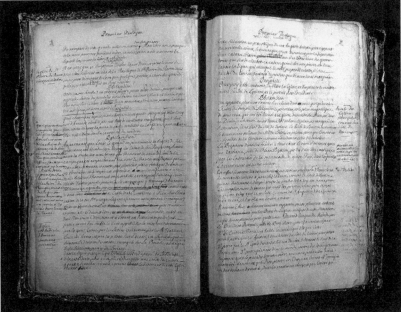

Fig. 11.1. (top) Amiens Cathedral and the city of Amiens. Photograph by Edouard Baldus, 1855. Copyright Réunion des Musées Nationaux/Art Resource, New York.

Fig. 11.2. (bottom) The manuscript of Jean Pagès's "L'Auguste Temple." Courtesy Bibliothèque Municipale d'Amiens.

II

According to a contemporary manuscript autobiography, Pagès was a native of Amiens who, as a boy, had been educated there by the Jesuits.[8] After a youthful spell as an apprentice in Paris, he lived his entire life in Amiens. His travels—all in northern France—were modest. Mostly, we know that Pagès was a pious man with a fierce enthusiasm for the history and monuments of his hometown: his manuscript on the cathedral is just one part of a mountain of notes, lists, and essays concerning Amiens that he wrote over the course of his life. Bound together in the nineteenth century, these manuscripts today fill three bulky volumes.[9] But his essay on the cathedral was his greatest work.

Pagès cast his description as an itinerant dialogue between two characters: Pariphile, who is a visitor to Amiens, a man with extensive book knowledge and well-informed about the city he is visiting; and Philambien, his host, a local man with an intimate knowledge of all things Amienois. These names each use the Greek *philo* (I love) to characterize their bearer, thereby associating one with Paris and the other with Amiens, which in Latin was called *Ambianum*.

Philambien is Pagès's real voice. For him the cathedral is a creation of incalculable greatness, the epitome of architectural achievement:

> I think that without exaggeration one could say that our august temple is built with more delicacy than all others[;] I well know that according to one modern writer the church of Saint Peter in Rome is far above all other churches, and that it surpasses in grandeur and magnificence all buildings both ancient and modern, not excepting the Temple of Solomon and the Hagia Sophia in Constantinople, but I doubt that the basilica of Saint Peter and Saint Paul [*sic*] in Rome surpasses that of Amiens in the delicacy of its architecture.[10]

In its absolute quality, a passage such as this reminds us of the architectural commentaries of medieval prelates. Pagès, through Philambien, refers to the cathedral on virtually every page as "our incomparable cathedral," and in a profound sense he means it.

The character of Pariphile is Philambien's foil. He is the mouthpiece for whatever an outsider could have known about the cathedral; that is to say, his knowledge is from books, not local experience. He is often used by Pagès to set up questions for Philambien to answer. Typically he will ask, "Didn't I read somewhere that the architect of this part of the church was named such-and-such?" Philambien will then confirm this and go on to explain the history in the sort of passionate and intimate detail only a local man could have known.[11]

After the two characters conduct an initial discussion of the church's exterior from a bench opposite the façade, they move inside.[12] There, over more than a hundred pages, an exhaustive inventory systematically details not only the architecture of the cathedral but all its furnishings and monuments as well. These pages remind us that the interior of the cathedral looked very different in 1709 than it does today. Relatively bright and empty nowadays, it projects a sense of structural logic and spatial dilation (fig. 11.3); but in 1709 the church was darkened by acres of stained glass, and cluttered with paintings by the hundreds, screens and ornate chapel enclosures, and countless ex-votos and tombs. The tiny fraction of this work that survives, for instance the funerary monuments of the local sculptor Nicolas Blasset, or the chapels of the *Pilier vert* and the *Pilier rouge* flanking the choir, offer only faint echoes of this busier and more jumbled church interior (fig. 11.4). As Philambien catalogs this multitude of works, prodded by the occasional question from Pariphile, he does so in a manner that frustrates the art historian; for he says little about their actual appearance. We learn, typically, of a painting only what story or personage it depicts and that it is "surpassingly beautiful." This beauty is presented not as a matter for analysis or delectation, but rather as that which gives the painting's evocation of a sacred story its power. He even remarks upon the distinction:

> If collectors esteem representations of nature done by skilled hands as master-pieces of the art, whether by sculptors or by the famous painters of profane antiquity, should we not esteem and admire all the more these images of the Holy Scriptures, which represent not only certain works of nature, but even more the marvels of grace, the most prodigious effects of which are exposed to our eyes in some of them.[13]

Philambien presents these works not only as aids to visualization but also as memory aids that recall the piety of his and his neighbors' ancestors. He exhausts Pariphile with information about the individuals whose pious acts led to the creation of these works. When he discusses the thirteenth- and fourteenth-century stained glass windows, it is chiefly the blazons that interest him, since they are what permit him to identify the specific mayors and aldermen who commissioned them.[14] Philambien proves himself capable of naming patrons right across the centuries, and far beyond the leading families of the city too, right down to minor canon lawyers at the bishop's court, officials of the nearby Abbey of Saint-Jean, barristers' assistants, deputy provosts, and minor guild officials. Some had given no more than a pennant or a plaque.

This social inclusiveness was a crucial aspect of the church for Pagès. Speaking again of the now-lost stained glass, Pagès has Philambien respond thus to Pariphile's expressions of admiration:

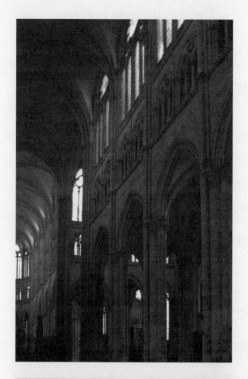

Fig. 11.3. The nave of Amiens Cathedral. Photograph by Richard K. Wittman.

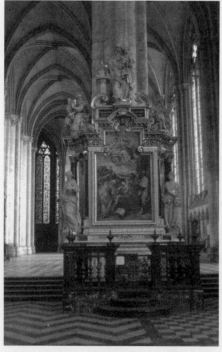

Fig. 11.4. The chapel of Notre-Dame-du-Pilier-Rouge (Chapel of the Puy Notre Dame Confraternity), Amiens Cathedral, 1627–28. Photograph by Richard K. Wittman.

What I find noteworthy regarding this subject is that not only rich and distinguished people gave abundantly of their goods for this enterprise, but also all
the *corps* and corporations of merchants and artisans had several beautiful
chapel windows made, upon which one sees representations in bright colors
of the different instruments and tools used in their labors and trades. Even the
lowest artisans offered striking marks of their liberality in the most elevated
regions of the choir. All contributed with pleasure to such a noble project.[15]

Such stories are a commonplace of medieval church construction narratives,
and they often misrepresented historical reality. What matters to us, though,
is that Pagès believed the story: the cathedral appeared to him as an image of
the community in whose great history his own identity was inscribed.

This becomes clearest in his discussion of the hundreds of paintings that
had been given to the church by the local Puy-Notre-Dame confraternity. Every
year since the late fourteenth century this confraternity had given a large painting to the church, and by Pagès's lifetime hundreds of these large and exqui-
site paintings, in fabulously intricate carved wooden frames, hung off the piers
of the cathedral (fig. 11.5).[16] These typically showed the Virgin surrounded by
the members of the confraternity and their families, occasionally with the
cathedral in the background. Philambien describes these richly individuated
works in great detail, fleshing out the astounding liveliness of the representations with anecdotes about the personages depicted. He also explains the various devises and patiently unravels the iconographic peculiarities of each picture.[17] Pariphile asks only the odd leading question.

After a while one begins to feel as though the visible surfaces of the cathedral were like a code that was incomprehensible to outsiders: thus where the
visitor Pariphile sees a mere coat of arms or inscribed name—for instance on
the tablets in the north transept, where all the heads of the confraternity since
1418 were named—Philambien sees personalities with whom stories, descendants, and specific, identifiable monuments of devotion and piety can be associated. For those with the knowledge to read this code, the beauty of these
works lent an uncanny authority to the long traditions of devotion practiced
in the town which had built the church and clustered around it for centuries.

It is rather startling to find, then, in the midst of this decidedly unmodern
text, several passages of sophisticated formal analysis—among the most sophisticated on Gothic architecture that had yet appeared in French. Here is
Philambien analyzing the architecture of the crossing (fig. 11.6):

The columns, or isolated pillars, are four feet and two inches in diameter, ex-
cepting the four largest, which support the great portal about which I have al-

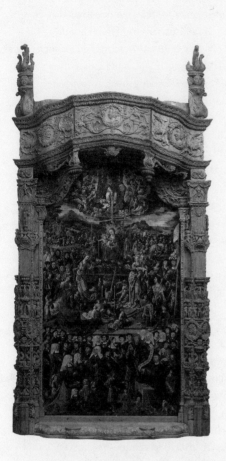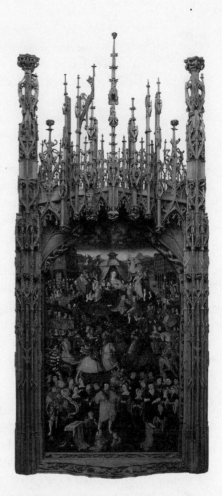

Fig. 11.5. Amiens Master (active in the first quarter of the sixteenth century), Puy of 1518: "Au juste poids véritable balance"; Puy of 1520: "Palme eslute du suveur pour victoire." Puy Notre Dame paintings from 1518 *(left)* and 1525 *(right)*. Courtesy Musée de Picardie, Amiens.

ready spoken to you, and are half engaged, holding to the body of the building by nearly a half of their diameter[;] but the four big columns which support the vault at the middle of the crossing are isolated, and each is posed upon its own square stereobate, which supports the bases[;] these columns each have four other medium-sized columns engaged to their four corners, giving them a square appearance, though they are in fact round. [E]ight other columns, arranged two on each side, much smaller than these four latter ones which I just spoke of, with yet another column fatter by half again the diameter, and placed in the middle of these eight others, surround these four admirable

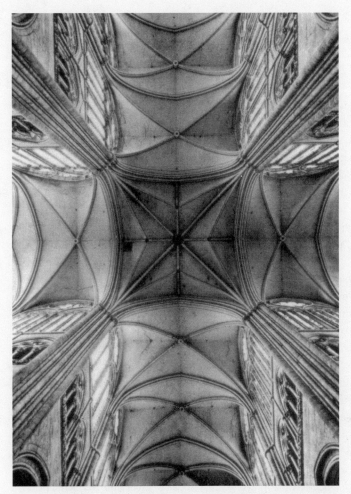

Fig. 11.6. The crossing vault at Amiens Cathedral. Photograph by Stephen Murray.

> bundled columns, against which all these medium-sized and small ones are en-
> gaged to about one-fourth of their diameter[;] these receive all the ribs of the
> vaults, whose center is embellished with delicate branches and crossing ogives,
> forming a sort of Maltese cross or cross of the Order of the Holy Spirit.[18]

The reader here feels as though a page from *Bulletin Monumental* has been ac-
cidentally spliced into Abbot Suger's *De consecratione*. Where had Pagès
learned to write about architecture in this manner? From books—the same
books from which he drew the dialogue of his well-informed visitor, Pariphile.
Through Pariphile's references, we learn that Pagès was familiar with Germain

Brice's innovative guide to Paris architecture,[19] Philibert de l'Orme's *Premier tome d'architecture*,[20] and—via an article in Bayle's *Nouvelles de la République des Lettres*—the artistic rulings of the Council of Trent.[21] But above all we learn that Pagès relied on the numerous theoretical works published in his lifetime by writers associated with the Royal Academy of Architecture in Paris: he refers repeatedly to Claude Perrault's translation of the treatise of the ancient Roman engineer Vitruvius (1673; second edition in 1684),[22] Nicolas-François Blondel's redoubtable *Cours d'architecture* (1675–83),[23] André Félibien's dictionary of art terms (1676),[24] and Jean-François Félibien's "Dissertation touchant l'architecture antique et l'architecture gothique" (1699).[25] These works lay at the source of Pagès's precocious, if incongruous, ability to analyze formally the architecture of his "incomparable" cathedral.

The publication of these books was part of a contemporary academic campaign to inculcate better architectural taste in literate Frenchmen, and was thus a facet of that larger process of acculturation evoked above. While we tend to think of seventeenth-century French architecture as overwhelmingly classical, in reality classical forms were then still widely rejected or ignored outside elite circles, or were handled in a spirit that owed more to Gothic traditions than to Vitruvius.[26] Men of taste and learning who knew Italy—for instance the *intelligents* of the 1630s[27]—had despaired that Frenchmen still built in this manner, which they considered ignoble, artisanal, and ultimately vulgar.[28] But it was only once Louis XIV harnessed the power of the state to his ambition of surpassing the age of Augustus, in the 1660s and 1670s, that architectural licentiousness became an official concern. From its foundation in 1671, the Royal Academy of Architecture was to be the headquarters of a kind of official anti-Gothic crusade, and from the start printing was its main weapon. Affiliated writers published thirteen new titles in the first twenty years of the academy's existence, covering everything from construction to decoration to architectural history. These works attacked the ignoble character of most recent building, decried the power of the guilds and masons' corporations, and announced the crown's new commitment to actively fostering a more noble (in every sense) conception of architecture.[29] These books promoted classical forms, to be sure, but more profoundly they sought to teach a more "modern" and analytical mode of viewing architecture, one capable of perceiving how properties like apparent solidity and orderly simplicity linked classicism to an ideal of nature and lifted it above other architectural traditions. By initiating readers into this disciplined contemplation of form, these books sought to preempt traditional emotional-religious patterns of architectural experience. Indeed, when Jean-François Félibien discussed the history of Gothic architecture in his "Dissertation touchant l'architecture antique et l'architecture gothique," he attributed its tenacious hold on popular French taste to the long dominance of that lower, less disinterested brand of architectural appreciation.[30]

Thus Jean Pagès was living in a time when it was possible for an energetic provincial to have an informed idea of the latest architectural thinking. In certain passages on the cathedral one can see Pagès trying gamely to apply his new knowledge of terminology and proportional analysis:

> The pedestals, which have several faces, forming a polygon, are also decorated with toruses and with moldings[;] the lower torus is fatter, the one being separated from the other by a *nacelle* or scotia of a well-proportioned depth. [A]rchitects call the fat rings on the bases of columns a "torus" because of its resemblance to the edge of a bed or a mattress. . . [.] [T]he little rings in the Ionic base are, however, named astragals. The diameter of the bases of these columns is equal to one half of the intercolumniations, which makes them seem quite ample and of a correct proportion.[31]

The irony, of course, is that the academy had not propagated this mode and vocabulary of formal analysis so that people might enrich their appreciation of their local Gothic church; quite the contrary, it was supposed to help them perceive the greater refinement and clarity of classicism. Pagès was hardly unaware of this problem, although he did not understand it quite as we would expect him to. On occasion, he confronted the academic critique of Gothic, as when Pariphile recites Félibien's account of the degeneration of Gothic architecture into overdelicacy, and Philambien responds, somewhat defensively: "Our incomparable cathedral, built in this same delicate manner which I have been describing to you, nonetheless has subsisted for some five hundred years, in all its power and beauty [*dans sa force et sa beauté*], despite the injuries inflicted by time, the impetuosity of the winds, and the violence of tempests."[32] Elsewhere, though, Pagès seems almost to concede the academicians' point. For instance, when Pariphile confronts Philambien with a typically academic condemnation of Gothic architecture (including a suggestion that the façade of Amiens would have been better off decorated with classical orders),[33] Philambien first defends the cathedral[34] before then joining Pariphile in a general attack on Gothic:

> The Goths introduced a heavy and massive architecture. These northern peoples had retained something of the rusticity of the caves and caverns that they had formerly inhabited, but later they imagined to polish and soften the grossness of their buildings. This Gothic architecture was in use for a long time, and was only abandoned because it corrupted itself from within, for the people became accustomed over several centuries to a manner of building which made the

270 RICHARD K. WITTMAN

buildings look light and delicate, and with a boldness of execution that could be astounding.[35]

These claims are reproduced almost verbatim from Félibien's "Dissertation touchant l'architecture antique et l'architecture gothique," an academic text which had analyzed the Gothic uniquely in order to define the essence of its inferiority.[36]

In effect, Pagès was caught between two authorities—that of the academicians and that of the cathedral. As long as "Gothic" remained an abstraction, within a theoretical discourse or historical narrative in which he accepted the authority of the academy, Pagès was happy to condemn it. But the translation of this discourse into concrete terms was another matter, because for Pagès his cathedral remained "incomparable" in the sense that its value was personal and absolute. This question of comparability is the essential difference between how Philambien experiences the place and how Pariphile experiences it. To take on academic criticisms of the cathedral was an option only for the erudite visitor, whose experience of the church was aesthetic and historical, not personal and memorial.

It is worth developing this last opposition with reference to the theorization of history and memory presented early in this century by the sociologist Maurice Halbwachs.[37] For Halbwachs, memory, and specifically collective memory, refers to the "depository of tradition" shared by a particular family, community, or other group dwelling together in a discrete time and place—a shared recollection of the group's past that plays an integral part in its present identity. This recollection is a present-minded social construction—one sustained not by objective analysis but by a dialectic of remembering and forgetting that unconsciously yet continually distorts the past to serve the needs of the present. Halbwachs theorized that the real places where a group has dwelled together sustain this dialectic: places offer the memory a stable, external record and reminder of the past of the group. They are like a text comprehensible only within the group—one whose meaning is perhaps reinterpreted and adjusted constantly, but which betrays no trace of this and therefore feels timeless to its "readers." This notion may be related to what we know of premodern mnemonic technique (a point Halbwachs does not make), in which memory training sometimes involved the construction of imaginary "memory palaces" where bits of knowledge could be mentally stored and accessed.[38] *Memoria* in this sense was also thoroughly present-minded: the training of memory was understood in premodern culture as a matter of ethics, and the memory itself as a workshop that one stocked and ordered so as to facilitate the quotidian production of moral judgments and actions.[39] Particular canonical readings of stories, places, and works of art of especial value to such a group can provide a touchstone for a kind of collective memory.[40] Pagès's account conforms in many ways to this model: his manuscript supplies his "reading" of the "code" of the cathedral, a code that both springs from and grounds the community that has gathered in that place for centuries. It reads images of the world within a continuum linking man and God, human history and sacred history.

Halbwachs differentiated memory in this sense from historical consciousness, which appears when "memory is breaking up" because past events have been "lost amid new groups for whom they no longer have interest." He argues that history, as opposed to memory, treats the past intellectually and critically, as a remote and neutral object with equal value for everyone. History in this sense is sustained not by the experience of place but via documentation, via the written word.[41] Clearly, Pagès was not untouched by this sort of consciousness either, as the very act of writing down his description shows. Yet he knew that the "code" of the cathedral addressed primarily a local audience (represented by Philambien) via its memory, and did not aspire to universal legibility (as evinced by the experience of the educated visitor, Pariphile).

The interest of Pagès's manuscript is not that we can extrapolate from it general conclusions about how French people experienced historical monuments circa 1700. Its interest is instead that it shows us how participation in the unifying, amalgamating discourse of the reading public left one reader caught uncomfortably between the authority of a prestigious discourse embodied in printed texts and the authority of a physical place, "*dans sa force et sa beauté.*" For if Pagès brings to life how a building could help ground the identity of the community in which it stood, his text also poses a question: What happens to one's experience of such a place when the paradigmatic community is dispersed, gathering only conceptually in the pages of books?

III

An answer to this question is suggested by an incident recounted at the end of Pagès's manuscript. At the outset of his epic inventory of the paintings of the Puy-Notre-Dame confraternity, in a passage written in 1709, Pagès remarked:

> I know that there are some persons who say that the paintings and marble and stone statues placed around the columns of our cathedral should be removed, offering as a self-evident reason that, without them, the building would seem brighter and more unencumbered [*dégagé*]; to them one may respond that this incomparable temple has been worked in such a delicate manner that the light easily shines even in its farthest corners.[42]

Against such claims Pagès invoked the arguments of the Oratorian Lamy, who defended the essential role of religious paintings as an aid to visualization and thus to spiritual understanding.[43] But if Pagès was able to resist aestheticism in his own thinking, he was powerless to counter its hold on others: throughout his manuscript, the annotation "*Oté en 1723*" (Removed in 1723) occurs in the margins, opposite his descriptions of specific paintings, written in Pagès's hand but in a slightly different ink. What happened in 1723? The answer is contained in a three-page appendix at the back of his manuscript.[44]

This appendix explains that the "*personnes*" to whom he had referred in 1709, who wanted to purge the church of its paintings, were a faction of the cathedral chapter. In 1723, in Pagès's final year of life—and the year in which the appendix was written—these canons were able to seize an opportunity afforded by the complaints of a visiting preacher who, afflicted by gout, had been unable one Sunday to mount the stairs to the pulpit. According to Pagès, the preacher blamed this on several adjacent picture frames, which, he said, crowded the stairway. The canons immediately removed the paintings in question. The Puy confraternity, which had given the paintings, was upset and sought an injunction from the bishop that would have returned the paintings to their place. A complex jurisdictional conflict over a legal technicality then erupted between the bishops of Amiens and Beauvais. Realizing that this legal deadlock presented them with an opportunity, the canons swiftly hired a team of workmen who worked through the night to spirit virtually all the other paintings out of the church. The workmen returned shortly thereafter to spend a night prying ex-votos off the walls and pillars. Finally, all the old medieval wall paintings were scraped and painted over. The church had, for all intents and purposes, become "*dégagé*" such as we see it today.

Pagès's account of these events is devastating. Leaving behind Pariphile and Philambien, it is written in a bitter first person, and concludes with a poem:

> What demon, full of malice,
> Has stripped, in a moment,
> This sacred, this superb edifice
> Of all its most beautiful ornament?

The poem suggests that the essential meaning of the church has been lost:

> This disfigured church
> Now presents in this place

> But a miserable mosque
> Instead of the temple to the true God.
> . . . .
> All the illustrious stories
> Painted by our feeble memories
> Have been destroyed in an instant.[45]

The canons are vilified, while the poet gnashes his teeth in solidarity with the confraternity, whose "vows," "gifts," and "presents" to Mary "are swept away with the wind":

> O powerful and just vanquisher,
> May your thunder and lightning
> Fall upon and pulverize
> Their enormous recklessness.
> Break open their criminal heads
> Explode and crush these rebels;
> Destroy the troop of ingrates;
> Let them recognize your power,
> That the world, by your vengeance,
> Might be purged of these villains.[46]

For all their baroque emotion, these are wrenching, moving passages; one wonders whether Pagès's death in November of that same year came of a broken heart. Categories like "Gothic" and "*dégagé*" fall away, and the center of this conflict is revealed as nothing less than the very role architecture is expected to play in the lives of its users.

The canons had surely been influenced in their actions by recent architectural publications. "*Dégagement*" had been the one formal property in Gothic mentioned somewhat favorably in certain publications associated with the academic milieu: Claude Perrault, most famously, had written in a note to his translation of Vitruvius that "[t]he taste of our century, or at least of our nation, is different from that of the Ancients, and perhaps in this it retains something of the Gothic: for we like openness, light, and *les dégagemens*."[47] "*Dégagement*" had resurfaced more recently as a key concept in the *Nouveau traité de toute l'architecture,* a treatise by the nonacademician Jean-Louis de Cordemoy first published in 1706 and reissued in an expanded edition in 1714.[48] Speaking specifically of churches, Cordemoy argued that the ponderousness and sterility of contemporary classicism precluded any sense of spiritual uplift, but that it was impossible to enter a great Gothic church without feeling "a certain and secret joy mixed with veneration and esteem, which obliges us to accord it our full approval."[49] He attributed this to the spatial *"dégagement"* of Gothic architecture and urged architects to strive for a more Gothic sense of space and structure. Cordemoy's polemic received broad exposure: not only was it widely reviewed in the press, but between 1710 and 1712 Cordemoy participated in a public dispute in the *Mémoires de Trévoux* with the engineer Amédée-François Frézier, who had ridiculed certain of his claims.[50]

There is ample reason therefore to think that, in clearing out their cathedral, the canons of Amiens were simply trying to highlight what they had learned to see as the best aesthetic qualities of their otherwise barbaric church. One conceives that they never saw it as a question of meaning—only of appearance, which is how the new architectural literature encouraged them to view it. But this division of meaning and appearance—of ethics and aesthetics—was itself a part of the development with which we are concerned here. The memory-based model of cognition which sustained Pagès's very different experience of the cathedral had endured a terrific attack in the seventeenth century from the likes of Descartes, Bacon, and others. The practice of relying on images, sensual experience, and memory to arrive at a knowledge of truth had been derided as corrupting knowledge—as mixing up the nature of things with the nature of the interpreting subject's mind. The new rationalist epistemology instead proclaimed that one could judge things properly only once one's interpretations were based on a fixed and objective logic that stood outside of one's own sense and emotion. In other words, once one's vision was stripped of the kinds of personal concerns that permitted Philambien to see things in the cathedral that were invisible to Pariphile.

Pagès, it is clear, was unable to strip down his own vision in this way: the hot and blinding immediacy of his deeply personal experience of the cathedral inevitably melted the cool disinterest that was required for a purer aesthetic beholding. But for others the situation was evidently different. Pagès's horror at the removal of the paintings stemmed from this inability to see that the prestigious forms of disinterested analysis he encountered in his reading depended, by their nature, on blanching the monument, on abstracting it from the very concerns that made it so valuable, so "incomparable," to him, in order that it might take its place in the universal aesthetic category of "architecture."

In its mistrust of the situatedness of the subject, in its quest for an objectivity free of the limitations of a vantage point—one that allows the object to belong "to everyone and to no one"[51]—the new rationalist epistemology was related to what Halbwachs termed a "historical" consciousness of the past. The parable presented in Pagès's manuscript reveals that this mistrust of the situated spectator has a sociopolitical component: for when self-interested, memory-based patterns of interpretation are declared illegitimate, a weakening occurs in the ways monuments can bond people into physically situated and necessarily exclusive communities. This, in turn, encourages a transfer of social identity to dispersed commonalities occupying the abstract conceptual spaces of a public or a nation. It is appropriate that the formalism that occasioned the destruction of Pagès's memory palace came to Amiens via printed books, as part of a public discourse launched by a consolidating, centralizing state.

Finally, Pagès's story helps us better to understand the discomfort of art history with those responses to art that are not those of a disinterested spectator. Traditional art history would, I think, reflexively interpret the incident of 1723 as nothing more than a sign of changing tastes. Our historical orientation certainly increases our intellectual mobility, permitting us to range comparatively across space and time. But it is also hard not to come away from Pagès's story envying him a little the intensity of his response to his "incomparable" cathedral, and feeling afflicted with a certain sadness that such responses seem so beyond our grasp.

NOTES

I am very grateful to have had the opportunity to present aspects of this work to audiences at the 2000 CAA Conference in New York, and at the Art History Departments of the University of Southern California and the University of Delaware. I would also like to thank Professor Henri Zerner of Harvard University for making several pertinent and encouraging comments on this essay.

1. For the claims advanced in this paragraph, see: Robert Muchembled, *Popular Culture and Elite Culture in France, 1400–1750* (Baton Rouge: Louisiana State University Press, 1985); Natalie Zemon Davis, *Society and Culture in Early Modern France* (Stanford: Stanford University Press, 1975); Jean Delumeau, *Catholicism between Luther and Voltaire: A New View of the Counter-Reformation* (London: Burns & Oates, 1977); John Bossy, "The Counter-Reformation and the People of Catholic Europe," *Past & Present* 47 (1970): 51–70.

2. Chandra Mukerji, *Territorial Ambitions and the Gardens of Versailles* (Cambridge: Cambridge University Press, 1997), 1–38. This new territory was also now mapped with unprecedented precision by official cartographers.

3. Muchembled, *Popular Culture and Elite Culture in France,* 279–311.

4. Ibid., 183–84.

5. I am not suggesting that the triumph of national paradigms of social identity over local ones occurred before the nineteenth century, but only that a process of cultural homogenization was already in full swing by 1700. On the concept of "the public" before 1700, see Elisabeth Noelle-Neumann, *The Spiral of Silence: Public Opinion—Our Social Skin* (Chicago: University of Chicago Press, 1984), 58–73; J. A. W. Gunn, *Queen of the World: Opinion in the Public Life of France from the Renaissance to the Revolution* (Oxford: Voltaire Foundation, 1995), 11–125; Jeffrey Sawyer, *Printed Poison: Pamphlet Propaganda,*

Faction Politics, and the Public Sphere in Early Seventeenth-Century France (Berkeley: University of California Press, 1990).

6. See for instance the recent works of Kevin Murphy: *Memory and Modernity: Viollet-le-Duc at Vézelay* (University Park: Pennsylvania State University Press, 2000); and "Restoring Rouen: The Politics of Preservation in July Monarchy France," *Word & Image* 11 (April–June 1995): 196–206.

7. Jean Pagès, "L'Auguste Temple, ou Description de l'Eglise cathédrale de nôtre Dame d'Amiens" (1708, with later interpolations through 1723), in vol. 1 of Pagès's "Notices historiques sur la ville d'Amiens" (Bibliothèque communale d'Amiens, ms 829 E [10 vols.]). The full title, as given by Pagès, is:

> L'Auguste Temple/ou/Description de l'Eglise cathédrale/de nôtre Dame d'Amiens,/avec des remarques./Dialogues entre Philambien, et Pariphile./Premier dialogue,/par Jean Pagés marchand d'Amiens./tôme Premier./Sancta uocant augusta patres: augusta uocantur/templa, sacerdotum rite dicata manu./Ouid Fast lib I vers vi ⁶ X./[device: Pagès's initials]/à Amiens./1708.

The text contains three separately paginated dialogues, each with separate "supplements." The nineteenth-century publication of Pagès's text is abridged and suppresses its dialogue format (Jean Pagès, *Manuscrits de Pagès, Marchand d'Amiens. Ecrits à la fin du 17e et au commencement du 18e siècle,* ed. Louis Douchet, 6 vols. [Amiens: A. Caron, 1856–64]). An informative though occasionally misguiding account of Pagès's life and work is found in: J. Garnier, "Notice sur Jean Pagès, Marchand et Historien d'Amiens (1655–1723)," *Mémoires de la Société des Antiquitiés de Picardie* 15 (1858): 103–28.

8. "Notice biographique sur Mr Pagès, donnée par lui-même," Bibliothèque communale d'Amiens, ms 829 E, vol. 1.

9. The other seven volumes at Amiens contain miscellaneous histories, ephemera, and collections of old documents, along with materials introduced after Pagès's death.

10. Pagès, "L'Auguste Temple," 1st dialogue, 34–35: "je crois que sans se flater, on peut dire que nôtre auguste temple est construit avec plus de delicatesse que tous les autres, je scay bien que suivant la pensée d'un écrivain moderne, l'Eglise de St-Pierre de Rome est fort au-dessus de tous les autres édifices, et qu'elle surpasse en grandeur, et en magnificence les batimens anciens et modernes, sans en excepter le temple de Salomon, et celui de Ste-Sophie à Constantinople, mais je doute que la Basilique de St-Pierre et de St Paul [*sic*] de Rome surpasse celle d'Amiens en délicatesse d'architecture."

11. See for instance ibid., 34.

12. Ibid., 1–30.

13. Ibid., 50: "Si les curieux estiment comme des chefs d'oeuvres de l'art la representation des choses de la nature faite par les mains scavantes, où des sculpteurs, où des peintres celebres de l'antiquité profane, ne devons [nous] pas estimer et admirer davantage ces tableaux de l'Ecriture Sainte, qui representent non seulement quelques ouvrages de la nature, mais encor les merveilles de la grace, dont une partie de ces tableaux exposent à nos yeux de si prodigieux effets."

14. Ibid., 40–42.

15. Ibid., 42: "Ce que je trouve de particulier sur ce sujet, est que non-seulement les personnes riches et de distinction donnèrent abondamment de leurs biens pour cette entreprise, mais encor que tous les corps et communautés de marchands et artisans firent faire plusieurs belles vitres des chapelles, sur lesquelles on voit représenté par de vives coulleurs différents instruments et outils qui servent à leurs manufactures et à leur métiers. Il n'est pas même iusques aux plus vils artisans, qui n'ayent donné des marques éclatantes de leurs libéralités dans les endroits les plus élevés du choeur. Chacun contribuoit avec plaisir à un si noble dessein."

16. A handful of these magnificent paintings survive at the Musée de Picardie in Amiens. See: Vivianne Huchard et al., *Le Musée de Picardie, Amiens* (Paris: Fondation Paribas, Réunion des musées nationaux, 1995), 66–83; Amédée Boinet, *La cathédrale d'Amiens*, 2d ed. (Paris: H. Laurens, 1931), 15–18. Sixteenth-century drawings of several of the lost paintings are reproduced in: Georges Durand, *Tableaux et chants royaux de la Confrérie du Puy Notre Dame d'Amiens* (Amiens: Yvert et Tellier, 1911). On other furnishings from the cathedral, see: Musée de Picardie, *La cathédrale d'Amiens* (Amiens: Le Musée, 1980–81), 121–265.

17. For example: "Ce tableau fut donné l'an 1504 par Mr Jean Le Prevost chanôine, procureur, et conseiller. Il est representé à genoux au bas du tableau avec l'écu de ses armes, Il porte d'azur à la bande d'or." Pagès, "L'Auguste Temple," 1st dialogue, 60. Countless such examples could be adduced.

18. Ibid., 35–36: "Les colonnes, ou piliers isolés ont 4 pieds et 2 pouces de diamètre, excepté les quatre plus gros, qui soutiennent le grand portail dont je vous ay déjà parlé, sont à demi-engagés tenant au corps du bâtiment par près de la moitié de leur diamètre, mais les 4 grosses colonnes qui soutiennent la voûte dans le milieu de la croisée sont isolées, et posées chacune sur leur stéréobate quarré, qui soutiennent les bases, ces colonnes ont chacune quatre autres moyennes colonnes adossées aux quatre coins qu'ils font paroître comme quarrées, quoiqu'elles soient rondes. huit autres colonnes, bien plus petites, disposées par deux de chaque côté, que ces quatres dernières, dont je viens de vous parler, avec encore une autre colonne plus grosse de la moié du diamètre, placée dans le milieu de ces 8 autres, composent le pourtour de ces quatre admirables colonnes en faisceaux, contre lesquelles toutes ces moyennes et petites sont adossées, et engagées environ sur le quart de leur diamêtre, elles reçoivent toutes les retombées des nervures de voûtes, dont le milieu est garni de ces délicates branches et croisées d'ogives, ou augives qui composent une espèse de croix de l'ordre du St-Esprit ou de chevalier de Malthe."

19. Pagès, "L'Auguste Temple," 1st dialogue, 46; 2d dialogue, 13. Brice's guide was the first that treated the architecture of Paris as an object for aesthetic contemplation. Germain Brice, *Description nouvelle de ce qu'il y a de plus remarquable dans la Ville de Paris,* 1st ed. (Paris, 1684). At least ten subsequent editions, under slightly different names, appeared between 1684 and Pagès's death in 1723.

20. Pagès, "L'Auguste Temple," 1st dialogue, 39.

21. Ibid., 100–105. Pagès also refers frequently to the *Journal des Savants,* although more with reference to theological and scientific questions.

22. Ibid., 5, 21, 39, 53, 56.

23. Pagès, *Manuscrits de Pagès,* 1:214–15. Blondel was the director of the Academy of Architecture. His *Cours d'architecture* contained the course he taught at the academy's architecture school.

24. Pagès, "L'Auguste Temple," 1st dialogue, 19; 2d dialogue, 13.

25. Pagès, "L'Auguste Temple," 1st dialogue, 16, 33. It is possible that Pagès drew the idea of casting his description as a dialogue from the work of Roger de Piles.

26. On this, see the many articles by Pierre Héliot, especially: "Remarques sur les survivances médiévales dans l'architecture française des XVIIe et XVIIIe siècles," *Bulletin de la société des antiquaires de l'Ouest,* 3d ser., 13 (1942–45): 287–301; "La fin de l'architecture gothique en France durant les XVIIe et XVIIIe siècles," *Gazette des beaux-arts* 38 (1951): 111–28; "La fin de l'architecture gothique dans le nord de la France au XVIIe et XVIIIe siècles," *Bulletin de la commission royale des monuments et des sites* 8 (1957): 7–159.

27. The *intelligents* were a group of court intellectuals (including the brothers Paul Fréart de Chantelou, Jean de Chantelou, and Roland Fréart de Chambray) associated with François Sublet de Noyers, *surintendant des bâtiments* under Louis XIII. They hoped to see

the Italian Renaissance ennoblement of art imported into France and adopted Poussin as their ideal. See Pierre Moisy, "Martellange, Derand et le conflit du Baroque," *Bulletin monumental* 110 (1952): 237–61; Claude Michaud, "François Sublet de Noyers, Surintendant des bâtiments de France," *Revue historique* 241 (1969): 327–64.

28. Before the foundation of the academy, this point of view was most clearly expressed by Roland Fréart de Chambray in his *Parallèle de l'architecture antique et de la moderne* (Paris, 1650). Fréart decried the vulgarity and ignorance of those in the building trades and complained that the forms of classicism were inevitably "Gothicized" by them (2–4).

29. Most importantly, see the dedicatory "Epitre" at the start of Blondel's *Cours d'architecture* (1675), Blondel's notes to the third edition of Louis Savot's *L'Architecture françoise des bastimens particuliers* (Paris, 1685), Félibien's "Dissertation" (1699), and (albeit with less venom) the royal dedication to Perrault's *Dix livres de Vitruve* (Paris, 1673 and 1684).

30. This officially sponsored discourse in turn had the unexpected effect of drawing forth architectural publications from other writers who were less in touch with official priorities. See my study "Architecture, the Press, and Public Opinion in Seventeenth- and Eighteenth-Century France," Ph.D. diss., Columbia University, 2001, 13–115.

31. Pagès, "L'Auguste Temple," 1st dialogue, 36: "Les piedéstaux qui sont à plusieurs faces formant un poligone, sont aussi ornés de tores, et de moulures, le tore inférieur à plus de grosseur, l'un étant séparé de l'autre par une nacelle, où scotie d'une profondeur bien proportionnée. les architectes appellent tores les gros anneaux des bases des colonnes à cause de la ressemblance qu'ils ont avec le bord d'un lit, où d'un matelas . . . , à la diference des petits anneaux, qui dans la base Ionique sont nommés astragales. Ces colonnes portent dans le diametre de leurs bases la moitié des entrecolonnemens, ce qui les fait paroitre bien dégagées, et dans une iuste proportion."

32. Ibid., 16: "Nôtre incomparable cathedrale batie de cette manière delicate dont je vous ai parle, subsiste cependant de puis pres de 500 ans dans sa force et sa beauté, malgré les jniures des tems, l'impetuosité des vents, et la violence des tempestes."

33. Ibid., 15. Pariphile's comments are probably drawn from another publication.

34. Ibid., 15–16: "Quoique les architectes ayent construit nôtre incomparable cathédrale suivant les règles de l'architecture gothique, on y trouve néanmoins partout cette solidité et cette beauté qui sont tous les jours admirées des plus habiles architectes."

35. Ibid., 15–16: "Les Goths introduisirent une architecture pesante, et massive; ces peuples septentrionaux avoient retenu quelque chose de la rusticité des antres, et des cavernes qu'ils habitoient autrefois, mais dans la suite ils songèrent à polir et adoucir la grossièreté de leurs édifices. Cette architecture gothique fut long tems en usage, et elle ne fut abandonnée, que parce qu'elle se corrompit d'elle même, car le peuple s'estoit accoustumé, depuis plusieurs siècles, à cette manière de bâtir, qui faisoit paroître les édifices légers, délicats et d'une hardiesse de travail capable de donner de l'étonnement."

36. Félibien, "Dissertation," 171 and 174.

37. Maurice Halbwachs, *The Collective Memory* (New York: Harper & Row, 1980). See in particular 78–82 and 128–57. See also the recent anthology of shorter texts: Maurice Halbwachs, *On Collective Memory,* ed. Lewis A. Coser (Chicago: University of Chicago Press, 1992), especially 46–51 ("The Reconstruction of the Past"), 52–58 ("The Localization of Memories"), and 193–235 ("The Legendary Topography of the Gospels in the Holy Land").

38. Mary Carruthers, *The Book of Memory: A Study of Memory in Medieval Culture* (Cambridge: Cambridge University Press, 1990).

39. Ibid., 1–15.

40. A point also made by Carruthers, ibid., 12.

41. Compare Carruthers: "It is my contention that medieval culture was fundamentally memorial, to the same profound degree that modern culture in the West is documentary" (ibid., 8). And while I have serious reservations about his attempt to extend Halbwachs's concept of collective memory to the dispersed and impersonal "community" of the French nation, Pierre Nora's celebrated essay "Between Memory and History" contains a very rich and suggestive evocation of the history/memory opposition. Pierre Nora, "General Introduction: Between Memory and History," in *Realms of Memory*, ed. Pierre Nora and Lawrence D. Kritzman, vol. 1 (New York: Columbia University Press, 1996), 2–3.

42. Pagès, "L'Auguste Temple," 1st dialogue, 50: "Je sçay qu'il y a des personnes qui disent qu'on devroit oster les tableaux et les statues de marbre et de pierres placées autour des colonnes de notre cathédrale, alléguant pour une raison apparante que les uns et les autres estant ôtés, l'édifice paraîtroit plus clair et plus dégagé; mais on peut leur répondre que cet incomparable temple est travaillé d'une manière si délicate que la lumière brille aisément dans tous les coins les plus retirés."

43. Ibid., 51–52. The Lamy text quoted by Pagès was a response to the excesses of Counter-Reformation (and Protestant) anti-idolatry, which Lamy viewed as a kind of reckless iconoclasm. It is surely revealing that the very distinct forms of antipathy toward images that confronted Lamy and Pagès both sprang at some level from centralizing, homogenizing movements.

44. Pagès, "L'Auguste Temple," Supplement after the 3d dialogue, 43–44.

45. Ibid., 43–44: "Quel démon, rempli de malice/Vient dépouiller, dans un moment,/Ce saint, ce superbe édifice/De tout son plus bel ornement? . . ./Cette église défigurée/Ne peut plus montrer en ce lieu/Qu'une misérable mosquée,/Au lieu du temple du vray Dieu. . . ./Toutes les illustres histoires/Peintes par nos foibles mémoires/Sont détruites dans un moment."

46. Ibid., 43–44: "Que ton tonnerre et que ta foudre,/Puissant vainqueur de l'équité,/Viennent réduire en poudre/Leur énorme témérité;/Brise ces testes criminelles,/Foudroye et écrase ces rebelles/Détruis cette troupe d'ingrats;/Qu'ils reconnoissent ta puissance;/Que le monde, par ta vengeance,/Soit purgé de ces scélérats."

47. Claude Perrault, *Les dix livres d'architecture de Vitruve, corrigez et traduits nouvellement en François avec des notes et des figures,* 2d ed. (Paris, 1684), 79, n. 16: "Le goust de nostre siecle, ou du moins de nostre nation, est different de celuy des Anciens, & peut-estre qu'en cela il tient un peu du Gothique: car nous aimons l'air le jour & les dégagemens."

48. Jean-Louis de Cordemoy, *Nouveau traité de toute l'architecture* (Paris, 1706; 2d ed., 1714).

49. Ibid., 175: "une certaine & secrette joye mêlée de veneration & d'estime, qui nous oblige à leur accorder une entiere approbation."

50. See Dorothea Nyberg, "La Sainte Antiquité: Focus of an Eighteenth-Century Architectural Debate," in *Essays in the History of Architecture Presented to Rudolf Wittkower,* ed. D. Fraser, H. Hibbard, and M. Lewine (London: Phaidon, 1967), 159–69.

51. Nora, "Between Memory and History," 3.

Settler Monuments, Indigenous Memory:
Dis-membering and Re-membering Canadian Art History

RUTH B. PHILLIPS

A monument is a deposit of the historical possession of power. Although it exhibits the traces of the particular historical will to memory that caused its creation, the monument cannot maintain that memory in a stable form. On the one hand, the physical monument is always subject to processes of destruction, erosion, and accretion. On the other hand, the cultural construction of a painting or other object *as* monument is altered by evolving narratives of history and art history. The processes of monument making and unmaking and the orchestration of memory and forgetting are most visible in the aftermath of major shifts in regimes of power. During the past century global processes of decolonization have produced many such shifts. In their wake the monuments left behind by four centuries of European mercantile expansion and colonialism have often become focal points for activist intervention.

In this essay I will address the kinds of negotiations that surround monuments belonging to settler societies like Canada, Australia, New Zealand, and South Africa.[1] More specifically I will focus on the particular issues that face internally colonized indigenous peoples within settler societies by examining several artistic projects undertaken during the 1990s by two First Nations artists working in Canada,[2] the Saulteaux-Ojibwa painter Robert Houle, and the Onondaga-Iroquois photographer Jeffrey Thomas. At the center of the discussion will be Houle's *Kanata* (1992) (fig. 12.1), a repainting of Benjamin West's *The Death of General Wolfe* (1770) in the National Gallery of Canada (fig. 12.2), and a series of photographic works in which Thomas interrogates the monument to Samuel de Champlain (1915–23) sculpted by Hamilton MacCarthy for a site adjacent to Ottawa's Parliament Hill (fig. 12.3). I will argue that both projects are pivotal postcolonial works within the artists' oeuvre of the 1990s because they intervene in settler constructions of monument and memory on two levels. They seek to revise a historical discourse that has silenced indigenous memory, while countering an art historical discourse that has constructed the indigenous artist as a primitive, and therefore as outside modernism. To understand the force of these interventions I will need to contexualize them within Houle's and Thomas's other, closely related artistic and curatorial projects.

Settler and Native Vectors of Decolonization

Before discussing Houle's and Thomas's revisionist work in more detail it will be useful to review briefly the particular politics that characterize decolonization in settler societies. Anticolonial movements generated by the desires of externally colonized settler populations for independence from imperial governments tend to trigger parallel movements among internally colonized indigenous peoples. In some external colonies, such as Canada and South Africa, decolonization is made even more complex by the desires for greater autonomy of historically subordinated European populations such as the Quebecois or the Afrikaners. These multiple vectors of decolonization are projected in characteristic ways onto and through expressive culture and the creation of national cultural institutions. The establishment of national museums, archives, and other institutions has been an integral part of the settler nation's self-construction. These institutions function both as architectural monuments in themselves and as agencies that make the nation's history visible to itself by producing certain visual and material objects as icons and landmarks that transmit the nation's origin story.[3] As Carol Duncan has put it, "like the traditional ceremonial monuments that museum buildings frequently emulate . . . the museum is a complex experience involving architecture, programmed displays of art objects, and highly rationalized installation practices."[4] By its acts of positioning, the museum endows certain images and objects with the seminal or summary significance associated with symbolic forms, allowing them to become shared reference points in the collective consciousness of the nation.[5]

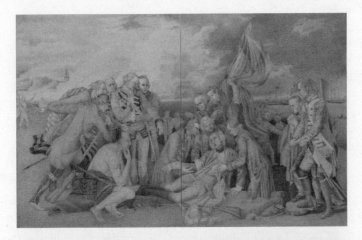

Fig. 12.1. Robert Houle, *Kanata,* 1992, acrylic and conte crayon on canvas, 228.7 × 732 cm overall, the National Gallery of Canada, 37479.1-4. Copyright Robert Houle. Reproduced by permission of Robert Houle and the National Gallery of Canada, Ottawa.

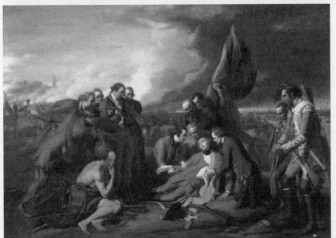

Fig. 12.2. Benjamin West, *The Death of General Wolfe,* 1770, oil on canvas, 152.6 × 214.5 cm, The National Gallery of Canada, 8007. Copyright National Gallery of Canada, Ottawa. Reproduced by permission of the National Gallery of Canada, Ottawa.

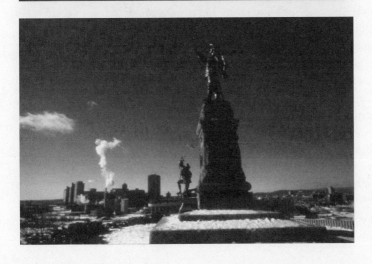

Fig. 12.3. Hamilton MacCarthy, *Monument to Samuel de Champlain,* 1915–23, Nepean Point, Ottawa. Courtesy National Capital Commission.

In order for the settler society to reinvent itself it must also create and display a cultural and artistic identity distinct from that of the imperial power. A characteristic syndrome, termed "borrowed identity" by Nelson Graburn, characterizes the processes of identity construction that accompany decolonization in settler societies and involves the appropriation of images of the indigenous population to the national self-image.[6] The first phase of Canadian nationalist cultural activism occurred during the early twentieth century and was informed by the progressivist period ideology that positioned the emergence of nation-states as a culminating achievement of modernity. It expressed itself, first, through evolutionist narratives of art and culture that denied the viability of indigenous peoples and their cultures in the modern world, and subsequently through the recasting of indigenous visual traditions as "primitive art." During the 1920s, for example, the Canadian national museums worked to foreground the expressionist landscape painting of the Group of Seven as a national school and to situate it within international modernism. Curators in these institutions directly promoted the paradigm of lost authenticity associated with the construct of primitive art and influenced artists to incorporate images of abandoned Native villages and totem poles that inscribed the trope of the Vanishing Indian.[7] During these years, too, the national museums and archives assembled a second tier "imperial archive" through government-funded collecting and documentation projects.[8]

In contrast to former external colonies, for internally colonized peoples there have been no definitive acts of political liberation, and no formal closure to the colonial era. In Canada, for example, indigenous people still live under the Indian Act, federal legislation first passed during the second half of the nineteenth century in order to engineer their assimilation into Euro-Canadian society through the appropriation of lands and the erasure of indigenous languages, cultural traditions, and memory.[9] The need to recover and restore indigenous accounts of the past to the national history is therefore at the heart of postcolonial politics in Canada, as it is in other settler nations. I would argue that the lack of formal closure on a political level has given special prominence to activist projects within the sphere of the visual arts.[10] The prestige and power of the national museums have led Native cultural activists to pressure the national institutions to be more inclusive by displaying contemporary Native art and working with indigenous curators.

Contesting the Allegorical Indian

The critical nexus of political activism, the national capital as monumental site, and art making can be illustrated anecdotally in relation to the artists considered here. Robert Houle first saw *The Death of General Wolfe* in 1969 when, as a rising member of a highly politicized generation of Native artists, he went to Ottawa to join a landmark protest against the government's plan to repeal the Indian Act (which, despite its oppressive legal features, continues to guarantee essential funding and government services). Jeffrey Thomas first saw the Champlain monument when he went to Ottawa to see the National Gallery's first exhibition of contemporary Native North American art, *Land/ Spirit/Power: First Nations at the National Gallery*, which was co-curated by Robert Houle.[11]

That these encounters proved to be defining moments in the artistic biographies of both Houle and Thomas is a function of the prior historical processes through which the West painting and the Champlain statue had been constructed as monuments. Both works celebrate major heroic figures of European settler history, and both were installed in the course of the key early-twentieth-century phase of Canadian settler nationalism and self-fashioning. The Champlain monument was created as a permanent marker of the Champlain Tercentenary, launched at Quebec City in 1908 with the most elaborate pageantry that had ever been organized by the Canadian government. As H. V. Nelles has recently shown, the celebrations repositioned a French colonial hero as a contributor to a triumphal history of British imperialism.[12] Over the years, however, the monument has also become a site for contestations of both Anglo-Canadian and settler empowerment. It has served as a rallying point for the patriotic St. Jean Baptiste Society at its annual celebration of the patron saint of Quebec, Ottawa's major public display of French Canadian nationalist and separatist sentiment. In the 1990s the monument became the target of demonstrations organized by the Assembly of First Nations, Canada's largest aboriginal political organization, to protest the subservient portrayal of the Indian scout, positioned on a plinth beneath Champlain's feet and rendered in reduced hieratic scale. In 1999 the National Capital Commission bowed to this pressure and removed the figure of the Indian scout from the monument to a park across the road.

The Champlain monument and its vicissitudes have been a central reference point of Jeffrey Thomas's photographic practice during the 1990s. He has photographed it from many angles, interrogating the monument in relation to the late-twentieth-century social realities of urban Indians like himself. In many of the images he draws out its contemporary resonances through the carefully calculated incorporation of reworked popular culture icons of Indians. In a 1997 photograph, for example, Thomas's teenaged son Bear sits in front of the bronze Indian, his head tilted back toward the scout at an interrogative angle (fig. 12.4). He is clothed in the fashions typical of contempo-

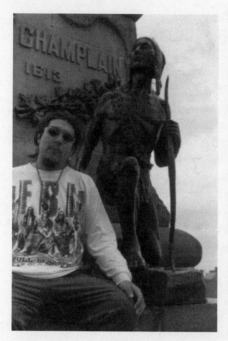 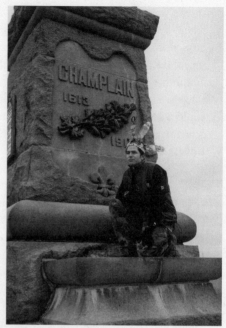

Fig. 12.4. (left) Jeffrey Thomas, "Bear Thomas Posed at the Samuel de Champlain Monument," 1997, gelatin silver print, 18 × 14 in. Artist's collection.

Fig. 12.5. (right) Jeffrey Thomas, "Greg Hill Posed at the Samuel de Champlain Monument," 2000, C-print, 30 × 20 in. Artist's collection.

rary Western youth culture, a baseball cap placed backward on his head, sunglasses, and a sweatshirt printed with an image of a nineteenth-century Plains Indian. The image has been doctored by the clothing designer; the Indian warrior also wears shades and is framed by the initials "F.B.I." and the words "Full Blooded Indian." In another image, made after the removal of the scout, Thomas photographed Greg Hill, a fellow Iroquois artist and curator, squatting in the scout's pose on top of the vacated plinth (fig. 12.5). Hill wears the camouflage pants and garments of any twenty-something Canadian man together with a traditional Iroquois *gustoweh* headdress made of cardboard cereal boxes. In both images the artifacts of fashion display the punning, ironic, pop sensibility of late-twentieth-century visual culture. They convey Thomas's commentary on the cumulative impact of a still-current tradition of romanticized imagery recycled through postindustrial mechanical reproduction into consumer culture. Both portraits speak to the ways that non-Natives are conditioned to see Natives and the crisis of identity many young Native people experience as a result. Both resonate with tricksterish resistance to this commodification and employ ironic juxtaposition as a strategy for interrogating stereotypes.[13]

Thomas has also used an image of the Champlain monument as the focal point of one of his most overtly political works, a five-part photographic installation entitled *Cold City Frieze* (1999–2001) (fig. 12.6). In this piece the monument is aligned with four other Indian figures from architectural sculpture and monuments. Each is constructed as an icon of a city that now occupies former Iroquois lands. Each is also made to stand as a "wampum icon" representing one of the five original nations in the Iroquois Confederacy, and the five images are placed in the same narrative order as are the symbols that represent the five nations in the historic Hiawatha wampum belt, a key sym-

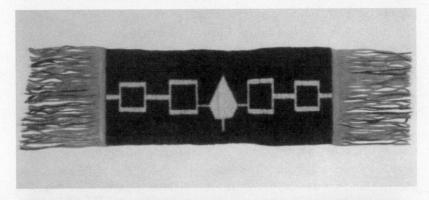

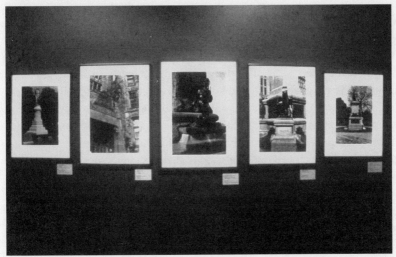

Fig. 12.6. Jeffrey Thomas, *Cold City Frieze,* 1999–2001, six C-prints. Artist's collection. (Temporary installation, Royal Ontario Museum, 2002.)

bolic expression of the Iroquois Confederacy.[14] On a third, autobiographical level each of the Indian figures is invested with meaning as a "personal icon," through associations made in the exhibit labels to people important to Thomas's own life. *Cold City Frieze* pulls Champlain's scout back into the indigenous structure of political power that preceded contact and colonialism *and* into a remembered history of twentieth-century Native life. Thomas announces this strategy in the artist's statement that accompanies the installation. "While living in the city of Toronto I came across an architectural frieze depicting a time-line of Canadian technological history. The first part of the frieze showed Indians riding on horseback and standing by tipis, images hardly relevant to the Iroquois experience. The rest of the frieze simply ignored the continued presence of the First Nations people in Canadian History. I designed *Cold City Frieze* to represent my urban Iroquois reality."[15]

Benjamin West's *The Death of General Wolfe,* which depicts the death in battle of the English general whose victory over the French in 1759 secured Canada for the British Empire, was one of five works given to the nation by the British government in 1921 as part of the Canadian War Memorials.[16] The gift was a gesture of Britain's gratitude for Canada's disproportionately great sacrifices during World War I. The transfer from England to Canada of important paintings related to its settler history can be read as an official recognition of Canada's "coming of age" as a nation. The painting quickly became a centerpiece of the National Gallery's collection and an icon of settler Canadian art history. Like Thomas's images of the Champlain monument, Robert Houle's repainting of West's masterwork also focuses on the marginalized figure of an Indian, the warrior who sits on the ground in the lower left-hand corner. Like the Indians in official state and provincial seals, or like the picturesque figures in the foreground of eighteenth-century topographical paintings, West's warrior frames the main scene of settler action and locates it in North America. On another level, as Vivien Fryd has argued, the figure—which she suggests is based on Dürer's *Melancholia*—is an initial and highly influential example of the topos of the Vanishing American in the iconography of Western painting.[17]

From his first encounter with the West painting, the warrior became for Houle the focus of crucial questions about identity and the position of aboriginal people in Canada—"Who are we? We're marginal, we're largely invisible, and ninety-nine percent of the time we're fictional."[18] In *Kanata* he renders the West painting as a cartoon in conte crayon on raw canvas, interpolating other Native figures into the background. Most importantly, Houle paints in only the Indian. By this gesture he shifts the focus of the painting away from the pathos of the dying English general in the compositional center to the impending tragedy of Native disenfranchisement and dislocation. "I created

Kanata because of a desire to invoke another history," he has written, "one based on underlining the historical marginalization of native people by heightening the allegorical reading of the Romantic 'noble savage' in the West painting. Nonetheless, it is a history based on an experience in the New World before there was a margin, the notion that 'our' lifeline here goes as far back as creation according to cultural memory."[19]

The settler origin story of Canada has defined the country's central historical drama as the struggle between the French and the English, the "two founding nations." Against this notion Canada's indigenous peoples have termed themselves the "First Nations." The strategies of Houle and Thomas are analogous. They complicate Canada's preoccupation with French and English historical perspectives, moving the European settler history of the country off center by manipulating the angles from which viewers can look at the canonical works of Euro-Canadian art history. By placing Houle's and Thomas's projects within the broader development of their work, we will be able to see how memory, history, and monument have been working on each other to inscribe new, postcolonial topographies in the commemorative landscapes of settler nations.

Robert Houle: Recovering Memory, Recuperating Newman

Robert Houle was born in 1947, grew up on the Sandy Bay reserve in Manitoba, and spent ten years of his childhood in a Catholic residential school. He has only recently, in his fifties, revealed the abuse that he, like so many other Native children, suffered there.[20] The highlight of his summers at home with his traditionalist family was attendance at the annual Sun Dance, but such duality carried a cost. Houle has recalled that he would attend a Sun Dance one day and have to confess his "paganism" in church on the next, and that it took years to rid himself of the imposed sense of guilt.[21] He went on to earn degrees from the University of Manitoba and McGill, falling under the sway of Mondrian, of his teacher, the Quebec hard-edge abstractionist Guido Mollinari, and, especially, of Barnett Newman and the New York School of abstract expressionism.[22] He accepted the rigorous discipline of field painting, recognizing both its spiritual content and its utility to the exploration of his own dual heritage of Christian and Saulteaux-Ojibwa spirituality. At crucial moments of his career he has used specific Newman works as points of departure for major projects of his own. His 1983 series *Parfleches for the Last Supper* was inspired by Newman's "Stations of the Cross" of 1958–66, and *Kanata* contains a direct quotation from a late Newman painting, the 1967 *Voice of Fire*.[23]

Kanata was painted in 1992, the year of the Columbus quincentennial, when many Native American artists were using their engagement with artistic modernism to confront the history of aboriginal people since contact, and it was purchased by the National Gallery of Canada in the same year.[24] By leaching the life and color out of the European figures and vivifying the Indian, Houle reverses the power relations of Canadian history, a revisionist gesture that cannot, of course, change the past, but only the future. In a 1992 interview Houle spoke of his hope that viewers would be drawn to his work, in the first instance "because of its beauty, because of its physicality and materiality," and that he could then, "somehow . . . teach them something, too."[25] This something has to do with how one sees the land and its history from a Native point of view. Quoting the remembered words of his grandfather he went on:

> And he would say *mii-aansh*. And that's just a narrative style of say-
> ing . . . "it has happened" or "used to happen" or "this is the way it was"—
> like fairytales from a long time ago. And then he'd say *ko aagiikidad*, "if
> something is going to happen," *anishnabec*, "native people will be there" and
> he would say *anishnabec*, "remember when this country was named, native
> people were present and native people signed treaties." And the reason for
> that he'd say is because we believe this is an integral part of our lifetime. We
> were given this land. We've always been here. So we firmly believe that we have
> this invisible contract with North America. That's my sense of history. And
> that's how I see myself even though I'm very open to the Canadian culture.[26]

Houle thrusts his image of a reempowered Native presence in between two large color fields of red and blue. In *Kanata* the red and the blue panels become emblematic of Canada's deadlocked French and English dualities. As noted, a key demand of aboriginal political leaders over the past two decades has been that the First Nations be recognized alongside the French and English as "founding nations" of Canada and that they be admitted to constitutional negotiations. *Kanata* thus plays on the multiple ironies of late-twentieth-century Canadian cultural politics. The fact that the Newman painting was first shown in the American pavilion at the Montreal World's Fair, Expo '67, held to celebrate the one-hundredth anniversary of Canadian confederation, was one such resonance. Canadian viewers would also have understood the reference made by its blue and red fields to Newman's *Voice of Fire*, whose purchase by the National Gallery in 1990 had raised an unprecedented nation-wide storm of controversy.[27] (It replaced *The Death of General Wolfe* as the Gallery's most visited work.) Of more serious and more recent import was the implicit reference to the Oka crisis which had taken place in the summer of 1990 when members of two Mohawk reserves in Quebec stood off the Quebec police and the Canadian army in a confrontation sparked by an unresolved claim to a sacred burial ground. The painterly qualities of the framing panels, whether read as expressionist symbolism or as pure visuality, became secondary. In *Kanata,* then, Houle moves from homage to manipulation, appropriating Newman's color fields in order to serve overtly political ends.

Yet the discipline of abstract expressionism also continues to lend to this painting and to a series of related prints a formal rigor and elegance that serve Houle's goal of attraction and persuasion. In this context Houle's use of abstract expressionist elements can be read as reinforcing his assertion of the survival of indigenous spirituality within the modern world. The quotation from Newman, I would argue, points to Houle's concurrence with the abstract expressionists' engagement with the mythic, the spiritual, and the mystical in general, and, more specifically, with Native American art as part of their own nationalist agenda. Newman, Rothko, Pollock, Gottlieb, and their colleagues were among the first artists to engage with Native American, as opposed to African or Oceanic, arts within the category of primitive art, and they made their debt clear in numerous statements and writings. As Jackson Rushing has pointed out, "these artists did not perceive themselves in a colonial situation vis a vis the use of Indian art, which, after all, was considered national cultural property. Moreover, modernism's self-defined universality seemed to justify its appetite for the cultural forms of Native American and other Others."[28] By these doubled references—to an alleged primordial system of meanings and to colonialist assumptions about Native people—modernist primitivism preempted the possibility of an unmediated use of their own formal traditions by the contemporary Native artists themselves. Houle's self-imposed task was, then, to recover the spiritual content of modernism silenced by formalist criticism during the 1960s and 1970s while at the same time countering its appropriative politics.[29] His reappropriation of abstract expressionism into a work of postcolonial critique is, then, an act of recuperation, informed by his desire to reverse the history of the exclusion of Native artists from the spaces of modernist art practice.

In 1993 Houle created an installation around his painting entitled *Kanata: Robert Houle's Histories* for the Carleton University Art Gallery in Ottawa within which he was able to play out the full range of his concerns. One of the most important was the complementary task of "rehabilitating" historic Native objects from anthropology museums, a commitment he had made to himself during a brief stint as curator of contemporary Indian art at the National Museum of Man in the late 1970s.[30] In the version of *The Death of General Wolfe* owned by the National Gallery West had omitted the Indian warrior's moccasins. By a striking coincidence, as Houle was planning his installation the National Gallery put on view a small loan exhibition from the British Museum of recently discovered historical Native objects that West had used as props—displayed, needless to say, in glass cases.[31] In his installation Houle parodies this treatment by "lending" his own moccasins—placed in an adjacent plexiglass box—to the painted warrior. At the same time he "freed" the ethnographic artifact by placing an offering of tobacco next to his parfleche (a painted rawhide container traditionally used to store sacred medicines, food, and other items) inside a circle inscribed on the floor. The circle demarcated a sacred space, open to the air, in which the parfleche could "breathe" and live.

A further element of the exhibition, *Contact/Context/Content*, introduced Houle's taped voice speaking his own history in Ojibwa and English, juxtaposed with photographs of the National Gallery's exhibit of West's Indian props.[32] The transcription of his spoken text, overprinted on reproductions of the contact sheets of the National Gallery's installations of West's artifact collection, activated the meanings of the diverse elements in the installation. It read:

> The historical relationship between the First Nations and Canada since CONTACT spans an empire and a post-colonial era. Today, the politics of multiplicity and the ideological grounding in listening to *other* voices has given me the opportunity to challenge authority—the CONTEXT upon which my work can have maximum empowerment for the viewer. Tomorrow, the politics of representation and the spiritual integrity of the past will govern the CONTENT to be found in my art.

On some of these prints Houle lettered the names of extinct North American indigenous peoples, written in reverse, over reproductions of *The Death of General Wolfe*. This textual/conceptual element connects *Contact/Context/Content* to several other major projects Houle worked on during these years that addressed issues of memory, commemoration, and monument even more specifically.[33] The series of works responded, in particular to Lothar Baumgarten's site-specific work *Monument for the Native People of Ontario*, commissioned as part of a 1985 temporary exhibition at the Art Gallery of Ontario. The work, which was subsequently acquired by the AGO, consists of an elegiac inscription of the names of "extinct" Native "people" painted in trompe l'oeil Roman typeface over the arches of the neoclassical Walker Court, one of the earliest parts of the AGO's building and now enfolded within several layers of more recent construction.[34]

Like the 1969 encounter with West's *Death of General Wolfe*, Houle's encounter with Baumgarten's installation was a pivotal moment. He was struck

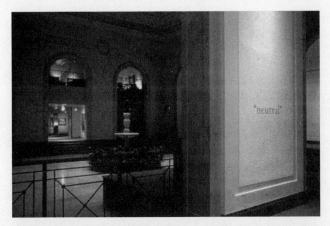

Fig. 12.7. Robert Houle, *Anishnabe Walker Court,* 1993, site-specific installation. Lothar Baumgarten's *Monument for the Native People of Ontario,* visible through the arches, has been installed in the Walker Court continuously since it was commissioned by the Art Gallery of Ontario in 1985. Typeface Perpetua [Eric Gill], tempera on painted concrete. Copyright Robert Houle. Reproduced by permission of Robert Houle and the National Gallery of Canada, Ottawa.

and disturbed by the white, German artist's appropriation of the right to mourn; by his confusion of the names of indigenous nations with those of language groups and regions; and by the fact that a number of the "Native People" named, such as his own group, the Ojibwa, are not extinct. In *Anishnabe Walker Court* (1993) Houle reappropriated the names by placing them in quotation marks and reinscribing them in lowercase on an outer wall that surrounds the Walker Court (fig. 12.7). He also included a photographic documentation of the changes to the Walker Court over the years that is itself a comment on the histories of change, memory, and forgetting that surround the museum-as-monument. The commissioning of Houle's intervention by the Art Gallery of Ontario, like the National Gallery of Canada's purchase of his *Kanata* in 1992 and its periodic hanging of the work adjacent to West's *Death of General Wolfe,* typifies the postmodern, reflexive culture of settler institutions during the 1990s. The handout accompanying Houle's piece states, for example, that the AGO acted, "being willing as an institution to exacerbate the contradictions Baumgarten's work asserts." The text stresses, furthermore, that Houle's work is situated within the discursive parameters of contemporary art: "Houle, incidentally, admires the installation as an 'eloquent European work which addresses our people.' . . . In the process, Houle has also taken as a subject the responsibility of an institution to site-specific works." The link between *Anishnabe Walker Court* and *Contact/Context/Content* is, then, that both retrieve from the limbo of the past images and icons of Natives who have been symbolically killed by premature acts of memorialization. Like *Kanata, Anishnabe Walker Court* works to alter the viewer's perspective on an existing work that has become monumentalized within a museum by the operation of art discourses, and by that change of perspective to insist on the vitality and agency of its subjects.

Jeffrey Thomas: The Quest for Identity and the Legacy of Curtis

Jeffrey Thomas also uses his camera as a tool for the discovery of lost histories. He regards the re-membering of the pasts of aboriginal people—pasts that have been overlaid with romantic and popular culture stereotypes—as an essential defense against the threats to indigenous identity. As I argued earlier, a key strategy of his interrogation of the Champlain monument is the juxtaposition of images that contrast the specificity and immediacy of living people and popular culture with the generality and romanticization of historic monuments. While the sculpted Indian scout gazes into the distance, Thomas's son Bear returns the gaze to the viewer and his friend Greg Hill looks beyond her, their expressions at once confident, quizzical, and cheerful. Ultimately, however, in these and other images, the focal point of the image is the portrait of the face of a contemporary First Nations person in all his or her individuality.

The portrait is one of two key photographic genres (or rhetorical modes, to use Barthes's taxonomy), to which Thomas has been drawn in his quest for historicized understandings of Native identity. The other is what he calls the "environment," the real, unromanticized, often gritty world that Indians have inhabited since contact, and particularly since the wave of economically motivated early-twentieth-century dislocations in which his own family was caught up—the world, that is, of urban modernity. The use of the camera as an investigative tool connects to the circumstances of Thomas's life. Jeffrey Thomas is a self-taught photographer born in Buffalo in 1956 to a family from the Six Nations Iroquois reserve in southern Ontario. Although he visited his relatives on the reserve regularly throughout his childhood, the fundamental condition of his life has been displacement. As an adult he has lived in cities—Toronto, Winnipeg, Ottawa—built on land that had been occupied for millennia by Native people. In the largest sense he set for himself the task of finding and documenting with his camera the traces of this occupation, historical and contemporary. He began taking photographs in the early 1980s as a founding member of NIPA, the Native Indian Photographers Association, an organization committed to countering the stereotypical representation of Indians through a new project of self-representation through photography.

Thomas's earliest photographs constituted a search for the traces of his family's history in the inner city neighborhoods of Buffalo in which he had grown up. He wanted, above all, to be able to visualize the world of his grandparents and great-grandparents, those who had first experienced out-migration from the reserves and who had first faced the need to reformulate and defend their identities. He found no answers to his most basic questions—how it had been for the first Indians who moved to the cities, what their world had looked like, how they had felt about becoming the objects of the non-Native gaze. What his quest revealed were paradoxical conditions of *in*visibility and *hy*pervisibility. As he walked the city streets his camera caught the fugitive traces of lives of alienation and displacement that lay outside of official histories. He found, on the one hand, a host of garish, highly visible, stereotyped images of Indians in advertising, on tee shirts, and on the covers of pulp novels, and, on the other hand, the more decorous but equally stereotypical images of the public monuments.

Both the absence and the excess produce the condition of nonrecognizability. Thomas has recalled the problems his initial inquiry posed. "I was curious . . . about the way Native people were depicted in pop culture. I found it very frustrating to see these depictions—on the Saturday afternoon westerns, for example. I wanted to investigate the history behind the stereotypes." He began to look for answers through historical research, and specifically in the visual archive of historical photography. Since the 1970s a large number of the images of Indians that circulate in popular culture have been derived from the early-twentieth-century photographs of Edward Curtis, who had set out to document the last traces of the vanishing American Indian. In an essay accompanying an exhibition of historical photographs he curated for the National Archives of Canada Thomas quoted Curtis's own description of his monumental, twenty-volume photographic project: "Above all, none of these pictures would admit anything which betokened civilization, whether in an article of dress or landscapes or objects on the ground. These pictures were to be transcriptions for future generations that they might behold the Indian as nearly lifelike as possible as he moved about before he ever saw a paleface or knew there was anything human or in nature other than what he himself had."[35]

As he viewed these early photographic images, however, Thomas was troubled by a sense of his own voyeurism. "There was a very limited amount of information that I could get from these photographs, and I felt guilty about staring at them. . . . I felt that I was on a field trip, staring at Indians."[36] He located his discomfort in the early photographers' erasure from the background of their subjects' actual historical existences. "The structure of the photographs produced this response in me," Thomas has said; "these people were living in poverty—they had no control over what was going on, over how the images were constructed. The results were very stylized images, tourist snapshots. On the other hand, there was a lack of environment revealed in the photographs, and this created a claustrophobic feeling for me because I was searching for information about that environment and these people."[37] Curtis's photographs belong to the primitivist current within modernism and to the intellectual movement of antimodernity, in T. J. Jackson Lears's sense.[38] Within this economy of signs, Curtis and others produced images of the almost vanished world of American Indians to be consumed by non-Natives yearning for an authenticity thought to have been lost through industrialization and urbanization. Antimodernist nostalgia (the sentiment that informs Baumgarten's *Monument for the Native People of Ontario*) denied to the depicted or referenced subjects a place in modernity. For Thomas, as for Houle, the retrieval of that denied modernity is a fundamental strategy for self-legitimation.

Thomas was blocked in his search for historical environments by the very conditions that had produced Curtis's photographs. He worked the problem out, as always, through photography itself, and specifically in his pow wow photographs, one of his major series of the early and mid 1990s. These images document contemporary pow wow dancers, the modern-day descendants of the romantic warriors Curtis had sought to record. For Thomas the pow wow photographs provide both a corrective to the artificial excisions of Curtis's work and an alternative body of imagery to his depictions of urban Indians. In pow wow dancers he found "a practice of that history [that] gives you that sense, that bearing in the world, that pride, that attitude"[39] that he had not been able to find in the city. It satisfied his need to explore the excess and messiness of actual environments and the ways that individuals negotiate divided subjectivities and complex modern identities. He photographed each dancer dressed both in everyday clothing and in dance regalia, their competition numbers clearly visible on their chests. He characteristically framed and displayed them in diptychs and triptychs to convey the complexity of modern Indian identities. In his 1996 exhibition *Portraits from the Dancing Grounds,* Thomas borrowed original Curtis photographs from the National Archives of Canada and incorporated them into his photographic groupings of modern pow wow dancers, finally returning these images back to Curtis.

As with Houle's use of color fields, the point of this inclusion was, however, more recuperative than deconstructive. In his continuing search for the traces of the past Thomas had come to regard Curtis's portraits as possessing an indispensable indexical relationship to the ancestral lives he himself sought to know. Curtis had written that his pictures "should be made according to the best of modern methods and of a size that the face might be studied as the Indian's own flesh."[40] Like Curtis himself, Thomas was drawn inexorably to the faces. He has said:

> The historic photographs, by Curtis and others like him, seemed to be an extension of that stripping away because they didn't provide a sense of place, time or history. If you are trying to take away someone's identity and impose a new one, of course you take the history away, the sense of place. . . . I also remember thinking, what if we had no record at all from the past? Although the images were lacking in many ways, they were nevertheless a record: the faces couldn't be changed. It occurred to me that there is no way that I can add a history to those early photographs. I can't make more than there already is, so, what can you do? For me, you become a photographer, and you become responsible for the time in which you are living.[41]

To find the faces of his own ancestors, then, Thomas has had to recuperate Curtis—at least in part—from the general poststructuralist condemnation of the modernist ethnographic and aesthetic movements that shaped his work. As Roland Barthes has written, "photography transformed subject into object, and even, one might say, into a museum object."[42] But, as he also writes, that same transformation is grounded in the photograph's fundamental "contingency," because of which "it immediately yields up those 'details' which constitute the very raw material of ethnological knowledge."[43] Curtis's portraits were intended to be commemorations of and monuments to the disappearing American Indian.[44] Thomas reaches back through this initial historical framing, through the reromanticized images of the calendars and the postcards, and through the reworked, ironic, postcolonial images, to reassert their essential evidentiary status. Ultimately, for Thomas this value is absolute and undeniable. For him, as for Barthes, "every photograph is a certificate of presence."[45]

Thomas regards his archival research as a form of archaeology, a "digging through the archives for the images of the past."[46] He has also pursued his quest as a curator of exhibits of historical photographs by working with an eclectic body of photographs taken by amateur, commercial, and ethnographic photographers. The resulting exhibitions are, increasingly, framed as the visual history he originally set out to find in city streets. His 2000 exhibit *Emergence from the Shadows* for the Canadian Museum of Civilization investigated what is perhaps the ultimate modernist project, ethnographic photographs deposited by early anthropologists, in this case those working for the National Museum of Canada. He found in the museum's ethnographic archives documentary evidence that showed that many of the sitters had carefully controlled their own self-presentations. This research has, finally, begun to answer the questions with which Thomas began, linking back, for instance, to some of his most treasured memories of childhood visits to his great-aunt Emily General. "When I was a child," he has said, "I stayed on the family farm at the Six Nations reserve in southern Ontario. At night or when people were visiting, I would sit in the kitchen and listen to the stories being told about people in the community. . . . There were no photographs of those I heard about, and none were needed because the stories created such a strong visual impression in my mind. During my research at the National Archives, I came across several photographs of people from my reserve. These photographs brought back memories of the vivid images I had as a child."[47] Thomas's photographic practice is intimately bound up with his archival project. Both are necessary to his goal of recovering identity through the restoration of memory to history. "I don't look at the historical photograph in a negative sense, but I think there's a place where my work as a photographer and the historical photograph come together . . . and they begin to expand upon the historical limitation and the pop cultural limitations, and you begin to find this ground that's very unique to who you are today."[48]

Bringing into History and Breaking History's Shackles

Thomas's and Houle's artistic projects are linked not by formal or generic qualities but by common critical and political purposes—purposes that are typical of their generation of indigenous North American artists. Both introduce into official spaces of display what Raphael Samuel has called "unofficial knowledge."[49] Both draw on a combination of individual, familial, and communal memory and of forgotten textual and visual documentation to alter the viewer's angle of vision on official settler monuments. Pierre Nora's central argument that history's absorption of memory is transformative has useful explanatory force in suggesting that these negotiations will construct new and equally rigid orthodoxies through the selective incorporation of orally preserved histories. Such incorporations both arrest organic, indigenous processes of reiteration and can bring into the public domain articulations regarded as proprietary and private in the originating societies. However, close readings of Houle's and Thomas's work also complicate Nora's formulation. By its very title, for example, Nora's essay "Between Memory and History" denominates a binary, which like other similar binaries—tradition and modernity or the sacred and the secular—colonizes discourse, limiting the terms in which the pasts of many non-Western peoples can be discussed.[50]

In his essay "History's Forgotten Doubles," Ashis Nandy has brought forward specific issues that arise around postcolonial history and memory. He argues that history marks all other modes of representing the past with a negative valence: "The historians' history of the ahistorical—when grounded in a 'proper' historical consciousness, as defined by the European Enlightenment—is usually a history of the prehistorical, the primitive, and the prescientific. By way of transformative politics or cultural intervention, that history basically keeps open only one option—that of bringing the ahistoricals into history."[51] He argues further that historical consciousness, once achieved, is totalizing; "for both the moderns and those aspiring to their exalted status; once you own history, it also begins to own you." He leaves open, however, a second possibility, presented as unstable and fugitive but nevertheless potent, for rupturing the hegemonic power of historical consciousness:

> You can, if you are an artist or a mystic, occasionally break the shackles
> of history in your creative or meditative moments (though even then you
> might be all too aware of the history of your own art, if you happen to be that
> kind of an artist, or the history of mysticism, if you happen to be that kind of
> a practitioner of mysticism). The best you can hope to do, by way of exercising your autonomy, is to live outside history for short spans of time.[52]

This possibility art offers for "breaking the shackles of history" is, I suggest, the second reason why the arena of visual art has been so important a sphere for postcolonial negotiation in settler societies (the first, as I mentioned earlier, being the lack of a formal political closure to colonialism). Both Robert Houle's and Jeffrey Thomas's interventionist works "bring into history," in Nandy's terms. But both also "break the shackles of history" to recover, experientially, alternate modalities that have existed historically and that survive today in fragmentary forms within the modern world. The work of recovery addresses itself not just to factual accounts forgotten in the archives or preserved in memory but never written down. It is, equally, a project whose goal is to recover that which has been lost through imaginative acts of projection and recreation. Such acts collapse time. Houle and Thomas engage Benjamin West, Barnett Newman, Hamilton MacCarthy, and Edward Curtis in dialogues that are impossible in historical time but that are enabled through the transtemporal physicality of the monument and the limitless potential for recontextualization present in the spaces that these works create around themselves.

Ironically, modernity's own archival and nostalgic impulses—its construction of an imperial archive and its creation of a romantic antimodernist

movement—have guaranteed the presence of collections of ethnographic artifacts and "primitive art," the documentary photographs, the literature of anthropology, and the ethnographic archive that continue to enable the production of these alternative views. Art, however, is not politics. In his analysis of
parallel examples of artistic intervention in New Zealand, Nicholas Thomas
has rightly asked, "Can indigenous art as a whole be seen to be placed in an
enabling situation," or do such interventions more often "[exhibit] an incom-
patibility between cultures and institution, and [attest] to the awkwardness of
combination rather than the prospects of partnership?"[53] Interventions similar to those discussed in this essay have steadily increased in major Canadian
institutions of art and culture for almost two decades, but they have not yet
destabilized the fundamental narratives in which settler monuments are embedded. Houle and Thomas, like their contemporaries, do not resolve the
problem of postcolonial memory but, rather, place quotation marks around
the monuments of settler historical memory. Their works leave behind impressions of their own ambivalence—the "awkwardness" of which Nicholas
Thomas speaks. Yet these multiplying moments of interrogation and opening
out are important, and for those who experience them the monuments they
call into question will never be the same. Perhaps Robert Houle's and Jeffrey
Thomas's ultimate, tricksterish, perspectival shift, however, is that their acts of
self-positioning within the history of artistic and anthropological modernism
reopen possibilities within the modernist tradition not only for Native but also
for non-Native subjects.

NOTES

1. Nicholas Thomas's *Possessions: Indigenous Art/Colonial Culture* (Thames and Hudson, 1999), which focuses on New Zealand and Australia, provides essential context for the
particular problem of monuments in settler societies, particularly Canada. See also Annie
Coombes, "Translating the Past: Apartheid Monuments in Post-Apartheid South Africa," in
Hybridity and Its Discontents: Politics, Science, Culture, ed. Avtar Brah and Annie E. Coombes
(New York: Routledge, 2000); and Paul Tapsell, Te Arawa, "*Taonga, Marae, Whenua*—Negotiating Custodianship: A Maori Tribal Response to the Museum of New Zealand," in *Na-
tional Museums, Negotiating Histories: Conference Proceedings,* ed. Darryl McIntyre and
Kirsten Wehner (Canberra: National Museum of Australia, 2001), 112–21.

2. The term "First Nations" is preferred in Canada to the term "Native American." It is
used interchangeably with "native," "aboriginal," "indigenous," and—by many members of
these communities—"Indian."

3. The National Museum of Canada was founded by a 1907 Act of Parliament that provided for the construction of the Victoria Memorial Museum, which opened in 1911. Its neo-
Gothic architecture closely resembles that of the Parliament buildings. Along with the physical
construction of buildings went an energetic project of assembling national collections. See

Victoria Dickenson, "A History of the National Museums from Their Founding to the Present Day," *Muse* 10, nos. 2 and 3 (1992): 56–63; and Edward Sapir, "An Anthropological Survey of Canada," *Science,* December 8, 1911, 789–93.

4. Carol Duncan, "Art Museums and the Ritual of Citizenship," in *Exhibiting Cultures: The Poetics and Politics of Museum Display,* ed. Ivan Karp and Steven D. Lavine (Washington, D.C.: Smithsonian Institution Press, 1991), 90.

5. I understand the monument as a symbolic form in Victor Turner's sense, as a multivalent form to which a relatively broad range of meanings can be attributed. See *The Forest of Symbols: Aspects of Ndembu Ritual* (Ithaca: Cornell University Press, 1967).

6. Nelson Graburn, "Introduction," in *Ethnic and Tourist Arts: Cultural Expressions from the Fourth World,* ed. Nelson Graburn (Berkeley: University of California Press), 19, 36–37.

7. On the involvement of the National Gallery and National Museum of Canada with the Group of Seven, see Charles Hill, *The Group of Seven: Art for a Nation* (Ottawa: National Gallery of Canada, 1995); Lynda Jessup, "Bushwackers in the Gallery: Antimodernism and the Group of Seven," in *Antimodernism and Artistic Experience: Policing the Boundaries of Modernity,* ed. Lynda Jessup (Toronto: University of Toronto Press, 2001); Leslie Dawn, "How Canada Stole the Idea of Native Art: The Group of Seven and Images of the Indian in the 1920s," Ph.D. diss., University of British Columbia, 2001; and Sandra Dyck, "'These Things Are Our Totems': Marius Barbeau and the Indigenization of Canadian Art and Culture in the 1920s," M.A. thesis, Carleton University, 1995. On the constructs of authenticity and primitive art, see Shelley Errington, *The Death of Primitive Art and Other Tales of Progress* (Berkeley: University of California Press, 1998).

8. See Thomas Richards, *The Imperial Archive: Knowledge and the Fantasy of Empire* (New York: Verso, 1993).

9. The Indian Act has been amended many times. One of its most oppressive features, the proscription of indigenous spiritual and ceremonial practices such as the Northwest Coast potlatch and the Plains Sun Dance, was not dropped from the act until 1951. The franchise was granted to status Indians in Canada in 1960.

10. The highly active late-twentieth-century phase of postcolonial indigenous political activism has, as I have argued elsewhere, been symbolically enacted by a series of contestations of important world's fairs and exhibitions. See Ruth B. Phillips, "Show Times: Decelebrating the Canadian Nation, Decolonising the Canadian Museum, 1967–92," in McIntyre and Wehner, *National Museums, Negotiating Histories,* 85–103. It is also represented by the successes of the Society of Canadian Artists of Native Ancestry (SCANA) during the 1980s in lobbying major Canadian museums and galleries to acquire and commission contemporary Native art.

11. The other curators were Diana Nemiroff and Charlotte Townshend-Gault. See *Land/Spirit/Power: First Nations at the National Gallery* (Ottawa: National Gallery of Art, 1992).

12. Over a two-week period thousands of citizens wearing period costumes enacted scenes representing not only Champlain's initial landing, but also other major events leading up to the British conquest of the French on the Plains of Abraham in 1759. H. V. Nelles writes: "There seemed to be some confusion as to who was being commemorated; was it Champlain, or Montcalm and Wolfe? Was it 1608 or 1759? Or was 1908 itself the object of celebration? Somehow a civic festival had taken on martial and imperial overtones. By a curious logic, the founding of a city in the seventeenth century had become connected in some way to its conquest in the eighteenth century and further linked to a celebration of imperial nationalism in the early twentieth century. Judging from these jumbled images and inscriptions, the festival seemed to be 'about' many things." *The Art of Nation Building: Pageantry and Spectacle at Quebec's Tercentenary* (Toronto: University of Toronto Press, 1999), 12.

13. For discussions of irony, humor, and trickster strategies in contemporary Native American art, see Lucy Lippard's chapter on "Turning," in her *Mixed Blessings: New Art in a Multicultural America* (New York: Pantheon, 1990); and Alan Ryan, *The Trickster Shift* (Vancouver: University of British Columbia Press, 2000). Hill wore the headdress to impersonate the Revolutionary War–era Mohawk leader Joseph Brant in his performance piece *Pocohaunt(s)us,* created with his partner Sue Ellen Gerritsen, which has had several incarnations since 1997. He addressed the Champlain monument in a video installation piece, "Joe Scouting/for Store Lasagne," as part of "In Control, Luminous Gravity," Ottawa, June 2001 (see also http: homepage.mac.com/gahill/).

14. For a discussion of wampum from an Iroquois perspective, see *Council Fire: A Resource Guide* (Brantford, Ont.: Woodlands Indian Cultural Centre, 1989).

15. The work was commissioned for the traveling exhibition *Across Borders: Beadwork in Iroquois Art.* I quote from the revised artist's statement displayed at the Canadian Museum of Civilization venue, Ottawa, summer 2001.

16. West painted three copies of the painting. The National Gallery of Canada version is the original. The other paintings transferred as part of the War Memorials were portraits of Mohawk chief and British ally Joseph Brant, explorers Sir John Franklin and Alexander Mackenzie, and British general Sir Geoffrey Amherst, by Romney, Phillips, Lawrence, and Reynolds.

17. Vivien Fryd, "Rereading the Indian in Benjamin West's *Death of General Wolfe,*" *American Art* 9 (spring 1995): 81. The figure has also been described as a "repoussoir" figure which replaces the temporally distanced trope of nobility identified with ancient Greek and Roman figures with an exotic, spatially distanced noble savage. See Edgar Wind, "The Revolution of History Painting," *Journal of the Warburg and Courtauld Institutes* 2 (1938–39): 116–27; Charles Mitchell, "Benjamin West's 'Death of General Wolfe' and the Popular History Piece," *Journal of the Warburg and Courtauld Institutes* 7 (1944): 20–33; and Alan McNairn, *Behold the Hero: General Wolfe and the Arts in the Eighteenth Century* (Montreal: McGill Queen's University Press, 1997).

18. Talk by the artist, Carleton University Art Gallery, Ottawa, during the showing of *Contact/Content/Context,* April 1, 1993.

19. Artist's statement in *Notion of Conflict: A Selection of Contemporary Canadian Art* (Amsterdam: Stedelijk Museum, 1995), 24.

20. Sarah Hampson, "Looking for Robert Houle," *Globe and Mail,* July 27, 2000, R3.

21. Talk by the artist, Carleton University Art Gallery, April 1, 1993.

22. Houle made a trip to Europe in 1980 in order to study Mondrian, but was already at that time also interested in Newman. Talk, National Gallery of Canada, October 5, 1995.

23. There is no attempt to bury the debt. Houle speaks of his own works as "homages" to Newman's art. Talk by the artist, National Gallery of Canada, October 5, 1995.

24. Two major exhibitions were held in Canada which dealt in different ways with this subject, *Indigena* at the Canadian Museum of Civilization, and *Land/Spirit/Power* at the National Gallery of Canada (see n. 11). Among the U.S. exhibitions were *First Encounters,* organized by the Florida Museum of Natural History, and *Submoloc Wohs,* organized by Atlatl, a Native-run artists' organization. See W. Jackson Rushing III, "Contrary Iconography: The Submoloc Show," *New Art Examiner* 21 (summer 1994): 33–34.

25. Michael Bell, *Kanata: Robert Houle's Histories* (Ottawa: Carleton University Art Gallery, 1993), 18.

26. Ibid., 19.

27. The controversy arose around two issues, first, an uninformed but noisy questioning of the merits of abstract expressionism, and, second, the expenditure of sizable public

funds on a painting by an American artist. See Bruce Parker, Serge Guilbaut, and John O'Brian, *Voices of Fire: Art, Rage, Power and the State* (Toronto: University of Toronto Press, 1996).

28. W. Jackson Rushing III, *Native American Art and the New York Avant Garde: A History of Cultural Primitivism* (Austin: University of Texas Press, 1995), 168.

29. See Michael Auping, *Abstract Expressionism: The Critical Developments* (Buffalo: Albright Knox Gallery, 1987); and Rushing, *Native American Art and the New York Avant Garde.*

30. See Robert Houle with Clara Hargittay, "The Struggle against Cultural Apartheid," *Muse* 6, no. 3 (1988): 58–63.

31. On the West artifacts, see J. C. H. King, "Woodlands Artifacts from the Studio of Benjamin West," *American Indian Art Magazine* 7 (1991): 34–47.

32. It also incorporated the voice of Simon Schama being interviewed by the Canadian Broadcasting Company about his book *The Death of General Wolfe, Dead Certainties: Unwarranted Speculations* (New York: Knopf, 1991).

33. For example, his series *Everything You Wanted to Know about Indians from A to Z,* and *The Only Good Indians I Ever Saw Were Dead.* See *Robert Houle: Indians from A to Z* (Winnipeg: Winnipeg Art Gallery, 1990).

34. See the exhibit catalogue, Germano Celant, *The European Iceberg: Creativity in Germany and Italy Today* (Toronto: Art Gallery of Ontario, 1985.)

35. Quoted in Jeff Thomas, "From the Collections, The Portfolio: Luminance—Aboriginal Photographic Portraits," *The Archivist, Magazine of the National Archives of Canada* 112 (1996): 9.

36. Quoted in Carol Podedworny, "New World Landscape: Urban First Nations Photography, Interview with Jeffrey Thomas," *Fuse* 19, no. 2 (1996): 35.

37. Ibid.

38. T. J. Jackson Lears, *No Place of Grace: Antimodernism and the Transformation of American Culture* (New York: Pantheon, 1981).

39. Interview with Greg Hill, December 13, 1995, Ottawa. MS, 2, Artists file for "Jeffrey Thomas," Library, National Gallery of Canada, Ottawa.

40. Quoted in Jeff Thomas, "From the Collections," 9.

41. Podedworny, "New World Landscape," 39. The beginning of the quote reads: "I thought that in looking at historical photographs I could understand how the people pictured there had lived, what their experiences were—like when they went to the cities, how they felt about being stared at by non-Native people, the hardships they endured when they moved into an urban environment. In viewing these photographs I might understand my own world. There isn't any information like that around—dealing with issues of identity and survival—it has been stripped away."

42. Roland Barthes, *Camera Lucida: Reflections on Photography,* trans. Richard Howard (New York: Hill and Wang, 1981), 13.

43. Ibid., 28.

44. Curtis's monumental compendium of photographs and information on language, oral history, art, and ethnographic information, *The North American Indian,* was published between 1907 and 1930. See Christopher M. Lyman, *The Vanishing Race and Other Illusions: Photographs of Indians by Edward S. Curtis* (New York: Pantheon, 1982).

45. Barthes, *Camera Lucida,* 87.

46. Podedworny, "New World Landscape," 38.

47. Jeff Thomas, "From the Collections," 7.

48. Transcript of an interview with Greg Hill , December 13, 1995, Ottawa.

49. Raphael Samuel, *Theatres of Memory,* vol. 1, *Past and Present in Contemporary Culture* (London: Verso, 1994).

50. Pierre Nora, ed., *Les lieux de mémoire,* 3 vols. (Paris: Gallimard, 1984). Nora's introductory essay was published as "Between Memory and History: Les Lieux de Mémoire," in *Representations* 26 (spring 1989): 7–24.

51. Ashis Nandy, "History's Forgotten Doubles," *History and Theory: World Historians and Their Critics* 34 (1995): 44.

52. Ibid., 45–46.

53. Nicholas Thomas, *Possessions,* 247.

||||||| Epilogue

The Rhetoric of Monument Making:
The World Trade Center

Final versions of the essays in this volume were due in September 2001. On September 11, two passenger jets, piloted by hijackers, crashed into the twin towers of the World Trade Center, two towers in the busiest commercial district in the country, Manhattan. Another plane hit the Pentagon in Washington. The events of September 11, 2001, as they have come to be called, overtook our project. We found our abstract categories imbued with life; our investigations of travel, time, and iconoclasm acquired new significance. Alois Riegl's definition, never inclusive enough before, seemed even more poignantly inadequate. A building need not last sixty years, or even survive at all, to become a monument. Some authors took advantage of our offer, a few days after September 11, 2001, to review their essays and make reference to the attacks in New York or Washington. The decisions and the responses of our collaborators to these issues varied, which is fitting and telling. As editors, we decided to append this epilogue.

The World Trade Center was not yet a monument when we were writing our original essays, because the building complex still existed as a functioning environment for the production of daily memories and meanings, a recursive loop that recycled, like a tape in a closed-circuit TV camera, the events of the recent past, the financial transactions of world commerce and the American stock market. It was gigantic, but not monumental. In a matter of minutes, the WTC changed from a *milieu de mémoire* to a *lieu de mémoire*. No longer the subject of architectural criticism and history, what is left of these modern skyscrapers is sacred ground and painful memories. The destroyed building became a national symbol and a means of memory making. Its memorial, whose specifics are not yet known at this writing, will further mold and focus social memory of the tragedy, in ways that scholars, critics, and architects will debate.

Our collage of primary quotations about and images of the World Trade Center chronicles the rhetoric of the building from its creation through the first months after its destruction: political compromise, urban renewal scheme, modernist extravaganza, postmodern failure, international symbol, and site of a future memorial, as yet only contemplated. Into these collected fragments we interject other discourses (differentiated typographically) to suggest context and encourage dialogue.

The narrative begins with the first destroyed complex of Minoru Yamasaki, a housing project in St. Louis, follows his World Trade Center from creation to ruin, and ends, not with architecture, but with people and their responses to the disaster. An office building thereby turns into a monument and a memorial. The reader of these excerpts will recognize many of the themes of the volume. Once the twin towers were a goal for tourists, especially from abroad, the site for a restaurant with a stunning view, and, on their highest floors, the home of powerful financial firms. Then photographs of the "missing" filled the streets and moved audiences around the world, who were mesmerized by televised pictures of the destruction. Tourists continue to come, but for entirely different reasons than before 9/11. The destruction of the towers proved the potential of iconoclasm to create monuments and increase their power.

Our epilogue bears the marks of the time of its composition, the autumn of 2001, and thereby becomes part of the record of the unmaking and making of a monument.

Prologue: Yamasaki's First Monument, Pruitt-Igoe, St. Louis

Two buildings by Yamasaki have become monuments through their destruction.

> One day Auguste Perret created the phrase: "The City of Towers." A glittering epithet which aroused the poet in us. A word which struck the note of the moment because the fact itself is imminent!
>   . . . In these towers which will shelter the worker, till now stifled in densely packed quarters and congested streets, all the necessary

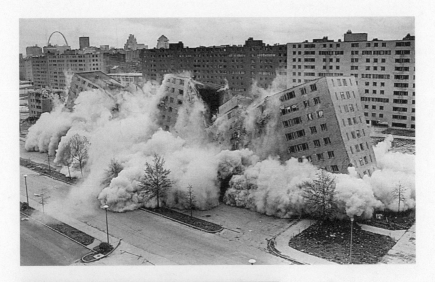

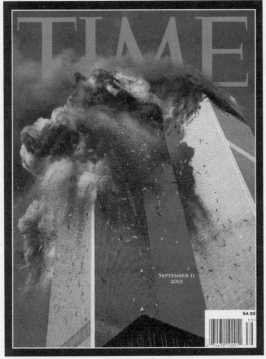

Fig. E.1. (top) Pruitt-Igoe implosion, 1972. Courtesy *St. Louis Post-Dispatch*.

Fig. E.2. (bottom) World Trade Center twin towers burning after terrorists crashed two commercial airplanes into the buildings. Photograph by Lyle Owerko-Gamma (9/11/2001). *Time* magazine, 9/14/2001. Copyright Time Inc./Timepix.

> services, following the admirable practice in America, will be as-
> sembled, bringing efficiency and economy of time and effort, and as
> a natural result the peace of mind which is so necessary. These tow-
> ers, rising up at great distances from one another, will give by reason
> of their height the same accommodation that has up till now been
> spread out over the superficial area; they will leave open enormous
> spaces in which would run, well away from them, the noisy arterial
> roads, full of a traffic which becomes increasingly rapid. At the foot
> of the towers would stretch the parks: trees covering the whole town.
> The setting out of the towers would form imposing avenues; there in-
> deed is an architecture worthy of our time.
>
> Le Corbusier, *Towards a New Architecture* (1931;
> reprint ed. Mineola, N.Y.: Dover, 1986), 54–58

Modern Architecture died in St Louis, Missouri on July 15, 1972 at 3:32
P.M. (or thereabouts) when the infamous Pruitt-Igoe scheme, or rather several
of its slab blocks, were given the final coup de grâce by dynamite. Previously it
had been vandalized, mutilated, and defaced by its black inhabitants, and although millions of dollars were pumped back, trying to keep it alive (fixing
the broken elevators, repairing smashed windows, repainting), it was finally
put out of its misery. Boom, boom, boom.

Without doubt, the ruins should be kept, the remains should have a
preservation order slapped on them, so that we keep a live memory of this failure in planning and architecture. Like the folly or artificial ruin—constructed
on the estate of an eighteenth-century English eccentric to provide him with
instructive reminders of former vanities and glories—we should learn to value
and protect our former disasters.

Pruitt-Igoe was constructed according to the most progressive ideals of
CIAM (the Congress of International Modern Architects) and it won an award
from the American Institute of Architects when it was designed in 1951.

Charles A. Jencks, *The Language of Post-Modern Architecture*
(New York: Rizzoli, 1977), 9

Though it is commonly accorded the epithet "award-winning," Pruitt-
Igoe never won any kind of architectural prize. An earlier St. Louis housing
project by the same team of architects, the John Cochran Garden Apartments,
did win two architectural awards. At some point this prize seems to have been
incorrectly attributed to Pruitt-Igoe. This strange memory lapse on the part of
architects in their discussions of Pruitt-Igoe is extremely significant. Beginning

in the mid-1970's, Pruitt-Igoe began increasingly to be used as an illustration of the argument that the International Style was responsible for the failure of Pruitt-Igoe. The fictitious prize is essential to this dimension of the myth, because it paints Pruitt-Igoe as the iconic modernist monument.

Katharine G. Bristol, "The Pruitt-Igoe Myth,"
Journal of Architectural Education 44 (May 1991): 168–69

World Trade Center: Intentional Phase

A project for Apartments or Flats, built as towers of 60 storeys and rising to a height of 700 feet; the distance between the towers would be from 250 to 300 yards. The towers would be from 500 to 600 feet through their greatest breadth. In spite of the great area devoted to the surrounding parks, the density of a normal town of to-day is multiplied many times over. It is evident that such buildings would necessarily be devoted exclusively to business offices and that their proper place would therefore be in the centre of great cities, with a view to eliminating the appalling congestion of the main arteries. Family life would hardly be at home in them, with their prodigious mechanism of lifts. The figures are terrifying, pitiless but magnificent: giving each employee a superficial area of 10 sq. yds., a skyscraper 650 feet in breadth would house 40,000 people.

Le Corbusier, *Towards a New Architecture*, 56

As soon as the concept of a World Trade Center was formerly [*sic*] approved by New York and New Jersey in 1962, a special Port Authority planning group under the direction of Malcolm Levy had begun the search for an architect. . . . From a list of prominent persons in the field, Minoru Yamasaki was chosen for the job. . . .

Representing the Port Authority as the "client," it was this group [Malcolm Levy and the World Trade Planning and Design Division] which established basic functional and design criteria for the project. The most important considerations were that this building be visible and identifiable throughout the world. . . .

To some members of the planning group, the quality of tallness was to be valued for at least one additional reason: it gave the structures greater visibility which would make it easier to attract tenants.

Leonard I. Ruchelman, *The World Trade Center:
Politics and Policies of Skyscraper Development*
(Syracuse: Syracuse University Press, 1977), 46–48

Today, you are looking down onto construction activity.
Tomorrow millions will look up to a new landmark.

> James C. Kellogg III, chairman of the Port Authority, September10,
> 1968. Quoted in Angus Kress Gillespie, *Twin Towers:*
> *The Life of New York City's World Trade Center*
> (New Brunswick, N.J.: Rutgers University Press, 1999), 110

Interviewer: Maybe, you can tell us how that height was decided?

Mr. Yamasaki: We have been accused of all kinds of things, like trying to beat the Empire State Building and so forth. But I was very interested in building these buildings. There was a way that we could have built a lower building which is a wall and had a courtyard inside, but that wouldn't have been very interesting for the skyline of New York. Beyond that I think there is a significance to world trade that the Port Authority recognized and the Port of New York is the single and most important port in the United States and World Trade symbolizes World Peace. Somehow if we made these buildings important enough that we might get across the idea that we are for World Peace.

> Meadow Brook Art Gallery, "Minoru Yamasaki: A Retrospective,"
> typescript of interview with Mr. Yamasaki,
> Art Institute of Chicago, pamphlet file
> [typographical errors corrected]

These are big buildings but they are not great architecture. . . . The Port Authority has built the ultimate Disneyland fairytale blockbuster. It is General Motors Gothic.

> Ada Louise Huxtable (April 5, 1973), *Kicked a Building*
> *Lately?* (New York: Quadrangle, 1976), 123

With the rise of modernism, the aesthetics of monumentality became both exaggerated and increasingly self-conscious. Many monuments of the nineteenth and twentieth centuries have been referred to as "monstrous" monuments, in which an aesthetic of size has become overwhelming at the expense of form.

> Marita Sturken, "Monuments," *Encyclopedia of Aesthetics*, vol. 3
> (Oxford: Oxford University Press, 1998), 274

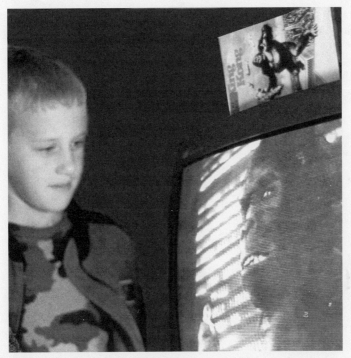

Fig. E.3. Snapshot, 9/11/2002. Photograph by Margaret Olin.

Unintentional Phase I: February 26, 1993

Americans were not accustomed to what so much of the world had already grown weary of: the sudden, deafening explosion of a car bomb, a hail of glass and debris, the screams of innocent victims followed by the wailing sirens of ambulances. Terrorism seemed like something that happened somewhere else—and somewhere else a safe distance over the horizon.

And then last week, in an instant, the World Trade Center in New York City became ground zero.

At 12:18 on a snowy Friday afternoon, a massive explosion rocked the foundation of the Twin Towers of the Trade Center in lower Manhattan—the second tallest buildings in the world and a magnet for 100,000 workers and visitors each day. The bomb was positioned to wreak maximum damage to the infrastructure of the building and the commuter networks below. And the landmark target near Wall Street seemed chosen with a fine sense for the symbols of the late 20th century. If the explosion, which killed five people and injured more than 1,000, turns out to be the work of terrorists, it will be a sharp reminder that the world is still a dangerous place. And that the dangers can come home.

Richard Lacayo, "Tower Terror," *Time,* March 8, 1993

Buildings are "forever," but memories of disasters are short-lived. Stories of the World Trade Center blast were front-page news around the world, only to be displaced within a week by the standoff in Texas between federal agents and David Koresh's Branch Davidians. The initial shock in the wake of an explosion caused by a few radicals is quickly forgotten. . . .

Unfortunately, with the passage of time there comes a return to openness and trust, a quality inherent to the human spirit. However, security and protection can be incorporated into buildings to act as a passive, nonintrusive shield to random terrorism.

Eve Hinman and Matthys P. Levy, "Protecting Buildings against Terrorism,"
in *The World Trade Center Bombing: Report and Analysis,*
ed. William A. Manning (Emmitsburg, Md.:
United States Fire Administration, 1993), 152, 154

The selection of the American embassies in Kenya and Tanzania as targets on August 7, 1998, for bombings allegedly arranged by Osama bin Laden followed a macabre tradition. Symbols of secular power were also chosen— perhaps again by bin Laden—when an American military residence hall in Dhahran, Saudi Arabia, was bombed in 1996 and when a truckload of explosives was ignited in the parking garage of New York City's World Trade Center in 1993. [Previous groups had targeted military installations, but] the actions of bin Laden . . . were aimed more broadly. They were directed not only at symbols of political and economic power . . . but also at other centers of secular life. . . . All of these incidents were assaults on society as a whole.

Mark Juergensmeyer, *Terror in the Mind of God:*
The Global Rise of Religious Violence
(Berkeley: University of California Press, 2000), 60

I never liked the World Trade Center.
When it went up I talked it down
as did many other New Yorkers.
The twin towers were ugly monoliths
that lacked the details the ornament the character
of the Empire State Building and especially
the Chrysler Building, everyone's favorite,
with its scalloped top, so noble.

The World Trade Center was an example of what was wrong
with American architecture,
and it stayed that way for twenty-five years
until that Friday afternoon in February
when the bomb went off and the buildings became
a great symbol of America, like the Statue
of Liberty at the end of Hitchcock's *Saboteur.*
My whole attitude toward the World Trade Center
changed overnight. I began to like the way
it comes into view as you reach Sixth Avenue
from any side street, the way the tops
of the towers dissolve into white skies
in the east when you cross the Hudson
into the city across the George Washington Bridge.

David Lehman, "The World Trade Center"

One of the problems working with stone is that although the material itself isn't that expensive, hauling it, fabricating it, having the tools to cut it, and
the manpower to work with it are very expensive. And if you make large
sculptures in wood, you can make small models in wood that really capture
the feeling of the material. You can't do that with stone. But stone has an integrity, and its natural qualities suggest the core of the earth. It also comes in a
huge variety of colors and textures, from limestone to marble to granite. I'm
interested in the fact that it's so enduring. I like to visit archeological ruins,
and what's left after many years is either terra-cotta or stone. Everything else
doesn't last.

Elyn Zimmerman, sculptor of "World Trade Center
Memorial," New York City, 1995, in Tracey Hummer, "An
Interview with Elyn Zimmerman," *Sculpture* 16, no. 5
(May/June 1997): 22

Unintentional Phase II: September 11, 2001

Hijackers rammed jetliners into each of New York's World Trade Center towers yesterday, toppling both in a hellish storm of ash, glass, smoke and leaping
victims, while a third jetliner crashed into the Pentagon in Virginia. There was
no official count, but President Bush said thousands had perished, and in the
immediate aftermath the calamity was already being ranked the worst and
most audacious terror attack in American history.

The attacks seemed carefully coordinated. The hijacked planes were all en route to California, and therefore gorged with fuel, and their departures were spaced within an hour and 40 minutes. The first, American Airlines Flight 11, a Boeing 767 out of Boston for Los Angeles, crashed into the north tower at 8:48 A.M. Eighteen minutes later, United Airlines Flight 175, also headed from Boston to Los Angeles, plowed into the south tower. . . .

Within an hour, the United States was on a war footing. The military was put on the highest state of alert, National Guard units were called out in Washington and New York and two aircraft carriers were dispatched to New York harbor. President Bush remained aloft in Air Force One, following a secretive route and making only brief stopovers at Air Force bases in Louisiana and Nebraska. . . .

The largest city in the United States, the financial capital of the world, was virtually closed down. Transportation into Manhattan was halted, as was much of public transport within the city. Parts of Lower Manhattan were without power. Major stock exchanges closed. Primary elections for mayor and other city offices were cancelled. Thousands of workers, released from their offices in Lower Manhattan but with no way to get home except by foot, set off in vast streams, down the avenues and across the bridges under a beautiful, clear sky, accompanied by the unceasing serenade of sirens. . . .

The twin pillars of the World Trade Center were among the best known landmarks in New York, 110-floor unadorned blocks that dominated any approach to Manhattan. It is probable that renown, and the thousands of people who normally work there each weekday, that led Islamic militants to target the towers for destruction already in 1993, then by parking vans loaded with explosives in the basement. . . .

The very absence of the towers would become a symbol after their domination of the New York skyline for 25 years. Though initial reviews were mixed when the towers were dedicated in 1976, they came into their own as landmarks with passing years. King Kong climbed one tower in a remake of the movie classic.

> Serge Schmemann, "Hijacked Jets Destroy Twin Towers and Hit
> Pentagon in Day of Terror: President Vows to Exact Punishment
> for 'Evil,'" *New York Times*, September 12, 2001

Three of the hijackers belonged to a terror group formed "with the aim of carrying out serious crimes together with other Islamic fundamentalist groups abroad, to attack the United States in a spectacular way through the destruction of symbolic buildings," Kay Nehm, Germany's top prosecutor, told reporters.

> *Chicago Tribune*, September 14, 2001

If you want to humble an empire it makes sense to maim its cathedrals. They are symbols of its faith, and when they crumple and burn, it tells us we are not so powerful and we can't be safe. The Twin Towers of the World Trade Center, planted at the base of Manhattan island with the Statue of Liberty as their sentry, and the Pentagon, a squat, concrete fort on the banks of the Potomac, are the sanctuaries of money and power that our enemies may imagine define us. But that assumes our faith rests on what we can buy and build and that has never been America's true God.

> Nancy Gibbs, "If You Want to Humble an Empire,"
> *Time,* September 14, 2001

Here is America struck by God Almighty in one of its vital organs, so that its greatest buildings are destroyed. Grace and gratitude to God.

> "Text of Statement from Osama Bin Laden,"
> *Los Angeles Times* (internet edition), October 7, 2001.
> [The text is from a videotape released October 7, 2001, released
> by an al-Jazeera network in Qatar, translated by Reuters]

With the invention of the passenger elevator in the mid-nineteenth century and the steel frame two decades later, an intimate connection was forged between the tallest tower in the city and the biggest corporation, the richest bank, or whatever financial entity wanted to be seen as running the place. Before there were skyscrapers, the horizon in most cites was dominated by church steeples. . . . The earliest skyscrapers wrested control of the skyline from God and gave it to Mammon, where it has pretty much remained.

> Paul Goldberger, "Building Plans: What the World Trade
> Center Meant," *New Yorker,* September 24, 2001, 76

A leading Germany [*sic*] fashion designer said yesterday there should be no regrets about the destruction of the World Trade Centre because it symbolised capitalism at its worst. "I don't regret that the twin towers are no longer standing because they symbolised capitalist arrogance," Wolfgang Joop, 56, told the Austrian magazine *Profil.*

When questioned by the tabloid *Bild,* he qualified his comments by adding: "September 11 set a learning process in motion because the twin towers, as symbols of capitalist arrogance, have fallen."

> Kate Connolly, "Twin Towers Symbolised Arrogance, Says
> Top Designer: Fashion King Says Schröder Policy Reminds
> Him of Nazi Era," *The Guardian,* October 16, 2001

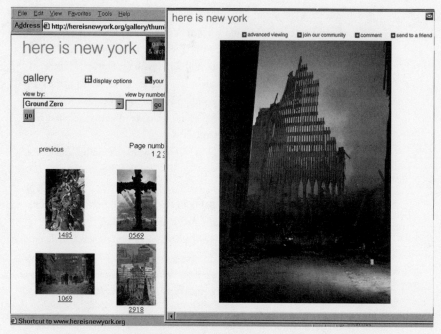

Fig. E.4. Website of Here Is New York. Photograph by Mickey J. Kerr.

Loss

> Mourning is regularly the reaction to the loss of a loved person, or to
> the loss of some abstraction which has taken the place of one, such as
> one's country, liberty, an ideal, and so on. In some people the same in-
> fluences produce melancholia instead of mourning and we conse-
> quently suspect them of a pathological disposition. . . .
>
>   . . . In melancholia the relation to the object is no simple one; it
> is complicated by the conflict due to ambivalence. The ambivalence is
> either constitutional, i.e. is an element of every love-relation formed
> by this particular ego, or else it proceeds precisely from those experi-
> ences that involved the threat of losing the object. For this reason the
> exciting causes of melancholia have a much wider range than those
> of mourning, which is for the most part occasioned only by a real loss
> of the object, by its death.
>
> Sigmund Freud, "Mourning and Melancholia,"
> The Standard Edition of the Complete
> Psychological Works of Sigmund Freud, vol. 14
> (London: Hogarth Press, 1957), 243, 256

We count on our urban symbols to be present. They are not supposed to
evaporate. . . . As the years passed, it seemed to take on the quality of a huge
piece of minimalist sculpture, and its dullness was almost a virtue. Now that
the Trade Center has become a martyr to terrorism, I suspect that architectural criticism of it will cease altogether. It has become a noble monument of a
lost past.

> Paul Goldberger, "Building Plans," *New Yorker,*
> September 24, 2001, 78

The World Trade Center towers never inspired the loyalty and affection
of New York's great skyscrapers of the past. A spectacular site but a lackluster
performance, at best a colossal piece of minimalist sculpture so ran the consensus. If anyone derived aesthetic pleasure from them, it was offset by the
pity they aroused for having been built during the early 1970's, that low-water
mark of architectural modernism. . . .

But the loss of the World Trade Center is something far different. It is an
instantaneous and convulsive change in the city's topography, transforming
the physical landscape violently and definitively, in a way we associate with
the greatest of natural disasters, like those volcanoes that explode and vanish.
It has let loose feelings far deeper—more primitive and instinctive—than
mere architectural nostalgia. It is the terror at the presence of uncontrollable natural forces, usually kept safely at a submerged level of human consciousness.

It is now clear that the World Trade Center towers occupied a far greater
position in the physical and psychological landscape of New York than anyone realized. They have now become what much of the world could plainly
see (and which New Yorkers could only belatedly see): the city's most conspicuous and symbolically freighted civic monument. . . .

. . . No one seems to have seen them as clearly as the men who destroyed
them.

In their absence, the World Trade Center towers are more a monument
than ever. The physical void they leave is itself a poignant memorial, an aching
emptiness that is the architectural counterpart to a human loss. Unlike the victims of our disposable architectural culture, they need not fear being dis-
lodged or overtaken. They now stand among the great and vanished monuments of the past. Like the Seven Wonders of the Ancient World—the
Colossus of Rhodes or the mighty Lighthouse of Alexandria—they have
reached their apotheosis through destruction.

> Michael J. Lewis, "In a Changing Skyline, a Sudden, Glaring Void,"
> *New York Times,* September 16, 2001

"The World Trade Center, though not aesthetically pleasing, was our anchor," said David Gallo, a Broadway set designer who is using an older New York skyline as the central element in a forthcoming stage version of the movie musical "Thoroughly Modern Millie." "It was there at the base of Manhattan giving us all a point of reference. Having lost that anchor, we are confused as a nation visually."

> Peter Marks, "A Skyline Is Conspicuous by an Absence,"
> *New York Times,* October 24, 2001

From: Interlibrary Loan, University of Chicago
To: Robert Nelson
Subject: Your Interlibrary Loan Request
Date: Tue, 16 Oct 2001

Dear Robert Nelson:
You recently requested the following material on Interlibrary Loan.
The architecture of the World Trade Center, 1973.
We are unable to fill this request. Document destroyed on 9-11-2001 in terrorist attack. NY Port Authority (One World Trade Center) was only holding library.
Thank you.

Monument for Monument

I feel that planting a park with trees and flowers commemorating our tragic loss symbolizes hope and rebirth.

We must remember that our loss was not of a great monument that represented architecture, commerce and tourism of the 20th century, but that we lost living and breathing people who once pulsed through that area.

> Genevieve Gochuico, Bedford Hills, N.Y., letter to the editor,
> September 26, 2001, *New York Times,* September 30, 2001

We don't need a monument. You see a monument and you don't think of anything.

> Joel Shapiro, sculptor and creator of the commemorative sculpture
> outside the United States Holocaust Memorial Museum in Washington,
> in Deborah Solomon, "From the Rubble, Ideas for Rebirth,"
> *New York Times,* September 30, 2001

> Let the memorial hill remember, instead of me. That's his job.
>
> Yehuda Amichai, *Amen: Poems,*
> trans. Yehuda Amichai and Ted Hughes
> (Minneapolis: Milkweed Editions, 1977), 37

But no matter what form the reconstruction of the site takes, New York should make a commitment now to preserving the searing fragment of ruin already so frequently photographed and televised that it has become nearly as familiar to us as the buildings that once stood there. This is the huge, skeletal and jagged steel fragment of the World Trade Center and its façade that still stubbornly stands in the midst of the utter destruction of ground zero.

Though tilted slightly, it somehow survived, emerging from the fire and smoke of Sept. 11—inexplicably durable, still pointing to the heavens and now a fitting, realistic and moving monument to those who died there. Already an icon, it should stand forever as a sculptural memorial, incorporated into whatever other structures or landscapes are chosen as fitting for this site.

Philippe de Montebello, "The Iconic Power of an Artifact,"
New York Times, September 25, 2001

Long after we are all gone, it's the sacrifice of our patriots and their heroism that is going to be what this place is remembered for. This is going to be a place that is remembered 100 and 1,000 years from now, like the great battlefields of Europe and of the United States.

Rudolph Giuliani, "Text of Mayor Giuliani's Farewell Address,"
New York Times, December 27, 2001

Witness

> People ask me, "How was it? What was it like?" All the words are wrong. So when I have to react in a word or two to casual, friendly inquiries, this is what I say: "Strangely enriching. You must go."
>
> Hershel Shanks, "The Strange Enrichment of Seeing
> Auschwitz," quoted in Jack Kugelmass, "Why We Go to Poland:
> Holocaust Tourism as Secular Ritual," in *The Art of Memory:
> Holocaust Memorials in History,* ed. James E. Young
> (New York: Jewish Museum, 1994), 175

I stop and look at a pile of papers in one disconsolate corner, at a team of firemen standing by their cars, silently changing out of their uniforms, at a bicyclist pedaling by with the American flag fluttering from her handlebars, at a fading bouquet placed before a side-mound of crushed cars and office debris.

I came to New York to bear witness, to pay my respects to a city I love and to people whose acts of sacrifice and compassion and courage embody ideals I have been raised with and have tried to impart to my own children. I came because I needed to be here, to make a palpable connection I could absorb and carry with me.

At times during this day I have felt awkward, inappropriate, profane, like an outsider intruding on a tribe's sacred ceremony. But now I know that I am part of this ceremony; we are all one family, and we all mourn what we have lost.

Don George, "Bearing Witness: A Report from Ground Zero,"
Lonely Planet Online, October 3, 2001

The scene at St. Paul's Chapel suggests a need for something right away—a large space near the site where people can leave flowers or poems or simply say a prayer. The crowds that press up against the fences to gaze at Ground Zero have come to bear witness. They deserve a formal place to end their pilgrimage.

"The Pilgrimage to Lower Manhattan," editorial,
New York Times, November 14, 2001

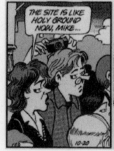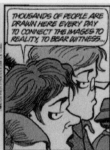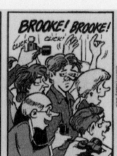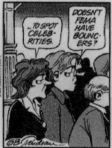

Fig. E.5. Doonesbury, October 20, 2001. Copyright G. B. Trudeau. Reprinted with permission of Universal Press Syndicate. All rights reserved.

Grief

At a banquet given by a nobleman of Thessaly named Scopas, the poet Simonides of Ceos chanted a lyric poem in honour of his host but including a passage in praise of Castor and Pollux. Scopas meanly told the poet that he would only pay him half the sum agreed upon for the panegyric and that he must obtain the balance from the twin gods to whom he had devoted half the poem. A little later, a message was brought in to Simonides that two young men were waiting outside who wished to see him. He rose from the banquet and went out but could find no one. During his absence the roof of the banqueting hall fell in, crushing Scopas and all the guests to death beneath the ruins; the corpses were so mangled that the relatives who came to take them away for burial were unable to identify them. But Simonides remembered the places at which they had been sitting at the table and was therefore able to indicate to the relatives which were their dead. The invisible callers, Castor and Pollux, had handsomely paid for their share in the panegyric by drawing Simonides away from the banquet just before the crash. And this experience suggested to the poet the principles of the art of memory of which he is said to have been the inventor.

Frances A. Yates. *The Art of Memory*
(Chicago: University of Chicago Press, 1966), 1–2

Mayor Rudolph W. Giuliani said yesterday that every family would receive something from the site. "We hope that we can recover remains," the mayor said, "but we will give every family something from the World Trade Center, from the soil, from the ground, so that they can take it with them."

Somini Sengupta with Al Baker,
"Rites of Grief, without a Body to Cry Over,"
New York Times, September 27, 2001

The only way I can transform the Photograph is into refuse: either the drawer or the wastebasket. . . .

What is it that will be done away with, along with this photograph which yellows, fades, and will someday be thrown out, if not by me—too superstitious for that—at least when I die?

Roland Barthes, *Camera Lucida : Notes on Photography*,
trans. Ron Howard (New York: Noonday Press, 1981), 93–94

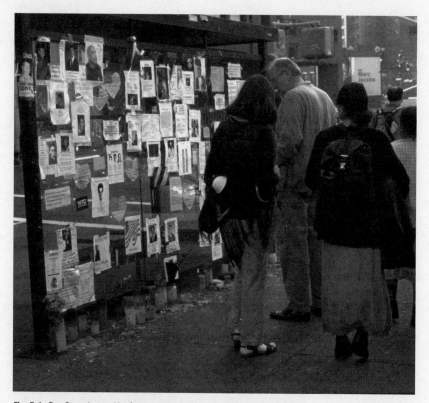

Fig. E.6. Bus Stop, Lower Manhattan, 2001. Photograph by Margaret Olin.

As our book ends, the memorial process continues. In the first months after the destruction of the World Trade Center, the discussion was already turning in several directions. Some proposals focused on a loss felt by all New Yorkers, the gaping hole in New York's skyline; these offered to fill the hole at night with ghostly, laser-produced beams. Others urged the building of real towers, less high, perhaps, and with an appropriate memorial. At the same time, a powerful visual symbol emerged. Attached to the barricades around "Ground Zero," or placed on bus stops, hospitals, and other public surfaces, fliers of the "missing" appeared, beginning on the day of the attack. Soon, makeshift memorials formed beneath and around these photocopied photographs. Scraps of paper were added, containing messages. Flowers, too, were taped to them or placed on the sidewalks below. Piles of candles sat in scrap heaps nearby. Sometimes wrinkled, lumpy plastic covered the entire ensemble. This attempt to preserve the fading words and images made them even less distinguishable from the garbage that lines the streets in the best of times. Two months after the attacks, some ideas for permanent memorials began to make reference to these unlovely, spontaneous outpourings. By the time the present book is published, other feelings will surely have had an airing. Channeled and directed by government agencies as it surely will be, the process once more confirms the primary tie that unites monuments of violence, destruction, and grief to the nation-state and its mechanisms of communal memory.

Stephen Bann is professor of the history of art at the University of Bristol. His earlier study of John Bargrave was published in 1994 with the title *Under the Sign: John Bargrave as Collector, Traveler and Witness.* His most recent book, *Parallel Lines: Printmakers, Painters and Photographers in Nineteenth-Century France* (2001), was awarded the R. H. Gapper Prize for 2002 by the Society for French Studies.

Jonathan Bordo teaches cultural theory and visual studies at Trent University. His recent publications include "Phantoms," in *On European Ground,* by Alan Cohen (2001), and "Picture and Witness at the Site of the Wilderness," in *Landscape and Power,* ed. W. J. T. Mitchell, 2d ed. (2002). His current project is *The Landscape without a Witness: The Wilderness, a Study in Critical Topography.*

Julia Bryan-Wilson is a Ph.D. candidate in the history of art at the University of California, Berkeley. She is currently completing a dissertation entitled "Art/Work: Minimalism, Conceptualism, and Artistic Labor in the Age of Vietnam, 1965–75." Her writing has appeared in the *Art Journal* and the *Oxford Art Journal.*

Jaś Elsner is Humfry Payne Senior Research Fellow in Classical Art and Archaeology at Corpus Christi College, Oxford, and visiting professor in art history at the University of Chicago. He is the author of *Art and the Roman Viewer* (1995) and *Imperial Rome and Christian Triumph* (1998), as well as edited volumes on issues such as pilgrimage, travel writing, collecting, and Roman biography.

Tapati Guha-Thakurta is professor in history at the Center for Studies in Social Sciences, Calcutta. She has written widely on the art and cultural history of modern India; on archaeological, art historical, and museum practices; and on popular visual culture. She is the author of *The Making of a New "Indian" Art* (1992). Her forthcoming book is

Monuments, Objects, Histories: Institutions of Art in Colonial and Postcolonial India.

Robert S. Nelson is Distinguished Service Professor of Art History and chairman of the Committee on the History of Culture at the University of Chicago. He has also edited *Visuality before and beyond the Renaissance: Seeing as Others Saw* (2000) and coedited the second edition of *Critical Terms for Art History* (2003, with Richard Shiff).

Margaret Olin is professor in the Department of Art History, Theory, and Criticism at the School of the Art Institute of Chicago. She is the author of *Forms of Representation in Alois Riegl's Theory of Art* (1992) and *The Nation without Art: Examining Modern Discourses on Jewish Art* (2001).

Ruth B. Phillips holds a Canada Research Chair in Modern Culture at Carleton University in Ottawa. She was director of the University of British Columbia's Museum of Anthropology from 1997 to 2003. Her recent publications include *Trading Identities: The Souvenir in Native North American Art from the Northeast, 1700–1900* (1998), *Native North American Art* (1998, with Janet Catherine Berlo), and *Unpacking Culture: Art and Commodity in Colonial and Postcolonial Worlds* (1999, coedited with Christopher B. Steiner).

Mitchell Schwarzer is associate professor of visual studies at the California College of Arts and Crafts in San Francisco. He is the author of *German Architectural Theory and the Search for Modern Identity* (1995), *Architecture and Design: San Francisco* (1998), and numerous articles on architectural theory, urbanism, and the historiography of the visual arts. His new book, entitled *Zoomscape: Architecture in Motion and Media,* will be published in 2004.

Lillian Lan-ying Tseng is assistant professor of art history at Yale University. She has published a number of articles concerned with diverse cultural issues in Chinese art, such as visual replication and political persuasion, pictorial representation and historical writing, and interchangeability of the self and the other. She is currently at work on a book tentatively entitled *Picturing Heaven: Visibility and Visuality in Early China.*

Richard K. Wittman is assistant professor of art history at the University of Delaware. He is currently completing a book on architecture, the press, and the concept of public opinion in eighteenth-century Paris.

Wu Hung is Harrie A. Vanderstappen Distinguished Service Professor in Chinese Art History and director of the Center for the Art of East Asia at the University of Chicago. He is the author of *The Double Screen: Medium and Representation in Chinese Painting* (1996), *Exhibiting Experimental Art in China* (2000), and many other books and essays on traditional and contemporary Chinese art.

Minerva, 212
misidentification, 137, 148–49, 151. *See also* identification; identity
Misrach, Richard, 197
Mitchell, W. J. T., 178
Mitra, Raja Rajendralal, 248
mnemonic technique, 270. *See also* Yates, Frances A., *The Art of Memory*
modernism, 2, 310; anthropological, 300; and art history, 2, 282; artistic, 290–91, 300; international, 284; and primitivism, 291, 296; secular, 68; spiritual content of, 291
modernity, 6, 65, 226, 284; archival impulses of, 299; historical transition to, 88; landscapes of, 85, 87; nostalgic impulses of, 299; urban, 294
Mollinari, Guido, 289
Mondrian, Piet, 289, 302n. 22
Montebello, Philippe, 319
Montreal World's Fair, Expo '67, 290
monument: and academic legitimacy, 2; animism of, 6; and antimonument, 105; appropriation of, 4; and art history, 2; artistic, 98; canonization of, by UNESCO, 4; cathedral as, 33; characteristics of, 60; and colonialism, 281; commissions, 74; and community, 207, 275; constructing memory of, 51; conventional, 194; creation of, 3–5, 12; and death, 105; designation of, 2; designers of, 2; destruction of, 3–4, 7, 15, 105, 205, 207, 281; of destruction, 323; distance from, 75; effect of guidebooks on, 12; etymology of, 4; historic, 4, 260; as hybrid, 6; imagined, 250; intentional, 2, 103–4, 148; making of, 2, 205, 281; and memory, 3, 4, 6–7, 38, 103, 198, 209–11, 281; modern, 61, 68, 74, 77, 128; monstrous, 310; and movement, 11; national, 60, 243, 251; natural, 98; as object, 2, 7, 210; people as, 84; photograph as, 104, 149; popular, 98; and power, 7, 281; preservation of, 1, 2, 4; public acceptance of, 2; reconstruction of, 5; representation of, 50–52; and

representation of past, 2, 4, 7, 38; and rhetoric, 3, 7, 103–5; as site of social conflict, 59; site-specific, 195; social aspects of, 3, 5–7, 11–12; and societal function, 3, 7; and sound, 104; of spectacle, 98; study of, 1, 4; sustenance of, 5; and technology, 98; and time, 5, 103; and tourism, 4; traditional, 194; transtemporal physicality of, 299; and travel, 5; underground, 98; unintentional, 2, 103, 149; unmaking of, 2, 205, 281; of violence, 323; visual, 104. See also *Denkmal;* Holocaust, memorials; monumental; monumentality; Riegl, Alois, and intentional monument; Riegl, Alois, and unintentional monument; ritual, desecration
monumental, 190, 194–95, 284; albums as, 38; architecture, 198–99; art history as, 148; commemoration, 226; discourse, 205; memory, 225; topos, 186. *See also* monument
monumentality, 12, 195, 211, 222, 225; aesthetics of, 310; architecture, 108, 120; conceptual bases of, 194; mechanics of, 186; and notion of public time, 107; notions of, 3, 107–9, 193; tropes of, 198; universal, 129. *See also* monument
Morris, Robert, 100
Mosque: of Hagia Sophia, 59–60; of Suleiman, 60, 65–66; of Sultan Ahmet (Blue Mosque), 60, 63, 65–67, 69. See also *masjids*
Mount Mang, 40
Mount Song, 37–38, 42–46, 52, 56n. 28
mourning, 316; and art history, 133; and Internet, 145; and John Bargrave, 13, 16; photographic, 135, 150
moving landscape, 83–101; and artistic landscape, 91, 96–97; and car commercials, 85, 91–97, 100; and consciousness, 83; and geographical landscape, 91; and memory, 99; and the past, 98; stillness in, 100; and technology, 97. *See also* landscape
Müller-Wille, Ludger, 171